The Automobile Revolution

The Automobile Revolution

The Impact of an Industry

Jean-Pierre Bardou, Jean-Jacques Chanaron

Patrick Fridenson, James M. Laux

Translated from the French by James M. Laux

The University of North Carolina Press Chapel Hill

Library of Congress Cataloging in Publication Data

Révolution automobile. English.
  The automobile revolution.

  Translation of: La Révolution automobile.
  Bibliography: p.
  Includes index.
    1. Automobiles—Social aspects—History—Ad-
dresses, essays, lectures. 2. Automobile industry
and trade—History—Addresses, essays, lectures.
I. Bardou, Jean-Pierre, 1935– . II. Title.
HE5613.R4213   303.4'83   81-11571
ISBN 0-8078-1496-2   AACR2

Contents

	Introduction	xiii
One	**The Genesis of the Automobile Revolution**	1
	1. The Birth and Youth of the Automobile	3
	2. The First Automobile Boom	14
	3. The Early Manufacturers	24
	4. An Expanding Market and Production Innovations, 1908–1914	51
Two	**The Spread of the Automobile Revolution, 1914–1945**	77
	5. Wartime Expansion	79
	6. American Dominance, 1918–1929	91
	7. Difficult Years	139
	8. Total War	159
Three	**The Triumph of the Automobile Revolution**	169
	9. The Universal Automobile	171

10. Automobiles and Technical Progress
   since 1945   208

11. Labor and Industrial Relations since 1945   230

12. The Automobile under Fire   272

General Conclusion   291

Notes   297

Bibliography   303

Index   321

Illustrations

1. Company notice to Ford workers   122

2. Berliet truck advertisement   123

3. The first Renault taxi, 1905   124

4. Ford, 1914: two of the three final
   assembly lines   125

5. Ford, 1914: the foundry   126

6. Ford, 1914: a semiautomatic machine   127

7. Panhard et Levassor advertisement, 1922   128

8. Service station in Atlantic City,
   about 1920   129

9. Renault: transmission assembly, 1938   130

10. Mercedes-Benz, 1930   131

11. Fiat Topolino ("Little Mouse"), 1936   132

12. VW "Beetle"   133

13. Volvo, 1974: cars assembled on
    individual carriers   134

14. Volvo, 1974: car assembly accommodated
    to workers   135

15. General Motors Technical Center,
    Warren, Michigan, 1975   136

16. 1980 Olds Cutlass and 1972 Olds Cutlass   137

Tables and Charts

Tables
 1-1 Automobile Production, 1891–1895   11

 2-1 Motorization in 1907   20

 4-1 Estimated Average Daily Wage of Automobile Workers, Selected Countries, Around 1910   66

 4-2 Motorization toward the End of 1913   72

 4-3 Estimated Production of the World's Leading Automobile Firms, 1913   74

 6-1 Number of Inhabitants per Car, Selected Countries, 1927   112

 9-1 Production during the Recession of 1973–1975, Selected Countries   190

 9-2 Annual Average Change in Motor Vehicle Production in New Producing Countries, 1970s   191

 9-3 Motor Vehicle Production in New Producing Countries, 1972 and 1979   192

 9-4 Number of Motor Vehicles per 1,000 Population, Selected Countries, 1950–1979   197

 9-5 World's Leading Motor Vehicle Manufacturers, 1979   207

Charts   3-1 The Automobile Industry in
the American Middle West before 1914   41

4-1 Ford and the United States Market,
1909–1917   55

7-1 The Automobile Industry in
Depression and Recovery   140

9-1 Fiat's Relations with Communist and
Underdeveloped Countries, 1970   189

11-1 Four Case Studies of Strikes   262

12-1 Annual Energy Consumption of
Different Forms of Transportation in
the United States, 1950–1976   284

Note on the American Edition

This work was originally published in French at Paris in 1977 by Albin Michel. During the course of the translation, however, the authors took advantage of the opportunity to accomplish considerable revision, especially in Part III to bring the contemporary story up to date. Several charts and tables in the French edition have been dropped and new ones added. The series in which the book first appeared called for few footnotes but an extensive bibliography. This format has been carried over in the present edition, with a thorough revision of the bibliography.

James M. Laux is the author of the Introduction and Part I, Patrick Fridenson of Part II and the General Conclusion, Jean-Jacques Chanaron of chapters 9, 10, and 12 of Part III, and Jean-Pierre Bardou of chapter 11. Serge Bonin and James Laux prepared the graphs and charts. Paul Burrell provided major aid in the translation, along with Frank Kafker and Roger Daniels.

Introduction
James M. Laux

Revolution? Did the invention of the automobile and its ultimate adoption almost everywhere on the planet produce a truly revolutionary impact? This is for the reader to judge, but the authors believe that it has, and this book offers considerable supporting evidence. The revolutionary effect of developments in technology is nothing new. Consider, for example, gunpowder, the clock, the printing press, and the steam engine. To these famous innovations, the automobile must be added. The French automotive engineer Maurice Norroy describes the revolution it has wrought in a few words: "The history of the automobile more than anything else is the history of a revolution. In only a few years industrial methods were transformed, and along with them the means of communication, and more, the nature of rural and urban life, the way goods are distributed, and the entire economic system."[1]

The genesis of this revolution can be placed in the Gay Nineties, when German and French engineers adapted the internal-combustion engine to road transport. In a few years, they managed to design cars that would run reliably and found a market for them. Then, the Americans, after first concentrating on electric- and steam-powered vehicles, began to produce internal-combustion models based on European designs. Manufacturers who made relatively small and cheap types discovered what appeared to be an unlimited market. To supply it, they introduced new production methods: standardization, intensive mechanization, and the assembly line. Artisanal production gave way to mass production. As Georges Friedmann explained it,

"One expression of man's technical genius disappeared over the horizon but another was born before our eyes."[2]

The several ramifications of the mass production of automobiles spelled revolution: 1) lower cost of production and lower prices, which in turn widened the market, a market that soon spread beyond national frontiers all over the world and that would require manufacturers to become multinational enterprises; 2) a sharp increase in labor productivity and higher wages; and 3) a precipitous decline in the need for skilled workers but at the same time a rise in the importance of highly trained engineers and technicians, who would take growing responsibility for planning and managing the production process.

Although in America the evolution of mass production and mass marketing of automobiles continued in almost unbroken steps into the 1920s, in Europe the First World War caused a diversion. Most auto firms there shifted to military production, especially of aircraft engines. Even though some of them worked out mass-production methods for their military orders, most fell further behind the Americans in this aspect of industrial technology. But, in the 1920s and the 1930s, mass-production and mass-marketing methods gradually were adopted in Europe, though not to the same extent as on the other side of the Atlantic.

In America, the innovations of the interwar period were less in the realm of technology than in improving the management of the large auto firms. During these years, while huge investments were being made in highways, the automobile, by expanding opportunities for leisure time, strongly influenced social life, ending rural isolation and fostering the beginning of urban congestion. Even at this time, a threat to the cities was perceived. As one farsighted observer remarked: "Already the automobiles are gnawing like termites at the bases of our skyscrapers."[3]

By the end of the 1930s, Europe had decided to adopt the automobile as a form of mass transportation and began to build expressways as well as small cars for a mass market. But, before this transition could occur, the Second World War broke out and interrupted the auto industry again. When it ended, Western Europe quickly turned to a policy of mass production and mass marketing, an approach that would spread to Japan in the 1960s, ultimately making that country the world's largest auto producer in 1980, and then to the Third World and the European communist countries in the 1970s.

But, as it did, two problems emerged in the heartland of the automobile, Europe and America, and in Japan as well. The huge numbers of cars in many of the world's cities made them a formidable nuisance, of which traffic accidents were the most urgent aspect. So serious did the automobile's side effects become that it began to appear as if the revolution was beginning to devour its own children. The growing recognition of the social costs of masses of cars would certainly affect research and innovation, but what form would this take? Would short-run marketing considerations continue to play a crucial role, or would manufacturers boldly seek new technical solutions?

Secondly, the labor problem became acute. As the process of further and further mechanization required fewer workers to produce a car, those who remained, especially those involved in assembly, found the repetitiveness and boredom of the job more and more distasteful. Would it be possible to incorporate more interest and meaning in the individual's job and yet maintain high productivity? Could the satisfactions of artisanal labor be joined to the low cost of production achieved by intensive mechanization?

To these problems of direct concern to the automobile industry was added that of petroleum. Although the growth of automobile transportation depended on this commodity, at first this new use took only a small share: only 20 percent of the petroleum produced in the United States in 1916, for example. By 1930 gasoline had become by far the most important petroleum product in America, taking nearly half, a proportion that remained steady after that date. In the rest of the world, the share of petroleum refined into gasoline has never come close to the American figure. Nevertheless, inasmuch as much of the world's transport was geared to a plentiful supply of gasoline and diesel fuel, the political and economic significance of petroleum supplies became crucial, a fact that some of the producing countries finally came to realize in the 1970s. The sharp increase in oil prices from 1973 on, joined to the side effect and labor problems, brought the automobile even more to the front of the public's consciousness all over the world. Somehow, this device in eighty-five years had brought a revolution to economic and social life. Now, some payments were coming due. This book tries to achieve a greater understanding of that revolution.

The authors have worked closely together in planning, writing, and revising this work. Two historians, an economist, and a sociologist, they have received different training and employ different methods. Thus, their appreciation of and approach toward the Automobile Revolution is not always the same. They have not simply repeated familiar material from earlier studies of the automobile, but have researched original sources for new information. Although they are not part of the automobile industry, they have carefully investigated its nature and operations, as well as those of the leading firms; the progress of production methods; and the role of workers, automobile buyers, and public authorities.

The authors are fascinated to watch a revolution going on in front of them, a revolution that began in the lifetimes of their fathers, and that will continue during the lifetimes of their children—a revolution whose twists and turns often are unpredictable and frequently are ironic.

One The Genesis of the Automobile Revolution

James M. Laux

1.   The Birth and Youth of the Automobile

The Automobile Revolution began with the appearance of automobile manufacturing, about the year 1890. By that time, Europeans and North Americans possessed the technology required to produce and successfully operate a mechanically powered road vehicle. A taste and a demand for such a device could then be created, building not only on two generations of public acceptance of railways, but also on the widespread interest in a more recent mechanical device, the bicycle. The opening stages of automobile production and marketing required nothing new in the form of business organization, factory operation, or selling methods. Nor did it require large sums of capital or large numbers of workers. Yet, ultimately, the growth of this industry would bring amazing changes in all these areas. Revolutions usually do not announce themselves at their first manifestations.

This one was first of all an innovation in technology. Those who introduced it brought together a wide variety of mechanical contrivances to create something new. The automobile might be considered to represent a marriage between a light-weight and portable power source and a sturdy road vehicle, a brilliant synthesis of two separate lines of technical development. The marriage of a carriage with an internal-combustion engine, the happiest and most prolific type, did not occur successfully until 1886. It was preceded by a long series of efforts since the 18th century to mate steam engines with road wagons in Britain (Trevithick, Gurney, Hancock, James, Todd), in France (Cugnot, Dietz, Bollée), in Italy (Bordino), and in the United States

(Evans). But the excessive weight of the engine, boiler, and fuel, together with a failure to perfect a system of suspension effective enough to protect the machinery from the rough roads of the period had discouraged or defeated these initiatives. Ultimately, steam cars and those powered by electricity would enjoy some success early in the twentieth century, but by that time the internal-combustion engine would already have demonstrated its superiority.

Some experimentation had also been done with the concept of burning or exploding some kind of gas in a cylinder to provide power. Again, British technicians were the most numerous, among them Street, Brown, Wright, and Barnett, but the Frenchman Le Bon and the Italians Barsanti and Matteucci had also investigated this approach. The decisive step came in 1860 when a Belgian mechanic and inventor working in Paris, Etienne Lenoir, was encouraged by a clever business promoter named Gautier to make an internal-combustion engine. Lenoir's machine of that year resembled a steam engine in design and operation; a mixture of illuminating gas and air exploded in turn at each end of the cylinder to drive the piston back and forth. In some ways, this internal-combustion engine marked a step backward technically, but its simplicity and resemblance to a steam engine made Lenoir's gas engine easier to sell than the more advanced but highly complicated machines of its predecessors. It did offer a major innovation, ignition of the fuel by an electric spark plug supplied by a battery and coil.

Lenoir may have used his engine to power a river launch and a carriage sometime in the early 1860s, bringing the gas along in a small tank, but these experiments led nowhere. His engines did. Several hundred of them were installed as power sources for small urban workshops in France and England. Their owners soon found that the engine's high consumption of gas and serious problems of overheating and lubrication made it unsatisfactory. Nevertheless, the engine was the first internal-combustion engine to be industrialized, and its faults encouraged others to improve on it.

In the United States, a Boston inventor of English birth named George Brayton devised a gas-fueled engine in 1872 and before long adapted it to burn petroleum vapor. It was a commercial success. Brayton even tried to fit it to road vehicles, but found it too large and heavy. George B. Selden, a patent lawyer of Rochester, New York, expanded on the idea. In 1879 he filed a patent application for a motor car using a Brayton-type engine of reduced size, and placed it over the front wheels. At this time, he did not construct a model of his car and purposely delayed the granting of his patent for many years by submitting amendments to it in an effort to gain rights to new developments.

In Cologne, Germany, self-taught inventor Nicholas Otto also contrived a gas engine more efficient than Lenoir's. He patented it in 1866, and soon began manufacturing it with financial support from Eugen Langen, the son of a wealthy sugar refiner. These men reorganized their firm into the Deutz Gas Motor Factory in 1872, and hired the academically trained and broadly experienced engineer Gottlieb Daimler to manage the factory. In 1876 Otto and Daimler perfected an entirely new design for a gas engine, embodying the four-stroke principle. This was an immense improvement over all the earlier types, and the company enjoyed much success with this "Silent Otto" engine, which it patented.

Other experimenters tried variant approaches. The Scottish engineer Dugald Clerk began working on two-stroke engines in the 1870s, and in 1881 introduced a design that offered commercial possibilities. Almost at the same time, Karl Benz, who operated a small machine shop in Mannheim, Germany, developed a similar two-stroke engine, and, aided financially by some local businessmen, began manufacturing it in 1883.

Thus, advances in gas engines occurred in a number of places, but the trail that actually led to the motor car began in Germany. Legal rulings there in 1884 and 1886 canceled the Deutz Company's patent rights to the four-stroke principle, an event that hastened the birth of the automobile industry by several years. For early in 1886 Karl Benz fitted a four-stroke gasoline engine of his own design to a large tricycle and drove it successfully. This machine is usually considered to be the world's first gasoline automobile. It featured a belt transmission, and two side chains provided the final drive to the rear wheels. The rather slow-running engine supplied about two-thirds of one horsepower and weighed 212 pounds. Its low power and unreliable electric ignition caused Benz much grief, and he did not make his first sale until 1888.

It would be incorrect to credit Benz alone as the "father" of the automobile, for in the meantime Gottlieb Daimler had left the Deutz Company to carry on independent experiments. In a workshop near Stuttgart, he and his assistant, Wilhelm Maybach, worked to perfect the four-stroke engine for use in water and road vehicles. Realizing that the basic problem was to obtain more power with less weight, they aimed to solve it by increasing the speed of the engine. Finding that neither electrical nor gas-flame ignition operated effectively at speeds over 250 rpm, they adopted instead an incandescent-tube ignition system. By 1885 Daimler and Maybach had built an engine that operated at 700 rpm. Weighing eighty-eight pounds, it supplied one-half horsepower, whereas the stationary Otto engine made by

Deutz weighed 1,450 pounds per horsepower. Late in 1886 Daimler and Maybach tested their engine in a crudely built motorcycle, but the results were only mediocre. By 1888 they had placed a more powerful engine in a carriage and demonstrated it publicly.[4]

By the late 1880s a number of inventors had clearly begun to explore the idea of a road carriage propelled by a gasoline engine. Not only the engine, but also various gearing and power transmission mechanisms, as well as suspension and steering devices, had been worked out by engineers and carriage makers over the course of the nineteenth century. Men with vision and skill were beginning to synthesize these elements. But more was needed: a belief that a large market existed for these horseless carriages.

The Role of the Bicycle

Crucial to this idea was the bicycle. The manufacturing of bicycles had begun in France, in the 1860s, when Pierre Michaux fitted a crank and pedals to the front wheel of a two-wheeled vehicle. In England, where bicycles caught on more than elsewhere, the safety bicycle appeared in 1885, a machine equipped with wheels of equal size and a chain drive. By making riding easier and safer, these improvements turned the bicycle movement from a sport for athletes into a craze for everyone.

The popularity of bicycling prepared a market for automobiles. Thousands of riders acquired a taste for speedy mechanical road transport, entirely under their own control. Those who had traveled where and when they wanted on bicycles might well prefer a car to a horse and buggy. Even before this stage arrived, and more important for the origins of the automobile industry, the bicycle must have encouraged hundreds of tinkerers, mechanics, and engineers to consider adopting some kind of mechanical contrivance to supply power for it.

The bicycle not only nourished the idea of lightweight mechanical road vehicles among both mechanics and the general public, but it exerted a powerful impact in other ways. Much of the technology used in automobiles first appeared in the bicycle industry, such as ball bearings, chain drive, various gearing systems, and pneumatic tires. Many of the early car manufacturers came from the bicycle industry, where they had adopted a new method of production: the assembly of many parts made in quantity on specialized machine tools. This method already was used to make watches, small arms, and sewing machines, but it is certain that it came to automobile manufacturing primarily through the bicycle industry.

Although some of the companies that engaged in bicycle manufacturing were large and experienced firms such as Peugeot in France, most were small metalworking shops willing to take a chance in this new business. Bicycles did not interest the large heavy engineering establishments, such as Schneider, Saint-Chamond, or Société Alsacienne in France, Krupp or Borsig in Germany, Vickers or Platt Brothers in England, or Baldwin in the United States. The same pattern repeated itself in the automobile industry.

The Early Development of Automobile Manufacturing

The process of merging the technology, the manufacturing ability, and the potential market to produce and sell reliable motor cars occurred in Germany and especially France around 1890. Daimler and Maybach had perfected their small, high-speed gasoline engine by 1885. In 1887 Daimler persuaded the Paris machine-building firm of Panhard et Levassor (P & L) to purchase a license to make a few of these engines. This company had produced woodworking machinery since the 1840s as well as some gas engines on the early Otto design in the 1870s and Benz types in the 1880s. Emile Levassor, a stubborn and taciturn engineer trained at the Central Engineering Institute in Paris, was technical director. Not long after P & L undertook to produce Daimler engines, it became acquainted with a Benz motorized tricycle that it assembled for Emile Roger, Benz's agent in Paris. Benz himself demonstrated this machine on the streets of Paris in the summer of 1888, but its lack of power did not recommend it. Levassor was not impressed, and Roger found no buyers for several months.

Later that same year, Levassor and Daimler discovered a prominent French client for the Daimler engines: Armand Peugeot, of the town of Montbéliard near the Swiss frontier. Peugeot and his cousin managed a large metalworking concern that made all kinds of hand tools. In the 1880s this company entered bicycle manufacturing on a large scale. But Peugeot was interested in power-driven vehicles also. In 1889 his firm made four small, steam-powered tricycles adapted from a design of Léon Serpollet, but found them unsatisfactory. Even before this, Peugeot had agreed to buy a number of the Daimler type engines made by P & L for use in vehicles. Peugeot's interest was crucial to the beginning of automobile manufacturing in France, not only because of his own firm's entry into the field, but also because his enthusiasm and faith soon would attract P & L to the business. Before Levassor made that decision, an event occurred that spread awareness, especially in France, of some new advances in mechanical transport.

This was the Paris Exposition, or world fair, of 1889. Among the exhibits were a Serpollet-Peugeot steam tricycle, a similar steamer made by Count Albert de Dion, soon to become an outstanding leader in the French automobile industry, a Benz-Roger gasoline tricycle, and several Daimler engines. As the exposition approached its close, Gottlieb Daimler arrived in Paris with a new four-wheeled automobile. It was rather crude and contained nothing remarkable except its engine, a new design in which two cylinders were arranged in a V. This engine turned at more than 600 rpm, and supplied almost two horsepower. It was a major step forward in the search for a lightweight power source for vehicles. Still, French entrepreneurs took advantage of Daimler's brilliant work on engines more quickly than did the Germans.

In 1890 the Peugeot Company constructed a small car powered by a one-cylinder Daimler engine made by P & L. At the same time, Levassor showed that he had been won over to the idea, for he also built a car. He employed chains to drive the wheels rather than gears, as did the 1889 Daimler and the 1890 Peugeot models. Neither the Peugeot nor Levassor cars of 1890 was successful enough to put on the market, but they showed that both companies had become seriously interested in automobiles.

What about their opposite numbers in Germany, Benz and Daimler? Once Benz managed to get a vehicle to run, in 1886, he gradually increased the power of his engines, but he was slow to improve his design, hesitant to learn either from his own experience or from the work of others. Benz's agent in Paris, Emile Roger, was his most successful salesman, finally disposing of some Benz tricycles in the period 1890–92. Upon Roger's urging, Benz introduced a four-wheeled car in 1892. It aroused much more interest than the tricycle, and Roger sold about two dozen of them in that year. Through 1893 the Benz company delivered a total of sixty-nine cars, but only fifteen of them were sold in Germany; Roger marketed forty-two in Paris. Germans were not yet prepared to buy automobiles, and Benz did not know how to provoke their interest. Daimler enjoyed much less success with automobiles in these years. In 1890 he found financial backing and formed the Daimler Motor Company. It concentrated on manufacturing engines, especially for motorboats. Soon

Daimler and Maybach quarreled with their associates, and for a time ceased any active role in the company. During this period, 1892–93, the company made about a dozen small cars designed by Schrodter. Crude and ineffective, they failed.

In France, the Peugeot and P & L companies enjoyed certain advantages over the Benz and Daimler firms. Both were well-established manufacturers whose high reputations were based on high-quality products. Their financial resources were substantial, and they were not troubled by serious disagreements among top management personnel. Both Armand Peugeot and especially Levassor were open to technical innovations for their cars, but they saw beyond mechanical improvements to the need to make standard models without diversifying their efforts too broadly, and they aggressively approached publicity and marketing matters. That men with this mixture of vision and practicality headed important metalworking firms does much to explain why France was the first major home of the automobile industry. But France offered something more: an excellent road system.

Leadership by the government's corps of civil engineers and legislation requiring local governments to maintain local roads at high standards had created a network that contemporary non-French observers found to be unsurpassed. The good roads encouraged bicycle manufacturing and touring. They also made it easier for French businessmen, such as Peugeot and Levassor, to imagine a sizable market for automobiles, for they were practical for residents of provincial cities and towns, whereas the wretched roads of the United States and Germany hindered early automobile development there. Moreover, the reliability of French roads inspired journalists and the early manufacturers to publicize their products by intercity demonstrations and races.

The first of these publicity efforts actually occurred during the first year of automobile manufacturing in France, 1891, when a light Peugeot car powered by a V-twin Daimler engine in the rear and equipped with solid rubber tires was driven by its designer, Rigoulot, from the factory near Montbéliard to Paris. Then it followed a bicycle race from Paris to Brest and back, which gave thousands of people and dozens of Peugeot hardware and bicycle dealers their first look at a horseless carriage. Rigoulot then drove the car to its buyer in Mulhouse, covering more than 1,200 miles on the entire trip.

In the same year, Levassor drove one of his cars from Paris to the Channel coast and back. A few months later, he sold five cars of a new design, in which the engine was positioned in front and drove the rear wheels. This arrangement would be adopted by most manufacturers by the end of the decade and remained standard until the 1930s, when front-wheel drive and rear engines began to reappear. These P & L and Peugeot models of 1891 remained in production for a few years and were gradually improved. Their competition forced Benz to introduce a new four-wheeled model in 1893, which was powered by a new engine of three horsepower. As table 1–1 indicates, it sold well, as did Benz's smaller Velo model of 1894.

These advances in gasoline cars did not discourage adherents of steam-powered vehicles. After making a few more tricycles in 1890–91, Léon Serpollet shifted his attention to steam omnibuses, but made little progress with them. Count Albert de Dion, a playboy aristocrat who demonstrated a passion for machines unusual for those of his social circle, had also been working with steam. In 1881 he had hired two Parisian craftsmen, Bouton and Trepardoux, to make a small steam carriage, but the various vehicles they produced did not reach the count's expectations. Finally, he abandoned these efforts in 1888, and experimented no more successfully with small steam engines for maritime use.

De Dion returned to dry land about 1892 when he and his associates built a steam tractor designed to pull a carriage. This machine incorporated the de Dion axle. To drive the rear wheels without chains, it ran the engine's power through the differential and then by transverse shafts to the wheels through universal joints. When de Dion's team finished this vehicle in 1893, the count convinced his associate Georges Bouton to turn his attention to gasoline engines and try to devise a small high-speed machine that might compete with Daimler's. After two years of effort he did, but much would occur in the interval.

One event came in 1894, the first major publicity effort to further the market for automobiles. This was a road trial to demonstrate the new horseless carriages to the general public. The enterprising journalist Pierre Giffard had promoted the Paris-Brest-Paris bicycle race in 1891 for the *Petit Journal*, and soon thereafter had established a daily bicycle newspaper, *Le Vélo*. He then staged a competition for horseless carriages in the summer of 1894. This affair would not be a race but simply a road test from Paris to Rouen, a distance of seventy-eight miles. That 102 vehicles originally were entered for the trial is striking evidence of the wide interest mechanical transport had aroused in France, but many, or most, of these entries never existed outside the minds of their inventors. When one Sunday late in July 1894 Giffard started the cars off, only twenty-one were ready for the trial. Six P & L cars took part, and five made by Peugeot, all

Table 1-1.
Automobile Production, 1891–1895

	1891	1892	1893	1894	1895
Benz	(7)	(12)	(45)	67	135
P & L	6	16	37	39	72
Peugeot	4	29	24	40	72

Sources: Benz—Siebertz, *Karl Benz*, pp. 170–72, and the author's
estimates in parentheses; P & L—company archives; Peugeot—
company archives.

eleven propelled by Daimler engines. Two others, too, used these
engines. A Roger-Benz car and seven steamers, including the De
Dion-Bouton tractor also participated.

Giffard awarded the first prize jointly to P & L and Peugeot, but
the result also represented a triumph for the Daimler engine, for
twelve of the thirteen cars using it finished the trial on time, as did
the single Benz, but only one steamer arrived within the time limit,
the De Dion. In France, steam never recovered from this defeat.
Those entering the new industry thereafter almost never decided to
tie their future to the steam engine, but chose internal-combustion,
though a few picked electrically powered cars. Well reported in the
Petit Journal, whose circulation was about a million, accounts of the
trial run also appeared in other widely read publications such as
L'Illustration and *La Nature*. The test not only brought the new
machines to the attention of the general public, but it in addition
identified for this public the serious manufacturers and the reliable
cars.

At the Second Bicycle Show, held in Paris in December 1894,
automobiles appeared again. P & L, Peugeot, Roger, and six other
firms displayed their wares. Also in Paris during this month, the first
magazine in the world devoted primarily to the motor car, *La Locomotion Automobile*, published its first issue. But already the leaders of
the infant industry were preparing a bold and spectacular new test
for their vehicles. Shortly after the Paris-Rouen trial, Count de Dion
suggested a race among horseless carriages. He organized a committee that in December announced the details of the competition.
It would extend from Paris to Bordeaux and back, some 745 miles,
nonstop, and the time limit would be a maximum of 100 hours. That
the first formal race in the history of the automobile should be this
demanding (even more than the Indianapolis races of the 1980s)
suggests not only the inexperience of its promoters, but also the

confidence the manufacturers placed in their cars and in the French roads.

Twenty-three automobiles began the race in June 1895. Eight of the nine that arrived within the time limit were gasoline powered, made by P & L, Peugeot, and Benz. An omnibus that Amédée Bollée had built in 1880 was the only steamer to go the distance. Driving one of his own cars, Emile Levassor finished first, in just under forty-nine hours, or an average speed of 15 miles-per-hour. This race clearly demonstrated the reliability of gasoline automobiles, and the three major firms soon found that their only difficulty was expanding production fast enough to satisfy the demand.

The last car to arrive, and it exceeded the 100-hour limit, introduced a significant innovation. This machine rode on pneumatic tires, and was driven by Edouard and André Michelin. These brothers had taken over the family rubber firm at Clermont-Ferrand in 1888, the same year that John Boyd Dunlop reinvented the pneumatic bicycle tire in Belfast, Ireland. The Dunlop Tire Company, headed by an energetic Dubliner, Harvey Du Cros, soon began to market pneumatic bicycle tires, and the Michelin Company entered the field in 1891. While Dunlop stayed with bicycle tires over the next decade as the British motor industry emerged only very slowly, the Michelins watched automobile production grow before their very eyes in France, and detected a future in it for themselves. They made their first public trial of a car equipped with pneumatic tires in the 1895 race. Skeptics, Levassor among them, soon were convinced that this innovation was feasible, and within a few short years nearly all French passaenger cars rode on pneumatics.

By the end of 1895, the pioneer entrepreneurs had demonstrated that gasoline automobiles could be reliable, and that in France a substantial market existed for them. About 350 were already operating in that country and 75 in Germany. The Automobile Revolution had commenced in these states, but had it emerged elsewhere?

In the early 1890s, British inventiveness did not extend to light motorized carriages, and exceptions were few. J. H. Knight built a simple gasoline tricycle by 1895, and others unsuccessfully experimented with electric cars. Frederick R. Simms obtained the British rights to Daimler engines in 1890, but did not go beyond selling imported engines, mostly for motorboats. He did not try to fit them to carriages. A few aristocrats imported a handful of cars from the Continent, and in October 1895 six of them were shown in the first public exhibit of motor cars in England, that country's response to the Paris-Bordeaux race. One can only speculate about the reasons for British disinterest in automobiles in this period: the tremendous prestige that steam engines enjoyed among engineers; the stringent government safety regulations on road locomotives (the Red Flag Law) that limited their speed to two miles-per-hour in towns and four in rural areas, which in turn inhibited experimentation with mechanical road transport.

In the United States, individual experimental activity seemed to be more extensive. Sylvester Roper and Ransom E. Olds built steamers in the 1880s and some inconclusive tests were made with electric cars. More significant, bicycle mechanics Charles and Frank Duryea, apparently stimulated by newspaper accounts of an early Benz motor tricycle, designed a gasoline automobile. They had it built by a machine shop in Springfield, Mass., and first ran it in September 1893, the first gasoline car built in the United States. The Duryeas did not sell any of their cars until 1896, and made hardly more than a dozen of them altogether. In 1894 Elwood Haynes had a gasoline car built on his design by the Apperson machine shop of Kokomo, Indiana, but the Haynes-Apperson Company did not make cars for sale until 1898. Others were tinkering, of course, among them Hiram P. Maxim in Lynn, Massachusetts, and Henry Ford and Charles B. King in Detroit.

The American echo of the Paris-Bordeaux race sounded at Chicago in November 1895. It was the first American automobile race, also sponsored by a newspaper. It covered a distance of fifty-two miles. Six cars started: two electrics, a Duryea, and three Benz cars, apparently imported from Paris. The Duryea won, averaging five miles-per-hour through snow and poor roads. Two Benz cars were the only others to finish. The Americans were still a long way from the best European practice. Part of the difficulty was that none of the earliest American experimenters was yet affiliated with a well-established business firm that could have placed its financial and technical resources at his disposal.

One possibility that might have led to this occurred when William Steinway, the German-born owner of the major American piano factory, obtained the United States rights to Gottlieb Daimler's engines in 1888. But Steinway did not market them very aggressively, and did not try to manufacture a motor car. So, unlike the situation in France, the Daimler engine did not directly ignite the Automobile Revolution in either England or the United States. Perhaps the American who kept closest watch on automobile trends was George Selden. In 1895, after sixteen years of cleverly amending his original patent application of 1879 to try to cover new improvements, Selden finally obtained his patent, which seemed to give him the United States rights to all gasoline automobiles until 1912.

2.   The First Automobile Boom

The period 1895 to 1908 marked the first automobile boom. During these years, France dominated the young industry. It was the leading producer for most of the period and the leading exporter throughout. From France as a center, technical and marketing methods spread to other European countries and to a lesser degree to the United States. This is not to suggest that in this period the French had nothing to learn from elsewhere, but on balance French contributions outweighed French receipts. The minor economic recession of 1907–8 brought a brief pause to the industry in Europe, but it also signaled a turning point. From this time until the First World War, the industry in Britain and Germany grew at a faster rate than in France and relied less on that country. More importantly, a challenge came from America, where manufacturers began to find a mass market for automobiles and sought to create new methods of production to satisfy it. These revolutionary innovations would make the United States the center of the industry from 1908 on.

Some of the reasons for French leadership during the period of the first boom have already been suggested: good roads and the fortuitous circumstance that two of the early French enthusiasts controlled major metalworking firms. In addition, some of the early firms were located in Paris, the center of the market for cars as well as for French journalism. It was convenient for the wealthy Paris sportsmen who bought the early cars to be able to take them to the factory for adjustment and repair. Actually, most of the Paris automobile firms eventually located in the western suburbs, close to the bourgeois section of the city where their clients lived. Automakers situated in the French provinces found themselves at a serious disadvantage if they sought to serve more than just a local market.

Paris set the tone, then, and the major way it did so was by the press. Paris journalism tends to promote what Paris does and what Paris makes. Motor cars and the wealthy men around them quickly attracted journalists who could easily visit the factories to see the industrialists and engineers. By the end of 1900, the French automobile press already included twenty-five publications, most of them in Paris. Day after day, week after week, month after month they spewed forth thousands of words, many thousands more than the 5,386 cars registered in France at the time. Would all this journalism have been devoted to a manufacturing activity carried on exclusively in the provinces? Or, in a broader sense, would the automobile have succeeded so quickly in France if none of the major producers had been located in Paris?

This leads to another reason for France's early lead in the Automobile Revolution: the reluctance with which the other industrial nations joined it. Special factors inhibited early development in Germany, Britain, and the United States. These shall be pointed out in the subsequent examination of the growth of the industry in these countries. In any event, their troubles left the field open to the French, and they took advantage of the opportunity.

In 1895 almost all the cars manufactured in the world were made by three firms. Benz made 135 in Germany, and P & L and Peugeot produced a total of 144 in France. Five years later, in 1900, French factories turned out about 4,800; the Germans produced about 800, Benz accounting for three-fourths of them; the British made about 175; and the Americans 4,000. By 1907 the French total was 25,200, not yet seriously challenged by the British figure of 12,000, the German of 5,150, or the Italian of about 2,500. But, in the United States, production overtook France in 1904–5 and reached 44,000 by 1907.

Marketing

This rapidly expanding output, especially in France and the United States, represented a response to a burgeoning market for cars. This market was potentially available, stimulated by the bicycle. But it had to be won over to automobiles. It was, by several methods used to generate favorable publicity and service to owners, all developed first in France: trial demonstrations, races, automobile clubs, and sales exhibitions or shows.

The trial run of 1894 and race of 1895 were followed by a Paris-Marseille-Paris race in 1896, Paris-Amsterdam-Paris in 1898, and dozens of similar events, culminating in a Paris-Vienna contest through the Alps in 1902 and a Paris-Madrid trek in 1903. The drama involved in men competing against each other, and against dangerous roads, blinding dust, and flimsy tires aroused wide excitement. The Gordon Bennett races of 1900–1905 pitted official representatives of countries against each other and so mobilized national rivalries to heighten interest. Over-the-road racing was a valuable marketing device, for it brought cars directly to the people in the most dramatic way possible.

Such races also permitted the more reflective among the public to compare speeds between cities among various forms of transport. Racing encouraged technical experimentation to increase power and endurance. But the danger to the public caused by racing on open highways soon led to either abolition or strict government control. The competitions on enclosed tracks that followed continued to exert a technical impact, but probably less directly affected marketing because of their artificial nature and because those who paid admission and watched the races were already converted to the automobile.

Another method to promote the sport and industry appeared in November 1895 when Count Albert de Dion and some of the other organizers of the Paris-Bordeaux race established the Automobile Club de France (ACF). Applicants flocked to join, 500 by March 1896 and 1,000 by June 1897. The club sponsored many of the early races, tests, and especially the annual auto shows. Because it was expensive, the ACF attracted rich and prominent persons. Others, from less exalted social circles, joined the Touring Club de France (TCF), founded in 1890 by bicycle enthusiasts and numbering 20,000 already in 1895. Many of the TCF endeavors—improving road signs, publishing maps, arranging for hostels, and urging improvements in provincial hotels—were helpful to early automobilists, and the club gradually increased the role of automobiles in its activities. Private firms in the industry also encouraged auto touring, most prominently Michelin, which began publishing its guide to cities and accommodations in 1900.

In France, automobile exhibitions were held in conjunction with bicycle shows in 1894, 1896, and 1897, but the ACF felt confident enough to inaugurate its own show in 1898. Held at the Tuileries Gardens, in the middle of Paris, that summer, it attracted 140,000 paying visitors. Conducted annually thereafter, the shows at first were retail markets and essential for the smaller firms that did not try to gain publicity by racing. Ultimately, as local sales agencies were established, direct marketing at the shows diminished.

In England, the first motor car reliability trial occurred in November 1896. Financial promotor H. J. Lawson staged it to celebrate the revision of the Red Flag Law to permit cars under two tons weight to travel fourteen miles-per-hour. This "emancipation run" from London to Brighton, marking the new freedom for motor cars, was so badly managed that it is not possible to determine all the cars that participated, or which ones traveled by rail for part or all of the distance. About twenty vehicles were engaged, most of French construction, but a scattering of German, American, and two or three English cars were represented.

Several years later, the 1,000 Mile Reliability Trial of spring 1900 produced a much stronger impact. This was a long demonstration run from London to Edinburgh and back that traversed many of the larger provincial cities. Of the sixty-five starters, twenty-three finished the entire trial, three of them British built. This event not only proved that automobiles were a serious enterprise, but also set off a boom in sales of motor cars, which in turn encouraged dozens of firms to enter manufacturing. Because of safety regulations, over-the-road racing was rare in Britain, and enthusiasts usually were forced to settle for closely controlled hill climbs or stage their competitions on the Isle of Man or in Ireland.

Frederick Simms founded the Automobile Club of Great Britain and Ireland in August 1897.[5] Membership grew more slowly in this organization than in the French ACF, reaching only 540 in November 1899, probably because cars were not yet readily available in Britain. The club and its able secretary, Claude Johnson, organized the 1,000 Mile Trial, and thereafter the organization expanded rapidly. From 1896 on, British followers of the industry could attend occasional auto shows, which were either rather small affairs staged by importers of French and German cars or were appendages to bicycle shows. Ultimately, the automobile club began to manage these shows.

In September 1897 some German enthusiasts founded the Mid-European Automobile Club in Berlin; prepared a small exhibit of cars made by Benz, Daimler, and Lutzmann; and organized a trial run to Potsdam and back. Two years later, the Berlin club put on a large show, in which a few foreign cars were represented, and Frankfurt began conducting shows not long afterward. Interest kindled only slowly in Germany. In 1902 the total membership of auto clubs in Berlin, Hamburg, Munich, and thirteen other cities reached only 900. In that year, the kaiser reversed his original opposition and began using automobiles. Others in the imperial family followed suit. The victory of a German Mercedes car in the Gordon Bennett race in 1903 brought this event to German soil the next year, and public interest began to mount. In 1905 came the first of the Herkomer reliability trials, in which eighty-nine cars started on a route 580 miles long.

Germans now were buying cars but only about half as many per year as Frenchmen. What held them back? Probably social conservatism, an attitude noted by many observers and often taking the form of a nostalgia for a rural, preindustrial past, incited perhaps by the traumatic problems springing from the extremely rapid industrialization and urbanization of Wilhelmine Germany.

In the United States, early runs to demonstrate reliability first were made as separate ventures by individual manufacturers or private owners. In 1897 Alexander Winton drove one of his cars from Cleveland to New York City, a distance considerably less than the trip made by the Peugeot car across northern France in 1891. Winton repeated the trip in 1899. In May 1901 a P & L car was driven from New York to Chicago, and in October Roy Chapin piloted a small Oldsmobile from Detroit to New York City. Two years later, several private owners made trips from San Francisco to New York, each taking about two months. They found that the wretched roads presented a more serious problem than mechanical faults in the cars. In 1905 and for several years thereafter, the Glidden tours involved groups of privately owned cars engaging in reliability runs through sections of the United States, rather like the Herkomer runs in Germany. By now dozens of local auto clubs were organizing innumerable endurance runs, races, and hill climbs to test and show off their cars.

The impact of racing was not so strong in the United States as in France, whether over-the-road or on closed tracks. Americans seemed more concerned about the dangers of racing than thrilled by its competitive aspects. But, for those who craved to watch the cars race around a track dozens or even hundreds of times, the Indianapolis race, begun in 1911, soon became an annual highlight.

The first successful automobile clubs began to appear in 1900, in New York and Chicago. Within a few years, nearly a hundred were organized. Those such as the Automobile Club of America (New York City) that followed the European example of socially restrictive membership, high dues, and elaborate club facilities usually failed to attract many members, but the more democratic clubs thrived. In

1902 the American Automobile Association (AAA) was established as a federation of local clubs, but it originally accomplished little, for the local clubs provided such services as motorists wanted.

The Automobile Club of America and the National Association of Automobile Manufacturers sponsored the first successful auto show in November 1900 at New York. About 48,000 attended, and they were held annually thereafter. Chicago and other large cities also conducted auto shows. The National Association of Automobile Manufacturers, founded in 1900, affected the industry only slightly. In a few years, it split into two trade associations that took opposite views on the Selden patent. Employer organizations that produced a more immediate impact on the industry early in the twentieth century were various associations aiming to weaken or destroy labor unions in manufacturing, such as the National Metal Trades Association and the Employers Association of Detroit.

One measure of the success of all these efforts in popularizing the automobile is the comparison in table 2–1 of the number of cars and trucks registered at the end of this period, late in 1907.

Methods of automobile marketing did not differ much among the various countries in these years. Usually the customer advanced about one-third of the price on account, and paid the balance on delivery. When a firm's output was small, it would often sell direct at the factory, especially in the case of Paris manufacturers, but ultimately it would delegate sales to agents. In Europe, such dealers early in the twentieth century bought cars from manufacturers at a 10–20 percent discount, paying part of the price on order and the rest on delivery. In the early days of the Ford company in the United States, it granted discounts of up to 25 percent to dealers. Established firms such as Peugeot and P & L originally sold through agents already handling other items for them, but new ones such as Renault Frères and Olds and Ford in the United States did not seem to experience difficulty finding dealers. Peugeot was probably the first to establish company-owned sales and service branches. Ford began to do the same in 1905.

The background of auto dealers was diverse. In Europe, they were often former racing drivers or bicycle salesmen. In America, it was more common for men who lacked experience with cars or bicycles to become dealers. This suggests that it took a shorter time for American businessmen to convince themselves of the seriousness of the industry, and shows the speed with which it grew in the United States. The larger the sales of a make of cars, the more valuable became the dealer's franchise, and the more requirements the manufacturers could place on the dealer. The Ford Company rather early

Table 2-1.
Motorization in 1907

	Automobiles registered	Inhabitants per car
United States	143,200	608
Britain	63,500	640
France	40,000	981
Germany	16,214	3,824
Belgium	7,800	924
Italy	6,080	5,554
Canada	2,100	3,053

Sources: United States—Flink, *America Adopts the Automobile*,
p. 58; Britain—*Autocar*, 27 July 1907, pp. 146–47; France—
Bulletin de statistique et de législation comparée 64 (1908):
143, but about 2,500 added so as to include untaxed vehicles;
Germany—*Statistisches Jahrbuch*, 1913, p. 129; Belgium—
author's estimate; Italy—*Autocar*, 2 May 1908, p. 649; Canada
—*Historical Statistics of Canada* (Toronto: Macmillan, 1965),
p. 550.

began insisting that its dealers handle no other makes of cars, and
that they carry large stocks of parts. By 1913 Ford dealers in the
United States numbered 7,000, and a year later nearly 1,000 in
Great Britain, but British (and Continental) practice allowed dealers
to handle several makes.

Dealers in England appear to have led the way in selling cars on
the installment plan. As early as 1903, Charles Rolls of London
offered P & L cars at 20 percent cash down, followed by four quarterly payments at 5-percent annual interest. In France, several small
banks soon specialized in making installment loans for automobiles,
and some instances of this occurred in the United States, but this
practice was not common before the First World War.

Export sales amounted to a substantial portion of early automobile
production in France; they rose from about one-third of output in
1899 and 1900 to more than half from 1903 through 1907. French
automobile exports of 144 million francs in 1907 well exceeded the
total of automotive exports from all other countries combined, as
had been the case since the beginning of the century. This demonstrated the overwhelming dominance of France in this industry's
international trade. By far the largest market for French exports was

the United Kingdom, which remained the biggest buyer from 1901 through 1913 and took more than half of French exports in the first four years of this period. This situation resulted from a rapidly growing demand for cars in Great Britain after 1900 that could not be supplied by local producers. Not until 1905 did British production exceed French imports, and by this time the French had won a place on the British market that only gradually declined. Because the total of French exports of cars slightly exceeded those sold at home from 1899 through 1907, the crucial importance of exports to the growth of the industry in France is clear. Yet the development of foreign markets, especially in Britain and other industrial countries, seems to have been caused more by the efforts of local importers than by French manufacturers.

In Europe, tariffs were not a serious problem in international trade. Entrance to Britain, the largest market, was free, and the tariff was 2–3 percent of the value for Germany, 4–6 percent for Italy, 8–12 percent for France, and 12 percent for Belgium. The high United States rate, 45 percent of the value, was reduced to 30 percent in 1913 for cars priced under $2,000 and for chassis and parts.

Taxicabs

About 1905 a new and specialized market for automobiles emerged: taxicabs. Earlier, in the late 1890s, a number of financiers had plunged into the electric cab business in New York, London, Paris, and other major cities. This effort fizzled out because the batteries and pneumatic tires of the electric cabs could not survive the heavy usage. Gasoline cabs were rarely used until the appearance of the taximeter, a mechanical device to render an accurate charge for the use of the cab, based on the time and distance. This machine guaranteed an honest accounting to both the client and the owner of the cab. French businessmen first took advantage of it on a large scale.

In 1905 a financial group associated with the Banque Mirabaud began to introduce gasoline taxicabs by the hundreds in Paris through their company Automobiles de Place. The same group repeated its innovation in London with the General Motor Cab Company and in New York with the New York Motor Cab Company. In all three cities, French-made cabs were used exclusively.[6] Other large- and medium-sized cities all over the world quickly adopted taxicabs, too, though not as eagerly as London and Paris. By 1911 more than 7,000 automobile taxicabs were operating in London, nearly 5,000 in Paris, and 2,000 in Berlin. These cabs whetted the appetite for cars among those who did not own them, and also affected the industry directly in Europe, for it was forced to expand to meet the sudden new demand for several thousand cabs of standard design annually. Such orders were instrumental in the growth of some firms, such as Renault and Unic in France and Napier in England.

Who Were the Clients?

In all countries, the earliest buyers of cars came from the same social groups: wealthy sportsmen, doctors, businessmen, and engineers. Sportsmen usually did not consider the original cost and the expense of operation as major factors in the decision to buy a car, but others were concerned about them. Automobile magazines frequently tried to demonstrate the financial advantages of mechanical transportation over the horse-drawn carriage. Some of these periodicals also tried to persuade manufacturers that a large market existed for reliable low-priced cars.[7] Most of the European and many of the American makers during this period preferred instead to aim at the wealthy with a limited output and a substantial profit per car. This attitude, however, should not be considered as solely the result of snobbishness or feeble entrepreneurship. Most of the early producers of cars were technicians or engineers. They aimed to make high-quality products to satisfy their own standards and those of their peers. Reflecting their training and experience, their interests focused on elegant design and technical innovation. Yet such attitudes made their cars expensive. Few of them recognized a challenge or potential profits in factory management or marketing, for these were "less noble" matters.

Governmental Reactions

When the automobile appeared, it quickly generated two kinds of opposition. Some feared it as a danger to life and limb, either because of careless driving or because of the many accidents that occurred from horses panicking when confronted by these vehicles. Many rural and small town residents were concerned about the terrible dust and damage to their roads caused by fast-moving cars.

Neither type of opposition prevailed, of course, but governments gradually did try to deal with both problems, first registering cars and drivers as well as regulating driving, especially speed, and then by covering roads with hard surfaces. Local officials usually acted first to regulate driving, sometimes within national rules, as in Britain. Public authorities did not hesitate to tax motor vehicles, charging fees for license tags and levying property taxes on them. The latter taxes tended to be higher in Europe than in the United States, for automobiles were more closely identified with the rich in the Old World. The adaptation of roads to the automobile came more slowly, for this would be expensive. The first step was to cover with asphalt the roads leading out of the large cities, but little progress in this endeavor was made before 1914.

Governments also moved slowly to adopt automobiles for their own purposes because bureaucracies played their usual retardant role. Cities usually led the way, acquiring motor vehicles for police work, fire fighting, and street maintenance. All armies were interested in automobiles, but not enough to transfer large sums from horses or other equipment to get them. The French Army, for example, owned only 220 automobiles in July 1914, including 91 trucks and 50 tractors for pulling artillery.[8] This situation even extended to the army's higher officers, for the military governor of Paris in 1913 still rode in a 1904 Panhard. In a letter to the Minister of War in May 1913, he complained that this old-fashioned model was unworthy of his position, especially because it was unable to keep up with the cars of other important personages in official parades. After a year, he finally received a promise of a new car.[9] Earlier, the German Army had devised a system to provide it with trucks in case of war. A regulation of 1908 authorized a government subsidy and annual maintenance allowance to purchasers of approved trucks in return for the army's right to requisition these vehicles in an emergency. France and Britain adopted similar schemes during the next few years.

As a whole, however, before 1914 governments did not recognize the revolutionary implications of the automobile and so concerned themselves little with it.

3.   The Early Manufacturers

Among the earliest automobile manufacturers, those who wagered on gasoline as an energy source would win out over those who favored steam or electricity. The French were the first to develop this industry, and they set the pattern.

Production

It was in the 1890s that France became the center of automobile production, and it retained its dominance in Europe until the 1930s. The earliest French firms in the business, Panhard et Levassor (P & L) and Peugeot, represent one type of company that entered the industry: established metalworking concerns looking for a new product line. P & L gained much prestige from its early racing victories, and built powerful and expensive cars. It offered a wide range of models, using engines of its own design, from 1899 on. After increasing production to 1,017 cars in 1902, the firm expanded its output little until 1910. Financially, its best years were 1903 to 1906, when it paid annual dividends of 50 percent.[10]

Armand Peugeot took his automobile business outside the family firm, Les Fils de Peugeot Frères, in 1896 and established a separate concern, Automobiles Peugeot, also largely family owned. In addition to a plant at Audincourt, in the Montbéliard region near the Swiss frontier, he opened an auto factory in Lille, where skilled labor was more abundant. The company began to use its own engines in the mid-1890s and produced 500 cars in 1900, but this was its last profitable year for some time. Because the firm failed to keep abreast of the rapid technical advances in automobiles, early in the century its old-fashioned models lost favor, as did also those of the Benz company in Mannheim at the same time. By 1905 Peugeot had recovered its lost ground, in that year making more cars (1,261) than P & L. Its vehicles were relatively light and low priced, a policy typical of producers who had been engaged in the bicycle trade. Sales revenue for Peugeot was much less than for P & L, and so were profits. The former paid no dividends from 1901 through 1904 and only 5 percent from 1905 through 1908.[11]

French companies entering automobile production from other sectors included Mors, Hotchkiss, and Delaunay-Belleville, all located in the Paris region. Mors had earlier moved from the manufacture of artificial flowers to electrical equipment. In 1896 it established an automobile department, and assigned Henri Brasier as its technical director. Following the lead of P & L, it gained a reputation for producing powerful racing cars, and sold its small output at high prices. After Brasier left Mors in 1901, its cars declined in quality and the firm experienced serious difficulties, even after the dynamic André Citroën took over its management in 1907. As Mors faded into the background Hotchkiss and Delaunay-Belleville entered the business, both manufacturing expensive and high-powered cars.

Hotchkiss had been founded in the Paris suburb of Saint-Denis by an American to make machine guns. A slow market for them early in the twentieth century led it to begin automobile manufacture, and it introduced its first cars in 1903. Yet Hotchkiss never fully committed itself to automobiles and never made more than 200 per year before the war. Delaunay-Belleville, also located in Saint-Denis, was a renowned manufacturer of boilers for ships. It, too, began to make cars when its primary activity suffered a slump, and showed its first cars in 1904. Delaunay took its new activity quite seriously and competed effectively with other luxury cars, such as Daimler-Mercedes and Rolls Royce. Annual output rarely exceeded 1,000 and was usually considerably less than this.

The bicycle industry contributed many firms to the French automobile industry in addition to Peugeot. Two leading bicycle producers in the 1890s, Alexandre Darracq and Adolphe Clément, soon began producing automobiles. In 1896 an English combine led by Harvey Du Cros of the Dunlop Company bought out the two bicycle firms. Darracq thereupon built a new factory near Paris, in Suresnes, to make bicycle parts. He also experimented with automobiles, and in 1900 offered a moderately priced one-cylinder model. It quickly caught the fancy of the public, which by September 1901 had purchased about 1,000 of them. In this early example of quantity production of a single model, Darracq made its own engines but seems to have obtained most of its other components from suppliers. Sales and profits grew in the following years, during which Darracq was probably second only to De Dion-Bouton in the number of cars produced. The firm's splendid results encouraged an English financial group to buy it out in 1903 for a handsome price; Darracq remained as managing director in Suresnes making 2,000–3,000 medium-priced cars per year. Most of these cars were exported, especially to Britain, but also to Germany and Italy.

Adolphe Clément's career followed a similar line. After he sold his bicycle company to the Du Cros group, he stayed with his company for a few years but also became chairman of the board of P & L until 1903. At the same time, he began making cars under his own name in Levallois, a Paris suburb. Many of these went to England from 1902 on, where they were sold as Talbot cars.

Other Paris auto manufacturers who entered the industry from the bicycle trade included Chenard et Walcker and Georges Richard. In 1904 Richard left the company he had founded, and it began to concentrate on racing and sports cars under the name Brasier. Richard established a new firm, Unic, which was financially supported by Henri de Rothschild, and found a good market in taxicabs, especially in London. Almost without exception the bicycle men entering the new industry in France chose to make large numbers of cars in only a few different models and to concentrate on the lower half of the price range. Their interest was stronger in production and marketing than elegance of design and luxury of appearance.

Some of the most successful automobile firms were founded by those completely new to manufacturing. One of them, Count (from 1901 Marquis) Albert de Dion, became the most significant personality in the French industry during the boom years. In 1895 his ingenious associate Georges Bouton devised a small, air-cooled, gasoline engine that operated at 1,500 rpm. Supplied with a new system of electric ignition, it proved to be very reliable and was used to power a large tricycle. In its factory in the Paris suburb of Puteaux, De Dion-Bouton made thousands of these engines annually in the late 1890s, about 1,100 per month in 1899,[12] and may have sold some 15,000 of its tricycles from 1895 to 1901. Those seeking the beginning of automobile mass production might well consider this instance. Dozens of auto firms bought De Dion-Bouton engines at the turn of the century, in France, the rest of Europe, and America. Others acquired licenses to manufacture the famous tricycle, and more imitated it and the engine. In 1899 the firm introduced its first four-wheeled gasoline car, at about $780, and soon about 100 of them left the factory each month. Early in the twentieth century, it produced more gasoline cars than any other company in the world.

As an aristocratic sportsman at the center of Paris society, de Dion might have been expected to turn his company toward the elegant and expensive vehicle so appreciated by his social circle, but this did not happen until after 1910. De Dion-Bouton concentrated on small one-cylinder cars until 1903, and abandoned this type only in 1912. De Dion frequently advised others in the industry of the current and future importance of the light and low-powered small car. However, he did not take the next step of concentrating all his production on one model. In France, Darracq and Renault enjoyed the same opportunity to adopt a one-model policy but made the same decision, to offer a wider range.

De Dion believed in thorough integration of production in his firm, making some of his own bodies from at least 1904 on, along with most other components. He continued producing a few heavy steam vehicles until about 1905, and ventured into electric cars. He added a line of gasoline trucks in 1903 but was more successful with his buses, widely used in Paris, London, and New York. In 1909 he installed a metallurgical research laboratory in his Puteaux factory and designated Léon Guillet as its director. Guillet, a recent graduate of the Central Engineering Institute in Paris, became the leading French expert in the chemical nature of special steels. De Dion-Bouton and P & L were among the first French automobile firms to use special steels for valves, shafts, gears, and other critical parts.

Amazingly vigorous, de Dion carried the flag for the entire industry. His role in the beginning of auto racing and the founding of the Automobile Club de France has been mentioned earlier. He also established a trade asssociation, founded the daily newspaper *L'Auto* in 1900, and in 1907 organized a machine tool company to provide auto firms with machines of French rather than German or American manufacture. This venture did not succeed. In time, de Dion seems to have involved himself and his company in too many different activities to become outstandingly successful at any one. His place in the leading circles of the new industry does not mean that aristocrats participated to any significant degree in auto manufacturing. In fact, his firm and Lorraine-Dietrich, a provincial establishment, were the only major French producers whose leadership was aristocratic. As De Dion-Bouton faded from the top rank in the French automobile business after 1905, Renault Frères came to the fore.

Son of a Parisian bourgeois family, Louis Renault exhibited strong mechanical inclinations, and did not follow his two older brothers into the family textile sales business. In 1898 he converted a De Dion-Bouton tricycle into a small car that featured the engine in front and direct drive in top gear. Financially supported by his brothers, he began making these cars in the same year in a small workshop located on some family property in suburban Billancourt. At first Renault Frères was almost entirely an assembly operation, but most of the large profits were reinvested to erect buildings and equip them. In 1903 the firm ceased using engines supplied by De Dion-Bouton and Aster in preference to those of its own manufacture. Moderate prices (from $1,000 to $1,500) and racing victories gained some repute for Renault cars, but the big opportunity came in 1905 when a Paris cab firm ordered 250 taxicabs. These worked so well that over the next five years orders for thousands more poured in. Although the company received considerably less for these machines than for ordinary passenger cars, the contracts were quite profitable, and the Renault brothers rapidly expanded their factory.

In quantity of output (3,066) and sales turnover (more than $6 million), the firm became France's largest auto producer in 1907, two years before Louis's last surviving brother died and he became sole owner of the firm. One of the most interesting aspects of the taxicab business was that it did not lead him to conclude that large scale production of one standard model was the route to rapid growth and success in the industry. Although he may have devoted more attention to questions of productive efficiency than most other French auto manufacturers of the period, he loved technical innovation, and he obtained hundreds of patents in his own name.

Lyon, the second economic capital of France, was also the second center of automobile manufacturing. Marius Berliet built a personal automobile empire there. A self-taught mechanic like Renault, he began with fewer resources but by 1901 had a sturdy model on the market. Berliet cars caught the attention of the American Locomotive Company, which in 1905 bought a license to assemble and eventually produce them in the United States. The license fee of $100,000 and the prestige of this transaction allowed Berliet to expand his operations and to rank with Rochet-Schneider, the other major Lyon producer.

The last of the four largest provincial automakers in France early in the twentieth century (after Peugeot and the two Lyonnais concerns) was Lorraine-Dietrich of Lunéville, a town near Nancy in French Lorraine. This railway car builder began to make cars in 1897, its output rising from 100 in 1899 to 311 expensive (more than $2,000) autos in 1903. While both its automobile and railway car businesses flourished thereafter, the company began building a new factory in the Paris suburb of Argenteuil (demonstrating the attraction of Paris to this industry), bought control of the Italian Isotta-Fraschini motor car company of Milan, and acquired still another auto factory in Birmingham, England. All this bold expansion looked like a mistake in 1908 when sales of the company's high-priced cars fell sharply in the recession of that year. Suffering heavy losses, it went through a reorganization that left it in the control of a Belgian financial group, which sold the Italian and British operations.

The four sizable provincial auto makers compare with about a dozen significant firms in the capital, where 70 to 80 percent of the cars were made from 1900 to 1907. Of course, dozens of other small French automobile manufacturers popped up during this period, many disappearing in a few years. Most of these just assembled components obtained from specialist manufacturers who quickly entered the business in the late 1890s. For example, in 1907 thirty-nine firms in the Paris region dealt in shock absorbers, springs, and axles for motor cars. All but four or five of the thirty largest French automobile producers in 1914 already had been in operation by 1907; those companies that started early had the best chance of survival.

Paris' dominance in the French automobile industry sprang from a variety of factors. Mentioned previously were the reciprocal influence of the original market of Paris sportsmen, early Paris manufacturers such as P & L, Mors, De Dion-Bouton, and Paris journalism. Some major bicycle firms were located in Paris, and, when some of them turned to automobiles, this further strengthened the capital's role. That it was not a center for producing the industry's raw materials—steel, aluminum, wood, and leather—was not important, for the cost of transporting these supplies did not bulk large in the cost of the final product. Of crucial significance, however, was the large number of small establishments engaged in a wide variety of metal and woodworking, firms that could supply the components needed in cars such as axles, springs, wheels, gears, carburetors, radiators, and electrical equipment. It was not difficult to begin automobile manufacturing in Paris with only a small amount of capital, as did Renault in 1898 or Delage in 1905, buying most of the components on credit from nearby suppliers. The many metalworking shops in the capital also provided a large pool of skilled and semiskilled labor for auto manufacturing to draw upon, an advantage no other French city could match.

Paris businessmen were fine salesmen, especially of expensive luxury goods, of which the city had been a center for centuries. The early automobile was a new Parisian toy, and Paris merchants knew how to market it. Did Paris as the financial center of France pose any significance? Probably only a secondary one. Most car makers tried to avoid recourse to financial institutions for long-term credit, but several smaller investment houses did supply capital to some Paris firms. To the major locational factors of the market, the presence of other metalworking firms, and the large labor supply must be added a fourth, capable entrepreneurship. Paris' leadership owed much to men such as Emile Levassor, Albert de Dion, Adolphe Clément, and Louis Renault. That major metal fabricating centers such as Saint Etienne and Lille took little part in the automobile industry despite certain favorable economic factors must be credited to a lack of entrepreneurship in those places at the crucial moment.

After France, widespread interest by businessmen in automaking appeared first in Belgium in the late 1890s. A surprisingly large number of companies entered the new industry at an early date, primarily metalworking establishments previously engaged in small arms, railway equipment, or bicycle manufacturing. Two of the more successful Belgian producers specialized in small, inexpensive vehicles. Alexis Vivinus of Brussels began producing a light car that was equipped with a belt transmission in 1899. He also licensed English, French, and German firms to make this car.

That same year, the National Armament Company (FN) of Liège entered auto production, soon making several hundred a year of a small and conventional design. Larger types on Daimler and P & L lines came from Germain, a producer of railway cars, from 1897 on, and from Minerva, a bicycle company of Antwerp, after 1900. By 1904 these and other Belgian manufacturers turned out about 1,500 cars per year. Local producers supplied most of the domestic market, while exports exceeded imports throughout these years, in sharp distinction from the British case.

As early as 1904, the number of cars registered in the United Kingdom (24,000 by the end of the year) surpassed those in France, though in that year the British made only about 3,000, compared to nearly 17,000 produced in France. This rapid rise in demand for automobiles in Britain after 1900 raises the question of why British manufacturers moved more slowly into the industry than the French, Belgians, and Americans. As already mentioned, the Red Flag Law speed limits may have helped discourage experimentation before 1896, along with the high prestige accorded to steam engines in the land of Watt and Stephenson.

More pertinent as a cause of delay were the financial manipulations of Harry J. Lawson, a London industrial promoter. In 1895 he formed the British Motor Syndicate to buy out the British rights to the Daimler patents, which were owned by F. R. Simms, who had not done much with them. Then, in 1896, Lawson licensed these rights to his Daimler Motor Company, a new firm established in a factory in Coventry to assemble a few cars from largely French components. He also obtained British rights to De Dion-Bouton and other automotive patents, and in turn licensed them at high prices to concerns that he floated or controlled, such as the Humber bicycle company. Burdened by over capitalization, eccentric management, and a lack of engineering talent, his companies did not engage in significant automobile production for several years, but his claims that he controlled the key patents in the industry may have discouraged some other firms from entering. By 1900, its fifth year of operation, the Daimler Motor Company had finally formulated its own designs and made about 150 cars.

Another key factor in British delay was the major engineering strike, or lockout, of 1897–98. Lasting from July 1897 into early 1898, it slowed or stopped production in numerous metalworking firms. When it finally ended, the owners of many of these companies may have hesitated to jump into the new automobile business, for they were under financial strain and preferred to fill orders that had been delayed.

Nevertheless, around 1900 British firms outside the Lawson system began to show interest in the new industry. Some bicycle makers jumped in. Two of them, in Wolverhampton, began making the Star and Sunbeam cars, at first following Benz designs and then adopting De Dion-Bouton engines and its drive system; the Swift concern, in Coventry, followed the same path. In 1904 and 1905, by which time the industry had proved that it was much more than a temporary fad, the Rover and Singer bicycle companies of Coventry also entered. By 1906 Humber and Rover ranked as the largest producers coming from the bicycle group, making about 1,000 and 500 cars in that year.

Moving into the new industry from elsewhere in the engineering trades were Wolseley in 1899 and Napier in 1900. Herbert Austin of the Wolseley Sheep Shearing Machine Company of Birmingham experimented with motor cars from 1895 on. In 1901, when the steel and arms maker Vickers bought the company, it put one of Austin's designs into production and made 323 in that year, doubling this output within five years. Austin then left Wolseley to set up his own firm near Birmingham. The Napier Company, an old machine and hardware maker in London, began working on a car in the late 1890s, encouraged by an enthusiastic motorist, S. F. Edge. Production cars appeared in 1900. Edge set up a sales company to market

Napiers, and publicized them by racing and making claims of technical innovations. In fact, Napier perfected a six-cylinder engine as
early as 1903. Although the firm concentrated on expensive luxury
cars, it also made a successful taxicab, which accounted for nearly
one-third of its production of 4,639 cars from 1908 through 1913.

Most British auto companies until about 1906 depended heavily
on France for their designs, raw materials, and components, but one
in particular preserved its independence: Lanchester. After the brilliant mechanical engineer Frederick Lanchester built his first car
in 1896, he continued experimenting for several years with original
and ingenious solutions to problems of vibration, carburetion, ignition, and transmission. Production began in 1900 in a small factory
near Birmingham. The combination of a complex mechanism, slight
dependence on outside suppliers, and an unorthodox design that
frightened away clients brought high prices and few sales. Frederick
Lanchester's insistence that design factors must outweigh concern
about cost of production and marketing made his excellent car a
curiosity rather than a major factor in the British automobile trade.

Far more fame came to the Rolls-Royce. Henry Royce was a poor
boy, for his father, a flour miller, died when he was ten. Lacking
much formal education but endowed with mechanical talent and
ambition, he became chief engineer for the street-lighting system in
Liverpool. In 1884 he established a shop in Manchester making
electrical equipment. In 1904 he made several two-cylinder cars as
an experiment, their design largely based on current French practice.
He did not sell them, but Charles S. Rolls, an aristocrat who held an
engineering degree from Cambridge, an enthusiastic and knowledgeable motorist who also operated an auto dealership in London selling
imported cars such as P & L, Mors, and the Belgian Minerva, tested
one of Royce's cars. Impressed by their quality, he contracted to sell
them under the name Rolls-Royce. Over the next two years, Royce
made about 100 cars in five different models, ranging from two to
eight cylinders.

In 1907 he found the Holy Grail, his masterpiece, the six-cylinder
Silver Ghost. The company, now Rolls-Royce, Ltd., settled in a new
factory in Derby, and until 1925 made only this model. Although
these cars achieved a high standard of excellence and elegance, they
were not revolutionary in any sense. The company only produced
about 2,800 altogether before the First World War. In the long view,
Rolls-Royce's later accomplishments with aircraft engines outweigh
its automobiles. The firm's move in this direction was foreshadowed
when Charles Rolls took up aviation in its pioneer period. In 1910

his Wright aircraft crashed, and he was the first Briton to die in an airplane accident.

Other early British automobile firms originating outside the bicycle industry included Arrol-Johnston, Argyll, and Albion in Glasgow; the Maudslay and Standard companies in Coventry; and Vauxhall in London. Another London company, Talbot, began in 1903 by importing Clément cars from France. By 1906 Talbot offered a British-built car along with French-made models. Many other small British engineering firms made automobiles in the period 1901–4, but most of them left the field within five or six years. The location of the early British auto industry, primarily in the Midlands, followed by London and Glasgow, should cause no surprise. It arose in areas already engaged in bicycle and other engineering work, where managerial experience, skilled labor, and nearby component manufacturing shops were available.

Not until 1906–8 did the British industry as a whole break loose from French domination. The big demand for cars that began with the Reliability Trial of 1900 was met in the first instance by French machines, Panhards, Darracqs, De Dions, and others, easily imported in this free-trade era. From the beginning, British automakers depended to some extent on French-made components, especially engines and cylinder castings, but gradually found local suppliers or began to make some of these parts in their own shops.

Although many of the British automobile engineers had connections with the bicycle industry, where large-scale output was common, they were less attracted to quantity production during these early years than was the case in France, to say nothing of America. Was this because they could not abide French leadership and wanted to do things differently, or was it because they prized technical perfection above market considerations? More likely the latter. The largest producers by 1906 were Humber (1,000), Argyll (800), Wolseley (629), and Daimler and Rover each made more than 500 cars. The following year, total output was about 12,000 cars.

Although in Britain automobile production expanded slowly despite strong demand, in Germany it grew even more slowly because of anemic demand. The Benz company remained the major producer through the 1890s into the new century, but not until 1899 did it sell more of its cars in Germany than France. After a fine year in 1900, when it delivered 603 cars, a crisis struck. Sales dropped sharply as motorists turned away from the old-fashioned Benz design to more powerful and reliable models that were based on French designs and components.

Karl Benz's hesitation to redesign his cars led to tension and bitter disagreement in the company's management when his colleagues hired a team of French engineers to modernize the output. He withdrew from the firm's activities and resigned from the board of directors in April 1903. After the company suffered heavy financial losses, he returned to the board when it offered some updated models that featured shaft rather than chain drive. From 1905 the firm began to expand, producing a variety of types and engaging heavily in racing. It stood ready to take advantage of the finally awakening German interest in automobiles. But Benz no longer played an active role in the firm. Indeed, he established another company in 1906, utilizing a small factory near Heidelberg. There, he and his two sons, under the name C. Benz Söhne, made cars in small numbers until 1926.

While Benz was turning out hundreds of cars in the late 1890s, Daimler was making dozens. From 1895 to 1897 Gottlieb Daimler and Wilhelm Maybach gradually regained managerial control of the Daimler Motor Company and produced a few cars, making only the engines in the Cannstatt factory. An engineer rather than an industrialist, Daimler kept busy adapting his engines to new uses, designing racing cars, buses, trucks, and rail cars. Like most European automobile engineers of this period, he found more satisfaction in design innovations than in identifying and solving production problems. During these years, his health failed and he died in March 1900.

As he faded from the company's leadership, Emil Jellinek rose in influence. His father had been a prominent rabbi in Vienna, but Emil eventually found success in the insurance business. He spent much time in Nice, on the French Riviera, and by 1898 was selling Daimler cars to his wealthy friends there. In fact, he was the major outlet for the cars, and joined the board of directors in 1900. He kept hectoring the company to raise the power of its cars and modernize their design. Maybach and Paul Daimler (Gottlieb's son) followed these suggestions, and early in 1901 began delivering the new Mercedes model, named for Jellinek's daughter. The 1901 Mercedes did very well in some races, and established a high standard for luxury sports cars. It popularized some new devices: the honeycomb radiator, pressed steel (rather than wood) chassis frames, an improved gearbox, and mechanically operated inlet valves. For the first time in Europe, a car that was not French set the fashion for automobile design.

But the Daimler company had remained quite small, making fewer than 150 cars a year and selling them at prices of more than $4,000. In 1902 it began to expand. First, it took over a small auto factory in the Berlin suburb of Marienfelde and concentrated its truck and bus operations there. Then, after a serious fire at its Cannstatt works in 1903, it moved to a new factory in Unterturkheim, another suburb of Stuttgart. Such expansion aimed at producing more parts in the firm's own shops rather than a large increase in cars manufactured. In 1907 sales were $1.9 million on an output of less than 500 vehicles.

In the late 1890s, other automobile producers appeared in Germany, stimulated by the success of Karl Benz and echoes from France. Among those that had been engaged in the bicycle business were Opel of Rüsselsheim (near Mainz) and Adler of Frankfurt. Opel began with a Benz-type car in 1898, then in 1902 began importing Darracq and some Renault chassis, for which it supplied bodies. Opel gradually introduced its own designs, and ended its French connections in 1906. Adler started operation in 1900 using De Dion-Bouton engines, but soon installed its own. Other early firms, Stoewer of Stettin and Dürkopp of Bielefeld, in Westphalia, were already engaged in metalworking, and August Horch was an engineer for the Benz company who left it to begin making his own cars in Cologne in 1900. In Berlin, a number of small auto firms appeared, but none of them gained much success. The giant electrical combine AEG entered the business by buying out two of these small Berlin shops in 1901 and 1902 and making gasoline cars on their designs, selling them under the NAG name. The other major electrical company, Siemens-Schukert, also entered the industry, making some electric and gasoline cars from 1906 and buying the Protos firm in 1908 to expand operations. Despite their huge resources, neither the AEG nor Siemens ventures into motor cars brought more than ordinary results. In this period, a metalworking concern producing cars as a sideline was rarely successful.

By 1907 automobile production in Germany was still in its infancy. Output was less than half that of Britain and one-fifth that of France. Some four dozen factories employing 12,000 workers and widely dispersed over the Reich manufactured about 5,000 vehicles. The geographic dispersal followed the same pattern as other metalworking activities. The low level of imports and exports indicated the weakness of demand at home and slight interest in German cars abroad, which was attributable either to unaggressive management or most of the cars' unimpressive reputations.

In Italy, as in most of the rest of Europe, the automobile industry followed French precedents. At the turn of the century, most of the cars sold there consisted of French chassis with locally constructed bodies. Not until about 1905 did domestic production exceed imports. The local market was small, but Italian makers enjoyed good export demand for their large luxury models, and exports exceeded imports from 1907 on.

From the very beginning, the industry was highly localized, established almost exclusively in Turin and Milan, each of which possessed a group of small machine shops, railway equipment builders, and carriage makers. Automobile production began in Milan in the late 1890s when the Bianchi bicycle works made a few cars and the Isotta-Fraschini company began importing and selling Renault cars. In Turin the candle maker Michele Lanza produced a handful of cars, beginning in 1895.

The Fiat company of that city made quite a different record. In 1898 Emanuele Bricherasio and some well-to-do associates backed two bicycle mechanics, Giovanni and Matteo Ceirano, in their effort to manufacture a few cars of their own design. Other wealthy Turinese industrialists and professional men grew interested, including Carlo Biscaretti di Ruffia and Giovanni Agnelli, the latter a wealthy young man who had earlier given up a career as an army officer and had dabbled in industrial enterprises. In July 1899 this group incorporated in a firm that soon took the name Fabbrica Italiana Automobili Torino, or Fiat. It was capitalized at 800,000 lire, or $160,000. Almost from the beginning, Agnelli made himself the dominant force in the company, in 1901 pushing the Ceiranos and the engineer Faccioli out of the firm and becoming its managing director. Once in power, Agnelli changed the thrust of the company from experimentation to production, and raised its output to 73 cars in 1901. He adopted the best foreign practice, offering models based on Mercedes lines. Fiat made a profit for the first time in 1902 and paid dividends in 1904, when it produced 268 cars.

At this point, an automobile boom occurred in Italy. The success of this industry in France and growing British and German interest began to infect Italian businessmen, especially in Turin, where after a slow start Fiat was showing the way and demonstrating that profits could be made. The Itala firm opened there in 1903, using De Dion-Bouton engines in small cars at first but soon turning to larger models. In 1905 the Rapid company entered the business, located in a former body making factory. The French firms, Clément and Peugeot, established subsidiaries for assembly and ultimately manufacture of cars, also in 1905. These were followed by Junior, Lancia, Scat, Spa, Aquila, and many others in Turin. The management of some of these companies wished to manufacture automobiles, but many were launched simply as speculative ventures by promoters who were more eager to sell shares than automobiles.

Fiat was in the midst of this speculation. In December 1904 the company split its 200-lire shares into eight parts, 25 lire each, apparently to make them more accessible to small investors. Fiat's good year in 1905 and the hope that dividends would be large encouraged buyers to demand these shares at almost any price, and by March 1906 the 25-lire shares were being exchanged at an astonishing 2,450 lire. At this point, Fiat's management declared a profit of more than 2 million for 1905 and a dividend of 50 lire per share (200 percent of the par value). As if this were not enough, the company was reconstituted financially; it was capitalized at 9 million lire, 8 million of which went to the stockholders on a basis of 2 1/2 new 100-lire shares for each 25-lire share. This gave a holder of an original share of 200 lire 20 shares of 100 lire each. This price for these new shares mounted quickly, reaching 1,885 lire by the middle of 1906.

Fiat management in this period engaged in a bold policy of expansion, buying control of other producers of automobiles or parts such as ball bearings and bodies. Agnelli visited the United States in 1906 to open a sales agency in New York and may have examined the American auto industry. However, his policy of expansion to control or participate in the production of parts and to make a wide variety of products, including industrial vehicles and engines for marine and aeronautical uses, does not seem to have been inspired by American examples, for this stage did not arrive there until several years later, when Durant and Briscoe began their empire-building.

In July 1906 the speculative boom in Italian automobile shares began to erode. Share prices dropped, Fiat's among them, sinking to 505 by January 1907. Even the announcement of a profit exceeding 5 million lire for 1906 on sales of 1,149 cars and a dividend of 35 lire per share failed to halt this downward slide, which reached 80 by October 1907. The appearance of all the new automobile manufacturers and the consequent expansion of production facilities, especially for high-priced cars, had overreached both the domestic and export markets, and investors came to realize this. Production in Italy in 1907 may have reached 2,500 vehicles. Many of the newly formed companies soon disappeared in the wake of the crash of automobile stock prices, though most of the Turin firms mentioned above remained in operation, and Itala reached respectable size.

Some of the gyrations of automobile stocks may have been caused by the occult manipulations of insiders and brokers, who hoped to fleece small investors attracted to the stock market by the growth and prospects of the new industry. When early in 1908 Fiat announced a financial loss of nearly 7.5 million lire for 1907 (despite sales of 1,420 cars), bitter criticism and serious charges resulted. These led to judicial proceedings against Giovanni Agnelli and his associates for financial fraud, and brought the resignation of the entire board of directors of Fiat.[13] Was this the end? Had the leaders of Fiat tried to grasp too much and brought their company to disaster?

Outside the European countries already mentioned, some additional motor car manufacturing occurred before 1914. In many towns and cities where there were machine shops or carriage makers, someone tried to construct automobiles: in Barcelona, Geneva, Zurich, Vienna, Prague, Budapest, Amsterdam, Copenhagen, and other places. None of these manufacturers made more than a few hundred cars a year, either because they tried to appeal to a small market of aristocrats with expensive models or because they could not make popular cars as cheaply as some French or German firms for lack of nearby specialized component makers. Among these countries, Switzerland had the most auto firms for its size, but their output was small because cars powerful enough for mountain driving were expensive to make. The Hispano-Suiza of Barcelona, Austro-Daimler of Vienna, and Spyker of Amsterdam probably gained the most esteem outside their own countries, for reasons of engineering excellence and innovation.

Early Production in the United States

In the United States, automobile manufacturing gradually began to get under way at the turn of the century, generally following a course somewhat different from the European industry. New England took an early lead. The leading bicycle maker there was the Pope Manufacturing Company of Hartford, Connecticut, whose "Columbia" bicycle enjoyed a national reputation. Deciding in 1895 to establish a motor carriage department, this concern hired Hiram P. Maxim as an engineer. He and his associates experimented with both gasoline and electric cars. Maxim himself believed that the internal-combustion engine was the best choice but he did not help his cause by failing to learn from European experience and spending several years working out solutions that had already been discovered there. His superiors convinced themselves that the electric type—cleaner, silent, and easy to operate—would better suit American tastes. In 1897 the Pope Company began selling its "Columbia" electric cars, and marketed several hundred over the next two years. It also made a few gasoline tricycles, and from 1899 on, four-wheeled cars.

That the Pope Company chose to concentrate its extensive engineering, manufacturing, and financial resources on electric cars was fateful for the industry. This delayed its growth for a few years by diverting onto a false path a firm that could have dominated the business. Another result was that other New England automakers were encouraged to stay away from gasoline engines, but they left the field open for Midwestern firms that did adopt this type of power. Still, the electric car looked like the right choice in 1899 when a New York City financial group bought out the Electric Vehicle Company, which operated 100 electric cabs in that city, and proceeded to establish a network of electric-cab companies in major U.S. cities. Early in 1899, this group ordered 1,600 electric cars from the Pope Company, and then acquired the Pope automotive department and merged it into the Electric Vehicle Company. This concern may have made as many as 900 electric cars in 1900, its best year. It also bought the Selden patent on gasoline automobiles to ensure that the company's future, in whatever direction it chose to go, would not be hindered by patent problems. Nevertheless, by the end of 1899 other difficulties had emerged. The electric cabs did not prove profitable to operate and questionable financial manipulations soon came to light that hurt the reputation of the Electric Vehicle Company. After 1901 it limited itself to manufacturing a small number of electric and gasoline cars, with limited success, and to exploitation of the Selden patent.

Also in New England occurred America's most successful effort with steam automobiles. Twin brothers who were in the photographic equipment business, Francis and Freelan Stanley, began manufacturing a lightweight steam buggy in Watertown, Massachusetts, near Boston, in 1899. Almost immediately, capitalists bought the brothers out and established two firms, the more important one, Locomobile, moving from Watertown to Bridgeport, Connecticut, in 1901. The cheapest Locomobile cost only $600. After producing about 5,000 of these steamers in four years, achieving peak output of about 1,600 in 1900, an example of quantity production little noticed by automobile historians, Locomobile switched to expensive gasoline cars in small numbers in 1903.[14] The Stanley brothers themselves improved on their design, and returned to manufacturing in Watertown in 1901. They made a few hundred steamers a year, but the complicated mechanism and the brothers' disdain for marketing limited the car's appeal, though the Stanley Company continued making them until 1925.

The heartland of the American automobile industry turned out not to be in New England—noted for its traditions of clever inventors, innovating metalworking, and aggressive financiers—but in some ten Midwestern towns and cities of northern Ohio, northern Indiana, and southern Michigan within a 200-mile radius centered at Fort Wayne, Indiana (see chart 3–1). Auto manufacturing on a significant scale in this region began in Cleveland, where the Scottish-born mechanic Alexander Winton operated a bicycle factory. After five years of experimentation, he began selling cars in 1898, and for several years led the American field of those who made gasoline types.

In Lansing, Michigan, Ransom E. Olds operated a shop making small stationary steam and gasoline engines. In 1897 he organized a company to make gasoline cars, but it lacked enough capital to engage in serious production. In 1899 he formed a new concern, the Olds Motor Works, financially backed by a wealthy Detroit businessman, and moved the automotive operations to a new factory in that city. Olds experimented with a number of different models, including electric types. Late in 1900 he decided to concentrate on the smallest and cheapest of his prototypes, a model that would compete directly with the popular Locomobile steamer. This car, the first Oldsmobile, was a horseless buggy, propelled by a small, one-cylinder engine under the seat and a single chain drive. Although low-powered, it was adequate for city driving, and New Yorkers bought it in large numbers. The Olds factory concentrated on assembling parts made elsewhere in Detroit: engines and transmissions by Leland and Faulconer and by Dodge Brothers, radiators and other metal parts by the Briscoe Brothers, and bodies by Byron Everitt—all firms that would eventually enter the industry with their own automobiles.

By the end of 1901, the company had produced 425 Oldsmobiles, which sold at the low price of $650. By this time, Olds had also expanded production facilities, finishing the first building of a new factory back in Lansing. Keeping establishments in both Lansing and Detroit operating through 1905, the Olds Company made 2,500 cars in 1902, 3,000 in 1903, and 5,500 in 1904. The 1902 figure was a U.S. record, and the 1903 total a world record. Like Locomobile and its steamers, Olds had uncovered a large market for an inexpensive car. His was the third American example of quantity production of a single model chassis, preceded by Electric Vehicle's output of some 1,200–1,500 electric cars in 1899–1900 and the Locomobile operation in Watertown and Bridgeport.

Early in 1904, Olds left the company he had founded. Differences over policy and authority had separated him from his financial backers. When they removed him as general manager, he sold his stock-

Chart 3-1.
The Automobile Industry in the American Middle West before 1914

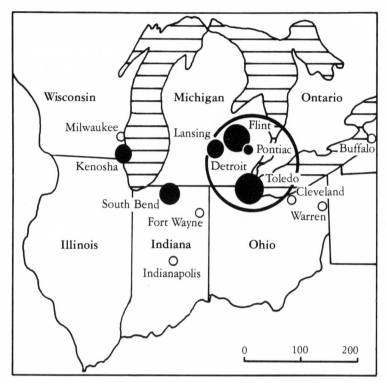

The number of cars produced in 1914 is represented by the circles (Pontiac, 6,100; Detroit, 335,000). Hollow circles represent other cities.

holdings in the company and established a new firm, also in Lansing, called the Reo Company, which produced its first car in March 1905. But Olds never repeated the spectacular early success of his Oldsmobile.

It took Henry Ford a longer time than Olds to establish himself in the automobile business. A farm boy from near Detroit, he became a machinist and self-taught engineer. In an interesting parallel with Henry Royce, Ford became chief engineer for an electric utility in Detroit in 1893. For several years, he tinkered with gasoline engines and in June 1896 he finished building a quadricycle weighing only 500 pounds, less than half that of a typical European car of this period. This machine was not the first constructed in Detroit, for Charles King, a consulting engineer and friend of Ford's, had operated one of his own manufacture three months earlier. Ford soon sold his first car, and by 1899 had built another. This machine operated creditably enough for Ford to find backing to establish the Detroit Automobile Company. This concern soon failed because Ford lacked experience in organizing production and made no more than twenty cars in the years 1899–1900.

Nevertheless, some of the same men who supported this firm again financed Ford in a new enterprise, the Henry Ford Company (1901), which backed his efforts in making some racing cars. He soon left this company, and his interest in racing lasted only until late 1902. Probably impressed by the success of the Oldsmobile in these years, Ford decided to make a small car to compete with it. In August 1902 he convinced a local coal dealer, Alexander Malcomson, to finance still another automobile venture. Ford and his assistant, C. H. Wills, built prototypes while Malcomson's associate James Couzens handled the business arrangements. All was ready by June 1903 when Ford, Malcomson, Couzens, and a few others organized the Ford Motor Company. It was capitalized at $100,000, of which only $29,500 represented cash paid in at this time.

Like the French Renault in 1898–99 and Olds in 1901, Ford began strictly as an assembly operation. At a price of $250 for each set, the Dodge Brothers machine shop supplied the crucial items for the two-cylinder car, including the chassis frame, engine, transmission, and axles. Carburetors, wheels, bodies, and other equipment also came from suppliers. Although this first Ford model was not outstanding mechanically, the demand for moderately priced cars was such that the firm easily sold 1,700 of them at prices ranging from $850 to $950 between June 1903 and September 1904. In this first year, the business made enough profit to pay dividends equivalent to 98 percent of the capital and build a large new factory, still primarily for assembly purposes. In 1904–5 the company employed about 300 men.

During the next few years, Ford offered improved versions of his two-cylinder car as well as a new four-cylinder model selling at $2,000. Ford himself wanted to keep his cars in the low-price range, but Malcomson preferred to follow most of the American manufacturers and make larger, heavier, and high-priced cars similar to French imports. Whereas disagreement with his financial backers led to Ransom Olds's departure from the Olds company at this time, Ford won the battle at his firm. Through some unfriendly financial maneuvers, Ford and Couzens forced Malcomson and his friends to sell their shares in the Ford Company in 1906–7. Ford emerged as the majority stockholder. At the same time, the company began to manufacture some of its engines, transmissions, and other parts, moving toward vertical integration.

In 1906 Ford introduced a new model, "N," a small four-cylinder car whose engine was in front, in hopes of moving into the low-price market that Olds was leaving. At first the price was only $500 but it soon had to be raised to $600. Yet the car was a good value, and sales soared to 8,423 for the year ending 30 September 1907, a U.S. and world record. However, the Renault company in France exceeded both Ford's sales revenue and profits in this year, disposing of 3,066 cars. Ford's sales revenue averaged $685 per car; Renault's $2,000 per car.

During these years, the Ford Company became a major protagonist in the Selden patent case. The Electric Vehicle Company had purchased this patent in 1899. When its electric cab business went on the rocks, it tried to earn an income by demanding royalty payments from other gasoline-automobile producers. To enforce its claims, it brought suit against the Winton Company and some others for infringement. Preferring to avoid the expense of a legal case, Winton and other major manufacturers, including Olds, Cadillac, and Packard, joined the Electric Vehicle Company in the Association of Licensed Automobile Manufacturers (ALAM). Member firms of this group paid a royalty of 1 1/4 percent on the price of each car sold; two-fifths of this money went to Electric Vehicle, one-fifth to George Selden, and two-fifths to ALAM. The ALAM firms hoped to use their power to grant licenses to limit entry to the new industry so as to protect their own firms from vigorous competition. A number of other companies refused to recognize the validity of the Selden patent, chief among them Ford in Detroit and the Jeffery Company of Kenosha, Wisconsin.

In the fall of 1903, ALAM, now comprising twenty-seven members, brought a patent infringement suit against Ford, a Ford dealer, a buyer of a Ford car, the French firm Panhard et Levassor (P & L) and its New York branch manager, and the Neubauer company, a Paris-based concern exporting French cars to the United States. All these suits were consolidated into one, commonly known as the Selden patent case. This affair dragged on for years in the courts. Ford used it as an advertising issue, portraying himself as the "little man" struggling to provide automobiles to the public against the greedy desires of the "trust." The hearing in federal district court in New York finally came in 1909 before a judge who lacked mechanical knowledge. After hearing oral arguments and examining the voluminous written record, the court held that, though the Selden patent referred to a two-cycle engine, it covered all gasoline-powered cars in the United States and that Ford and the other defendants had infringed on it. Although most of the non-ALAM manufacturers gave in, paid royalties on cars they had sold since 1903, and joined ALAM, Ford and P & L refused and appealed the judgment to the federal circuit court of appeals.

At this stage, Ford and P & L were well served by the talented attorney Frederic Coudert. He pointed out to the court that Dugald Clerk, the Scottish expert on internal-combustion engines, had testified as a key witness for ALAM in 1906 that Selden's patent was strikingly new and opened a fresh chapter in automobile history. Coudert then showed that the 1909 revised edition of Clerk's textbook on engines contained not a single mention of Selden or his car, but credited Daimler and others with the development of the automobile. In a decision handed down in January 1911, the three circuit judges unanimously found the Selden patent to be valid only in a very limited area and that Ford and P & L had not infringed on it. The industry had finally been freed from a legal effort to smother competition. Despite the heavy expenses the Ford Company had incurred in this case, about $250,000 in direct costs, it certainly benefited from its part in it because of the publicity value of its stand against the monopolists. The case also became a key ingredient in the personal legend of Henry Ford.

The Selden case produced some other long-run results for the industry. Recognizing from this case and similar patent struggles in the bicycle and pneumatic tire businesses that the lawyers were the only real winners in such controversies, in 1915 the automobile industry established a cross-licensing arrangement. This provided that, with some exceptions, all present and future automotive patents held by member firms would be fully available to the others. This system spread technological innovations quickly through the industry and thereby served consumers. Until 1955 it was renewed periodically. Ford and Packard stayed out of this patent pool, but the former usually acted as if it were a member and never exacted tribute for the use of its automotive patents. An even more significant, though less direct, result of the Selden case was standardization. ALAM had begun to move toward standardization of automotive parts and materials. In 1910 the Society of Automotive Engineers took responsibility for this activity, and gradually put into effect a comprehensive program. Again, the consumer benefited from lower prices and ease of repair and replacement of parts.

Because of the success of the four-cylinder Model N, Ford became the leading producer in the United States in 1907, its output in that year reaching 19 percent of the national total, but it lost this lead to the Buick company over the next three years. In 1899 David Buick had sold out his interest in a plumbing supply business in Detroit to enter gasoline engine manufacturing. In 1903 his firm became the Buick Motor Car Company, and was moved to Flint, a small town northwest of Detroit. This company made only a handful of cars before William C. Durant bought control of it late in 1904. A dynamic salesman, he had made a fortune managing a carriage and wagon factory in Flint, where he assembled thousands of vehicles from components made in other specialized establishments. At Buick, he used the same method of production and dealer network built up in his wagon business. Buick soon became a ranking member of the industry. The sensation of the automobile show at New York in November 1907 was the new Buick 10, a small four-cylinder design somewhat larger and heavier than Ford's Model N and selling at $900. In 1908 Buick made 4,000 of the 10s and about 4,500 of other types for a total that surpassed Ford's by more than 2,000 cars.

Ford responded to the challenge, for during 1908 his firm prepared a new low-priced four-cylinder model, the "T," and deliveries began in October. They would stop only in 1927, 15,458,781 cars later. The Buick 10 and the Ford T uncovered for the American industry a large, apparently unlimited market for inexpensive, reliable, four-cylinder cars. The next problem would be to manufacture them in quantities sufficient to meet the demand.

Marketing considerations, then, were fundamental at the Buick and Ford concerns, but the Cadillac Company espoused a different philosophy: high-quality workmanship. Actually, Cadillac's germ was the Henry Ford Company of Detroit, which Ford had left in March 1902. The owners called Henry M. Leland to appraise the value of the factory preparatory to selling it. A skilled machinist, he had learned to use precise measurements and first-class materials while working for the Brown and Sharpe machine tool firm of Providence, Rhode Island. Later, he sold the products of this company throughout the Midwest, and in the process visited hundreds of metalworking shops and factories. His experience had made him an expert in machine tools and organizing them for production. In 1890 he established his own machine-building company in Detroit. It soon specialized in making gears and gasoline engines, which it supplied for the early Olds cars.

When Leland inspected the Ford Company in 1902 he saw it not as something to be liquidated but as an opportunity. He persuaded the owners to recommence automobile production, using a new engine he had designed. They reorganized the firm in August 1902, naming it Cadillac after the French explorer who had founded Detroit. The first

Cadillac prototypes, built in Leland's factory, featured a five horse-power, one-cylinder engine placed in the middle of the chassis. Offered at $750, 1,895 were sold in 1903. Leland made the major components and had them assembled at the Cadillac factory. In 1904 the two companies merged under the direction of Leland, and Cadillac continued as a leading firm in the industry.

The year 1908 was not only a turning point because of the advent of the new Buick 10 and Ford T models, it also marked the founding of General Motors (GM). This holding company controlled Buick, Olds, Cadillac, and many other firms, the first large merger in the industry. The two events signaled the beginning of a new and a revolutionary phase in automobile development. But why did they take place in Detroit?

In 1902 a Detroit businessman, Henry B. Joy, became interested in the Packard Company, a small automobile manufacturer in Warren, Ohio. He invested in it, and moved it to Detroit the next year. The company specialized in expensive luxury cars, making nearly 1,200 in 1907 and more than 5,000 in 1913. Packard's move to Detroit in 1903 underlined the city's evolving leadership in the industry. It offered no particular advantage over other Midwestern cities, such as Cleveland or Indianapolis, as far as transportation facilities or the supply of capital, marketing, or manufacturing experience were concerned. But it was the first home of the Olds Motor Works, of Cadillac, and of the Ford Motor Company, all of which engaged in what was then quantity manufacture.

Olds and Ford relied on other shops in Detroit to supply most of the components for their early cars. The rapid growth of these parts makers attracted other assemblers of cars to the Detroit area, initiated many young men in the locality to the automobile manufacturing business, and finally led some of these component firms to make their own cars. Men made Detroit the center of the automobile industry, not impersonal geographic factors.

All this was not so clear at the time, for late in 1903 Benjamin Briscoe, who operated a factory in Detroit making auto parts, and Jonathan Maxwell, an experienced automobile engineer, joined to create the Maxwell-Briscoe Motor Company. They began operations not in Detroit but in Tarrytown, New York, where they found a well-equipped factory that had once produced the Mobile steam automobile. Maxwell cars sold so well that branch factories were acquired in Rhode Island, in Indiana, and in Detroit. From 1906 through 1911, Maxwell was a major contender for leadership among American producers.

These producers made 44,000 cars in 1907 and 65,000 the next year. The United States was rapidly expanding production to meet the demand stimulated by the appearance of reliable automobiles. Behind this especially strong demand lay a higher average per capita income and its more even distribution than in Europe. Estimated average per capita income for the United States in 1914 was $335, compared to $243 in the United Kingdom, $185 in France, and $146 in Germany.[15] The vast free-trade area of the United States, comprising 92.2 million people in 1910, has often been emphasized in this regard, too much so.

After all, the United Kingdom market was open free of tariffs to European automobile manufacturers, and tariffs elsewhere in Western and Central Europe were quite low. A French manufacturer, for example, in 1910, had free entry to his own country of 39.9 million and to the United Kingdom of 41.8 million. In addition, the German market of 64.6 million (tariff of 3 percent) and the Italian of 34.4 million (tariff of 5 percent) were available, not to speak of smaller countries, though nationalist sentiments sometimes hindered such trade. Consequently, the size of the population does not seem to have been a major factor, but the average income certainly was.

Other reasons added to the strong demand in the United States. Americans recognized the utilitarian advantages of automobiles. Cars were judged to be more reliable, safe, and sanitary than horses. Also, in these early years, they seemed a cheaper way to improve urban transportation than mass transit on rails. And automobiles seemed to fit perfectly into certain American culture traits: individualism and mobility.[16] However, if it is assumed that such traits were in some way unique and that they were crucial to the American passion for motor cars, then what accounts for the widespread adoption of automobiles—and passion for them—in non-American cultures, especially after 1945? The desire for personal transportation seems to be universal and not restricted to certain national groups, but it was close to the surface in the United States before 1914, and it generated an effective demand because of higher average incomes there than elsewhere.

As yet, American methods of production differed little from the European. Table 2–1 shows that motorization in the United States in 1907 was not materially different from that in leading countries of Western Europe. But 1908 was the point where a rapid divergence between the industries of the two regions began to occur. The United States was about to launch a new era.

Canada

The Canadian automobile industry evolved essentially as a branch of the American. Although a few experimenters were active at the turn of the century, serious operations began in 1904 when Gordon McGregor established the Ford Motor Company of Canada in Walkersville, Ontario, just across the border from Detroit. The American Ford Company granted this firm the right to manufacture Ford cars in return for a controlling interest in it, though most of the money invested in it came from Canadian businessmen. Although this company soon emancipated itself from American-made parts, most of the other Canadian branches of American firms did receive their major components from across the border. In 1914 Ford of Canada sold more than 14,000 cars, 31 percent of which were exported; Buick, Willys-Overland, and Studebaker were also well represented in Canada. The Russell and Tudhope companies, which had no direct connections with the United States automobile firms, experienced several years of success, but competition was severe and both left the business about the time the war began.

The Demise of Steam and Electric Cars

During these early years of the industry, internal-combustion engines triumphed over steam and electric. The early races and reliability trials in France demonstrated the gasoline engine's superiority for passenger cars over long distances, and the French precedent determined the outcome in the rest of Europe. Still, some persisted. In Paris, Léon Serpollet designed an outstanding steam car and sold about 1,000 of them from 1900 through 1906. Their high price and Serpollet's death in 1907 terminated this last French effort with steam. In Germany, stringent saftey regulations on steam boilers deterred work with steam cars. Steam trucks and buses found wider use in Britain than elsewhere in Europe. A Belgian design derived from the Serpollet system was the most popular model there.

Electric cars did even less well than steam in Europe. Problems of short range, heavy weight, and fragile batteries could not be overcome. The few in service were used as cabs in the major capitals, especially Berlin.

In the United States, both steam and electricity found broader acceptance and hung on longer than in Europe. In part, this stemmed from the decentralized character of automobile making in the early days. Knowledge of successes and failures elsewhere was less common, and "follow the leader" was not so prevalent in automobile design. The lightweight Stanley steamers were the most successful of all, for 7,000–8,000 were made before 1914. The White Company of Cleveland made almost as many of more elaborate designs until it converted to gasoline types after 1911. The complexities of starting and maintaining steam cars and their higher cost than gasoline models of equivalent performance settled their fate.[17]

Unlike the situation in Europe, electric cars sold well in the larger American cities up to 1914. This occurred because of the poor state of American roads and the comparatively large number of women drivers. Electric cars' short range did not place them at a serious disadvantage when most country roads were so bad they limited almost all cars to city driving. Starting a gasoline engine by hand cranking could be difficult and dangerous, so the electric type was especially suitable for women driving alone, as they did in America, for chauffeurs were less common than in Europe. These two factors began to lose their significance just before 1914, when the roads began to be improved and the self-starter was invented.

Many experimenters in Europe and America had employed compressed air, springs, electricity, or acetylene gas to start gasoline cars automatically. None had proved reliable when Henry Leland set Cadillac engineers to work on the problem in 1910. In a few weeks, they devised a starter to operate on the engine's flywheel. For an electric motor to drive this, they called upon Charles F. Kettering, who was to become the most eminent inventor in American automobile history. An Ohio farm boy, he had earned a degree in engineering from Ohio State University in 1904. Strongly inclined away from theory and from traditional authorities and toward experiment by an independence of mind and probably by poor eyesight that hindered reading, he first worked for the National Cash Register Company of Dayton, Ohio. There he perfected a small electric motor with high torque and a special clutch to power cash registers electrically.

In 1909, in his spare time, Kettering devised an improved ignition system for automobiles. After selling it to Cadillac, he established himself as an independent consulting engineer. Early in 1911, he provided Cadillac with an electric motor and clutch analogous to the cash register system to operate the new starter. The power for this motor was supplied by a system of lead-acid battery and generator that also operated the headlights instead of the usual acetylene. Cadillac introduced the new starting and lighting arrangement on its 1912 models, and it was soon adopted by most other manufacturers in the world. In a few years, Kettering joined Cadillac's parent, GM, as director of research.

The electric self-starter conquered what seemed to be the most serious difficulty with gasoline engines at this time and their major disadvantage vis-à-vis electric cars: starting them. Now the gasoline car could be operated by those not mechanically inclined or physically strong, and so the market could expand. The self-starter also made it possible to offer to the public cars having eight or more cylinders and to increase compression ratios. Ironically, an electrical device doomed the electric car. The internal-combustion system triumphed because its limitations were fewer than those for electricity. It provided greater range and speed, was not so fragile, and could be made in all sizes.

The self-starter was the most important single American technical achievement in motor cars before 1914. Two others of importance were the lightweight steam car of the Stanley brothers and the rotary valve engine of Charles Y. Knight. Neither of these exerted a lasting impact, and all such American technical refinements recede into the background before the accomplishment of mass production of low-priced gasoline automobiles.

4. An Expanding Market and Production Innovations, 1908–1914

American automobile production grew rapidly after 1905. From then until 1914, only twice was the annual increase less than 20 percent. In 1913 production reached 485,000 cars and trucks, more than ten times that of the leading European country, France, and more than three-fourths of world output. As production rose to these massive proportions, two basic characteristics emerged in the American automobile industry: the establishment of very large business organizations, and the perfecting of manufacturing techniques to make and assemble huge numbers of identical parts without using an enormous work force, especially of highly skilled workmen.

Corporate Combinations

As the Ford Motor Company would soon come to exemplify the firm grown to gigantic size through internal expansion, General Motors (GM) would represent the large enterprise resulting from a combination of separate entities. W. C. Durant, head of the Buick Company, founded GM in September 1908. The economic motives for this combine—spreading the risk in a volatile business by acquiring many different firms making cars or parts—were secondary to Durant's personal thirst for power and a desire to gamble for high stakes. GM's core was the Buick Company, which it bought for nearly $3.75 million in GM stock. Durant went on to buy Olds, also for stock, and ten more automobile companies, most of them small and unproven, except for Cadillac, which cost $4.5 million in cash. He also acquired about a dozen parts and accessory manufacturers.

A few of these concerns were profitable, but Buick and Cadillac were the really valuable properties. Buick was the largest car maker in the world in 1909, and Cadillac was enjoying its most profitable year so far by disposing of 6,000 cars. Cadillac's new four-cylinder model, priced at $1,400, was remarkably successful. Durant also tried to buy the Ford Motor Company, but lacked the $8 million in cash that Henry Ford asked. Before long, a shortage of funds threatened to bring down the structure that Durant had hastily thrown together. Many of the constituent firms were losing money, and, when Buick failed to generate enough cash in 1910, GM tottered on the edge of bankruptcy. To obtain desperately needed working capital, Durant finally was forced to give up his control to a group of Boston and New York financiers in return for a loan of $15 million.

The new management team, headed by Boston banker James Storrow, provided more order and improved methods. It rectified Durant's expensive blunders; encouraged operations that gave promise of profits, such as the Oakland Company of Pontiac, Michigan; and placed capable men like Charles Nash and Walter Chrysler in key executive positions. Chrysler had begun as a locomotive mechanic in Kansas and worked his way up to managing the Pittsburgh works of the American Locomotive Company. It was unusual for a railway man to win success in the automobile business because the methods of locomotive manufacturing did not have much in common with automobiles. But Chrysler had learned to watch costs and to schedule production carefully. This was exactly what Buick needed at this point. He mastered the new business quickly, drove hard, and became one of America's foremost automobile industrialists.[18]

The Storrow management of GM consolidated some of the parts-making operations, and tried to increase coordination among the several companies. Nevertheless, GM continued as a confederation of autonomous firms. [How it was to be molded into a decentralized and yet integrated organization is one of the success stories of American capitalism in the 1920s and is described in chapter 6.] The bankers' cautious management saved GM from collapse, but by 1915 it looked as though they had missed some opportunities. In 1910 the group had produced 21 percent of the country's cars; by 1915 this had dropped to less than 8 percent, while Ford had soared from 11 to 43 percent in the same period.

Benjamin Briscoe entertained the same idea as Durant, and also tried to construct a large combination of automobile firms. Under the name of United States Motor Company, in 1910 Briscoe began collecting a variety of concerns around the nucleus of his Maxwell-Briscoe Company. Within two years, some 150 enterprises became associated in some way with the United States Motor Company. There were not enough profitable ones to keep the structure solvent, however, and in 1912 it went into receivership. Creditors forced Briscoe and Maxwell out, and brought in Walter Flanders, an experienced motor car manufacturer, to take charge. He eliminated the losing operations, concentrated production in fewer locations, and renamed the result the Maxwell Motor Company. This firm would become the Chrysler Corporation in the 1920s. Both Durant and Briscoe had gone too fast, buying up almost everything in sight with little technical or financial discrimination. By 1914 it looked as if merger was the wrong path to growth.

Two other large automobile companies appeared in this period: Willys-Overland and Studebaker. John N. Willys was a bicycle salesman who organized a company to sell cars at Indianapolis in 1906. He soon took control of two small automobile makers, and in 1909 bought an automobile factory in Toledo, Ohio, from the Pope interests. This establishment became the center of Willys-Overland operations. In 1910 Willys introduced a low-priced ($850) four-cylinder model like the Buick 10 and Ford T, and his output rose to 15,600 cars. This company continued to compete with Ford in the low-price range (unlike Buick) and made 48,500 cars in 1914, second to Ford.

The Studebaker Company of South Bend, Indiana, began manufacturing horse-drawn wagons in the 1850s, and grew to become one of the world's largest wagon companies by the end of the century. From 1902 it began offering electric and then gasoline cars in small numbers. When it finally decided to enter large-scale automobile production, it moved quickly by buying out a Detroit maker, EMF, in 1909. Utilizing major facilities in South Bend and Detroit and a dealer network of more than 1,000 built up in its wagon business, it became a leader in the medium-price range. Its output was about 35,000 cars in 1913 and again in 1914.

Ford and the Single Model at a Low Price

The growth of Buick, Willys-Overland, and Studebaker seems astounding enough in comparison with the European experience, but the Ford Motor Company overshadowed them all. The foundation for its expansion after 1908 was the full-sized four-cylinder car at a low price that Buick and Ford had introduced in 1907–8. The Ford entry, the Model T, weighed less than the Buick 10, but its wheelbase was eight inches longer. Sturdy, simple in design, and easy to maintain, it had a wide appeal, especially to farmers who appreciated its high clearance, which made it easier to drive on unpaved rural roads. Its relatively high power-to-weight ratio gave it a long life, for most drivers could obtain all the performance they wanted without pushing the engine to its limit. First introduced at a price of $825, the Model T sold well, but the 10,607 Fords disposed of in 1909 fell short of the 14,606 Buicks marketed that year.

Despite his largest profit ever in 1909 and his abandonment of all but one model, Ford raised the basic price of the T to $900 in October 1909, apparently to help pay for the new factory he was constructing at Highland Park, just outside Detroit. But he was not looking for a quick profit by raising the price of a popular model; from a long-range standpoint, he really wanted to cut his price so as to expand the market and thereby lower his unit cost by longer production runs. In October 1910 he slashed the basic price for the 1911 roadster to $680. (The Model T price in chart 4-1 refers to the touring car price.) Sales responded immediately, reaching 34,528 for 1911 and making Ford the national and world leader by a wide margin. When he cut the price to $590 in October 1911, sales rose to 78,440. Year by year, he continued this policy, selling 248,307 in the year ending September 1914, at a basic price of $500. This gave him about 45 percent of the American passenger-car market. Yet, to make this huge number of cars in 1914, the firm employed an average of only 12,880 people in its Detroit operations. Ford's growth and its relation to the annual wage are shown in chart 4–1.

Ford and his associates, especially Couzens, worked harder at reducing costs than most automobile men. One technique that Ford pioneered in the United States was branch assembly plants. In 1909 the company erected an assembly hall in Kansas City. The Detroit factory shipped parts there by rail at one-half the freight cost of fully assembled cars. Assembly at branch plants reduced congestion at the Detroit works and generated local goodwill. This physical separation of assembly from component manufacture echoed prior examples by Renault, Olds, and many other firms in their early days, including

Chart 4-1.
Ford and the United States Market, 1909–1917

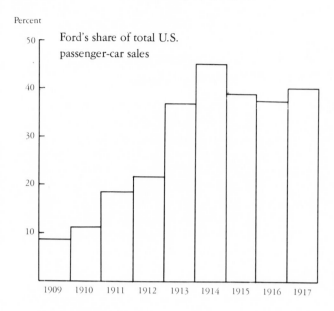

Percent

Ford's share of total U.S.
passenger-car sales

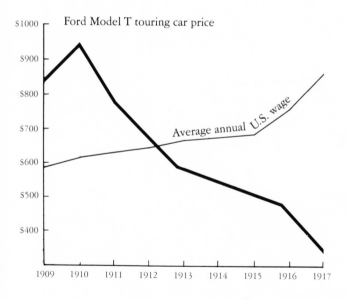

Ford Model T touring car price

Average annual U.S. wage

As Ford's price fell below the annual wage, its share of the market
rose rapidly.

Ford itself. It made possible further specialization of labor and equipment to take advantage of economies of scale. When the Kansas City venture demonstrated its success, Ford established other branch assembly operations, eighteen in all by August 1914. In addition to these domestic branches, Ford maintained two foreign ones. The Canadian subsidiary has been mentioned. In England, assembly began in 1911 at Manchester, and in 1913 this factory turned out 7,310 cars to lead all British firms.

Ford's insistence after 1908 on retaining the same model year after year featuring only minor changes also brought lower costs. Not only did the long production runs cut expenses per unit, now Ford engineers did not design new models but concentrated their talents on improving production methods and tools so as to make the standard car more cheaply. This orientation and the need to supply the huge demand aroused by low prices brought a series of production innovations climaxed by the famous moving assembly line. To appreciate these changes, a survey of the traditional methods is warranted.

Artisanal Production

The word "artisanal" is often used to describe early automobile manufacturing in Europe and America. It means that production was small, from 200 to 2,000 cars per year, or 4 to 40 per week. Frequently, many of the finished components were obtained from suppliers: commonly wheels, radiators, springs, and axles, and oftentimes engines and transmissions. Parts purchased as well as those made in the factory usually were not interchangeable and required individual fitting with hammer and file. Skilled craftsmen did most of the work, machining parts of the engines and running gear and then putting them together, helped by unskilled laborers, who held parts for them and moved pieces from one area of the factory to another.

Cars were assembled in batches of 5 up to 100. Small teams of workers would first put the frames together at separate stations, and then add the various components brought to them by hand or on carts. Assemblers, usually skilled workers, used small benches and forges nearby on which to adjust ill-fitting parts. Open bodies were often supplied with cheaper cars, in Europe as well as America, but usually in Europe and sometimes in America buyers of expensive automobiles had bodies made to order by specialist body builders.

Characteristic of the artisanal system was the high proportion of skilled labor involved and the low output per man, oftentimes less than one car per worker per year, though the proportion of components received from outside suppliers would strongly affect this ratio. For example, the Daimler works near Stuttgart was almost completely integrated with its own foundry and body shop. In 1909 it employed some 1,700 production workers. Those rated as skilled numbered 1,175, semi-skilled 200, and unskilled 325. Total employment may have reached 2,000 persons, but the factory produced less than 1,000 cars in this year.[19] The revolution in automobile production changed all this. It replaced artisanal methods by a further mechanization of production, leading to a much higher proportion of unskilled and semiskilled labor and an amazing increase in the output per man. How did this come about?

New Production Methods

Almost from the beginning, automobile manufacturers worked to find methods to simplify and speed production. When they began to require hundreds or thousands of copies of exactly the same part annually, they looked for cheaper ways than casting, cutting, or hand forging pieces of metal to the right dimensions. Shortly after 1900, cold stamping or pressing of parts, from chassis frames to axle housings to wheels, began to appear at Krupp in Germany and Forges de Douai (Arbel) in France, both of which already had been stamping parts for railway equipment; at Rubery Owen and Sankey in Britain; at Fiat in Italy; and in the United States at Briscoe Brothers of Detroit, A. O. Smith of Milwaukee, and J. R. Keim of Buffalo. The heavy investment required for presses and dies in these stamping operations could be offset by long production runs; the Americans took the most advantage of this.

Although pressed-steel parts replaced some pieces formerly made by metal-cutting tools, the automobile industry did create a tremendous demand for these kinds of tools, especially specialized ones operating at high speeds for quantity production, such as turret lathes, milling machines, grinders, vertical borers, and radial drills. For this demand, the American machine tool industry was well armed. It had already produced such devices over the course of the nineteenth century for the quantity manufacture of firearms, sewing machines, and bicycles.[20] American machine tool firms, taking advantage of the large domestic market, had come to specialize in one type—lathes or milling machines, for example—much more than was the case in

Europe, where a machine tool company preferred to make a variety of tools for a smaller market. This meant that the better American firms could quickly supply high-quality tools for quantity production. And the Europeans bought them, despite the lack of aggressive American marketing of such tools in Europe.

The majority of machine tools used by French and Italian automobile makers was of American origin, and in some factories the proportion reached 70 or 80 percent.[21] The machine tool industries in Germany and Britain were larger than in France and these two countries made fewer cars, so they relied less on the Americans. By 1905 some British machine toolmakers had learned their lesson and offered machines competitive with the Americans.[22] In the United States, the automobile industry became the largest single buyer of machine tools, taking 25–30 percent of output after 1900. The need for quantity auto production and the use of harder steel brought stronger, more specialized, and faster-running tools. They were designed to operate with more precision, but required less adroitness on the part of the worker. The Ford Company, for example, used a machine in 1914 that drilled forty-five holes in the engine block from four different directions at the same time.[23]

In an effort to improve the reliability and reduce the weight of cars, manufacturers about 1900 began to adopt special steels for crucial parts, such as gears, valves, shafts, and springs, to make them more durable. Special steels had begun to appear in the 1860s for cutting tools, and then navies adopted them for shells and armor plate in the 1880s. Special steel alloys contain, in addition to carbon, other elements deliberately added to achieve certain properties. Metallurgists in this period most commonly used nickel, chromium, tungsten, and manganese to make harder steels. Although the Pope Company in the United States used nickel steel in its bicycles in the 1890s, the use of special steels for cars apparently began on a large scale in France, and gradually spread elsewhere. In 1907 the Ford Company adopted vanadium steel alloys for some parts and trumpeted this loudly in its advertising, but eventually found other alloys to be superior.[24] It had become possible to machine these harder steels when the American Frederick W. Taylor devised his high-speed cutting tools, demonstrated publicly at the Paris Exposition of 1900.

Early motor car factories in Europe and America were organized on traditional lines. They usually comprised several buildings, sometimes more than a dozen, often several stories in height. Machine tools were placed together according to type so that all the lathes would be in one shop and all milling machines in another, regardless of the function they performed in the production process. When output began to reach several thousand cars annually, it became clear that such orthodox arrangements required an immense amount of wasteful movement of materials back and forth among departments. The essence of production came to be recognized as a flow of materials through the factory—raw materials and externally made parts coming in at one end and cars emerging at the other. If the factory made one kind of product, machines should be placed according to their function in this flow. Large, well-lighted, one-story buildings that provided huge rooms or halls to provide flexibility for manufacture and assembly would become standard. The gradual evolution toward these principles came most rapidly in the United States, where large-scale automobile production made the flow idea more obvious than in Europe, and where production in new factories rather than converted ones was more common. Even so, the one-story concept did not prevail before 1914.

The organization of the Olds factory in Detroit already showed some attention to the flow-of-materials principle, as did the Packard works of 1903. designed by Albert Kahn.[25] The White steam car factory in Cleveland featured a central hall 600 feet long by 30 feet wide that served as a transportation artery. The various departments branched out from it.[26] In France, the new Lorraine-Dietrich automobile works of 1907, in Argenteuil, was more advanced than most American plants, though this firm made less than 1,000 cars annually. Léon Turcat designed this factory. Underground galleries carried electric lines along with pipes for water, steam, oil, and compressed air. Maintenance crews could repair them without interfering with production. Individual electric motors powered the machines and so eliminated the usual noisy and dangerous thicket of belts coming from overhead shafting that so darkened many factories. The flow of production determined Turcat's arrangement of machines, rather than the nature of the machines. The assembly line, not moving, was supplied with stores of parts located at strategic points.[27] What was lacking was a bold marketing strategy to expand the demand for Lorraine-Dietrich cars.

The Ford Accomplishment

It was the Ford Motor Company that first put together a synthesis of these technical improvements and achieved mass production, exceeding the output of one or two thousand cars a year first accomplished by De Dion, Darracq, and Renault in France, and by Locomobile and Olds in the United States. Mass production in the automobile industry meant turning out a high quantity of cars identical in their essentials and so organized that unit costs declined. It was accomplished by maximum mechanization of the manufacturing process, which required standardization of product and the use of interchangeable parts made by precise machining; and then continuous assembly of these parts through close synchronization of their movements.

Ford's introduction of the moving assembly line was the most dramatic event in the evolution of mass production of automobiles, but it had to be preceded by standardization of output and interchangeability of parts, which Ford and several other American auto firms had attained by 1907–9. Then, in 1910, Ford moved into its spacious new Highland Park factory, which was designed by Albert Kahn and Ford engineers, who kept the flow of production in mind. Overhead cranes and other mechanical devices handled materials. However, much of the plant was several floors high, moving assembly lines were not contemplated, and the machines were operated by the old shaft-and-belt system.

Soon it became clear that at the low prices asked, Ford could sell as many cars as it could make, so pressure mounted to expand output through further innovations that would not require heavy capital investment. This pointed directly at a need to raise labor productivity, that is, to return to the profound insight of Adam Smith: market expansion made possible further steps in the division of labor.

One area that seemed susceptible of improvement was moving materials among the manufacturing operations. The idea of conveying products continuously and mechanically through the course of production had been recognized for decades, but had been used only sporadically. Historians have pointed to the grain mill of Oliver Evans, built near Philadelphia in the 1790s, which used various types of conveyors to move grain from one operation to another; the mechanization of baking ships' biscuit in England beginning in 1804; and mid-nineteenth-century meat packing in Cincinnati, where hog carcasses were hung from overhead trolleys and moved by hand from operation to operation.[28] The packing companies had adopted this "disassembly" system to speed production in the face of a large market, a short winter slaughtering season, and a shortage of labor.[29] Thus, the moving production line began in the processing of standardized food products.

By 1890 the Westinghouse Air Brake Company of East Pittsburgh employed a mechanically operated conveyor to move molds for parts of air brakes through the casting process.[30] The Crane Company in Chicago adopted this system for casting valves. Ford engineers inspected these two facilities and then set up their own lines in the foundry at Highland Park late in 1912. The first of these consisted of an endless belt that conveyed foundry sand mechanically to the core molders. Then, for light castings, chain-driven carriers were installed in February 1913 to move molds past the pouring ladles.[31] Elsewhere in the factory, engineers constructed a variety of slides and conveyors to move parts from one process to another. A significant advance occurred in May 1913 when a magneto assembly line was organized. As in the foundry, manufacturing operations were performed on a moving product, but this time a variety of different operations were required. It had taken one man twenty minutes to assemble a magneto. Now the job was divided into separate tasks for twenty-nine men as the magneto moved past them. This reduced assembly time to thirteen man-minutes. After a year's further refinement, the line required only fourteen men and it took just five man-minutes per magneto.[32]

The success of the magneto line encouraged application of the division of labor principle to larger and more complicated activities. In the fall of 1913, experiments began with chassis and engine assembly. By April 1914 chains pulled three parallel rows of chassis six feet per minute along 300-foot lines, and on one day 1,212 were assembled. Using the moving line required an average of 93 man-minutes to assemble one chassis, compared with 840 seven months earlier. The assembly line for engines cut the time from 594 man-minutes to 238 by May 1914.[33]

Such spectacular results in raising labor productivity resulted from requiring the workers to pace their actions to the speed of the line. They devoted their time and energy to one particular productive task rather than spending moments walking about picking up tools and materials and wondering what to do next. In addition to these mechanical improvements, Ford management also took steps in 1913 and 1914 to stabilize its work force, notorious for its high rate of turnover. These measures contributed to higher labor efficiency.

The increased productivity brought a sharp drop in costs, which allowed price cuts, along with substantially higher wages and profits. The profits were large, but accrued from a smaller amount for each car. In the years 1911 and 1912, Ford made about $187 profit per car; after the innovations just described, the figure was $116 in the period from October 1914 through July 1916.[34]

Several revolutions were occurring at once. The adaptation to complex metalworking of a manufacturing method that had evolved earlier for rather simple food processing made possible a huge expansion of automobile production and soon of many other durable consumer goods. These products found wide markets because of price cuts and because labor benefited from the productivity gains by rapidly rising incomes, first of all at Ford. A salient feature of the assembly-line technique that minutely divided manufacturing operations into simple tasks was that this permitted the use of semiskilled labor for the large majority of factory jobs.

The high level of production could not have been achieved by traditional methods using a high proportion of skilled workers because these persons simply were not available. But the new methods enabled Ford to expand production so that sales rose from 183,000 cars in 1913 to 355,000 in 1915, while average employment in the Highland Park plant increased only from 14,366 to 18,892. By adopting production techniques that could be employed by a majority of semiskilled workers Ford pointed the way to the future of automobile manufacturing.

The European Pattern

In Europe before 1914, the lack of enough pressure from the demand side to stimulate a huge increase in production meant that traditional manufacturing methods, using much skilled labor, could be maintained. The narrow extent of the market did not yet permit a thorough division of labor. Nevertheless, startling news came from America about 1912 telling of gigantic increases in auto output. This, along with the competition that low-priced American cars now began to exert on the British domestic and overseas markets alerted some European industrialists to the possibilities of new methods. Of course, some European concerns did have considerably lower production costs than others, but the low-cost firms tended to maintain their prices close to the standard and earn high profits. These earnings often went back into the business, but usually into expensive experimentation, racing, and design work, which hardly affected production costs; or into expanded production facilities that rarely took full advantage of possibilities to raise labor productivity.

To be sure, there were some exceptions. These included the Lorraine-Dietrich factory; some of the shops at Renault; and the Berliet works in Lyon, where much mechanization of materials handling and assembly took place, and where, like Ford, the company made its own specialized machine tools. In England in 1913, the Sunbeam factory in Wolverhampton assembled chassis by moving them mechanically from one group of specialist fitters to the next. This verged on moving assembly, but Sunbeam's annual sales of less than 2,000 cars hardly required it. In Turin, the large Fiat works was also developing flow assembly in 1913, but its wide variety of products, trucks and marine engines as well as several models of cars, precluded the standardization that would take best advantage of it.[35]

The European firms moved only slowly toward standardization of product and mass-production methods for a variety of reasons. The current level of demand failed to require it, and the firms did not anticipate or vigorously stimulate such demand. Also, management was reluctant to invest in new machine tools as well as new methods and was less familiar with the practice of using interchangeable parts. Finally, skilled labor acted as a strong force to maintain the traditional methods of production. Management rarely seemed to question the principle that its direct responsibility did not extend into the shops, where the parts were made and assembled. There, the foremen and older skilled workers ruled. Academically trained engineers were unwelcome, and sometimes modern machine tools were also, for they were perceived as a threat to the power of labor.

Any change that reduced the skilled worker's autonomy or that subordinated him to the rhythm of a machine or to the dictates of an outside "expert" was resented and stubbornly opposed by European workers more ardently than by American ones. Management, believing that these skilled employees were essential to the factory's operation, usually did not try to press the issue, or compromised. An American observer touring European metalworking factories in 1908 noticed that frequently shops failed to achieve as much production from American machine tools as they could have, and that in some cases skilled workers refused to operate modern semiautomatic tools for reasons of craft pride and fear that they would bring unemployment.[36]

Hence, the shift from skilled labor using artisanal methods to mass production employing semiskilled or unskilled labor was slow in Europe. The idea began to germinate just before the First World War, fertilized in part by the American example, but the war itself, which created sudden huge demand leading to the mass production of some kinds of munitions by unskilled (even female) labor provided a more graphic and persuasive demonstration.

Labor

Rarely did the early automobile firms experience difficulty in finding labor. The majority of these concerns were already engaged in some kind of metalworking and simply shifted their workers from bicycles, sewing machines, or whatever to automobiles. Those companies starting de novo were easily able to hire enough experienced craftsmen to make the small number of cars they produced. In this period, especially in Europe, the large majority of these workers were highly skilled, and for several years had served an apprenticeship and worked as journeymen. To help them, a few apprentices and unskilled laborers were sufficient. When output rose to several hundred or even thousands of cars per year, opportunities (and problems) arose and changes began to occur. Now production of hundreds of exactly similar parts was possible, and manufacturers introduced semiautomatic or automatic machine tools to make these parts. These machines were highly specialized and limited in their actions, in contrast to the universal type of machine that could be adapted to cut or form metal in many different ways. The specialized machines could be tended by semiskilled or unskilled workers.

Such men, and occasionally women, were paid at lower rates, and followed orders with fewer disputes than skilled craftsmen. This situation allowed little room for apprentices, who traditionally had spent several years learning every facet of a particular type of metalworking. Their broad skills were needed less and less in the auto factories, and the apprentice system was fading out in them by 1914. Skilled workers naturally resented the influx of untrained laborers to the factories. Where metalworkers' unions were strong, such as the Amalgamated Society of Engineers in Britain, they opposed the assignment of unskilled workers (handymen) to specialized machine tools, but they usually lost such disputes. Where unions were weak, as in France and the United States, the process moved ahead somewhat faster.

This happened especially in the factories of the American Midwest, where the industry grew so rapidly from 1905 on. There, the skilled men did not suffer seriously because they usually could find positions as toolmakers or supervisors. The unskilled recruits at first came from the farms and the declining lumber business of the area and Canada, then in rising numbers from the flood of immigrants coming to the United States from Eastern and Southern Europe during these years. Detroit soon became a polyglot city, and the Ford company posted some notices in at least eight different languages, including Greek and Arabic. In 1900 Wayne County, in which Detroit lies, had 112,000 foreign-born inhabitants. By 1920 this figure had tripled to 345,000, or 29 percent of the total population. The 76,000 Poles made up the largest contingent, followed by Canadians, Germans, Russians, British, Italians, and Hungarians. During the First World War, the movement of American blacks from the south to Detroit began, and 44,000 lived in Wayne County by 1920. The Ford Company made a special effort to employ workers with physical handicaps and those released from prison. In sum, the American automobile industry set a pattern of using marginal labor as a large part of its work force, a pattern that already could be seen in the earlier European textile spinning mills, and that would be adopted by automakers in Europe in the following decades.

Ordinarily, the workers' day lasted nine to eleven hours, five and one-half or six days a week; and a trend toward fewer hours occurred. Everywhere, auto laborers tended to be among the highest paid factory workers in their communities. Employers offered good wages to attract workers, and the piecework payment systems often used allowed them to earn relatively high incomes. The successful firms enjoyed large, sometimes huge, profits, and managements conceded some of these earnings to labor, consciously or not passing on some of the productivity gains. Around 1910 automobile workers received the daily wages indicated in table 4–1. Although these figures are estimates, they do indicate orders of magnitude. An interesting aspect is that the national ranking of wages is the same as the author's impression of labor productivity in the auto factories.

In France and the United States, the rate of wage increases for automobile workers in the period 1900–1914 exceeded that in all other industries, and this may have been true in other countries. One reason was the spread of piecework, or payment by results. Most manufacturers were convinced that this method increased labor productivity and tried to institute it wherever possible, both for the individual worker and for teams of men engaged in assembly. Such arrangements usually provided that a worker was guaranteed his rated hourly wage regardless of his output, but would be awarded a bonus if he surpassed the piecework norm. In most cases, workers on piecework earned more than those on a time-payment method, and the majority of unskilled and semiskilled workers accepted the system.

Skilled men often opposed it. They argued that the speedup exhausted workers; that rates would be cut if many workers exceeded them, and they often were; and that quality suffered in the rush for quantity. All these consequences might occur, but none was inevitable. What really upset the skilled men was the threat to their

Table 4-1.
*Estimated Average Daily Wage of
Automobile Workers, Selected Countries,
Around 1910 (in dollars)*

United States	2.70
France (Paris)	1.90
Britain	1.57
Germany	1.30
Italy	1.06

Sources: United States—Paul Brissenden, *Earnings of Factory Workers, 1899 to 1927* (Washington: Bureau of the Census, 1929), p. 124; France—calculated from P. Combe, *Niveau de vie et progrès technique* (Paris: Presses universitaires de France, 1956), p. 606, but about 1 franc added to the figure for Paris metal-workers; Britain—calculated from the figure of 35 shillings for a 54-hour week, suggested by several sources; Germany—based on the average daily wage at Daimler of 5.45 mark, from Schumann, *Auslese und Anpassung*, p. 45; Italy—a slight reduction from the 5.7 lire daily wage for 1911 given by Castronovo, *Agnelli*, p. 53.

power in the factory. Piecework, as well as the scientific management movement already on the horizon, implied that company management would gain more control over shop operations, and reduce the privileged and independent status of the skilled workers.

By 1914 about half the British automobile workers were on piecework, and probably a higher proportion in France, Germany, and the United States. The Ford Company did not use it because Henry Ford strongly disliked it. But his method to ensure results from his workers before late 1913 was more brutal than piecework. His foremen were empowered to discharge workers without appeal, they did so massively, on occasion firing 500 men in a single day. The factory's monthly labor turnover reached a towering peak of 48 percent in December 1912.

Piecework was essentially an effort by management to extend its control over factory operations to raise productivity. Another step toward this end in the automobile industry was centralized hiring by an employment office rather than by individual foremen. The subcontracting system, in which a skilled worker contracted to finish a specific task in the factory and then hired his own team of men to accomplish it, also faded away. The trend toward tighter management control eventually found a name (scientific management), a prophet (F. W. Taylor), and some basic principles: apply scientific procedures to determine the most mechanically efficient way to perform tasks, insist that employees follow these methods even if they contradicted traditional usages, and reward workers liberally. Although scientific management was often called "Taylorism," it was more than a one-man crusade and would probably have evolved without the presence of Taylor at all.

In automobile manufacturing, it began in America, where engineers were more oriented toward production problems than in Europe. Taylor himself never installed his system in an automobile factory, but he did exert an indirect influence through his speeches, writings, and disciples. This is a complicated matter, however. For example, the Packard factory in Detroit employed about 6,600 men to make 2,320 cars in 1912, an astonishing ratio of 2.84 workers per car. Then, after a reorganization said to rest on Taylor's principles, it used 4,525 workers to produce 2,984 cars in 1913, a ratio of 1.5, still surprisingly high in comparison to the figure at Cadillac (.17 workers per car), or Chalmers (.39). In a letter to Charles de Fréminville on 27 January 1914, Taylor indicated that Barth and Merrick, two of his associates since 1911, had gradually been introducing the Taylor system in the factory of the Franklin automobile company of Syracuse, New York. It produced cars in the medium- and high-price ranges, and never grew to more than secondary importance in the industry.[37] Further, the innovations already described at the Ford plant owed nothing to Taylor directly.

In Europe before 1914, Taylor and scientific management received more publicity in France than elsewhere through the efforts of some savants—led by Henry Le Chatelier and Léon Guillet—who were deeply interested in applying scientific method to industrial production, and some engineers, Georges de Ram of Renault and Charles de Fréminville of P & L. In France, the adoption of Taylor's methods before 1914 frequently was limited to standardization of tools and to time study so as to better calculate piecework rates, and this led to strikes in several auto factories. Yet Taylor's message was heard, for on 4 January 1914 a prominent preacher in Paris, Father Sertilanges, began his sermon with the statement that "The love of God is the Taylor system of our spiritual life."[38]

Across the channel in Britain, skilled workers also felt harassed by "feed and speed men" telling them how to do their jobs. German interest in scientific management came with a rush after the war. Yet European employers tended to ignore Taylor's insistence that gains from increased productivity should be shared generously with the workers.

Although skilled workers clearly disliked the nature of factory work after the introduction of intensive mechanization on the models of Ford and Taylor, unskilled workers raised fewer objections. Their pay was relatively high, and because of their low status in the factory and lack of craft pride, they had little to lose. However, many intellectuals echoed the complaints of the skilled workers. They criticized what seemed to be the growing dehumanization of factory work, and used the automobile assembly line as a convenient symbol. Perhaps they were unaware that the unskilled laborer in a low-wage, nonmechanized occupation might also lack mental stimulation, such as the attendant deep in the champagne cellar who turned by hand 30,000 bottles every day. And yet such criticism led to a fruitful dialogue about mechanization and the worker. It soon revealed that both Taylor and his early critics viewed matters too simply, and ultimately produced wise and searching analyses of the complexities of industrial society by investigators such as Georges Friedmann and Michel Crozier.[39]

Strikes tended to be infrequent in automobile factories in the period before 1914. Conditions were usually better than in older industries and the unions were less entrenched. In Britain and the United States, automotive unions of machinists enrolled only skilled men, and so their influence progressively diminished. In France, Italy, and Germany, the unions did not follow such exclusive policies, but experienced trouble recruiting members in France, split over the issue of revolutionary or reformist tactics in Italy, and busied themselves administering welfare programs in Germany. In all these countries, employers began to use their own associations to counter the power of trade unions.

In Britain, the Employers' Federation of Engineering Associations led management to victory in the long lockout in the metalworking trades in 1897–98, and thereby won greater latitude in hiring practices and setting working conditions. Automobile manufacturers were thereafter relatively untroubled by strikes. A similar situation prevailed in the United States. Local groups such as the Employers' Association of Detroit and broader-based organizations such as the National Metal Trades Association managed to weaken the power of unions in the first years of the twentieth century, before automobile factories employed much labor. When the industry suddenly expanded, the unions refused to bestir themselves to organize the unskilled laborers. No major strike in the American industry took place before 1914.[40] In France, strikes occurred more frequently, but they were rarely led by the unions. The largest wave came in May 1906 in the eight-hour-day movement, and most of them failed. A series of conflicts erupted in 1912–13 over time study, climaxed by an unsuccessful six-week strike at Renault.

The most significant event concerning labor in the entire period was the announcement on 5 January 1914 that the Ford Motor Company would reduce the working day to eight hours and pay a minimum of $5 per day. This startling event capped a new labor policy that Ford had initiated in October 1913, in the midst of the experiments with moving assembly lines. Foremen lost their right to discharge workers (and labor turnover dropped sharply), the wage scale was simplified, a promotion system was established, and a 13-percent wage increase was granted. But these progressive actions were soon dwarfed by the $5 wage, which nearly doubled the rate of pay for American auto workers. Eligible for the new wage were workers twenty-two years and older who had worked for the company for six months and whose home life met certain standards of acceptability. Most Ford workers met these qualifications, 57 percent by the end of March 1914, and 76 percent of the rapidly growing labor force by the middle of 1916.

Labor turnover was no longer a problem at the time the new wage was introduced, and henceforth it became even smaller. Critics of Henry Ford have imputed discreditable motives for this step, but the evidence indicates that he and his associates felt they were sharing the huge profits that the firm now made, and possibly believed that it would convince workers to ignore labor-union organizers. The company had doubled its net income over 1912 to $27 million in 1913 and had declared a special dividend of $10 million in June of that year. The $5 wage was a dividend for the workers, originally estimated to cost at least $10 million in 1914.[41]

This massive pay increase demonstrated how a share of the large financial rewards resulting from mass marketing and gains in labor productivity could be passed on to workers. When generalized, as ultimately would happen first in the United States, it would produce the mass-consumption society typical of the industrialized western world in the mid-twentieth century. The role of the Ford Company in this achievement should not be overemphasized. Other auto firms were groping toward the moving assembly line after 1910 (in the United States, Buick and Willys-Overland); automobile wages already were high and rising everywhere. Henry Ford, in this period of his life, simply was bolder, and his intuitive sense of publicity encouraged him to make his moves a little ahead of his competitors.

European Developments after 1908

If the recession of 1907–8 barely affected the American automobile industry, the contrary was true for Europe. Those manufacturers there who aimed at the luxury market with expensive cars, and this meant most of them, suddenly found their sales sharply reduced when their clients postponed purchases. Because the recession was brief, relatively few of the major firms failed, but most tried to broaden their market by producing some smaller and cheaper cars, and to cut costs by reducing the gamut of models available. The appearance of the Ford and other low-priced American cars on the European market further stimulated this trend, but was not essential to it. None of the European manufacturers were courageous enough to plunge into the low-price field by producing thousands of cars and offering them at a notably lower price.

France remained the leading European producer throughout these years, its 1913 output of 45,000 exceeding Britain's 34,000 and Germany's estimated 23,000. But the French industry's rate of growth had slowed down considerably. Production rose at an annual rate of 9.7 percent from 1907 to 1913, compared to an annual rate of 20 percent from 1901 to 1907. This slackening resulted in part from growing competition on the export market. In 1907 the value of French automobile exports, $28.6 million, easily surpassed the totals of the other major producers, Britain, the United States, Italy, and Germany ($19.3 million total). In 1913 France, whose exports amounted to $43.9 million, remained the leader, but by this time the total of the other four countries, $82.1 million, was almost twice as great. The proportion of French production exported declined from about half in 1907 to just under 40 percent in 1910 and 1911, and then recovered to 44 percent in 1912 and 1913. While exports could not be expanded so easily as earlier, the domestic market after 1910 also slackened its expansion.

A look at which firms grew most rapidly in this period may explain why. From 1910 to 1913 Peugeot, Berliet, Darracq, and Unic increased their output the most. In 1912 Peugeot introduced a small four-cylinder car, the Bébé, selling in the low-price range, and the other three emphasized sturdy cars in the lower half of the medium-price range. Such policies brought growth. Firms that continued to offer a wide variety of expensive models, such as P & L, Lorraine-Dietrich, Rochet-Schneider, or diverted their interests to aviation or heavy vehicles, such as Renault, Clément-Bayard, De Dion-Bouton, and Delahaye, took a smaller share of the passenger-car market. A close observer might have predicted that the small four-cylinder car selling at under 5,000 francs ($1,000) would become the center of the market, but most French entrepreneurs could not accept that fact, and only about 6,000 of the 45,000 automobiles produced in 1913 fell into this class.

The British automobile industry moved ahead rapidly after 1909, finally beginning to take advantage of the large domestic market that French firms had first exploited. British exports became substantial, but nearly 60 percent of them went to the empire in 1912 and 1913, especially Australia and New Zealand. Except for France, the British had difficulty penetrating the Continent. The British annual rate of growth of production averaged 17.5 percent from 1907 to 1913. Prices tended to be high; few models sold for less than £250 ($1,250). This left plenty of room for Ford, which began assembly of Model Ts in Manchester in 1911, and immediately became the leading seller at £135 ($675) and up.

Some of the smaller British motor firms soon challenged Ford, and beginning in 1912 a rush started toward small four-cylinder cars, led by the Singer 10 at £195 ($975) and the Morris Oxford at £175 ($875). Both these companies had started in the bicycle business. The first Morris cars in 1913 were assembled entirely from externally made components, but Morris experienced so much difficulty obtaining what he wanted at low prices in England that he made two trips to the United States in 1914 and ordered engines and other major components for a new model car from American suppliers. The war halted this arrangement. Of the largest British producers— Wolseley, Humber, Sunbeam, Rover, and Austin—only the first one listed had a car ready for the low-price market when the war began.

Similar trends marked the German industry: expansion of production from 1908 and a sharp increase in exports. The German rate of growth in the period 1907–13 averaged 25 percent annually, and an increasing proportion went to exports, about 36 percent in 1912. Such exports were slightly under half the value of the French. German cars far outsold French ones on the Russian and Austro-Hungarian markets and had begun to appear in strength in Argentina and Brazil, but offered no serious threat to the French business in Britain, Belgium, Switzerland, Italy, and Spain.

Benz and Daimler-Mercedes continued to aim at the upper half of the price range. The two firms followed a similar policy of offering a wide variety of passenger cars and trucks. Like Daimler, Benz established a separate truck factory, in Gaggenau near Baden-Baden, and both engaged seriously in racing. Benz expanded more rapidly, raising its capital from 4 million marks in 1909 to 22 million in 1913, and employing up to 9,000 workers to make about 4,500 vehicles

Table 4-2.
Motorization toward the End of 1913

Country	Automobiles registered	Inhabitants per automobile
United States	1,258,000	77
Canada	50,600	151
Britain	250,000	165
France	125,000	318
Germany	70,615	950
Italy	17,000	2,070

Sources: United States—National Automobile Chamber of Commerce, *Facts and Figures of the Automobile Industry* (New York, 1933), p. 10; Britain—calculated from Society of Motor Manufacturers and Traders, *The Motor Industry* (London, 1932), p. 41; Canada—*Historical Statistics of Canada* (Toronto: Macmillan, 1965), p. 550; France—author's estimate; Germany—*Statistisches Jahrbuch*, 1915, p. 144; Italy—author's estimate.

in 1913. Daimler's employment and output were about half these figures. The powerful and prestigious cars made by these concerns sold well in Russia, where the aristocracy had slight interest in the small and light cars designed for a middle-class market. In the German case, it was almost a rule that those automobile firms once in the bicycle trade would be the ones to develop small cars, as proved by Opel, Brennabor, NSU, and Wanderer. Small cars made by the first two of these sold well, showing that in Germany, too, the market was good for this type. Yet this country still had a long way to go to reach the level of motorization of Britain and France, as seen in table 4–2.

In Italy, the recession of 1907–8 hit the automobile industry hard. Already prices of automobile stocks had crashed on the stock exchange in 1906–7, and then the orientation of almost all Italian production toward the high-priced luxury market, especially for export, made the industry especially vulnerable to swings in the business cycle. The leading Milanese firm, Isotta-Fraschini, was saved only when the French Lorraine-Dietrich company bought a controlling interest in 1907 and advanced large sums to keep it running. Lorraine-Dietrich finally cut Isotta-Fraschini free in 1911 after suffering heavy losses. Thereafter this company prospered, making 400–500 large cars per year in many models. In Turin, Itala and Lancia (the latter founded by a former Fiat racing driver in 1906) enjoyed moderate success. They made a few hundred large and powerful cars annually for the wealthy in Italy and for export. But Fiat overshadowed these small companies and the handful of others that had survived the recession.

Fiat had suffered a severe shock in 1908 as a result of public revelations of heavy financial losses the previous year, official charges of fraud against Giovanni Agnelli and some of his associates, and the resignation of the entire board of directors. The legal case against Agnelli dragged on for years and was not finally settled until the court in 1912 and 1913 found him innocent. He had resumed his position as managing director of Fiat in 1909 and continued his policy of vertical integration on the one hand and a wide range of products on the other. Fiat's taxicab of 1909, driven by a small four-cylinder engine, was a success, but the company did not concentrate on this model, and it also began to make engines for aircraft and then diesel types.

To retain its market in the United States, Fiat established a manufacturing branch in Poughkeepsie, New York, to produce small numbers of its more expensive models. In 1912 Agnelli came to the United States again and visited the Ford factory. He did not thereafter standardize Fiat's output, but did improve its factory organization and planning. Company production of vehicles rose from 1,300 in 1908 to 3,050 in 1913 and took a big jump to 4,644 in 1914, ranking it with Peugeot, Renault, and Benz among the major European producers. Twenty-two of the largest producers are listed in table 4–3.

Conclusion

By 1914 the first phase of the Automobile Revolution had been accomplished. A synthesis of several lines of technical development occurred in France and Germany around 1890 to produce the motor car, an interesting innovation, hardly more than a toy at first, but not a revolution. For the next decade, production expanded gradually as manufacturers worked out methods to publicize and market their vehicles. By 1900 automobile designs and manufacturing techniques were spreading rapidly in the industrial areas of

Table 4-3.
Estimated Production of the World's Leading Automobile Firms, 1913

1.	Ford (USA)	202,667
2.	Willys-Overland (USA)	37,442
3.	Studebaker (USA)	31,994
4.	Buick (USA)	26,666
5.	Cadillac (USA)	17,284
6.	Maxwell (USA)	17,000
7.	Hupmobile (USA)	12,543
8.	Reo (USA)	7,647
9.	Oakland (USA)	7,030
10.	Hudson (USA)	6,401
11.	Chalmers (USA)	6,000
12.	Chevrolet-Little (USA)	5,987
13.	Peugeot (France)	5,000
14.	Paige (USA)	5,000
15.	Renault (France)	4,704
16.	Benz (Germany)	4,500
17.	Rambler-Jeffery (USA)	4,435
18.	Darracq (France)	3,500
19.	Opel (Germany)	3,200
20.	Fiat (Italy)	3,050
21.	Wolseley (Britain)	3,000
22.	Berliet (France)	3,000

Sources: James J. Bradley and Richard M. Langworth, "Calendar Year Production: 1896 to Date," in *The American Car since 1775*, edited by Automobile Quarterly (New York: Dutton, 1971), pp. 138–139; Laux, *In First Gear*, p. 199.
Note: the least reliable figures are those for Benz, Darracq, and Berliet. Buick, Cadillac, and Oakland were all owned by General Motors.

Europe and North America, and production began to climb rapidly to meet the demand of the wealthy for the new luxury.

After 1906 in America, automobile makers began to seek earnestly for a market for low-priced cars, something that European producers also attempted, but much more hesitantly. The Americans found it and soon the question no longer was how to sell the cars they made, but how to organize production so as to meet the apparently un-limited demand. Here was the beginning of a revolution: the dis-covery of a widespread desire for individual private mechanical trans-portation, and the adoption of new methods of production to make cars to satisfy this demand.

But how was this new industry financed? Where did the capital required to manufacture automobiles come from? Was the new industry an agency of so-called finance capitalism? The answer is "no" because the source of capital in the early automobile industry was not a major problem. To enter it before 1914 did not require much money. Many firms started simply as assemblers of parts made by specialist manufacturers, and some of these assemblers—Renault, Ford, Morris—became the most successful. For them, the long-term investment in manufacturing facilities had already been made by the component suppliers, and the short-term capital came from deposits made by purchasers or credit extended by suppliers and sometimes by commercial banks. Ultimately, the assemblers of cars began to manufacture some components themselves, usually financing this out of their own earnings, or less frequently by the sale of securities. Firms already in business that entered the new industry—for example, Delaunay-Belleville, Napier, Pope, Studebaker—could use facilities and equipment they already owned in their new activity.

However, someone starting new in the industry and wishing to manufacture most of the parts of his car himself needed a large sum of long-term capital from the beginning. Banks and private investors were hesitant to invest in such untried enterprises, knowing well that more of such firms failed than succeeded. Therefore, companies following this sort of strategy, such as Fiat and Daimler-Mercedes, were forced to start on a small scale, and they grew rather slowly in their early years.

Usually, banks were of minor importance in supplying long-term capital to the French, British, and American industries, though in the French and British cases small investment banks and financial houses sometimes helped to market stocks and bonds to the public. Bank control of GM from 1910 to 1915 was based on a large medium-term loan. It was unusual and did save the firm from failure. Banks provided more capital and exerted more influence on the automobile industry in Italy, certainly, and in Germany, probably. Such was the style of industrial growth in these two countries, but the state of present historical research does not yet permit any conclusion as to whether or not the closer banking connections in them help explain the slower development of the industry. The revolution in production methods first carried out by the American producers ultimately would sharply raise the capital requirements for automaking, both for production facilities and for marketing networks. The industry would become highly capitalized, but it did not begin that way.

By 1914 a revolution was apparent in the way automobiles were produced, but the industry had not yet wrought a revolution in the daily lives of most people. In the entire world, only about 1.8 million motor vehicles were in circulation, not enough to exert any large impact on social conditions. But, hardly more than a decade later, more than thrice this number of automobiles would be supplied to the market in a single year. The social revolution was just over the horizon.

Two   The Spread of the
Automobile Revolution,
1914–1945

Patrick Fridenson

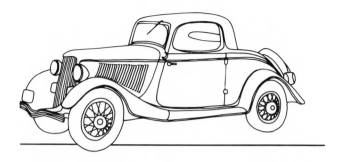

5. Wartime Expansion

The First World War did not halt the irresistible growth of the automobile manufacturers. It even expanded their working capital and their productive plant. It was an unequal expansion, however, for it benefited most of all the American companies. They took advantage of these years to increase their lead over Europe because the United States did not enter the war until 1917.

Europe's Conversion to War Production

The war brought destruction and pillage to the European belligerents. For example, in France the Panhard et Levassor (P & L) factory in Reims was shelled and demolished; the Germans plundered the Peugeot factory in Lille of its machinery. Other firms operated on a reduced basis such as the Belgian FN at Herstal near Liège, which was requisitioned by the Germans and turned into a major truck repair facility. Other negative aspects of the war included the rapid deterioration of equipment and of roads in the combat zones.

The war also held back the appearance of such new models as the Morris Cowley, the first really mass-produced European car, which was ready in 1915, but the introduction of this British response to the Ford T had to be postponed. The war also ended Europe's supremacy in exports, for the well almost ran dry. Finally, it opened European markets to American car manufacturers, for munitions production occupied the Europeans almost completely. The American penetration, spearheaded by Ford, was so strong that almost everywhere tariff duties were raised. Even free-trade Britain decided to seek protection with the McKenna Duties in 1915.

Still, the positive effects of the war on the automobile industry outweighed the negative. Automakers managed to shift into munitions production rather quickly, often with a remarkable adaptability and technical flexibility, especially striking in the cases of Fiat and Renault. The industry continued to produce passenger cars, but often in small numbers and largely for military use. It greatly expanded truck production and to a lesser degree, that of tractors. Above all, it plunged into manufacturing war materials. The nature of these was not exactly the same for each country and firm, but aircraft engines were clearly the major new product. The industry supplied a large part, even a majority, of those ordered by the Allies, and sometimes this led to their manufacture of airframes as well.

To produce various kinds of munitions, the auto firms needed to hire many more engineers and supervisors. This led them to expand and renovate their stock of machine tools, often with the financial aid of their governments; encouraged their technical staffs to look for better products; stimulated the spread of the Taylor system of scientific management so as to meet the need for mass production; and required more employment of women workers (called munition-nettes in France, where they often comprised over a quarter of a factory's labor force), rural people, and in France, of immigrants to meet the labor shortage. Consequently, the proportion of unskilled workers in the automobile industry rose, most slowly in Germany. Often the war encouraged manufacturers to make for themselves or to have made under their control parts that formerly they had bought elsewhere. Finally, the war brought large profits to the automobile manufacturers, probably not at a higher rate than before the war, but larger totals.

In France, the automobile industry quadrupled its buildings, machinery, and employees. It accomplished this under the auspices of the Automobile Manufactures Association, where Louis Renault presided after October 1913. The manufacturers organized themselves into several industrial groups, each specializing in fabricating a particular military item. Hispano-Suiza led a group of fourteen companies, mostly from the automobile industry, which made aircraft engines. A similar arrangement operated for tanks. These machines required entirely new equipment, new methods for working with armor plate, and great speed to design and produce the 3,200 tanks that were delivered. The two leaders of the prewar industry, Renault

and Peugeot, dominated the groups, and during the war years reinforced their strong positions in the French economy. They decided
to adapt to the increasingly varied military needs by widely diversifying their output.

André Citroën did the opposite. He left his position as general
manager of the small Paris firm of Mors to establish his own new
factory, built nearby on the bank of the Seine from February to June
1915. There his policy was to make only shells and equipment for
shells, such as tubes and high-speed tool steel. In contrast to the
diversification policy of his competitors, who entered into quite different lines of production with varying profitability, he chose a strategy of risk, probably inspired by Ford, and wagered on the profits to
be made from large-scale production of shells alone.

During the four war years, France apparently was the belligerent
country where the automakers turned out the widest variety of munitions along with the 65,592 cars and trucks sold to the army and
2,500 to the private sector. Berliet, the top supplier of trucks, produced several thousand per year. The size of their orders led some
automobile firms to introduce aspects of the moving assembly line.
Delage did so for shells, and Berliet in 1917 installed two assembly
lines "on conveyor belts as at Ford"[42] in his new factory in Vénis-
sieux, near Lyon. At the Renault works in Billancourt, beginning in
May 1915 moving conveyors appeared in some shops. These were
chains traveling at 1.35 meters per minute. Nevertheless, such methods were not ordinarily used.[43]

The automobile industry in Great Britain also expanded its potential, though probably not at so fast a rate as in France. Firms diversified into fewer activities, and automobiles remained the larger share
of their output. Ford of England increased its supremacy by concentrating on cars, trucks, and ambulances. During the four war years,
its production totaled 50,000 vehicles, far ahead of such other firms
as Leyland (6,000) or Morris (1,344). The war also saw the rise of the
Associated Equipment Company (AEC), which supplied 40 percent
of the military trucks. It annually produced about 4,000, using an
assembly line installed in 1915. Beyond motor vehicles, the automakers moved gradually into aircraft-engine manufacture.

Before 1914, Britain had practically no aviation industry. By 1918
the automobile firms at Manchester, Conventry, Birmingham, Derby,
London, Sheffield, and the Clyde had made aircraft engines a separate industrial sector and had prepared the technical foundations for
the postwar English automobile boom. Among these firms was Rolls
Royce, which, like Hispano-Suiza, shifted from luxury motor cars to
aviation engines and also like it remained in this new line after the

war. Among the automobile firms making munitions, Austin in Birmingham benefited the most, for its labor force rose to 20,000 in 1918, about 10 percent less than Renault.

At first a neutral, Italy entered the war on the side of France and Britain in May 1915. Giovanni Agnelli of Fiat warmly supported Italian intervention, and the war brought him a marvelous harvest. In 1918 Fiat ranked third among Italian corporations behind the iron and steel firms Ilva and Ansaldo. Its automobile production continued above the prewar level, in 1917 equaling that of Ford of England, and in 1918 surpassing it with 16,542 vehicles, including the sturdy 18BL military trucks. Fiat's growth required construction of a new factory in the Lingotto section of Turin beginning in 1916, the first Italian factory built of reinforced concrete. There Agnelli began a renovation program, including assembly lines in a few departments.

Like Renault, Fiat had manufactured aviation engines since 1908 and expanded their output sharply, reaching a wartime total of 15,380. Military demand also brought Fiat into aircraft construction, and it produced 1,336 in two years, one of the many ways that Fiat, like Renault, moved beyond automobile making in this period. The consortium of auto factories that from 1911 included such smaller firms as Itala and Lancia enjoyed wartime prosperity, but could not reduce the gap in size between its members and Fiat. In Milan, on the contrary, the engineer Nicola Romeo enjoyed thundering success managing the old Darracq factory. In 1918 his company's capitalization reached 30 million lire, and a few months later 50 million ($10 million).

In Russia, the automobile industry performed well, but did not play such a decisive role in the war economy. This stemmed from the small number and size of the firms that had been created before the war (especially in comparison with the iron and steel industry), and also from the tsarist regime's policy of placing massive munitions orders with foreign producers. The Russo-Baltic Company, in Petrograd, made aircraft, and other auto firms, from Citroën's gear works to Fiat's truck-making licensee in Moscow, expanded vigorously. Indeed, three new factories were built during the war. One at Jaroslavl was erected in 1915 and was scheduled to make 1,500 English Crossley cars per year. Another plant, which opened in 1917 at Moscow, was managed by a new company, AMO, and was equipped with up-to-date American machines, whose operation would require 6,000 employees. Renault activities, however, were especially striking. This company had decided in January 1914 to establish a plant in Russia. Its Roussky-Renault subsidiary put up the buildings in Petrograd, equipped them with American machine tools along with those made locally, and taught Russian workers, both men and women, to operate them. In 1916 Renault established a new factory for auto and aeroplane parts at Rybinsk, on the upper Volga.[44]

The same combination of growth and conversion occurred among the Central Powers, though full information on it is lacking. Although automobile production declined in most of the Allied countries from 1914 to 1918, in Germany it apparently rose. The 1913 level of output could not meet the military need for trucks, armored cars, and staff cars. Because the Germans had fewer auto companies than the Allies, and most of the car orders went to Adler, Benz, Mercedes, and Opel; and truck requisitions to Benz, Bussing, Mercedes, Opel, and Krupp. As elsewhere, the automobile industry began producing aircraft engines, making 40,500 in four years, the majority by Benz and Daimler-Mercedes.

Unlike the French case, however, the war did not bring much change in production methods. The German expansion into aircraft engine manufacture was a little less than half that of France's, and required no major change in shop practices. In addition, German management chose not to recruit a higher proportion of unskilled labor. The Daimler-Mercedes Company earned the largest war profits, but, when it refused to open its books to the War Ministry, the government placed it under military control in March 1918. The six largest German automobile companies at least doubled their dividend payout from 1914 to 1916, and Daimler-Mercedes quadrupled its capital.[45]

In Austria-Hungary, the war boom particularly benefited the Czech firms Laurin-Klement, Nesselsdorf, and Praga. The last of these began producing a heavy-duty, six-ton truck in 1917, and continued this model for nearly twenty years. Praga also ventured into aviation engines. Austrian companies did well too, especially Austro-Daimler but also Gräf und Stift and WAF.

So the motor car makers in the European belligerent countries profited from the new and temporary circumstances. But their growth did not angle as steeply upward as that of manufacturers in the neutral countries.

Expansion in the Neutral Countries

The outbreak of the war in Europe represented a bonanza for American automobile makers. It not only removed their major competitors from the market, but it also created an economic boom that spurred the automobile industry. Domestic demand expanded as purchasing power surged upward. Foreign demand followed suit as European governments placed orders for munitions. Total demand became so strong for all types of cars that the average selling price stopped falling after 1915. In 1914 America produced 548,139 passenger cars: in 1917 the figure was 1,745,792. Ford, naturally, profited most of all from this windfall, for the heaviest demand was for low-priced cars. The company even strengthened its domination of the market by cutting the price of the Model T without any reduction of quality. It thereby reached new levels of consumers, which allowed it to increase its profits on an investment that was paid off rapidly. In 1916 the price of a Ford T fell to $360, a level that none of its competitors could match and which assured Ford a monopoly of the mass-market cars.

The continuing drop in the price of the Ford T left an opening in the American automobile market. There was room for a car selling at $700–800 that would outdo the Model T in power and style and that would provide what the T lacked: a self-starter, electric lights, and detachable wheels. Three major companies decided to move into this market gap. The first of these, Willys-Overland, already had made cars for several years. Employing bank financing obtained in New York and its home, Toledo, it made the necessary investment. During the first three years of the war, its output tripled, and the company became the second largest American producer. In 1915 it was the first to set up its own finance company to handle installment loans, and soon Studebaker, Chalmers, Maxwell, and Paige followed its lead.

The $750 price range also attracted two new firms, Chevrolet and Dodge, which entered the industry along with a growing flood of new automakers (167 from 1914 to 1917 alone). The helmsmen of Chevrolet and Dodge were not new to the industry. Chevrolet owed its success to a phoenix springing from the ashes, William Durant. The Dodge brothers had previously made various parts for Ford and completely understood production methods peculiar to automobile making.

In his quest for high profits, Durant worked out a new system of production and distribution. In key locations throughout the country, he bought or established assembly plants. Then he organized parts making factories that sent their output directly to the assembly plants and near them he established wholesale sales offices. By using regional factories, he could sell his Chevrolets at prices attractive to local consumers while making most of his profit by billing the sales outlets for the fictional cost of delivering a complete car from the factory in Flint, Michigan. Durant, therefore, did not try to create an integrated factory, as Ford was doing at the Rouge at that very moment, nor even build a central assembly plant like many of his competitors.

Durant recognized that the bulk of savings made from mass production came from the manufacture of parts and accessories rather than from their assembly. The simultaneous growth of production and profits testifies to the soundness of his method. Durant continued it as the head of General Motors (GM), where he resumed control in 1915–16 by using money made by Chevrolet and with financial backing from the heads of the Du Pont de Nemours chemical company. On the one hand, he organized a holding company, United Motors Corporation, to buy up several major parts and accessories makers and placed talented manager Alfred P. Sloan at its head. On the other, he vigorously pushed his policy of mass production of low-priced cars.[46] In 1917 GM climbed to second place in output by producing 203,119 cars.

The Dodge brothers enjoyed even more success than Chevrolet, but it was easier for them. All they needed was a design office and national distribution network. By producing virtually one model only, the first to feature an all-steel body, they managed to reach third rank in 1917.

These changes first of all gave a small number of automakers a stronger hold on the market. Ford, making 664,000 cars in 1917, captured more than 46 percent, and the companies selling in the $750 price bracket won 20 percent. Around 1917, Willys, Dodge, and Chevrolet each turned out about 100,000 cars per year. To do this, they, and Buick also, gradually adopted the production methods created by Ford, especially assembly lines. Consequently, labor productivity in the automobile industry climbed by 40 percent between 1914 and 1918. Seeking to cut costs even more and to obtain more reliable delivery of better quality parts, the larger companies moved to make a higher proportion themselves. Vertical integration in the industry advanced some 20 percent during the war years. As a result, for cars costing under $1,000 automaking was ceasing to be strictly an assembly business. All the companies increased in size, but the largest ones grew the most. As in Europe, this expansion required more employment of immigrant workers. The companies had to adapt them to the conditions of mass production, which they did by establishing various procedures pertaining to selection, education, and welfare.[47]

A second outcome was a growing distinction in the nature of the competition among firms according to the type of car. For those selling below $1,000, vigorous competition prevailed in both price and quality. Price reductions came from increasing the level of production, that is, through economies of scale. But model changes and product improvement also resulted. Producers of medium-priced cars, those selling between $1,000 and $1,500, no longer emphasized price, but quality. They rang all the changes on which one of them best adapted the novelties developed by the makers of expensive cars. By 1918 such rivalry meant that henceforth the American car could be driven in any kind of weather, in all seasons, at any time; it had become easier to buy and to drive, thanks to the installment plan and to the spread of self-starters and detachable wheels; and, in the medium-price range, it had a permanent roof and electric lights. Finally, the makers of large cars and luxury models in the price range above $1,500 competed over esthetic and technical refinements.

A third change during this period of prosperous neutrality occurred in automobile distribution. Ford firmly insisted that his dealers handle his car exclusively. This implied sales quotas and dealers' observance of Ford recommendations. Although this tight control reduced the dealers' freedom, it did not limit their profits in good years. Chevrolet and Buick tried to imitate these arrangements, for they simplified the manufacturer's operations, but most companies did not follow Ford's lead.

A growing awareness of traffic problems came as a fourth and last result. Detroit was the first city to erect a "stop" sign in 1914, and in August of the same year Cleveland installed the first electric traffic signals. To improve rural roads, in 1916 the Congress passed the first law of the automobile age providing for federal aid for highways. The implications of this legislation were not immediately apparent because American entry into the war impeded its fulfillment. Its importance resided in the following principle: if the nation needed better roads, the national government must help provide them.

Although in the United States the war years staked out the path for later fundamental changes, in other neutral countries their effects were fleeting: a temporary revival of prosperity for their automobile industries and the replacement of European auto imports by American. In Sweden, two companies merged to create Scania-Vabis. Switzerland's automobile industry had suffered a serious crisis just before the war, and its smaller producers quickly closed their doors, but the larger firms—Pic-Pic, Martini, Saurer, Berna, FBW, and Arbenz, some of which specialized in trucks and buses—succeeded in maintaining normal operations by filling the orders of the Swiss Army and by exporting some 500 cars annually. In Spain and to a lesser degree Denmark, the decline of firms slowed down.

About the same thing happened in two non-European allies of Britain and France, Japan and Canada. In Japan, two domestic producers already had begun before the war. Two more took advantage of the situation to enter the industry: Ishikawa and Mitsubishi. In 1918 auto registrations still amounted to only 4,523, however.

In Canada, auto production enjoyed a boom parallel to that in the United States, stimulated by rising purchasing power and by military orders. Such orders came not only from the Canadian government, but from everywhere in the British Empire. From 1914 to 1918, Canada ranked second in the world in automobile production. In 1917 its output attained 93,810 units, and the capital invested in its eleven important auto firms doubled from 1915 to 1917. The favorable circumstances encouraged more American companies to locate branches in Canada. Willys acquired Russell, and GM bought out and reorganized the McLaughlin Company, in Oshawa. Leadership went, of course, to Ford of Canada, which enlarged production by 275 percent. This branch exported 41,288 vehicles during the war, almost all for the armed forces. As did Ford of England, the Canadian division made few military items and concentrated on cars, trucks, and ambulances. On the contrary, American Ford plunged into a much more varied output when the United States joined the war.

America in the War

For the automobile industry, the United States entry in April 1917 did not mean a sharp break. For the previous three years, the war had already made its presence felt in several ways. European war orders took a good share of the output of the industry's suppliers. Truck making, just reaching maturity on the eve of the war, quintupled to satisfy European needs primarily. It rose from 24,900 in 1914 to 128,000 in 1917. The luxury car makers, such as White, Packard, Peerless, and Locomobile, took the lion's share of these orders, for the chassis of a luxury car could be converted easily to support a two- or three-ton truck. And, finally, in 1915–16, a group of automobile engineers mounted a national campaign for the industry to prepare itself for probable war. At the head of this movement marched Howard Coffin, vice-president of the Hudson Motor Car Company, former president and renovator of the Society of Automotive Engineers, and an untiring evangelist of standardization. Later, in 1917, he became a leader in American war production.

A second factor of continuity was that, after the United States entered the war, motor car production did not stop and only began to decline after a considerable delay, quite unlike the European precedent. This situation sprang from a deliberate policy of the manufacturers, and it would be repeated in 1940–41. They wanted to do their part in the war effort, but only if they could also continue their ordinary activity, making cars. The most integrated firms felt this most strongly, and continued to make deliveries on previous orders. So it was that in 1917 the industry achieved a record output of passenger cars.

But in the following year car production dropped 45 percent to 943,500 and truck output nearly doubled to 227,500. The repeated efforts of the War Industries Board did not cause this reduction in car production. What turned the companies around was the scarcity of essential raw materials and their own analysis of the market. In an agreement signed in late August 1918 by the manufacturers, their dealers, and the board, production for the last half of 1918 would be 25 percent of the number of vehicles produced throughout 1917, and the automakers would submit their production plans to the board. In reality, the board accepted the decisions taken by the manufacturers on their own.[48]

They prepared for the reduction in output by raising their prices an average of 42 precent from 1917 to 1918. Their profits did fall and the government levied an additional 5-percent tax on automobiles, but most of the companies remained profitable in 1918 because the vigorous demand for cars absorbed the higher prices. Manufacturers even found it possible to improve their cars by installing heaters in those with closed bodies in 1917, and Loughead—the future Lockheed—introduced four-wheel hydraulic brakes in 1918.

So huge was the capacity of the American industry that it could also engage in war production. General Motors and Dodge made ammunition; Chalmers antiaircraft guns; Ford shells, tanks, helmets, caissons, and submarine chasers. In addition to trucks, ambulances, and field kitchens, the largest scale production was of Liberty aircraft engines, developed primarily by a Packard engineer. Packard, Cadillac, Buick, Marmon, Ford, and a new firm, Lincoln, founded by Henry Leland in 1917 after he left Cadillac, began to produce Liberties.

Unlike European auto firms, the Americans did not engage heavily in shell making. At the end of 1917, they grouped themselves in several boards to standardize models and designs for the army and navy. The large military orders resulted in many company mergers as well as numerous increases in capital. As in Europe, the American firms hired much female labor.[49] One automaker who was deeply involved in war production was Charles Nash. He presided over GM from 1912 to 1916, then left it when Durant came back to power and bought the Jeffery Company, renaming it Nash in 1917. It quickly turned to army truck production and became the largest American supplier of these vehicles in 1918.

American entrance into the war demonstrated clearly that the country needed a network of national highways rather than simply piecemeal improvement of local roads. Overwhelmed, the railways soon were clogged with freight, making it impossible to ship military trucks to ports of embarkation for France. At this point, Roy Chapin, president of Hudson, suggested that trucks be driven from the Midwest to the East Coast. The army approved, and from the end of 1917 to autumn 1918 some 18,000 of them made the trip. This episode provided a striking demonstration not only of the possibilities of road transport even under poor conditions, but also highlighted the urgent need to transform the entire road system.

The war also encouraged the automobile companies to consider new products so as to fully employ their plant capacity and to keep their marketing networks in business. Henry Ford finally could fulfill his dream of mass producing tractors on an assembly line. The sudden shortage of foodstuffs had sharply increased the demand for this kind of relatively new agricultural machine. During 1917 and 1918, Ford's River Rouge plant at Dearborn turned out 6,000 tractors for Britain. In April 1918 it also began to supply them to private customers in the United States and from this point until the armistice it produced 26,817 Fordson tractors selling for $750 to enthusiastic farmers at a profit of 24.4 percent.

Over at GM, Durant also began to make tractors. But he also bought the Guardian Frigerator Corporation, and GM began to sell refrigerators. This expansion of activities only increased GM's internal organizational problems. Aware of this difficulty, in February 1918 the Du Ponts initiated GM's first administrative reorganization, following the precedent set in their own company. They established an executive committee composed of the heads of the major divisions, and gave it full authority and responsibility for corporation policy and results. Attached to it was a specialized finance committee.

Although the Du Ponts did improve coordination and supervision over the divisions, GM was still only a growing conglomerate.

Conclusion

During the First World War, public opinion and governments continued to consider passenger cars as luxuries. In October 1917 the War Industries Board in the United States categorized automaking as a "non essential" industry along with luxury goods, and the surtax imposed on cars in 1918 was a luxury tax. In Britain, several similar taxes were proposed, and a newspaper in 1916 demanded an end to passenger-car use, which was deemed unpatriotic. Once again, public attitudes lagged behind economic realities. In fact, the war forced the world to recognize the usefulness of the automobile as a method of transportation, as these examples illustrate: the recourse to Paris taxicabs at the Battle of the Marne in 1914; the supply of Verdun in 1917 over the "sacred road"; and the omnipresence of the Ford T on battlefields all over the world, including Arabia, where Lawrence replaced his camels with "Tin Lizzies." All these demonstrated the value of automobiles to the most dubious and made them a familiar sight. In the United States, auto registrations in 1920 totaled 8,132,000 cars and 1,108,000 trucks. The Automobile Revolution had won its spurs; now it only had to fight the battle of dissemination.

Just about everywhere, from 1916–17 onward thoughtful automakers delighted in their rosy prospects for the postwar years: in the United States, a continuation of the industry's expansion; elsewhere, a leap forward by using American methods; and, everywhere, a highway improvement program. They were preparing to make cars "meeting the real needs of a majority of buyers."[50] Yet, perhaps they underestimated the organizational and management problems created by large-scale production.

6.   American Dominance, 1918–1929

During the 1920s, the model of mass production initiated by Ford began to spread around the world. Yet, in the United States, where replacement demand came to provide the bulk of the market, General Motors (GM) dethroned Ford. Everywhere, automobile production achieved unprecedented levels, though at a more subdued rate of growth in America than elsewhere. All this progress brought a major change in the daily habits of people living in the developed countries.

The New Foundation for American Supremacy

At the war's end, American manufacturers optimistically prepared to resume the expansion that had characterized the preceding decade and that had depended on the growth of national income, the constant improvement in car technology, and the downward trend of prices. From 1919 to 1923, production rose by 110 percent, setting a record of 4,034,012 vehicles, while sales revenue grew 44 percent, reaching just over $2.5 billion. After 1924, however, annual sales stopped expanding, and the market remained rather steady. The explanation is that the growth of national income became more and more cyclical, few major improvements had been added to cars between 1918 and 1924, and the price of the Ford T reached its nadir. The number of those who did not yet own a car had much diminished, which reduced the group that had formed the bulk of the market for the major automakers. The producers now moved from a situation of excess demand to one of excess capacity, or what one of them, Alfred Sloan, described as a shift from a mass market to a mass-class market with increasing diversity. The task was to encourage replacement demand by offering better quality and variety. The former strategy of growth, centered on innovations in production and finance, was losing its relevance in favor of a new competitive strategy emphasizing management and marketing.

Automakers took several years to adapt to this fundamental change in the market. At the very beginning of the postwar period, they could depend on their earlier momentum. The limitations on automobile construction in 1918 created by restrictions on raw materials had created a strong demand, which came into play after the armistice. Its strength enabled the companies to sell cars at the high wartime prices. They took little time to reconvert production. Ford only required three weeks to modify his Model T to provide the options of a self-starter and electric generator and to resume production. If total production in 1919 did not quite fulfill the expectations of the industry's leaders, the difficulty came because it took a while for the economy to convert from war to peace and because a wave of strikes hit producers of raw materials and accessories.

All the auto companies tried to expand their factories as quickly as possible. Ford continued building his giant new complex at Dearborn on the River Rouge, which he had begun in 1916, and which included a steel mill. His borrowing of $75 million from Boston and New York bankers was not to pay for the Rouge plant but to exclude his minority stockholders, the Dodge brothers, by buying them out. GM announced the largest expansion program, aimed at doubling its capacity. William C. Durant inaugurated it in December 1918. Flush with financing coming from Du Pont, which had invested $42.6 million of its wartime profits in GM stock, he was confident in the chances of increasing GM's capital. All over the United States, he enlarged factories and built new ones, especially assembly plants.

Durant also bought into many of GM's suppliers, most importantly Fisher Body of Detroit, then (and now) the largest body manufacturer in the world. On the suggestion of John J. Raskob, chairman of GM's finance committee and former treasurer of Du Pont, Durant established a financial subsidiary, the General Motors Acceptance Corporation, to help dealers carry their inventories and to help consumers buy cars on credit, a system that Ford would not countenance. Durant organized a large research laboratory in Detroit, and invested considerable sums in housing for workers in Flint, Detroit, and near other GM plants.

Then suddenly, in April 1920, the market began to collapse. Earlier recessions (1903, 1907, and 1913) in the American automobile industry had only slowed down the growth rate. This one, on the contrary, led to a drop in production that lasted until July 1921 and forced automakers to lay off 84 percent of their workers. The recovery when the general economy revived was abetted by a policy of drastic price cuts that Ford had begun in September 1920. Most of the other firms followed suit, but only in May 1921 and with considerable reluctance. At that point, GM, long opposed to any such move, cut more deeply than Ford and slashed Chevrolet prices by 21.3 percent. This set off a price war between Ford and GM lasting until October. The price differential between the Ford and Chevrolet shrank to $90 from $245 in September 1920. Now Chevrolet competed directly with the Ford T. It had completed the strategy that Willys, Dodge, and Durant had tested between 1914 and 1917. Because Ford was unbeatable on his own ground, attack him from above with slightly better cars that would carve out an increasing share of the market to allow a reduction of prices. In reference to prices, the recession of 1920–21 provided the last major case of price flexibility in the American automobile industry.

To all appearances, Ford emerged from the recession as the victor. He had been the first to cut his prices. He had managed to divert the burden of the recession onto his 17,000 dealers by sending them in January 1921 all the cars he had in stock (125,000). They needed to pay in cash, a policy that Ford continued regardless of the recession. As the economy began to revive, his financial position surpassed that of his competitors. He held a dominant place on the market, more than 55 percent of sales in 1921. His leading rival, GM, had only 12 percent and had barely skirted disaster. Its president, the fast-dealing Durant, for the second and last time, was forced to resign. On 1 December 1920 the vigorous, shrewd, and cautious Pierre Du Pont, whose company now owned 36 percent of GM's shares, replaced him. Willys-Overland had tumbled into permanent difficulties. Maxwell went into receivership, and survived only when taken over by Walter Chrysler, who retired as vice-president of GM.

Other than these large firms, the major victims of the recession were the small manufacturers of luxury cars that the war had left with excess productive capacity in the face of a rapidly shrinking market. They suffered severe losses and several (including Lincoln, later bought by Ford) went through bankruptcy. Only some of the makers of medium-priced cers, such as Hudson, Dodge, Studebaker, Nash, and Reo, survived the recession undamaged, simply because they had not thrown together grandiose schemes of expansion.

The revival that succeeded this recession was strong but short. In 1924 another slump occurred and automobile demand slackened again (as it was also to do in 1926–27). This time, the policy of price cuts that Ford and the others repeated failed to bring back the customers, and American production fell 12 percent. But there were three exceptions to this rule. Maxwell (renamed Chrysler in 1925), Dodge, and Hudson raised their output in 1924 by 20 to 46 percent. This progress against the current is explainable by factors common to the three companies. They had introduced new models and they emphasized closed cars. In short, they were the first to react correctly to a fundamental change in the market. This change occurred under the pressure of four conditions.

The used-car market experienced a lively advance. From now on, the sale of a new car usually involved taking a used car in trade, and each used car was owned by two or three people before it was scrapped. Those drivers who wanted a car simply for transportation no longer needed to buy a functional new car, such as a Model T. They could get what they wanted from a used car. On the other hand, those who sold their old functional car for a new one asked for a model possessing more modern design, comfort, power, and style.

They could now afford it because of the expansion of installment selling. Around 1920, some 65 percent of cars and trucks were bought on time (one-third down and the rest paid in twelve monthly installments at variable rates of interest). These convenient arrangements encouraged consumers to aspire to better-quality goods and made them more easily available.

These two factors raised serious problems of adaptation for both dealers and manufacturers. Derived in part from them was a third, the increasing desire for cars with closed bodies. Earlier these had been available as special models, made to order. But, since 1919 a rising proportion of buyers, infatuated with comfort, agreed to pay more to drive a closed car. From 10 percent of the market in 1919, this style rose to 56 percent in 1925 and 85 percent in 1927. Open-body cars suffered a devastating blow, most of all the Ford T.

A final innovation, also partially a response to the first two trends just mentioned, consisted in the annual model change to stimulate demand. Beginning as a frequent practice, the annual changeover became a formal policy. Such makers of luxury cars as Cole offered new models each year from 1921 on so as to justify their necessarily high prices. Gradually other companies took this path, including GM in 1923. Ford and other firms that stuck with one basically unchanging model could not take advantage of the attractiveness of novelty and were condemned to lose ground.

Together, these four innovations completely changed the nature of the automobile market. As the manufacturers expanded their output of closed-body cars and moved toward the annual model change, demand rose well above the basic level needed to replace worn-out machines. The new policies required lavish investment, especially in tooling for the annual change. This strengthened the position of the large companies, for they could pay off the cost more quickly and over a larger number of cars. Yet, the initiative for the changes came from the medium-size companies making medium priced cars: Hudson, which marketed its closed-body Essex, Dodge, and Chrysler. Large enough to take advantage of most of the anticipated economies of scale, they were still small enough to follow a flexible and aggressive product policy. Neither Ford nor GM could do this.

After the 1920–21 recession, Henry Ford chose to maintain his traditional policies: production of a functional car, along with one-man management of the firm. Those officials in the company who held different views were dismissed, except for his son Edsel. So Ford persisted in his strategy of compressing costs, but this reached its limits.

To cut costs in spite of rising wages, Ford invested heavily. He bought or built forests, sawmills, blast furnaces, a railway line, textile mills, coke ovens, a glass works, a cement company, coal mines, and rubber plantations. He also established seven new assembly plants in the United States. The capital invested in plant doubled from 11 cents per dollar of revenue in 1913 to 22 cents in 1921. The time to fabricate a car fell from fourteen days (1913) to four (1924), and inventories shrank by half. The production process became more and more integrated and mechanized. All this raised the amount of capital invested per dollar of revenue to 33 cents in 1926, a figure representing a sharp rise in fixed costs, which made profits harder to achieve. In addition, to meet the competition, Ford was forced to add new devices to the Model T. These not only reduced its performance, for its weight rose by 25 percent from 1915 to 1925 even though the engine was unchanged, but also raised the cost of production. The result was declining profit margins for Ford beginning in 1923. The cost of producing a Ford touring car reached 93 percent of the selling price by 1926, and some models were sold to dealers at less than cost.

The second limit also flowed from Henry Ford's policy: the company was too narrowly specialized. One example will show this. Because of the Model T, Ford was oversupplied with wood capacity but lacked facilities for glass and body work. The workers, engineers, management, and technology were prepared to make Model Ts only. Any model change would require much time and money.

This led to the third limitation: a decline in ability to innovate because the complexity of the productive organization made it more expensive to change it and also because Ford had cut costs by slashing the numbers of supervisory personnel from 5 percent of his employees in 1913 to 1.2 percent in 1925. Innovation also became less intensive, being confined more and more to the transfer of tested technologies to different operations.

It is known today that any policy reducing the price of a product through regular increases in the numbers produced will ultimately encounter the same three limitations: rising fixed costs, hyperspecialization, and a declining capacity to innovate. In the metal fabricating trades, Henry Ford probably was the first to experience this phenomenon. At first, the decline of his market share, which had begun in 1922, seemed compensated by greater output (from 1.3 million cars in 1922 to 2 million the next year). But, from 1924 on, his falling share was matched by an absolute reduction in production.

By 1926 Ford had receded to under 40 percent of the market and 1.6 million cars. In vain, he had cut the Model T price six times between 1921 and 1925; nothing worked. Sizable profits continued to come in, but these arose from spare parts and accessories, not from auto sales. The "Tin Lizzie" had aged. The fraction of consumers who had never purchased a car shrank steadily. Finally, Ford no longer enjoyed the exclusive advantage of his production methods; from 1915 on, his competitors, one by one, adopted them. Hudson took only ninety minutes to assemble an Essex in 1926, even less time than Ford. Because Chevrolet, Buick, Dodge, and Willys-Overland were almost as efficient as Ford, the spread between their prices and that of the Model T had narrowed considerably. Was Ford over the hill?

During these years, GM carried out a complete reorganization based on principles totally different from those of Ford: the production of a complete range of cars to fit every purse and every purpose, and management of a decentralized firm by committees. Both these principles bore the impress of the calm and cold Alfred Sloan, Jr. This methodical engineer at first was the chief assistant of GM President Pierre Du Pont. Then, in the spring of 1923, Du Pont turned over the presidency to him but remained as chairman of the board. Sloan held his position until 1937. The new management that had taken over from Durant in December 1920 had spent only a surprisingly brief seven months to determine its new system of management and its new policies.

First, it needed to reorganize the enterprise, as yet only a formless aggregate of diverse companies. How could a system of coordination and internal hierarchy be set up that would preserve the efficiencies of the earlier decentralized system? Sloan's plan, adopted by 30 December 1920, depended on a combination of autonomous and decentralized divisions, best capable of solving day-to-day problems, directed by a central staff, competent to make crucial long- and short-range decisions. As the system was put into operation from 1921 to 1925, Sloan redrew the boundaries between divisions, defined the precise responsibilities of each one, and pruned off dead branches. He decided to give up Durant's old policy of vertical integration, and, contrary to Ford, to invest only in businesses directly related to automobiles. His chief financial administrator, Donaldson Brown, prepared a battery of statistical and financial controls, which, combined with a system of forecasting demand, gave the central staff a full understanding of its own operations and of the activity of the divisions in light of a dynamic market.

Finally, the new management established an advisory staff, which consisted of sections that specialized in various branches of activity, such as research, marketing, manufacturing, and purchasing. This staff's duty was to help the division heads as well as the central management. The importance of the advisory staff specialists rose when Sloan created interdivisional committees, to which they belonged. The corporate organization conceived by Sloan was running smoothly by 1925 and allowed top management to maintain efficient control over its huge industrial empire. GM would come to serve as an organizational model for many large American, and later, European companies.[51]

GM also needed a product policy. From Durant's leadership, it had inherited the largest variety of cars in America. But, of the seven different makes, all except Buick and Cadillac were losing money and some competed with each other. GM stood out by its absence from the low-priced, high-volume market. On 9 June 1921 the Executive Committee laid down the principles that were to allow GM "to make money, not just to make motor cars."[52] Henceforth, it would have one model, and only one, for each level of the price scale. To cut costs by taking advantage of long production runs, it would restrict the number of models and use interchangeable parts. This golden rule has brought success to GM up to the present. It showed up immediately in the firm's profits, but its real merit came when GM in quick succession adopted the annual model change (1923) and the closed body (1924). It was also reinforced by a constant effort to raise quality and to introduce technical improvements cautiously. Thus, the company had established a policy that was both coherent and adaptable to changes in the market.

Meanwhile, Sloan had improved the marketing side of his enterprise by consolidating the largest network of dealers in the United States and instituting a rigorous inspection system. Results followed quickly: from 1924 to 1926 GM rose to become the largest American automaker. From 1924 to 1928 it tripled its sales while its share of the market climbed from 18 to 47 percent.

In these circumstances, Henry Ford decided to come out with a new model. So rigidly specialized was his organization that he had little choice but to take the draconian step of closing all his factories for several months beginning in May 1927 so as to completely retool. Actually, almost a year went by before he could resume his normal level of production. The new Ford Model A featured a modern four-cylinder engine that performed well. Along with it, Ford changed his strategy. He did keep the single model, of course, but he dropped his traditional policy of cutting prices by shaving production costs. From that time until the present, every year the company improved the performance of its cars in return for a higher price. It ended up following the GM strategy: a better quality product offering better performance.

But Ford's resources were inadequate. For one thing, despite massive investment, he could not regain the high levels of labor and capital productivity of his earlier peak. Secondly, although the Model A was successful, it was still a functional car of a single type, an outdated conception. In the Chevrolet, GM offered something better at a price only slightly higher. In 1929 Ford's share of the market dropped to 31.3 percent.

When Ford shut down the River Rouge plant and forty-eight other factories all over the world in 1927–28, he not only left the field open for Chevrolet, but he also opened it to Chrysler. The latter company now climbed to rank as the third major producer. In the old Maxwell organization, Walter Chrysler had lacked the plant and dealer network necessary to produce a mass-market car at a low price. He obtained them when he bought Dodge after it ran into difficulty. So he possessed all he needed to launch the Plymouth against the Ford Model A in 1928. By this time, he had adopted the GM principles. He marketed a complete line of cars—in ascending order Plymouth, Dodge, De Soto, Chrysler, and Imperial—and he tried valiantly to offer clients a better car than his competitors at a price scarcely above them.

From a structure made up of one large firm, several medium-sized, and many small ones, the American automobile industry had moved on to another, much more concentrated, where a few large firms dominated. Their growth could come only at the expense of the others, nibbling away at the clientele of their rivals at each price level. Competition no longer revolved about price but about the product.

Several innovations improved the comfort and performance of cars. An independent body manufacturer, Budd of Philadelphia, in 1924 designed an all-steel body, quicker to make and much lighter. Most of the changes emanated from GM, however, because of the effectiveness of its research laboratories, directed by Charles Kettering and provided with a testing center in 1924. From them came cellulose lacquer, which made it possible to extend the range of colors offered to buyers and which, drying quickly, allowed more rapid production of auto bodies. To improve engine performance, compression ratios needed to be raised. GM found the answer in 1922 with ethyl gasoline, which was created by adding tetraethyl lead. It ended engine knock. At the time, no one measured its pollution effect.

How to better transmit the engine's power to the wheels? GM inaugurated the synchromesh transmission, and began work on an automatic transmission. In 1922 the tire companies introduced low-pressure balloon tires, which lasted longer than their predecessors. These and other improvements gave American cars their character: comfortable, large, powerful, and stylish. Style became a serious matter with the advent of the closed car, for the early ones were not very graceful. In 1927 GM set up the Art and Color Section under Harley Earl. Its time had come. Auto buyers more and more frequently based their choices on style, not mechanics.

Marketing also needed new ideas. Early in the 1920s, it suffered a crisis. Under the twin impact of a flood of used cars and manufacturers imposing quotas of new cars on dealers, the latter had suffered heavy losses. Some failed or went out of business. The partial cure that the industry had discovered in 1915, establishing a regional, then a national price list for used cars, had stabilized prices at that time, but no longer was sufficient. Therefore, the manufacturers began to pay more attention to their sales networks.

Now the local dealer became valuable to them, for if he left the business often the make went down with him unless a successor willing to accept the risks of the trade could be found. Beginning in 1921 manufacturers began to advance capital to their dealers to permit them to survive. Gradually, they began to supervise all aspects of the dealer's operations. They laid down rules on after-sale service, accounting, advertising, and location. They extended the system of exclusive dealerships. By 1929 the dealer had no choice but to follow strictly the instructions coming from the factory, of which his business had become an extension.

The automakers also had to innovate if they wished to squeeze production costs even more and reduce those for closed bodies. The installation of giant hydraulic presses to shape metal into wide and complex curves allowed them to make thousands of identical chassis frames and body panels and eliminated individual fitting. Techniques of continuous electric welding were worked out. Early in the 1920s, the A. O. Smith Company of Milwaukee established the first production line using transfer machines for chassis frames. Completely automatic, it performed an average of 550 separate operations in the course of one cycle of an hour and a half.

This further mechanization reduced the need for both skilled and unskilled labor, but increased the proportion of semiskilled. As a result, wages leveled out. Management boosted labor productivity in many ways. Skilled professional workers were assigned to more specialized tasks. Earlier, each machine had required one person to operate it, but manufacturers now managed to build a battery of machines so that one person could handle several. This raised the speed of production. Management tried all kinds of payment systems, especially team bonuses.[53] To control rising wage costs, the industry encouraged company unions and supplied paternalistic welfare systems for workers. More important than these policies, however, the ethnic heterogeneity of the labor force worked against unionization efforts. Because immigration from Europe had practically ended, recourse to southern blacks increased, to 25,895 by 1930, or 4 percent of the labor force of the entire automobile industry. They were assigned to the jobs requiring the least skill except at Ford, which employed three times as many blacks as all other companies combined.

Exports were a final way to reduce overhead costs per unit and increase the market. Between 1918 and 1923, American producers sold abroad about 4 or 5 percent of their output. When the domestic market reached saturation after 1923, they grew more attentive to foreign buyers and exports took a larger share of production, reaching 10 percent between 1927 and 1929. Faced with rising freight costs and tariffs, companies followed Ford's lead and set up assembly plants abroad. In 1929 eight companies (Ford, GM, Chrysler, Willys-Overland, Studebaker, Durant, Hudson, and Graham-Paige) operated such establishments, which assembled 48 percent of American automobiles exported.

Since before the war, Canada had been the favorite location for these moves, and the trend continued. In 1919 United States capital controlled 61 percent of the Canadian automobile industry, a proportion that rose to 83 percent by 1929. Almost all the authentically Canadian automakers left the industry. Ford, unlike GM, kept its Canadian branch entirely separate from its other foreign ventures. It expanded its manufacturing facility in Walkerville, and added four assembly plants in Montreal, Toronto, Winnipeg, and Vancouver. It used Canada primarily as a bridgehead into the British Empire.

During the 1920s, Ford-Canada created five assembly plants and a body factory in Australia, along with assembly operations in India, Ceylon, Malaya, and South Africa. In 1918 GM obtained full control of its Canadian branch, and in 1929 bought its major supplier of parts, McKinnon. Chrysler inherited a Canadian operation from its predecessor Maxwell, and its purchase of Dodge in 1928 brought it a factory there. The "Big Three" followed the same policies in Canada as at home, with similar results. Ford held first place until late in the 1920s, when GM overtook it.

The automakers operating in Canada exported about 42 percent of their output, a much higher proportion than that of their parent companies in the United States. More than two-thirds of these exports went to the British Empire. Ford exported the most, both in proportion to output and in absolute amount, but GM and Chrysler sold abroad nearly 40 percent of their Canadian production. The domestic and foreign demand raised Canada to the rank of second largest producer in the world; it produced 132,580 vehicles in 1924 and 263,000 in 1929.

The Spread of the American System

Outside North America, no other country reached a saturation of its automobile market. A massive demand for cars arose everywhere in the world. This forced manufacturers to give their primary attention to production problems and allowed them to sell their cars at progressively lower prices. Two kinds of situations arose: one in Western Europe, a second in other areas.

In Western Europe, helped by the rise of average purchasing power, most countries managed to maintain a local automobile industry protected by high tariffs. A few European producers tried the American recipe for success, particularly the technical principles dear to Henry Ford. They adopted interchangeable parts, intensive division of labor in the productive process, assembly lines, and one mass-market model. In the area of sales, they adopted the policies of distribution through exclusive dealers, installment credit, and the use of advertising campaigns. In these ways, they could reach most of the middle-class clientele and strengthen their dominance of the market. But, despite continual progress, they could not equal the productivity of the American giants. In 1927 the manufacture of a car represented 300 man-days of labor in France, compared with 70 in the United States.

The more numerous small manufacturers in Europe continued to restrict themselves to assembling finished parts and preparing chassis for well-to-do buyers. Their number declined after 1924 because frequent modifications in their cars made them too expensive. As had been the case before the war, both large and small European automakers exported a larger share of their production than did the Americans. The four leading European producing nations made about three-fourths of the cars purchased in these countries. A growing share of the remaining quarter consisted of American imports, assembled more and more frequently in plants established in Europe or in European factories purchased by the Detroit firms. So strong was the American attraction that in the 1920s both Austin and Citroën tried in vain to sell out to Ford and GM.

Elsewhere in the world, average incomes were often much lower, highway systems sketchier, and industrialization too weak to permit profitable operation by local automobile manufacturers. These countries could only import complete automobiles or those ready for assembly. Taking advantage of the momentum gained from the war boom, American firms worked quickly to displace their European competitors in these states, except in some colonial areas, and to win the favor of the local clientele. These countries became heavy buyers of trucks, tractors, and taxis. Automobile owners kept their machines much longer and sought durable vehicles, which made the Ford T a favorite among them.

In addition to protective tarrifs, in Europe two specific obstacles deterred the American invasion: high gasoline prices and a tax system that penalized large engines. As a result, during the period when American cars were raising their engine size, power, and comfort, European makers directed most of their efforts toward small- and medium-sized cars, light in weight and economical of fuel. In 1923 some 55 percent of the cars made in France had only 10 fiscal horsepower or less, and in 1928 this proportion reached 80 percent. Despite the steady European adoption of American production and business methods, these years witnessed a growing divergence between American cars, overstuffed and extravagant, and European models, smaller and cheaper.

France remained the leading European producer. It was third in the world after the United States and Canada. It still retained the second best highway network in the world after the United States. Car production in 1919 amounted to only 18,000, a level below that of 1913, but it rose to 254,000 in 1929. This growth depended especially on rural and small town buyers. As in the United States, production soon came from a smaller number of companies. Among the leaders, just as before the war, were Renault and Peugeot. But Renault, which held 25 percent of the market, maintained a comfortable lead over its old competitor, for Peugeot reached little more than half this figure. André Citroën, prewar manager of the Mors company, now ruled his own concern and outdistanced both of these with more than 30 percent of sales. These three totaled 63 percent of the new-car business in 1929. Foreign automobile companies owned some assembly plants in France: the leading English firm Morris; the Italians Lancia and Fiat; and Ford, which operated one at Asnières near Paris. They satisfied only a small fraction of the demand.

Citroën aimed at the mass market, which implied a modern product but a limited range of cars. He did it by being the first to import the latest American methods, such as moving assembly lines that he introduced from 1919 onward. His competitors had begun to adopt this practice during the war, but were slow to employ it throughout their factories. Berliet did so in 1920[54] but his financial troubles and the aging of his company's management hindered him from profiting from his quick reaction. Renault waited until 1922 and Peugeot a little later. A similar delay occurred in the adoption of installment selling by the French "big three" (though some of the smaller companies used this technique before the war).

The other side of the coin to Citroën's aggressive style was his financial instability, reminiscent of Durant in the United States. Renault lacked such marketing and technical boldness, but his company did possess a more solid and extensive network of dealers than its competitors. It also supplied a broad range of products—passenger cars, commercial vehicles, tractors, aircraft engines, railcars, and tanks—which allowed a wide spread of risks and higher profit margins. Peugeot followed a policy similar to Renault's, though in the early 1920s it operated from a smaller base.

Beyond the Americanization of their methods of production and marketing, the three large French companies used several other growth strategies. To assure their supplies and guarantee markets, they all substantially increased their vertical integration.[55] None went so far as Louis Renault, however, whose systematic efforts in this line resemble, but hardly equal, those of Ford. To finance their investments, the automakers turned more to banks and the financial markets, for their augmented need associated with mass production paralleled a shrinking of profit margins. To expand sales, they all recruited more dealers and established more sales branches at home, in the colonies, and abroad. They set up assembly plants outside France, a practice already begun before the war. Peugeot led off at Milan in 1925 and then at Mannheim in 1927. Citroën moved more boldly and raced ahead of his competitors, spending more money in the process. After considering a factory in the United States in 1923,[56] he established one in Britain in 1926, then others in Italy, Germany, and Belgium. Renault set one up in Belgium in 1926 and in England in 1927.

The small firms retained two characteristics of the earlier period: a lively capacity for innovation, as evidenced for example by a Louis Delage and a Gabriel Voisin in France; and a fervent interest in racing, everywhere in Europe. French exports, nevertheless, began to slide downward from 1926, tilted by American and to a lesser degree Italian competition, and the profits earned from auto manufacturing declined. Among the "big three," Renault experienced this the earliest; in 1928 he suffered sales losses for the first time. The first to react, he did not stop with appeals for more tariff protection as did his colleagues. In the summer of 1928, he decided to build an entirely new factory on Seguin Island, in the Seine at Billancourt.

The second-ranking European producer in this period, Great Britain, owed its position in part to foreign capital, unlike France. English Ford continued as the country's leading producer until 1924. Thereafter, it lost this position because of Henry Ford's obstinacy in continuing production of the Ford T, a car that had aged and become too expensive after the tariff duties imposed in 1915 and then the motor car tax of 1920. Other American auto companies nevertheless decided to follow Ford's example. GM opened an assembly plant in London in 1924. In contrast to Ford, it understood the necessity to adapt to the European market, and so it tried to buy the second largest British firm, Austin. Failing in this, it settled on a small company, Vauxhall, whose dealer network it expanded, but GM hesitated as to the product policy it should follow. Chrysler, too, maintained assembly operations, for it had inherited Maxwell's factory for cars and in 1928 that of Dodge for trucks. The real problem for Ford and then for GM and Chrysler came with the conversion of the leading

British companies to the fundamentals of mass production for their light and low-powered cars. The new tax, which hit the powerful American cars hard, worked to their advantage by strengthening the British trend toward small-engined vehicles.

William Morris pointed the way. He successfully revived his twelve-horsepower Cowley model of 1915, and, as production mounted, he cut his prices. In 1924, making 32,918 cars, he passed Ford and in 1929 he reached 63,000, an output in the same range as Citroën and Renault. He established a subsidiary to extend installment credit in 1925, and arranged with America's Budd Company to introduce the all-steel body. His major error occurred after he bought the Bollée auto works in Le Mans. He tried to compete with the large French firms by making the Bollée models rather than introducing his own twelve-horsepower type.

At first, Sir Herbert Austin did not have such a magic touch. In 1918 he concentrated his efforts on a twenty-horsepower model in the middle of the price range. Then the recession of 1920–21 shifted demand to the lower end of the scale. Austin barely escaped failure. He recovered only by turning in the opposite direction. In 1922 he introduced his famous and indestructible Seven, resembling a soapbox on wheels, and he managed to slash this "Baby" Austin's price almost 50 percent in seven years. Morris and Austin made more powerful cars, but the key to their growth lay in the longevity of their basic models, the Morris Cowley and the Austin Seven. Austin was a technician; Morris a salesman. Austin used an integrated production system. Morris always preferred to obtain as many parts as possible from outside suppliers.

Other motor car firms of lesser size also offered small cars: Singer, Clyno, and Standard. In 1924 Austin, who had failed in a 1920 bid to sell out to the Americans, proposed a merger with Morris and Wolseley. Morris, who would have become head of the new group, turned him down; he valued his freedom of action too much. In 1927 Morris decided to buy Wolseley nevertheless, but he paid a higher price than Austin had offered.

In Britain, as elsewhere, the industry took giant steps toward concentration. By 1929 Morris, Austin, and Singer controlled 75 percent of production, while Ford's share had shrunk to 5.7 percent. Morris and Ford dominated the commercial-vehicle market. Because mass-production methods made the competition too unequal between the large and small firms, the number of manufacturers dropped sharply from 1925. On the other hand, the motor car equipment industry grew stronger during these years, when the Joseph Lucas company was especially impressive as a supplier of electrical parts.

The British industry by 1929 suffered some handicaps in comparison with the French: a less dynamic domestic market; a wider diversity of models, which hindered it from profiting fully from economies of scale; and a less thoroughgoing adoption of American mass-production methods. But the British automakers cannot be charged with backwardness. The same William Morris who did not add a moving conveyor to his assembly line (unlike Austin) introduced the first transfer machine designed in Europe in 1923–24. This venture failed because the machines were not yet perfected. The English also divided jobs more and more narrowly so that the share of semiskilled labor expanded from 30 percent in 1921 to 57 percent in 1933. Production rose from 60,000 in 1920 to 239,000 vehicles in 1929, pressing the French. The same was true in exports, 42,000 to 49,000, which went primarily to the empire and Scandinavia.

Much less progressive was the course of the German automobile industry during this decade.[57] GM experts reported in 1929 that the German market at that point had reached "about the same state of development as the United States in 1911."[58] Only one automaker, Opel of Rüsselsheim, managed to introduce assembly-line methods, beginning the process in 1924. In four years, it succeeded in replacing 70 percent of its machine tools, making it the most up-to-date factory in Germany. It also enjoyed the best sales network in the country, consisting of 736 dealers. Even so, Opel had not yet established the interchangeable parts system. Although it turned out 44 percent of German cars in 1926, it garnered only 26 percent of the nation's auto sales. Its best selling model, introduced in 1924, copied the five-horsepower Citroën of 1922.

The slow growth of the industry can be explained first of all by insufficient demand. The middle classes saw their savings melt away during the war and in the subsequent galloping inflation, so they could not buy so many cars as their counterparts in France or England. Throughout the 1920s, German farmers were in a touch-and-go economic situation, and motorization spread very slowly in the countryside. The government also held the industry back. It retained the high prewar taxes levied on cars as luxury goods, and made little effort to improve one of the worst highway systems in Europe. Most seriously, it reopened the frontiers to imports, keeping tariffs at a rather low level. Consequently, foreign cars sold at lower prices, including tariff duties, than their German competitors. In 1928 some 40 percent of new automobile sales in Germany were imports. Even an American car cost 10 percent less than its German rivals. This explains why Ford, General Motors, and Chrysler each built truck and car assembly plants at Berlin in 1926. But, as was also the case in

Britain and France, they did not win one of the top three places on the market.

Regardless of that, the German parliament reacted to this invasion. Late in 1927 it raised the tariff, blowing the whistle on the American assembly plants. GM faced up to this first when, on Sloan's initiative, it bought 80 percent of Opel's capital in 1929. GM decided that Opel should produce an average-sized car suitable for the European market. Many of the small firms that had proliferated in the early 1920s collapsed under pressure from imports and from Opel's growth. Some older ones adapted by merging, such as Daimler and Benz in 1926. As head of engineering from 1923 to 1929, Daimler employed the talented designer Ferdinand Porsche. Benz innovated by producing diesel engines with precombustion chambers, first for tractors in 1922 and then for trucks in 1924. These ultimately led to the modern Mercedes-Benz diesel automobiles.

The German motor industry ended the 1920s more concentrated, more Americanized, and better equipped than it had entered them, turning out 140,000 vehicles in 1929 compared with 40,000 in 1923. In the years 1923–24 and again in 1926–28, Germany even showed the world's fastest rate of growth in the industry. Nevertheless, the number of registered vehicles was relatively small, and the most widely used means of individual motor transport in 1929 was not the motor car but the motorcycle. Production of these was 196,000, or 15 percent more than passenger cars. In 1928 two motorcycle companies entered the auto business. BMW, at Eisenach, acquired a license to make Austin Sevens from the Dixi company, and in Berlin DKW adopted in its cars the principle of the two-cycle engine, which it used in its motorcycles.

The fourth major European producer, Italy, was penetrated the least by the American motor firms, but not for want of trying. The Italian companies won government protection on nationalist grounds. This reaction led the French, and especially the Americans, to maintain their markets by establishing assembly units there. In 1928 Ford planned to build one at Livorno and a second in association with Isotta Fraschini, at Milan. But in October 1929 Mussolini shut down Ford's plant in Trieste, and denied it authorization to build at Livorno. He also cooled off similar plans by GM. Then, in September 1930, he quashed the Ford-Isotta agreement. So once again the Italian producers received the protection they wanted.

Behind this wall, however, the Italian market could absorb only a small number of cars. Accordingly, the manufacturers exported from two-fifths to three-fourths of their output, no longer to America—Fiat sold its factory in Poughkeepsie—but to France, Britain, Spain, and Central and Eastern Europe. Fiat also set up assembly plants in Spain (1919), Austria (1921), and Britain (1927). At home, it strengthened its dominance. Its share in new car sales rose from 60.2 percent in 1922 to 73 percent in 1928. In the latter year, its production of 47,000 cars amounted to 80 percent of national output, way ahead of Lancia at 3,000 and Italian Citroën at 2,000.

Giovanni Agnelli successfully surmounted labor troubles, financial maneuvering by his enemies, and political perturbations. He brought young people into his management, where next to the engineer Guido Fornaca an economist, Vittorio Valletta, took his seat. Continuing the momentum of his wartime expansion, Agnelli followed a strategy of industrial integration and product diversification. The parallel between Fiat and Renault, already apparent during the war, continued apace. Agnelli organized a steel consortium, a company to make auto glass, a financial holding company (IFI), and extended the range of his products to include gasoline railway engines, airliners, and diesel engines for ships. He even bought control of a major newspaper, *La Stampa* of Milan.

But his adoption of American methods came later than his French competitors. He took up assembly lines only after Citroën; he introduced a mass-market car, the 509, only in October 1925 after six years of preparation, though the three large French companies had been delivering their five- and six-horsepower models since 1922. He waited until 1926 to establish an automobile credit company, four years after Citroën. This slower movement indicates problems of adaptation in the Italian labor, auto, and financial markets. It also shows the relative fragility of Fiat's supremacy. That company's exports varied widely from one year to the next. It needed external financial support, and in 1926 Agnelli was forced to negotiate a $10 million loan from the American Morgan bank. Despite its recent construction—it was finished in 1921—the model factory at Lingotto soon reached the limits of its possibilities. To produce more in better working conditions, Agnelli decided in 1928 to erect a completely new factory where he could install the latest improvements in American methods. Italy produced 54,000 vehicles in 1929 against 37,000 in 1924.

Beside these four traditionally large producing countries in Europe, in the postwar era a new nation entered the market: Czechoslovakia.[59] The auto industry there first encountered serious difficulties. Despite strong tariff protection, from 1920 to 1925 high luxury taxes penalized automobiles. Laurin and Klement, the leading firm, decided not to market a cheap car analogous to the Ford T that it had readied. It finally sold its factory to Skoda in 1925. This iron and steel concern, majority owned by French capital, constructed a new factory from 1925 to 1930. Equipped on American lines for mass production, it even bore the name "America." The Tatra Company offered a low-priced car in 1923. Designed by its technical director Hans Ledwinka, it had only two cylinders but was unusually rugged, a necessity on the poorly maintained Czech roads. That same year, the company also introduced a broad range of commercial vehicles. The most notable of the other, less important, Czech firms, Praga, made cars, trucks, and airplane engines. In 1928 the country produced a total of 13,150 vehicles.

Czechoslovakia's vigor contrasts with the sharp decline of automobile making in other small European states, where it had begun earlier. A rather similar picture emerged everywhere. Local manufacturers ran into serious difficulties in both their domestic and foreign markets because of American competition especially, but also that of the major European producers. Ford usually set up an assembly operation, followed by GM a little later, and sometimes by the larger European firms. Many local producers just could not survive this competition, and closed their doors.

In Denmark and the Netherlands, all the indigenous firms disappeared. In Sweden, only one company, Volvo, begun in 1927, remained by 1929. In Spain, the fourteen local concerns could not buck the invasion by Ford and Fiat, and left the scene in the 1920s. In Switzerland, the healthiest of the survivors, Martini, saw its share of Swiss-made cars rise from 38 to 60 percent over the period 1922 to 1931, but its proportion of total new car sales fell from 5.5 to 1 percent. In 1927, to hang on, it had to begin making a German car, the Wanderer, on license. Belgium, which had already endured the German occupation, became a favorite target of the mass producers. Ford, GM, Citroën, and Renault all began assembly there. By 1929 only five local firms of the earlier fifteen remained in business. Austria, turning out 9,160 vehicles in 1928 while the domestic producers in Belgium made 7,000, was hardly in a more comfortable position. A few small concerns limped along for a while in Norway, Poland, and Hungary.

In short, the smaller European countries one by one surrendered to foreign domination, especially to the Americans. This held true even for the Soviet Union. In the first year for which statistics are available, 1924, a mere ten vehicles were produced, a figure that rose to 1,700 in 1929. The Soviets did not keep in operation the well-equipped factories that had survived the revolution. So they looked abroad, importing trucks, tractors, chassis, and parts, supplied in large part (47.7 percent) by the Americans, and by Fiat (19.1

percent). Taking another step in 1928, they began negotiations with four American automakers to build an up-to-date factory capable of producing 100,000 cars per year. They finally chose Ford. The May 1929 agreement provided that it would extend technical assistance in the construction of a factory at Nizhni Novgorod (later renamed Gorki), which would make Ford trucks and Model A cars. The Soviets agreed to buy $30 million in Ford cars and parts up to 1933. Even here, American technology conquered.

Elsewhere in the world, except for the French and Italian colonies, the Americans systematically won markets. China was the only one left untouched. Sun Yat-sen's appeal to Ford in 1924 to set up a factory there received no response. Just about everywhere else, Ford opened the way, first installing an import agency or rehabilitating an old one. Then, when motorization began to thrive, it established an assembly plant. Shortly afterward, GM would also begin an import company and less frequently, assembly operations. Until 1927 Ford clearly led GM outside the United States. In Latin America and the Far East, it still maintained this leadership in 1929. The extent of these overseas sales should not be minimized. In 1926 Ford marketed more cars in Latin America and the Far East than in Europe. Sales revenue for Europe was greater, however, because many more trucks were purchased. Ford now was operating on six continents, rather than the two of prewar days.

Latin America emerged as the biggest success of Ford's world policy. The largest markets were Argentina and Brazil. In the other countries, average incomes were too low and road networks too poor to expect rapid motorization. The original base of Ford's empire in Latin America was Argentina. The first assembly works on the continent were installed in a former cigarette factory in Buenos Aires in 1916.

Full-scale auto manufacturing in this city dates from 1920, when Ford built a large and entirely new plant. Three and then four stories high, it was a scaled-down version of the mother factory in Highland Park, Detroit, as was its sister auto works in Sao Paulo, Brazil, put into operation that same year. The creator of both was Ellis Hampton, a bold manager assigned by Ford to direct Latin America operations from Buenos Aires. He detected the future demand for cars on this continent, and succeeded in convincing the home office in Detroit of it. By 1927 Ford had eleven subsidiaries in Latin America and a network of 1,172 dealers. It operated additional assembly plants in Chile, Mexico, and Uruguay. Named by Ford headquarters, Americans managed these concerns, and paid their workers wages higher than local norms. At the same time, GM maintained assembly operations in Argentina, Brazil (where it had one plant to Ford's four in 1927), and Uruguay.

Many of the local dealers were located in rural areas and were illiterate. But they quickly learned to sell to clients eager for automobiles—the symbol of progress—and especially to provide the all-important service after the sale. This commercial penetration by the automobile companies fits into a larger process, the seizure of control of the Latin American economies by large multinational companies based in the United States. This phenomenon grew so quickly that from 1925 to 1929 Argentina was the next largest foreign market for Ford after Canada. Ford sold more cars and trucks there than in old England.

The second blossom on the American growth was Australia. The vast distances to cover on that continent stimulated the demand for motor cars. Behind a protective tariff, a body-making industry was founded to finish off imported chassis. Ford of Canada did not wait long, and established a body works and five assembly plants in 1925. GM followed a different tactic. In 1923 it made an arrangement with the Holden Company of Adelaide, a leather firm that had converted to auto-body making during the war. Holden's production costs were lower than Ford, so the latter gave ground both in its share of the market and in absolute sales revenue. From 30 percent of the market that Ford held in 1922, it fell off to 14.7 percent in 1925 against 16.9 percent for GM. When, in 1926, GM began its own assembly operations in cooperation with Holden and strengthened its sales network, its share climbed to 35.1 percent in 1927 to Ford's 9.6 percent of a total yearly sales of some 130,000 cars. Whereas in the Latin American market European automakers made only a nominal showing, in Australia the outmanned English fought doggedly against the Americans, for the primary benefit of the dealers, who received substantial concessions.

A third major geographic area, the Far East, bought an increasing number of cars. Ford of Canada in 1926 created four assembly works in India and Ceylon (Bombay, Calcutta, Madras, and Colombo) and one at Singapore. The parent in Detroit took the lead in Japan. There, the motor car met some serious problems: an unsuitable road system and the priority given to railways. The earthquake of 1923 was a turning point, for it put the train- and street-car tracks out of service in Tokyo and Yokohama. The Tokyo city fathers bought 1,000 Model T Ford chassis and organized a bus service.

These machines familiarized the Japanese with automobiles, and a boom followed. Ford benefited the most, and in its Yokohama assembly plant, built in 1925, it installed an assembly line. Soon recog-

Table 6-1.
*Number of Inhabitants per Car,
Selected Countries, 1927*

United States	5.3
New Zealand	10.5
Canada	10.7
Australia	16
Argentina	43
France and Britain	44
Germany	196
Soviet Union	701

Source: National Automobile Chamber of Commerce, *Facts and Figures of the Automobile Industry* (New York, 1927), p. 44.

nizing that this was too small, Ford opened another factory with a capacity of 35,000 cars per year instead of the 16,000 of its predecessor. Meanwhile, GM had chosen Osaka for its large assembly works, inaugurated in 1927. In this way, the two giant American producers forced the European firms out of the Japanese market. Because of the low Japanese living standards, the Americans supplied mainly trucks, buses, and taxis. A few Japanese firms tried to establish a local automobile industry but made little progress for want of an extensive enough network of metal fabricating shops to supply parts.[60]

By the end of the 1920s, the motorization of the world had entered a new phase. The United States owned 80 percent of the world's automobiles, and 55 percent of American families owned a car. Ranking behind it among the most motorized nations were other rapidly developing countries that had a low density of population, countries built by European immigrants who had come to conquer gradually thinly populated territory (see table 6–1). The motor car was now beginning to shape human culture, but unequally according to country and social class.

Automobiles and Social Change

The enormous economic, social, and cultural impact of the spread of automobiles appears to have provided greater benefits to the private interests of individuals and business firms than to their collective interests. The automobile's economic effect demonstrates this clearly. It worked to the benefit of the large firms. In the United States, automobiles had become the largest industry by 1925, absorbing 80 percent of the rubber industry's production, 75 percent of glass, 25 percent of machine tools, and 20 percent of steel. Cars consumed 90 percent of the gasoline refined. They fed the prosperity of the construction industry and of real estate agents, for street and highway building was the second largest expenditure of state and local governments. Automobiles encouraged a boom in housing in suburban areas and another for small businesses operating service stations and what were then called "tourist courts." The industry also often generated revolutionary changes in processes used in other industries. These included the inauguration in the 1920s of continuous strip steel rolling mills and continuous cast window glass.

On the other side of the coin, the automobile caused considerable harm to the railways. In the United States, railway passenger traffic dropped regularly from 1921 on. Private motor cars carry the major blame for this because travel in them was more convenient, cheaper, and readily available. Although buses increased in number and comfort, their competition had less to do with the railway traffic decline, for they competed only over shorter distances. Railway freight traffic in America also fell off, especially in short hauls and for high-value goods that trucks could move in a more flexible, often more rapid fashion, and frequently at lower cost. Along with waterways, railroads remained masters of long-distance freight traffic, where trucks rarely were employed before 1939, and of course for movement of heavy goods. In most cities, automobiles also struck a heavy blow against public transit by street car and trolleybus. The few survivors balanced their deficits only with public subsidies.

In Europe, similar patterns occurred: various industries were affected by the enthusiasm for automobiles, and the railways experienced difficulties. But they came later, with less force, and with two significant differences. Railway traffic did not decline in the 1920s, though its growth slowed down. The toughest competition the railways had to face did not come from individual passenger cars, still not numerous enough, but from buses. These took the fight to the railroads, especially to the single-track lines, where traffic was light.

Another common feature everywhere was highway building, though at different intensities. Automobile clubs and the car manufacturers were the most energetic promoters. Far behind other countries at the beginning of the automobile age, the United States now made the most vigorous efforts at road building. Paved roads doubled between 1921 and 1930, a national system of highways was built with financial aid from Washington, and four-lane parkways allowing easier movement in and out of large cities appeared. In this happy country, drivers accepted without much complaint state taxes on gasoline to pay for highway improvements. These levies paid for about 60 percent of such construction. In Britain, on the contrary, strong opposition arose when the Chancellor of the Exchequer diverted into the general funds some of the gasoline taxes earmarked since 1905 for roads. All over Europe, highways were improved. The most novel initiative came from Italy, which in 1924 opened the first limited access expressway, a road restricted to passenger cars traveling at high speed.

The economic influence of motorization extended beyond these measurable effects. The results were also qualitative. Considering only the central fact of increasing individual mobility, motorization allowed business firms to extend the area of recruitment of their labor force, strengthened the hold of large cities over their hinterland, and raised the value of land located near good highways.

In this period, the public became even more aware of the social impact of automobiles. They multiplied to the point that in the major countries they profoundly changed living styles. In the United States, where the automobile reached its acme, this grew to the dimensions of a revolution in daily life. The public noted especially the advantages gained by individuals; it paid much less heed to the social costs attendant to operating all these cars.

Nowhere were the changes more positive than in the rural areas of the United States. Farmers could now expect the same quality of services as city folk. Physicians owning cars made calls more quickly and visited more patients, and it became much easier to move the ill to better places of treatment. Automobiles allowed the replacement of the one-room schoolhouse by the large diversified school located at a greater distance but accessible by car or school bus. City high schools were opened to rural students. The post office department could offer rural free delivery, allowing farmers to receive mail every day and encouraging, for example, a rapid expansion of mail-order merchandising.

Rural isolation ended, for easy travel now became available to those of all incomes, reducing the monotony, loneliness, and even boredom of farm work. Vividly recalling this period, an Ohio farmer wrote Edsel Ford in 1938: "Until your father provided low cost transportation, the vast majority of these families had scarcely been five miles from home. Every time such a family group met my eyes, I would reverently say, 'God bless Henry Ford.'"[61] Farmers not only used cars in many ways around the farm and went to the nearest town for business or pleasure, but joining the rest of the populace, they discovered the joy of touring America. Anxious to enjoy nature without spending too much money, many people took up family camping.

During the 1920s, American farmers flocked to buy trucks. Henceforth, all those near a good highway were better integrated into the overall economy. By 1930 farmers owned 900,000 trucks, or one per five cars or per thirty farmers. Finally, land prices rose sharply. The magnitude of all these constructive upheavals explains why Henry Ford became the hero of many American farmers and why he received tens of thousands of letters from them on every subject under the sun. Still, the coming of the motor car and then the truck and tractor did not end either the movement of rural people to the cities or the decline of the family farm. Outside of North America, in countries where distances were shorter and motorization less intense, the life of farmers changed much less.

In U.S. cities, the multitude of cars also revolutionized the way of life. During the week, the motor car, formerly a luxury but now easily available because of its low price and modest operating expense, became a family necessity. Basically, it allowed one to escape from the crowded public-transit vehicles.[62] It found a variety of uses: more and more often as transportation to the job, but also to run errands, visit friends, and take advantage of such city services as schools, hospitals, and churches. Women began to drive more and more, and the car became an aspect of their growing autonomy. Business began to adapt to the new means of transportation. The first drive-in restaurants appeared, beginning a long line of establishments to which the customer enjoys access without leaving his machine. On Sundays, owners took their cars to escape the cities or simply for pleasure drives.

Gradually the weekend emerged as an institution, including plodding Sunday drivers. When they began to receive vacations, city dwellers, as well as their rural cousins, traveled in their cars. Tourism, especially for short periods, enjoyed an unprecedented popularity. Visitors to the national parks sextupled over the decade. Service stations, garages, restaurants, and hotels sprang up along the major routes. In addition to travel, cars encouraged the development of new residential suburbs, poorly served by public transit because routes there were unprofitable and these areas were occupied exclusively by the well-to-do. People gave up apartment-house living for private dwellings, and before long would obtain household supplies from new locations where several retail businesses were grouped: the shopping centers, situated away from the central business districts. Three of these existed in the United States in 1929.

Both in Europe and America, the ubiquity of automobiles aroused problems that only a few people recognized. The cities experienced difficulty handling the flood of cars. Automobiles amplified the usual nuisances of big-city living. They increased noise, air pollution, and traffic congestion, especially at rush hours. They often weakened public-transit systems, including those using buses. They encouraged a decline in the central parts of cities, which exchanged a good share of their shops and homes for office buildings and slums. In the United States, the reaction of the municipal governments was often to establish city planning departments and through them adapt the city to the motor car. Bureaucrats were convinced that better highways and streets benefited the entire population. But hardly had an urban street system been improved than the increase in traffic brought congestion back again. Subsidies paid to public-transit systems rarely were enough to maintain the quality of their service.

Certain negative features of the automobile affected both cities and rural areas. Most obvious were the accidents, which were accompanied by damage, injuries, and deaths. As cars increased in numbers and speed, accidents multiplied. Highway accident fatalities rose in the United States from 15,000 in 1922 to 32,000 in 1930, and in Great Britain from 4,886 in 1926 to 7,300 in 1934. Population experts stated that highway driving had become the principal cause of the currently rising rate of violent deaths. Most responsibility for accidents fell on driver errors and poor highways.

Public authorities reacted by improving the roads and instituting better regulation of traffic, not without some success. The number of deaths per million miles driven by cars declined during the 1920s in both Europe and the United States. In Europe, traffic laws were revised; for example, the French highway driving code was issued in 1921–22.[63] Just about everywhere, police forces were strengthened. Many drivers arranged for insurance coverage, but nowhere did campaigns to make it compulsory succeed. Highway accidents were a clear social cost linked to automobile usage.

Contemporaries also imputed to the motor car part of the responsibility for the loosening of social ties. The car and the greater distances between home and work made encounters between neighbors less frequent and less close. The car weakened parental authority over children. Young drivers became much more mobile and found it easier to escape family control. Cars also reduced the supervision of the relations between the sexes; cars became a place for courtship and even love. Despite all this, the automobile was far from the only reason for changing social norms during the "roaring twenties." And opinions are divided on whether the diminution of family controls was all bad. In any event, by 1929 outside the United States the trends just mentioned appeared only as slight tendencies.

When contemporaries calculated the automobile's costs and benefits, they deemed the result to be favorable. Middle-class families, and in the United States those of the working class, strained their resources to buy a car. For it indicated they had "made it," that they owned something that formerly was identified only with the rich. A family's expenses to maintain the car became a budgetary necessity that could not be cut. A rather simple hierarchy developed between those with low incomes who obtained their cars through the used-car market and those receiving medium or higher incomes who wanted new cars to keep up with technical progress and fashion and who were helped by consumer credit arrangements. Two- and even three-car families began to appear. In 1929 some 10 percent of American families owning cars had two or more of them.

In the long run, the cultural impact of the automobile was probably the most significant. It did much to accustom people to technical progress, innovation, and modernization. The unusual mobility that it brought, its amazing accomplishments, and its regular improvement gave daily evidence that technology was preparing a new era of prosperity and that the spread of durable consumer goods required the adoption of mass-production techniques. Then came Henry Ford's best-selling book, *My Life and My Work*, written in 1922 and translated into many languages. One surprising result was that Ford, the capitalist multimillionaire, gained immense prestige in the Soviet Union, almost equaling that of Lenin or Stalin. Towns and children received the name "Fordson" after Ford's tractor. "Fordizatsia" became a term for economic modernization. Even in distant Asian and Latin American villages, Ford's name was not unknown.

While the automobile helped spread the ideology of economic growth through intensive work, it fostered the cause of productivity. Even more easily, it directed desires and energies toward consumption. "To live is to consume," declared automaker Louis Renault.[64] To push the obsession with consumption into becoming a dominant value of society, manufacturers supported the massive growth of advertising. The advertising budget of American automakers alone tripled between 1920 and 1927, attaining 1 1/2 percent of their sales revenue. In France, it reached 2 percent.

The tone of advertising changed also. Instead of the former emphasis on the reliability and performance of the car's mechanical elements, now it highlighted the pleasure and psychological benefits of driving it. A small American producer, Edward Jordan, introduced this new theme in 1923 to promote his Playboy model. "Step into the Playboy when the hour grows dull with things gone dead and stale," read one of his ads, "and start for the land of real living."[65] The automobile was presented as more than simply a useful machine; it was a way of escape and an essential factor of status. Orienting his advertising on the romantic aspects of a car, which takes one to distant horizons "somewhere west of Laramie,"[66] Jordan raised his sales 61 percent.

The rest of the auto companies picked up this theme, and the industry became the largest advertiser in the United States. The manufacturers no longer emphasized the real qualities of their products, but how motor cars brought together the advantages of city and country living and how they reinforced the family unit. At the same time, the auto companies, recognizing that often the wife chose the model to buy while the husband paid, emphasized style and color in the annual model change, making these the difference between models that mechanically were the same. The Auburn Company offers the most striking example of this. In trouble in 1923, its bankers entrusted the management to a Chicago salesman named E. L. Cord. Inheriting a stock of 700 unsold cars, he retouched the body style lightly and painted them in bold colors. They sold like hotcakes.

The final encouragement to consumers was installment credit, much more common in the United States than Europe (it was used in only 14 percent of French auto sales in 1929). In the United States, installment sales of cars led to the extensive growth of consumer credit. Finance companies tried to diversify their risks and urged the use of time-payment plans for other kinds of products that a decade earlier had been considered luxuries but were now part of the average American's life-style. Consequently, the character of family budgets and saving habits changed considerably. In 1926 California buyers of cars on credit devoted 18 percent of their monthly income to their car payments.

The priority given to consumption rested on the glorification of the individual. Motor cars gave to their owners total freedom of movement. They offered privacy. Everyone was expected to select a model that gratified his, and only his, tastes. On the highway, differences of class or race disappeared; only personal driving ability counted. Roads became a field for individual competition; the winners were those who achieved the highest average speed, selected the best route, or mounted the most spectacular accessories. Owners of sumptuous cars entered them in weekend competitions that rewarded the most elegant.

Yet the automobile is a complex cultural artifact. For each of the values it carries with it, it also spreads the opposite value. While fostering individualism, it gives rise to anonymity. There is the anonymity of working on the assembly line that produces it. The assembler is as interchangeable as the parts that he uses. The qualities expected of him are dexterity, diligence, regularity, quick reactions, and nervous endurance to carry out his rhythmic, monotonous, and fatiguing tasks. He has very little hope of promotion; mobility is forbidden to the auto worker but reserved for the client. To compensate for all this, the pay is good and the workday shorter.

In 1926 Ford even introduced the forty-hour week. This satisfied the labor unions, won over to the ideal of productivity, but workers tended to lose initiative. Despite the spread of mechanization, they continued to quit their jobs, to restrict output, to slow down, in Europe as well as the United States. Occasionally, in Europe, wildcat strikes protested the faster production schedules brought by time study and assembly lines.[67] The result was the moral devaluation of labor. Less and less did it serve as a form of personal fulfillment; more and more it became simply a source of income.

Leisure, the periods when individuals exercise the freedom to consume, gained a new importance for those who worked in large-scale industry. Anonymity also began to characterize consumption, for the concentration of manufacturing into just a few firms reduced buyers' choices. Differences among models diminished; in each price range, cars resembled each other more closely. A French automobile worker who also worked for Ford in the United States, Hyacinthe Dubreuil, brought into common use a key word of the period: "standards."[68]

The apotheosis of individual freedom, the motor car still needed to call for help from a force in apparent contradiction to this freedom: the state. Cars are only one of the thousand and one causes for its growing power, but not the least of them. Increasing traffic brought higher taxes to pay for more highways and more police. It also entangled motorists in a more and more complex network of rules on driving, on parking, and on the size and design of vehicles. It led city governments—in the United States, at least—to plan city growth. It encouraged automakers to ask their governments for higher tariffs, restrictions on foreign-owned assembly plants, and support of exports or of measures to ensure supplies of raw materials.

Because the success of the automobile promised a future of abundance, it became an effective propaganda tool for capitalist business. This was the meaning of the wave of Fordism during the 1920s. In the same way that its predecessor, Taylorism, had focused on the engineer, vaunting the rather utopian merits of science applied to the modern world, so the new Ford mystique stressed industrial efficiency in preaching the much more conservative cult of the head of the firm. It included in the same favorable aura another agent of efficiency, the technocrat.

Conclusion

By 1929 the automobile had conquered the world, and American manufacturers dominated this new empire. They turned out 85 percent of the world's production. In the United States, the automobile had carried out its revolution. It merged mass production, individual transportation, and the orientation of society toward consumption. The automobile enjoyed such a cultural hegemony in this country that the French writer Roland Barthes could declare in *Mythologies* that he saw in it the "rather close equivalent of the great Gothic cathedrals: that is, the supreme creation of an era, conceived with passion by unknown artists, consumed in image if not in usage by a whole people which almost absorbs it as a thoroughly magical object."[69]

Everywhere else, rosy prospects for expansion stretched out for the automobile, which often became the symbol of those who demanded the right to "happiness." Yet, in the other countries, American methods were never adopted without change; some delay always occurred as well as some adaptation to local conditions. This is the way of all innovations; when diffused beyond their place of origin, they experience inevitable changes. In this case, differences between American and European automobiles in the areas of size, weight, power, and use began to show up during the 1920s. Such differences did not cease to grow stronger until the 1960s. Their explanation rests in divergences of geography—distances, highway networks, character of city development—as well as income levels, tax policies, and industrial organization.

However, something was rotten in Denmark. The beginning of the longest economic depression in the twentieth century occurred in 1929. Did the automobile revolution contribute to its outbreak in the United States? Such is the provocative interpretation of American historian James J. Flink. He alleges that it created the most important of the necessary conditions out of which the Great Depression arose. The boom of the 1920s, he argues, was fueled especially by the huge capital expenditures required to adapt the economy and society to the multiplication of automobiles, a transformation largely completed by the end of the decade. These changes directed a majority of savings toward investment. Family incomes did not grow enough to absorb all the increased durable goods produced, and these could count only on a weak replacement demand. As a result, mass production methods, despite the prodigies of modern marketing, led to overproduction.

Two additional factors can be added to this interpretation. The growth of automobile exports managed to mask the effects of the stagnation of the domestic market and encouraged an expansion of productive capacity, though the resources devoted to this would have been better employed to improve the quality of the cars and the financial soundness of the dealers. Large profits led some manufacturers to divert a part of them to stock market speculation. This, in turn, brought more profits and pushed up the share prices of the auto companies without reference to actual production of goods.[70] However valid this interpretation of the depression may be, inasmuch as it does not rest on a thorough statistical analysis, it is not yet fully proved that the automobile played a crucial role in the origin of the world economic crisis. Historians will continue to debate the matter.

In the 1920s the United States held the center of the stage. There, a new strategy—Sloanism—was worked out to ensure the survival of the giant automobile companies. This system combined a new concept of management: replace the autocratic risktaking entrepreneur with the safety-first technician who could work well in a group; and a new encouragement to the market: the planned obsolescence of products. Europe did not have available such good recipes, but it would take the spotlight in the 1930s with the small car.

ΕΙΔΟΠΟΙΗΣΙΣ ΠΡΟΣ ΟΛΟΥΣ ΤΟΥΣ ΥΠΑΛΛΗΛΟΥΣ

"Οταν ἀλλάσσετε διεύθυνσιν, νὰ εἰδοποιῆτε ἀμέσως τὸν ὑπάλληλον εἰς τὸ Τμῆμα ὅπου ἐργάζεσθε ἢ νὰ τὸ ἀναφέρετε εἰς τὸ Γραφεῖον τοῦ Γουάτσμαν διὰ νὰ συμπληρώσῃ τὸ δελτίον ἀλλαγῆς διευθύνσεως. Παράλειψις τοῦ νὰ μᾶς εἰδοποιήσετε περὶ τῆς ἀλλαγῆς τῆς διευθύνσεως, εἰμπορεῖ νὰ συνεπιφέρῃ ἀπώλειαν τῆς θέσεώς σας.

ΜΑΘΕΤΕ ΝΑ ΔΙΑΒΑΖΕΤΕ ΚΑΙ ΝΑ ΓΡΑΦΕΤΕ ΑΓΓΛΙΚΑ
Ford Motor Company.

Объявленіе Для Всѣхъ Служащихъ

Въ случаѣ перемѣны вашего адреса, извѣстите конторщика того Цеха, въ которомъ вы работаете, или объявите въ контору сторожа и просите выполнить для васъ бланкъ для перемѣны адреса. Вамъ могутъ отказать отъ мѣста, если вы не извѣстите насъ о перемѣнѣ адреса.

Научитесь читать и писать по-англійски.

Ford Motor Company

ZAWIADOMIENIE
do wszystkich pracowników

Jeżeli zmienicie swój adres, zawiadomcie natychmiast pisarza w Departamencie, w którym pracujecie, albo donieście o tem do Biura Szwajcara i odnotujcie zmianę adresu na właściwym druku. Zaniedbanie zawiadomienia o zmianie adresu, może spowodować utratę posady.

Uczcie się czytać i pisać po angielsku.

Ford Motor Company

NOTICE TO ALL EMPLOYEES

If you change your address, immediately notify the Clerk in the Department you work or report to the Watchman's Office and have change of address blank made out. Failure to notify us of change of address may mean a loss of position.

LEARN TO READ AND WRITE ENGLISH

Ford Motor Company

اعلان لجميع العمال

فاذا غيرت عنوانك فالحال بلغ كاتب الادارة التي تشتغل بها أو صرح بذلك في مكتب الحارس وعنك بان تملأ ورقة تغيير العنوان بعنوانك الجديد. ان سهوك عن ابلاغنا بتغيير عنوانك ربما ادى الى خسارتك شغلك

علم ان تقرأ وتكتب الانكليزية

Ford Motor Company

AVVISO AGL'IMPIEGATI

Quando si cambia di casa bisogna avvisare immediatamente lo scrivano del Dipartimento in cui si lavora, o farne rapporto all 'Ufficio del Custode, e far riempire il modulo del cambio d'indirizzo. La mancanza di questa notificazione di cambiamento di domicilio può cagionare la perdita dell'impiego.

Imparatevi a leggere e scrivere Inglese

Ford Motor Company

AVIS PENTRU LUCRĂTORĬ

Dacă vĕ mutaţi şi vĕ schimbaţi adresa, ınştiinţaţi ındată biroul Secţieĭ în care lucraţĭ saŭ biroul păzitorului, dându-ĭ noua voastră adresă scrisă pe una din formularele din biroŭ pentru acest scop. Cine nu se va conforma acestuĭ avis póte să-şi pearză locul.

Invăţaţi să cetiţĭ şi sĕ scrieţĭ ın Englezeşte.

Ford Motor Company

ZUR BEACHTUNG
AN UNSERE SAMTLICHEN ANGESTELLTEN

Bei Wohnungsänderungen haben die betreffenden Angestellten unverzüglich dem Bureaubeamten der Abteilung, in der sie beschäftigt sind, Anzeige zu erstatten, oder sich im Bureau des Fabrikwachters (Watchman's Office) zu melden zwecks Ausfullung eines Wohnungswechsel-Formulars, widrigenfalls Entlassung aus ihrer Stellung erfolgen kann.

Lernet englisch lesen und schreiben

Ford Motor Company

1. *Company notice to Ford workers in eight languages, about 1914. (Editions Albin Michel)*

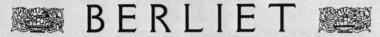

2. *Berliet truck advertisement claiming the truck will replace twelve horses, 1913. (Editions Albin Michel)*

3. *The first Renault taxi, 1905. The first major success with taxis and a key to Renault's early growth. (Editions Albin Michel)*

4. Ford, 1914, *two of the three final assembly lines. (Editions Albin Michel)*

5. Ford, 1914, the foundry. Casting in moving molds. (Editions Albin Michel)

6. Ford, 1914, *a semiautomatic machine that drilled forty-five holes at once in four sides of a cylinder block. (Editions Albin Michel)*

7. *Panhard et Levassor advertisement, 1922, weekend touring. (Editions Albin Michel)*

8. *Service station in Atlantic City, about 1920. (Motor Vehicle Manufacturers Association of the United States, Inc.)*

9. Renault: transmission assembly, 1938. (Renault)

10. Mercedes-Benz, 1930. Formal transportation for the well-to-do. (Mercedes-Benz of North America)

11. *Fiat Topolino ("Little Mouse"), 1936. Europe prepares to adopt the small car. (Fiat Motors of North America)*

12. VW "Beetle." The 1951 edition of the best-selling car of all time.
    (Volkswagen of America)

13. Volvo, 1974, cars assembled on individual carriers. (Volvo)

14. Volvo, 1974, car assembly accommodated to workers. (Volvo)

15. *General Motors Technical Center, Warren, Michigan, 1975. The largest automotive research laboratories in the world. (General Motors Corporation)*

16. *1980 Olds Cutlass and 1972 Olds Cutlass. American cars begin to shrink. The 1980 model, which is nine inches shorter and 140 pounds lighter, is also powered by a smaller engine. (L.J.A. Villalon)*

7.   Difficult Years

Prosperity, a French magazine devoted to automobiles that was published by the Michelin tire company, did not appear during the year 1930. This might symbolize a new era that the world economy and the automobile industry had entered. Difficult times, however, did not bring the same reactions throughout the world. America, fully convinced of the wisdom of its methods, girded itself and waited for better days. Its production stagnated. Europe and Japan, on the other hand, sought to adapt to their clientele's lower incomes by making innovations in cars, trucks, and highways. Everywhere, the state took advantage of the depression to increase its influence over the automobile, and in at least two major countries the depression and political changes allowed auto workers to engage in mass unionization.

The Effects of the Depression

The drop in production occurred unequally, and so did the revival. During both phases, developments in some countries moved contrary to the general trend, as chart 7–1 indicates. This chart should be completed by an interesting fact: in 1938, the last normal year before the Second World War, four countries still had not regained their 1929 levels of production. These were France, Italy, Canada, and, above all, the world's leading producer, the United States.

Chart 7-1.
The Automobile Industry in Depression and Recovery

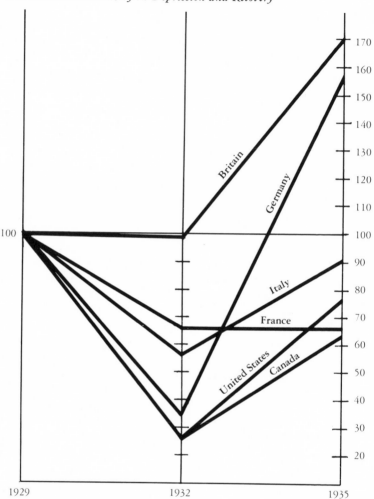

Curves indicate changes in vehicle production in 1932 and 1935 with index 100 in 1929.

The immediate effects of the depression were not surprising. Motorists kept their cars longer, and relied more on used cars. In the United States, this led to a 10-percent drop in the number of cars registered; elsewhere, to a slackening in the growth of registrations. Manufacturers cut prices. They also reduced wages, hours, labor skill requirements, and numbers of workers. Profits still declined in most

cases, and some firms disappeared. The number of automobile manufacturers in France fell from ninety to twenty, in Germany from
twenty-seven to seventeen, in Britain from one hundred to forty,
and in the United States from twenty-three to eleven. Some of the
smaller firms sought to survive by entering another industry. In this
way, the depression worked powerfully to strengthen the tendency
toward concentration already apparent in the 1920s because, except
in Britain, the largest firms held on more successfully and increased
the strength of their position.

Prospects for the industry were so gloomy that it begged for public
assistance. Everywhere, the state responded to these pleas by raising
tariffs, both for the countries themselves and for their colonies,
colonies that now received a growing share of exports. In addition,
governments made business difficult for foreign-owned assembly
plants, except in Switzerland. In Italy, they were proscribed. England, Germany, and France required them, with public approval, to
make a rising proportion of parts locally and to use more domestic
products and labor. In Japan a law of 1936 reserved auto manufacturing to domestic concerns. The government determined the number of cars to be assembled in Japan by the American companies, and
then progressively cut this total.

In Europe also, the state sought to encourage domestic producers.
In Italy, it reimbursed tariffs on raw materials and semifinished products that they imported; in France and Italy, it paid subsidies on
exports; and just about everywhere, it temporarily cut taxes on car
ownership and even on gasoline and worked as well to improve high-
ways. Governments placed military orders with automobile firms in
Germany, Italy, Japan, Czechoslovakia, Britain, and France. The state
tried to keep afloat those companies that drifted into difficulty. In
France, it vainly asked Renault to take over the faltering Citroën. In
Germany, it played a vital role in creating Volkswagen. Finally, in
Poland and the USSR, it even entered the business itself, and, in
Italy, it nationalized the struggling Alfa-Romeo.

The automakers did not approve all of the state's efforts. In the
United States, the government filed charges of antitrust violations so
as to allow dealers to choose their own spare-parts and credit companies. In the U.S., Germany, and France, it tried to begin regulation
of used-car sales, and succeeded in the first two countries. In the
U.S., France, and Italy, the state intervened in labor-management
relations. The American NIRA legislation of 1933 gave labor the
right to organize and bargain collectively with management. However, the importance of this law and its application to the auto industry was more apparent than real. In 1934 President Franklin D.

Roosevelt interpreted the law in a way favorable to management on an important issue of labor representation. In Italy, the state acted at the behest of the Fascist unions to curb the extension of the Bedaux system of payment by results. In France, during the unceasing labor-management conflicts from 1936 to 1938, the state tried to mediate before finally taking the side of management in November 1938. And, lastly, in some countries where the railways had been losing, the state tried to limit competition between railways and trucks. This involved schemes to coordinate transportation systems and so limit the activities of trucks.

Hence, the effect of the depression was to make the state a full partner of the automobile manufacturers, dealers, and workers. It also consecrated the affection of consumers for their automobiles, for most refused to dispose of them, despite difficult economic circumstances. It also happened that the most highly developed organizations, in this case those in the United States, which had reached the point of earning respectable profits, reacted with less flexibility and vigor than their rivals in other auto manufacturing countries where demand had not yet reached saturation.

Renovation in Europe and Japan

Europe was persuaded by the depression that it could no longer be satisfied, as in the twenties, to follow the paths traced by America. Two methods were discovered by which the auto industry might continue its strong rate of growth: mass-market cars (people's cars) and expressways. Different countries did not adopt these policies at the same time, which among other things explains how the British and German auto industries overtook the French. In many areas, nevertheless, automakers recognized that they had an original card to play. Among them, and this was new, the European branches of the American companies designed new models adapted to the local market and gained considerable success. The Europeans also played a third card, the diesel engine, to promote truck sales. Its high technical efficiency made more economical both long-distance trucking and bus service involving frequent stops.

Britain climbed to the rank of the second largest automobile producer in the world and first in Europe. This ascent came in two phases. During the depression, the British economy held up more firmly than the others, primarily because the drop of average real income was less pronounced there than in other industrial countries. Automakers also moved more quickly than those in other nations to adjust their output to the reduced means of their clientele. Preferring to see demand shift toward the bottom of the price scale rather than into used cars, and not wanting to leave the market entirely, they supplied a wide variety of low-priced cars. Morris was first with his Minor in 1929. Ford followed in 1932 by producing an eight (fiscal) horsepower model, its first designed expressly for the British market and made in the new Dagenham factory near London. The public responded enthusiastically. Small cars of eight horsepower or less increased from 16 percent of new-car sales in 1927 to 30 percent in 1938. From 1932 on, models of ten horsepower or less always totaled more than half of sales. General Motors (GM) annexed a large share of the next higher price range with its Vauxhall Cadet.

Automakers also used other tactics to keep their customers and win over a larger section of the middle classes. They introduced the annual model change, and competed vigorously over quality and over who supplied the best quality for price. In this regard, it appeared as if they had learned the lessons of the recent American experience. They added a particular feature: a large number of models. English automakers' conversion to the idea of the small and low-priced "people's car" also brought them favor in export markets. Sales abroad rose from 42,000 in 1929 to 59,000 in 1937, or 15 percent of national production. Three-quarters of these sales were made in countries where British vehicles received special tariff concessions: in the Commonwealth where Imperial Preference prevailed, as well as in Sweden and Denmark.

In the second phase, British producers tried to compress their production costs. Morris and then Ford gave up the annual model change. Bodies made of pressed steel became standard, and unitized construction of the entire car was more widely adopted. Morris reorganized his production methods from 1933 to 1935 and rebuilt the Cowley factory near Oxford, installing a moving assembly line in 1934. Austin and Morris brought new people into top management positions.

Total British production soared from 238,805 vehicles in 1929 to 507,000 in 1937. The principal beneficiaries of this remarkable expansion were the American subsidiaries, Vauxhall and especially Ford, which introduced models very modern in appearance and of high quality. Other firms that raised their share of the British market included two domestic ones, the Rootes group (including Hillman) and Standard. They avoided the strongest American competition by offering nine- to ten-horsepower cars. As the only large firms in this range until Ford introduced its ten horsepower in 1935, they had no trouble doubling their share of British production.

In 1929 two major British motor car companies dominated the market; by 1939 the number was six. Morris, followed by Austin, still led Ford, Standard, Rootes, and Vauxhall. But the two principal concerns had seen their share of total sales on the British market shrink by almost half compared to 1929. Together the six accounted for 90 percent of the total.

The commercial-vehicle business experienced fewer disturbances. Ford and Morris retained their supremacy in light trucks, but now were joined by Bedford, a GM subsidiary. Trucks carried larger and larger loads. Leyland led in the heavy truck division, followed by Albion, Guy, and AEC. This sector was revitalized by the introduction of the diesel engine for trucks in 1929 and for buses in 1931. Adopted by the four companies just mentioned and by two firms that had produced steam trucks (Atkinson and Foden), the diesel also permitted the rise of two new truck makers: ERF and especially Seddon. In 1939 the latter company built the first light diesel truck. Its Perkins engine would challenge the three large light truck makers that relied on gasoline engines.

Germany boosted itself to the position of third largest producer in the world, developing even more vigorously than Britain. Production of vehicles tripled from 1933 to 1938, cars increasing at the rate of 40 percent a year, trucks at 49 percent. By 1937 more than twice as many automobiles as motorcycles were registered, and the proportion of foreign cars had dropped to 9 percent. Exports increased also, and in 1936 Germany became the world's third largest automobile exporter.

What accounts for this revival of the German automobile industry? The severity of the depression turned out to be helpful. It speeded up industrial concentration, provoking the formation of Auto-Union in 1930, a merger of Horch, Audi, Wanderer, and DKW. The automakers, enjoying up-to-date equipment and large, recently built factories, found themselves in a good position to profit from an economic revival. This stemmed from several forces. The Nazi state played its part, as has been seen, but other factors were involved. Demand jumped upward, coming from big business, the public sector, professional men, and farmers. The revived prosperity stimulated this demand, of course, but another element was the need for a transportation system adequate for the rapidly growing economy.

Vehicles also changed. A German creation, the diesel engine was well suited for a country poor in petroleum resources. It was installed extensively in large trucks as the trucking industry grew rapidly, comprising 35,000 companies by 1937. Automakers continually improved their cars, using more special steels; quickly adopting aluminum, bakelite, and other plastic materials; and even developing front-wheel drive. In emulation of their British colleagues, some German firms, such as Auto-Union, began a policy of making "people's cars." Ford, utilizing a new factory built in 1931 at Cologne, did the same, first making the eight-horsepower English Ford type in 1933 and then producing its own design, the Eifel. Helped by the latter model, by a managerial reorganization carried out by officials from Detroit, and by a gradually increasing number of orders from the Nazi government, German Ford went through a startling revival. By 1938 it ranked fourth among passenger-car makers with 23,969, behind Opel (114,020), DKW (50,340), and Mercedes-Benz (25,330), but placing ahead of Adler. In trucks, Ford reached second place in 1936, behind Opel and ahead of Mercedes-Benz.

Hitler was not satisfied with the industry's accomplishments. From 1934 on, he urged the manufacture of a car for the masses, a "Volks Wagen." After the revolutionary design conceived by Ferdinand Porsche was adopted and capital accumulated by public subscription, factory construction began in 1938. The Volkswagen plant was supposed to commence operations in 1940 with an output of 150,000 cars and reach 1.5 million in 1942.[71]

Already, in 1933, Hitler had launched a major highway building program. This included renovation of existing roads and building expressways, the Autobahnen. By 1939 about 1,860 miles of the latter had been finished and 10,500 miles of other roads rebuilt. The objective of this policy was much more civil than military; it aimed to stimulate economic revival. By encouraging a strong demand for vehicles, it allowed producers to cut their prices and reinvest most of their profits.

The situation of the French industry was not so good as the British and German in the 1930s. Still, tendencies prevalent in the other major European states were apparent. The industry also moved into the production of diesel trucks when the Berliet Company began to specialize and use them as a basis for an unexpected revival. The major producer of commercial vehicles, Renault, did not disdain this new technology, and in 1938 even began to build a plant to assemble diesel trucks in China.[72] The idea of a network of expressways was broached by Louis Renault in 1932 and also by French highway engineers, but only a tiny stretch of the Western Expressway (from

Paris) was opened before the war. The plans of the engineers succumbed to the higher priorities given to military expenditures and to the good quality of the existing highways.

A "people's car" was a continued topic for discussion here also. It even appeared, for from 1930 to 1935 the fourth and fifth largest French producers, Mathis and Rosengart, made cars of this type. Rosengart's was an Austin Seven made on license. In 1936 Fiat's new French subsidiary introduced a twin sister of the Italian Topolino, the small Simca 5, priced at only 9,900 francs ($650), whereas the cheapest Renaults and Peugeots sold at 13,300 ($880). This car, helped by its younger sister, the Simca 8, boosted the company to fourth place among French automakers.

In 1936 the new president of Citroën, Pierre Boulanger, began preparations for an even more unusual model, the 2CV, and it was ready for the October 1939 auto show. Meanwhile, Matford, the reorganized Ford subsidiary in France, had been arranging to make a small car derived from a German Ford model. Moreover, the three large firms, Renault, Peugeot, and Citroën, had each prepared a prototype five-horsepower small car. They agreed not to market these models, however, because they feared that their dealers, many of whom were losing money, could not adequately promote them. Because none of the "big three" offered a "people's car," the French auto industry was hard hit by the financial difficulties of its rural and small-town customers, and this was the main cause for its problems.

Even so, many of the firms improved their facilities during the 1930s. Renault, Citroën, Peugeot, Matford, and Simca all built or renovated factories. They established modern research departments, the one at Renault headed by Jacques Pomey.[73] France also made the first mass-produced front-wheel drive car. This was a Citroën model, in production from 1934 to 1957. Exports revived toward the end of the thirties. Renault arranged for a Romanian company to produce its tractors and tanks; licensed production of its trucks in Poland and its cars in Japan; and undertook to build a truck factory in China.

The three largest firms strengthened their dominance to 73 percent of production. While Renault and Citroën battled for first place with varying success, Peugeot advanced regularly by applying caution, care, and capital investment. In 1938 it even moved up to second place in passenger car sales because of its model 202. A sign of the times was that the "big three" were followed by two subsidiaries of foreign producers, Simca and Matford.

The Italian industry at first experienced a sharp decline during the depression because the thinness of its home market left it in a weak position in the face of falling exports, but it recovered and gained new ground. In 1937 it produced 77,740 vehicles, 84 percent of them passenger cars. This represented a growth of 43.9 percent over 1929. Giovanni Agnelli, like Louis Renault, extended his industrial and financial empire beyond automobiles during these years, but moved more cautiously within the industry. At the end of the twenties, he had been interested in front-wheel drive but gave it up in the face of the financial and technical difficulties involved. In 1932 he introduced a small car, the Balilla (six fiscal horsepower, four seats, and two doors), with considerable success even though it was too expensive for most Italians.

Then the 70-year-old Agnelli made two bold decisions. After a trip to the United States, he built a new factory at Mirafiori, a Turin suburb. Manufacturing in this plant was all on one level, using the latest methods and best machines from America. Finished in 1936 after two years of construction, the factory extended over 1 million square meters (nearly 11 million square feet) of floor space, three times the size of the Lingotto works.

Concurrently, hoping to reach a new stratum of consumers, Agnelli had his engineer Antonio Fessia prepare a three-horsepower two-seater powered by an engine of only 569 cc. (34.2 cubic inches) displacement. It appeared in 1936 at the low price of 9,750 lire ($711). Responding enthusiastically, the public gave it the name "Topolino" (little mouse). Fiat's total automobile production rose 50 percent in one year.[74] This won for it 84.9 percent of Italian output in 1937. Its chief rivals, Alfa Romeo and Lancia, restricted themselves to luxury cars. Lancia's founder died in 1937, but his company retained its prominence in automobile engineering.

Part of Fiat's success came from its methodical policy of expanding exports during the 1930s. By then plants assembled Fiats in Poland and in Batavia, in the Dutch East Indies; and built them from locally made parts in France (Simca). Export results varied sharply from one year to the next, and the Fascist regime's policies often held back the growth of the domestic market. Consequently, Fiat's position was unstable and it did not seem impossible that the firm of Agnelli and Valletta might end up as a dependency of German, British, or American companies. The only governmental action that provided long-range aid to the industry was the construction of 310 miles of expressway, and this was partially supported by private capital.

Among the smaller European countries, Czechoslovakia stood out even more than earlier. Tatra also created a "people's car," in the 1920s, and introduced a new range of models in 1934. They were characterized by aerodynamic lines and unitized construction, which preceded and influenced the design of the German Volkswagen. The major firm, Skoda, did even more in design and production, building the steel works it needed in 1930 and giving up its traditional designs, which were equipped with rigid axles, for a new line of light, fast, and inexpensive cars. The most noticeable innovation on them was independent suspension of all four wheels. These cars carried the names Popular and Rapid. In 1938 the country produced 14,000 vehicles, 6 percent more than in 1929. Only the German invasion in 1939 interrupted the advance of the Czech manufacturers.

Inversely, automakers in other small countries (except for Sweden's Volvo) did not recover from the depression. It completed their downfall. By 1937 the only surviving Austrian producer was Austro-Tatra, a subsidiary of the Czech Tatra. In Belgium, two makes hung on: Imperia and Minerva. The last Swiss car builder, Martini, closed its doors in 1934 after several years of mortal illness, but a Swiss truck maker survived by introducing diesel models. During these years, Chrysler and GM set up assembly operations in Switzerland.

As for the Soviet Union, it enjoyed a brilliant period of growth by borrowing Western methods and capital and by establishing the Five Year Plans. Its expansion was especially fast during the years of depression elsewhere. Production reached 96,700 vehicles in 1935, soon exceeded by 211,100 in 1938 and 201,700 the following year. The USSR managed to do this the same way the other major European countries did, by rejuvenating its industrial potential. Two factories dating from the tsarist period were expanded and completely reequipped with the latest American machine tools. The Brandt Company of Detroit aided the conversion of one of these, AMO of Moscow, in 1929–31, to the manufacture of trucks, buses, and other large vehicles. Using ultramodern machines, its 40,000 workers turned out 68,128 vehicles in 1940, or 46 percent of the country's production. Another American concern, the Hercules Motor Corporation of Canton, Ohio, modernized the AOV works in Yaroslavl between 1929 and 1933. It specialized in heavy trucks and buses and employed 15,000 to make 2,377 vehicles in 1938.

Unlike these factories, two plants were entirely new. One was planned by Ford in accordance with the contract mentioned in the preceding chapter. The Austin Company of Cleveland actually built the one in Nizhni-Novgorod (renamed Gorki); it began operating on 1 January 1932. In 1938 its production reached 117,392. In 1930–31 Ford also built an assembly plant geared to produce 24,000 cars annually in Moscow. The Soviets employed American, and some Swiss and Italian, firms to establish from the ground up the indispensable domestic parts and accessories industry. Finally, the regime had three huge tractor factories built at Stalingrad, Kharkov, and Chelyabinsk. These plants also produced military tanks.

The period 1929–34 was spent readying and starting up all these factories, aided by American engineers, technicians, and workers on the spot (among them the Reuther brothers at Gorki in 1934–35).[75] Some were employees of the industrial-architectural firm of Albert Kahn, Inc., of Detroit, designer of most of the factories. During the following years, 1935–40, all this productive capacity was developed. Everything in the Soviet automobile industry was foreign, especially American: Ford cars and trucks, International Harvester and Caterpillar tractors, and military tanks based on American and English designs. Trucks comprised the bulk of production.

In Japan as well, a domestic automobile industry reached the stage of quantity production. It, too, continued to grow during the depression years. Production rose from 1,200 units in 1929 to 57,524 in 1939; vehicles registered from 97,071 to 217,563 over the same years. From 1937 on, domestic production surpassed imports, but exports remained feeble. The heads of the auto firms were neither feudal barons, nor from prominent families, nor leading merchants, but small businessmen or farmers.

Actually, the industry did not seem to be a very sound venture. In 1942 the average rate of profit was 11.3 percent, below that of naval construction, railway equipment, or electrical equipment. This ensued from the heavy fixed investment needed; it usually exceeded the resources available to company owners. Therefore, they applied to the government, whose investment in the industry reached 160 percent of the private capital invested. Because mechanization lagged behind that of western manufacturers, the technical division of labor was not so extensive, and production depended primarily on skilled labor. The proportion of female labor did rise in the 1930s, however, reaching 3.4 percent in 1937. As elsewhere in the world, Japanese auto workers earned the highest wages of all industrial workers.

To compensate for an underdeveloped machinery industry, the auto manufacturers followed two policies: they imported most of their machine tools, often secondhand; and they subcontracted work to the artisanal sector of the economy, where labor costs were much lower. Nissan became the largest producer of passenger cars. Trucks amounted to some 50 percent of output because of military needs, which ran counter to the desires of the automakers. Most trucks employed diesel engines.

Already at this early stage, small cars had found a strong market. The Datsun of Nissan held the lead. Owners of these types of cars were not required to possess a driver's license, and traffic and parking regulations were not so strict for them as for others. Similar privileges were extended to very small delivery trucks, leading to the popularity of the small, three-wheeled type. Although the pre-Second World War Japanese industry remained closely dependent on its government for orders and for loans, and on the United States for its equipment, it already had staked out the route that would bring it to success.

Stabilization in America

The situation in America was complex and different from that elsewhere. First, the United States must be distinguished from Canada. In the case of the United States, several interrelated factors were behind the loss of vigor in the automobile industry. Since the 1920s, stability had characterized the automobile market, which was based primarily on replacement demand. The manufacturers' strategy was gradually to improve the quality and performance of their products. This ruled out both price-cutting and radical innovations. During and after the depression, U.S. producers kept investment at a low level, unlike the European firms. Another difference from the European practice was that the Americans managed to make profits during the depression; therefore, they were not forced into the major policy changes that occurred across the Atlantic. Efforts to introduce small European cars—the Austin by Bantam in 1930 and the Mathis by William Durant—resulted in complete failure.

Still another characteristic was less rigorous competition than in Europe. Most of the remaining small manufacturers went out of business. The rest survived only by moving into specialty vehicles, such as Reo with buses, into parts making, or even by leaving the industry entirely. More serious, the share of the "independents"—Nash, Studebaker, Hudson, Packard—dropped to about 10 percent of the market. Their decline benefited those divisions of the major producers that aimed at the medium price range: Oldsmobile and Pontiac for GM, De Soto and Dodge for Chrysler.

The major companies also exerted pressure in a less direct manner. They controlled the parts and accessories makers who were less dispersed than in Europe. Body makers numbered only three, and wheel manufacturers only three. In fact, the Big Three placed their own machine tools in these suppliers' factories and carefully watched their operations and their production costs. The major firms, of course, obtained from these suppliers discounts from the prices charged to the smaller firms.

The different evolution of the industry in the United States and Europe during the 1930s allowed Europe to begin to catch up. By 1939 the variance between the number of cars there and in the United States was back to the 1913 proportion. That the American industry lacked dynamism does not mean that the Big Three evolved in the same fashion. Chrysler performed the best. During this period, despite the depression, it not only increased the number of Plymouths sold (139.8 percent of the 1929 figure in 1932 and 545 percent in 1937), but it also raised the dollar sales even more, to 563 percent of the 1929 figure in 1937. Until 1936 this rapid growth allowed it, unlike Ford and Chevrolet, to cut its costs of production systematically. In consequence, it earned especially high profits.

Chrysler's specialty in this decade was to lead in technical innovations developed in its own research center. In 1931 it offered the floating engine, attached with rubber mounts, that gave a smoother ride. In 1934 it introduced overdrive, which saved fuel at high speeds. In the same year, it offered the first car designed on aerodynamic lines, the Airflow De Sotos and Chryslers. This design proved too advanced for its time, and Chrysler was forced to return to less advanced but still modern styling. In 1933 the company took over second place among American producers and held it until the war. Walter Chrysler retired in 1935, basking in the prestige of his success.

GM held first place, though its achievements were not remarkable. Over the course of the 1930s it managed to surpass its 1929 level only once, and just barely, in 1937. Whatever those who praised it may have said, it was not going anywhere. But two of its innovations are noteworthy: the semiautomatic transmission, introduced in 1937, made fully automatic in 1940; and independent front-wheel suspension in 1933, deriving from a French patent. Both of these made driving easier.

The most impressive aspect of GM was its financial results. Except for the single year 1932, it continued to show net profits equal to or greater than 10 percent of sales revenue. The structure and strategy devised by Sloan and his team remained effective. Although the 1920–21 recession had hit GM severely, the Great Depression posed no threat to its existence. Sloan improved the committee organization; he established a Design Office complementary to the Research Division and a Dealer Council in 1934, with which GM management held useful consultations.

The real industrial triumphs of GM in the 1930s did not occur in automobiles but in other activities. Following a tentative European lead, it began to produce diesel-electric locomotives on a large scale. GM's achievement here deserves considerable credit for helping the railroads to survive financially in the United States. The company also improved its refrigerators, aided by its research director, the untiring Charles Kettering. The Frigidaire, mass-produced and sold at a low price, became an essential feature of American homes. GM also bought and developed aviation engine and airframe companies. Reserves built up during the 1920s not only financed all this expansion, but also sweetened stockholders' dividends. Sloan left the presidency in 1937, when he was sixty-two, but remained chairman of the board. The manager of Chevrolet, William Knudsen, replaced him.

Ford stumbled along in third place, losing money most years. Yet it continued its policy of adapting to changes in the market that it had inaugurated in 1927. A crucial step came in 1932. From one unchanging model, Ford switched to the annual changeover. Thereafter, instead of the single engine of twenty horsepower, it made two or more types of more than fifty horsepower. From one size wheel, it moved to two or more. These changes improved the Ford's comfort, performance, and safety, but the increased costs raised prices for cars of the same weight. Still, in these years, except for 1935, Ford's share of the market shrank, and the financial results were poor. At the same time, as happens in a transition from a policy of reducing costs to another policy, even less innovation occurred than earlier.

Two major exceptions should be noted. In 1932 Ford offered the first low-priced V-8 car. Mass production of V-8 engines at a low cost depended on innovations in foundry technique that allowed casting the engine block and transmission in one piece. The higher average power of American cars in the 1930s was attributable primarily to the V-8. More significant, in 1937 Ford succeeded where the Englishman William Morris had failed; his company developed the first successful transfer machines, an important step toward automating the machining of metal. Still, old Henry Ford had not changed his management methods. He owed his survival during the depression to the hard core of clients and dealers who obstinately remained faithful to the Ford name.

At first glance, during the 1930s major changes did not take place in American firms' products or methods. There seemed to be simply a downward trend of prices throughout the entire range of cars. Their power and comfort steadily grew, which widened the distance between European cars and American ones, which were more complex but easier to operate.

A closer look reveals a change in the shape of cars. Two major principles stand out. The first was the aerodynamic line. Until about 1930, the auto's esthetic principle was that of terrestrial architecture, characterized by a search for stability as suggested by sharp angles and straight lines. Thereafter, the model became the airplane, suggestive of movement. People said the Studebaker was as pretty as an airplane. Suddenly, curved lines were in; right angles were out. The Chrysler Airflow of 1934, which was designed by a committee, consecrated the new style. This auto featured a raking chassis, sloping front and rear windows, headlights recessed in the fenders, and overall fluid lines. The aerodynamic style not only expressed a desire to achieve better performance by reducing wind resistance, that is, an effort to make the body work functional, but it also brought the esthetic of the automobile into its baroque age. Forms began to proliferate, often playing roles independent of the function of the vehicle. This approach has predominated up to the present.[76]

The other salient principle was to simplify the car's silhouette. The stylists managed this by lengthening and lowering it. While Chrysler emphasized aerodynamic lines, GM, led by Harley Earl, deliberately and gradually transformed body styles. The different parts of the car lost their independent character to a more compact body shell that enveloped everything and disguised the various components. The companies found two advantages in this change. The long and low look appealed to the clientele. The new style also reduced the number of pieces that made up the body. The top for a body built in 1929 comprised some thirty pieces; in 1935 only a single piece of pressed steel was necessary. The modification in the automobile's appearance brought by the stylists forced the engineers to seek new solutions that turned out to cut production costs. Often the designers that began this process were from Europe, Raymond Loewy, for example, or were women.

Management methods also evolved. The practices that GM had pioneered spread throughout the American automobile industry with the exception of Ford. The companies learned to adjust their purchases and production to variations in short-term demand. To respond to the medium term, they worked out systems of market research that projected current trends and predicted possible future changes. They improved their knowledge of production and distribution costs by careful budgeting, and maintained a detailed and continuing control of them. Following the GM practice, experts and specialists in other firms now worked together in committees. They made decisions that more and more became collective efforts.[77]

American automobile sales abroad naturally suffered from the difficulties of these years. Yet, in some cases, expansion continued despite the hard times. GM profited from the growth of Vauxhall and Opel and from its subsidiary in Japan. In 1931 the firm consolidated its position in Australia by buying the body maker Holden and merging it into its local branch. The new company began to make a larger proportion of parts locally.

Even more striking were Ford's overseas operations. During the 1930s, the company continued to establish assembly plants in new countries, in Turkey in 1929, the Netherlands in 1932, and Romania and New Zealand in 1936. It opened new factories in countries where it already was established, in Germany and England, and also in Mexico, Argentina, and Australia. The best region of Ford's industrial empire, especially on the financial level, remained Latin America. Despite competition from GM and even from Chrysler, Ford held first place in sales. The 1930s brought high profits from this area, though Ford's business in the United States continued in deficit.

These differences in results sprang from the fact that Latin American subsidiaries made few investments, and sent their gross profits back to Dearborn. During the 1930s, nevertheless, Ford's sales in this continent were not so large as those of its factories in Europe and Canada. Unlike the situation elsewhere, in Europe Ford's rate of sales was higher in the later thirties than in the twenties because of new models designed for the European market. Exports by Ford of Canada and operations by this branch's subsidiaries also generated healthy profits. In all of Ford of Canada's export markets, it did better than GM except for Australia, and even there Ford rose to 22.6 percent of the market in 1939. On all these foreign markets, Ford's V-8 won major success.

While the United States remained the world's leading producer during the decade, Canada fell from second to fifth place. No outstanding reasons are apparent for this drop. Production in Canada stabilized for the same reasons as that in the United States. Canadian output in 1929 was not far above production by its competitors in Europe. Then the industry declined less in Europe, and, when it revived there, in most cases it advanced faster than in Canada. Consequently the European countries experienced little difficulty in overtaking Canada. In its best year, 1937, Canadian output of 207,000 vehicles did not reach the 1929 level. As was the case in the United States, Chrysler mounted the most vigorous Canadian initiatives. The most important was a model prepared expressly for the Canadian market, the "small Dodge" introduced in 1933. This car's success, along with sales of other Chrysler cars, raised the firm to second rank in sales in Canada from 1937 until the war.

GM waited four years before following the example of its trium-
phant rival. In 1937 it offered its own Canadian model, the small
Pontiac. Ford did not follow suit. This was one reason for its decline
in Canada, a drop slightly more serious than in the United States. In
1935 it lost first place on the Canadian market to GM and held
second for only two years. Without earnings from its exports, Ford
of Canada would have lost money. These exports allowed it to remain the largest automobile company in Canada. To adapt to producing the V-8, Ford of Canada itself financed a large modernization
and expansion program from 1935 to 1939, including two new assembly plants. The facilities of the company were now relatively
modern but it lacked the dynamic entrepreneurship of its sister Ford
operations in Europe. The first North American expressway, the
forty-mile Queen Elizabeth Way between Toronto and Hamilton,
opened in 1939.

Mass Unionization

The Great Depression not only brought changes in the
auto companies' industrial policies. It also aroused a collective awakening among automobile workers. To be sure, this came out in the
open only in the democratic countries, but it was latent in the authoritarian states also. This is clear from the worried reports submit-
ted by Fascist agents concerning labor in the Fiat works in Turin.

In Britain, as usual, changes came through evolution, not revolution. The metalworkers (engineers) union began to enroll most semiskilled workers. Their massive entry was the primary reason for the
increase in this union's membership. From 1913 to 1939, it rose
from 190,000 to 390,000, and the semiskilled amounted to some 36
percent of the membership. Workers at Austin, Morris, and Standard
were largely unionized. Because of its new power, the union won
better wages and working conditions.

In France and the United States, unionization achieved an unprecedented advance, and the unions tried a new way to pressure management: sit-down strikes. The reasons for these trends are similar in
the two countries. Firstly, in both a new political climate existed that
was much more favorable to the Left and to working-class action.
This made it possible to consider seriously tactics that formerly had
been thought to be unrealistic or utopian. In addition, the depression
had grave consequences for auto workers. It often brought massive
unemployment, a reduction of the skill requirements in jobs to

which skilled workers were assigned, lower wages, poorer working conditions, and managerial arbitrariness.[78] The result was a wave of discontent that unified a heterogeneous labor force.

In turn, this led a larger and larger fraction of workers to give stronger support to certain dynamic minorities among them. The leadership of these groups came from the skilled workers, the category traditionally the most alert to labor conditions and the most politicized. In the United States, historians recently have emphasized the actions of this group of socialists and communists rather than middle-of-the-roaders such as the Reuther brothers. In France, it was crypto-communist or communist unionists who in 1935 worked out on their own the tactic of sit-down strikes in response to earlier failures. They tried them out at Panhard, Simca, and in aviation factories.[79]

The wave of sit-down strikes in France in May-June 1936 and those that to some extent echoed them at GM near the end of the year have much in common in outbreak, course, and result. The two major similarities were the massive increase in union members and the recognition of the unions by management. Henceforth, the determination of working conditions no longer would be unilateral but the consequence of bargaining in most cases. In the United States, managements of individual firms signed contracts with the union; in France the contracts covered all firms in the entire industry. The agreements dealt with hiring, wages, promotions, and dismissals. They ratified in each case the dominance of one large union: in the United States, the United Automobile Workers; in France, the Metal Federation of the General Confederation of Labor. The latter, unlike the UAW, organized technicians and supervisors as well as manual workers.

The economic consequences of this wave of unionization still are not fully known. They certainly include, however, a reduction in seasonal unemployment, improvement in working conditions, wage increases (large in France, slow and regular in the United States), and a reduction in weekly hours, especially in France. Managements in some firms tried to compensate for their higher labor costs by improving production methods. Less clear are the results of unionization on the spread of wages (it probably narrowed in France) and on the share of the value added allotted to wages (did it increase?).

Until these major strikes occurred, management fought the union movement by all kinds of legal or illegal means. Afterward, the American firms (except for Ford, which gave in only in 1941) recognized the fact of unionization. Union contracts could assist management in its planning by making wage increases predictable and could reduce wildcat strikes. The union became an instrument, antagonistic to be sure, by which labor might be controlled. Matters went differently in France. There, management tried to crush the new mass unionization but failed to do so. In both countries, labor unions now organized a large working force, concentrated and profoundly changed by the transformation in production methods. These changes had made semiskilled workers the large majority of the total; in the United States in 1940, this category represented 73 percent of automobile workers.

Conclusion

The European and Japanese automobile industries evolved quite differently from the American in the 1930s, with one exception, the Soviet Union, which transplanted wholesale methods and models from across the Atlantic. Still, upon close examination, Europe manifested a new version of an earlier phase in the growth of the American automobile manufacturers, the era of Fordism. From 1929 on, the small European car, which had made only a timid appearance in the 1920s, began an irresistible rise. Its dominance of the field would last about as long as the Ford T, some twenty years (if one deducts the period of the Second World War). As happened in the United States, ultimately it would be replaced at the end of the 1950s by a shift to a diversified range of models, that is, by Sloanism.

Some commonalities were apparent among the automakers everywhere during these years. Research activity increased. Management viewed it as a new way to arouse interest among consumers. Engineers who specialized in improving the product and in innovation gradually became a distinct group in the technostructure, and exerted an influence on decision making that surely weighed more heavily in Europe than America. Also, the major manufacturers depended more on subcontracting. The production of buses reached a profitable level. The state became for the manufacturers a partner both annoying and obstructive but essential withal. Finally, labor organized itself in what emerged as mass unionization.

In the short term, in the last years of the decade the most significant change was the rising share of military orders in the companies' business. Although amounting to a small share of total sales (except probably in Japan), around 15 percent in France, still it was welcomed and even considered essential in the face of sharp economic fluctuations. The manufacturers did not, however, push eagerly into armaments production, for such a conversion appeared to them expensive and unprofitable in the long run, as well as outside their true calling. This conversion, repugnant to most of them, would be forced on them by their governments from 1939 to 1945.

8.   Total War

At first glance, the Second World War presents many similarities with the First. The United States and Italy once again entered the conflict well after it had begun. The two principal military products made by the automobile industry were trucks and aviation engines. The industrial potential of Britain and America (Roosevelt called the United States the "arsenal of democracy" and the auto industry was an important part of this) was greater than that of Germany and its allies, and its weight determined the ultimate balance of military strengths.

Closer examination, however, reveals sharp differences between the two war situations. The automobile industry on the Continent was dominated by Germany and no longer by France. Germany's economic contribution to the war was less than that of the United States. On the other hand, the Soviet Union made an immense industrial effort. This was a total war in which the belligerents sustained much more serious damage, and it forced them to make more thorough industrial conversions. This time, the automobile industry halted practically all production of cars for civilian use. Yet, at the height of the struggle, the manufacturers, guided by the experience of the earlier war, prepared models and strategies for the return of peace.

Adapting to the War

The state exercised a closer direction of the automobile firms than during the 1914–1918 War. Of course, it did listen to the advice of the manufacturers, and even borrowed some of them to staff its industrial production departments. William Knudsen of General Motors in the United States, Patrick Hennessy of Ford in Britain, and François Lehideux of Renault in France filled administrative or political posts. These industrialists, however, are often, for many reasons, reluctant to comment about their role in the war effort.[80] The state surrounded the industry with a whole system of government bureaus, and stationed permanent representatives in the factories. In this war, it took over distribution of energy, raw materials, and labor. It intervened directly in the location of factories. It rationed fuel.

The state not only acted differently, but the whole business and political situation was also changed from that in the First World War. This required the automakers to alter their procedures. They organized themselves much more tightly on the national level. In France, the Automobile Organization Committee, instituted 30 September 1940 (after the defeat), presided over the thoroughly regulated industry and acted as an intermediary between the companies and the German occupation authorities.[81] In the United States, the Automotive Council for War Production coordinated the industrial mobilization through its twelve sections. The German regime even tried to reorganize the industry on an international scale through the European Automobile Committee.[82]

The manufacturers decentralized their operations, in Britain with the program of replacement "shadow" factories begun in 1935, and in the Soviet Union, Germany, France, and Italy with schemes to locate new factories far from the traditional areas so as to avoid bombing attacks. Labor shortages led the industry, as during the earlier war, to recruit from reserve supplies: women everywhere (the proportion of women workers rose from 10 to 30 percent at General Motors (GM) and to even higher figures in the USSR and Japan); blacks in the United States; and foreigners, including prisoners of war and forced labor, in which the Germans specialized.

Because this labor lacked experience and manifested a high rate of turnover, companies tried to rationalize further their production methods and use more specialized or even automatic machines, within the limits of their funds and available equipment. In some countries, raw material shortages forced companies either to extend the life of their machines as long as possible, which led to an abnormal increase in the average age of machine tools, or to use new materials, frequently of lower quality, to replace those unavailable. The scarcity of liquid fuels, most acute in Europe and Japan, turned manufacturers toward substitute energy sources: alcohol, city gas, electricity, or gasogenes (devices burning wood, charcoal, or coal). The most widely used substitute, the gasogene, became the specialty of two auto-parts suppliers, Imbert of Cologne in Germany and SEV in France.[83]

The war not only brought temporary palliatives of this sort. It also led to permanent innovations. The wide-ranging nature of the conflict encouraged the appearance of off-the-road vehicles. Two American officers, Captain Howie and Colonel Herrington, finished designing the Jeep in 1940. Some 660,000 were built, a majority by Willys-Overland, aided by Ford. In Germany, the new Volkswagen factory at Wolfsburg doubled its capital and in 1940 introduced a similar machine, the Kubelwagen, of which 50,435 were built by 1945. In 1941 the company produced an amphibious Volkswagen with four-wheel drive. Volkswagen and Porsche of Stuttgart made 14,283 of these.[84] The war also caused further refinement of diesel-powered vehicles. The development of products for military use was unceasing. At GM, for example, 20 percent of the military items were designed in cooperation with military personnel, and 35 percent were designed elsewhere but improved by GM. Many spin-offs from wartime technology ultimately benefited the automobile industry, such as synthetic rubber, synthetic gasoline, and the principles of numerically controlled machine tools.

The needs of war sometimes worked to the advantage of the auto industry in countries where it was small or engaged only in assembly. The Americans and British fully utilized their multinational companies. Canada became a reservoir of transport and arms production for the British Empire. The other Dominions to a large degree assembled vehicles made in Canada. Production in India doubled; lesser increases came in South Africa, Australia, New Zealand, and even Malaya before 1942. Australian auto firms did not stop at assembly, but took advantage of the situation to increase their capacity to make complete vehicles and other military items. New Zealand tried to follow suit. Auto plants in Argentina, Brazil, and Mexico also aided in the Allied war effort, but on a smaller scale. This industrial aid rendered by the British Commonwealth and Latin America shows that between the Anglo-Americans and their opponents the game was not an equal one.

The Anglo-American Supremacy

In Great Britain, the automobile industry's expansion in the 1930s and the careful preparation for wartime industrial mobilization aided the conversion to military requirements. Of course, production of passenger cars fell to a low level, but output of industrial and commercial vehicles beat all records. The automakers did not stop at full utilization of their productive capacity, but built or acquired new factories and new machines and expanded their labor force. A large part of this additional capacity eventually would support the postwar growth. The firms also improved their designs of commercial vehicles. In addition to them, they delivered aviation engines and aircraft, munitions, and tractors. They transferred mass-production methods successfully from automobiles to the nonautomotive products.

The American automobile industry, however, gave the most convincing demonstration of the skill and adaptability of the manufacturers. Two-thirds of all GM military production consisted of products the firm had never made before. Auto factories in the United States produced 4,131,000 engines (mostly for trucks), 5,947,000 guns (mostly rifles and machine guns), 2,812,000 trucks and tanks, and 27,000 complete aircraft. As in all the auto-producing countries, truck and bus output bounded upward, quadrupling from 1940 to 1944.

Also particularly noteworthy was American success in aviation manufacturing. This result was not a foregone conclusion. Although production methods in the two industries had been quite similar in 1918, by 1940 they had diverged considerably. The aircraft manufacturers, in addition, feared that the war might lead to their own absorption by the large auto companies. Nevertheless, cooperation between the two industries began in 1940. Auto firms used their industrial capacity and their mass-production techniques to make planes designed by the aircraft companies. All did not go well, however, as the misadventures of the Ford bomber plant at Willow Run, Michigan, reveal. Begun in 1941, this factory reached full production only in 1944.

After the United States entered the war, the auto companies, as in 1917–18, converted slowly to military production, each in its own way. The flexibility and strength of the organizational system worked out by Sloan at GM and adopted by most of the other manufacturers largely explain the successful conversion. If the large companies managed to "refit many large plants and retrain hundreds of thousands of workers"[85] to work on materials with which they were completely unfamiliar, it was because of their decentralized structures. Each division of the major firms sought its own contracts. If they could keep up with the continual changes in the nature of their output (caused by the shifting needs of the armed forces), it probably was due, as Alfred Sloan suggests, to the practice of the annual model change which "gave them know-how and flexibility."[86] If they succeeded in finishing orders on time and maintaining high quality, it was attributable to the system of periodic reports on the process of production derived from the reporting systems established in the 1920s.

The practice of subcontracting, including that among divisions of the same corporation, was continued and extended to cope with the flood of military orders. As the manufacturers gained experience in working with war materials and increased the volume of their output, their costs of production declined. GM consequently reduced the prices of its military products either by voluntarily cutting them during the course of a contract, or at its renewal. Demand was so strong that sales of the major companies reached levels considerably above those of peacetime.

In the United States, as in Britain and the Commonwealth, this intense industrial activity brought a moderation in but not an end to labor-management conflict. Unionization spread into new factories, such as Ford in England (1944) as well as in Canada and the United States, where the UAW led the way. Supervisors in the United States began to unionize, and the public authorities stepped in to regulate working conditions.

During the war, despite immense difficulties, the Soviet automobile industry continued to expand its industrial capacity and kept its technical links to the United States. In Rostov, at the mouth of the Don, a new vehicle factory was built, and two tractor factories making Western models were established at Robtovsk and Vladimir in 1943–44. The Soviet auto industry turned out a remarkable number of tanks and aircraft engines. In 1941 the monthly average was 1,000 tanks and 1,800 airplanes. By 1943 the figure for aircraft reached 2,080. In 1942 tank output doubled over 1941, and rose to 29,000 for the year 1944. United States Lend-Lease aid supplied the Soviet Union with even more: 14,018 aircraft, 6,196 tanks, and 460,772 other vehicles, mostly trucks.

In the Axis countries and the occupied nations, the automobile industry suffered much more from shortages and rationing than occurred among the Allies. In Germany, Opel and Ford, subsidiaries of American companies, took an active part in the Nazi war effort. They produced trucks and other war material, and through agents controlled operations of sister subsidiaries in the occupied countries. American entrance into the war broke the ties between these companies and Detroit. Hitler placed them under the control of the Nazi government, but this produced slight effect on their operations.

Like the other German auto firms, Opel and Ford took part in a system that looted the conquered countries and integrated the auto firms there into the German war production machine as subcontractors. Because of a smaller capacity to start with and difficulties in supply, the German auto industry during the war always remained smaller than the British. In the case of some companies, output even fell below the prewar level. Daimler-Benz (which operated ten factories, including one in Austria and one in Hungary) and BMW (five plants) specialized in mass producing aircraft engines. Daimler-Benz turned out some 70,000 from 1939 to 1944.

The effect of the German occupation on the automobile industries in the conquered countries has been closely studied in the case of France.[87] During the nine months of war to June 1940 the automakers achieved a production level above that of peacetime, but from the time of the defeat on they fell back to a rate well below that of 1913, or a total of 138,356 cars and trucks produced during the occupation, of which 117,470 went to the Germans. To the difficulties due to bombing and shortages were added anti-German resistance efforts by workers and some management personnel.

The Germans seized a third of the French stock of automobiles. They expropriated some firms, and forced their production programs and sometimes their technology on others. They disoriented the market by artificially setting prices for vehicles. They made away with some high-output machine tools from Peugeot and Citroën, and transferred a large number of skilled workers to Germany. They centralized production in the factories of seven large producers, while the others received orders for tractors and repaired automobile and tank engines.

The Italian auto industry profited from the war. For example, by March 1941 Fiat's production of buses, tanks, and other vehicles had quintupled from the winter of 1939, and the output of aviation engines had tripled. The company expanded further in 1941–42 when Agnelli raised the productive capacity of his various factories, took control of firms in areas occupied by Italian forces, and extended his operations beyond automobiles, among other things taking over the Italian branch of Esso. Nevertheless, the Germans gradually began to direct the operations of the Italian automobile industry and even began importing Italian labor.

Lastly, Japan's automobile production continually shrank from 1940 to 1945, vehicle output dropping from 57,524 to 7,762. As the war expanded, Japan could not import enough oil or raw materials. The auto firms increased their capital to meet high costs of production. The end of foreign deliveries of machine tools forced the auto manufacturers to make their own. Toyota, for example, in 1940 established a machinery-making subsidiary that began building machines for large-scale production, and other companies followed its example. As for war production, the Japanese firms converted successfully to the manufacture of large numbers of aviation engines and airframes.

The Results of the War

The reinforcement of the American and British supremacy during the course of this "war of materiel" can be explained by the initial superiority of the Allied economic potential, which was further consolidated as the war continued. North America also benefitted from its geographic location, which protected its factories from aerial bombardment.

The destruction and looting that Europe and Japan suffered during and after the war also boosted the American predominance. By 1945 the buildings and machinery of automakers in these countries had suffered serious but not irreversible damage. The human capital of skilled workers and supervisors built up by the companies was partly destroyed. On the morrow of victory, the Soviets especially, and the Anglo-Americans to a much lesser degree, requisitioned from the Axis countries the best machines and engineers.

But the war did not only bring its usual heap of ruins. It also gave auto firms the opportunity for profits. These wartime profits likely reached relatively lower levels than in 1914–18 because of more effective tax systems, more difficulties in obtaining supplies, and the voluntary limitation of profits by American companies to 10 percent before taxes. GM's net profits each year from 1942 through 1945 came to a lower dollar figure than in the immediate prewar years. The same situation prevailed at English Ford. However, profits made by Ford-Canada and its subsidiaries in the Commonwealth were higher than earlier. It is surprising to discover that all of Ford's branches on the European Continent made profits during the war, except in 1943. The French automobile industry even raised its real profits from 1940 to 1942. Although the American subsidiaries in Latin America were forced to restrict themselves to repair work primarily, they too made healthy profits.

The record of the war does not stop here, however. It also comprises vigorous preparation for the postwar period by manufacturers and by governments. In the United States, GM especially worked on plans for the return of peace. Even before Pearl Harbor, top management had begun to think out these matters and to prepare its reconversion to civilian activities. Its planners began with the assumption that the world economy would expand strongly after the war, and anticipated the need for heavy investment to modernize equipment and to retool. They also prepared an expansion plan for those foreign operations of GM that were not in the Soviet sphere of influence. Adopted in 1943, this plan urged a further internationalization of the corporation and anticipated that the Australian subsidiary would shift to complete manufacture of vehicles. Also, in this period, the firm analyzed its wage policy and studied formulas for automatic cost-of-living wage increases during a postwar period of inflation.

In Britain, the state (in this case, the Board of Trade) opened contact with the automakers in 1941 to study how to return to normal conditions. Most of the predictions, however, were quite conservative. Car models, rates of taxation, and tariffs would be the same as prewar. Sir Roy Fedden's proposed three-cylinder, air-cooled, rear-engined car, developed independently of the automakers, aroused skepticism and was allowed to die.

In occupied Europe, on the other hand, innovation was welcomed, but usually carried out in deep secrecy. Unknown to the Germans, the Czech company Avro prepared a low-priced car powered by a two-cycle engine. In France, during the occupation, the engineer Pierre Bezier designed his transfer machines; and several prototype cars, very successful later on, were designed, built, and tested by Renault, Panhard, and Peugeot. These models not only incorporated some important technical improvements devised by the engineering staffs, but their designers, including F. Picard and J. A. Grégoire, also took into account their analyses of the postwar economic situation. These seemed to require completely different cars than earlier, those that were inexpensive to make, buy, and maintain.

The French firms even planned for the future in public, in the subcommittees of the Automobile Organization Committee. This committee expected to discipline the trade, to control and standardize automobile design, to allocate among the major firms production of different types of vehicles, and to reorganize marketing networks. F. Lehideux wanted to make this committee a sort of constitutional convention of the automakers for the postwar period. The Pons Plan—the first postwar French government scheme for reorganizing the auto industry—did in fact enunciate some of the ideas proposed by this committee.

Conclusion

The Second World War did not cause a fundamental change in the orientation of the world automobile industry as it had evolved from 1914 to 1939. The war ratified the strength and dominance of the North American companies, the second-place ranking of Europe, and the growing potential of Soviet Russia and Japan. The only new aspect was the increased reliance upon the British Commonwealth and Latin American countries. Also established was the basis from which these areas could move from assembly plants to complete automobile manufacturing.

Already before the war, observers as clear-sighted as the Italian philospher Antonio Gramsci foresaw the spread to the entire world of the American economic and social model as incarnated in the automobile industry. His prison notebooks dating from 1934 called Taylorism and Fordism "progressive efforts to overcome" the long-term tendency of the rate of profit to fall. The spread of the new methods would continue and would cause a series of recessions "as long as the limit was not reached in, (1) the strength of materials, (2) the introduction of new automatic machines, and (3) the industrial saturation of the world."[88]

The war had demonstrated the vitality of the Fordist model of production, to which Sloanism had given a second wind and an essential flexibility, while retaining its principle of growth based primarily on a firm's own earnings (self-financing). The war also confirmed, in secret, the growing movement toward "people's cars" in Europe. It also raised the question of who would take over the auto firms. Sir Herbert Austin died in 1941, Louis Renault in 1944, Giovanni Agnelli in 1945, and just after the war, in 1947, Henry Ford. The men who had created the automobile and had then brought it to the rank of a mass-production industry had finished their duty. The time for a new team had sounded.

Three   The Triumph of
the Automobile Revolution
Jean-Jacques Chanaron and
Jean-Pierre Bardou

9.   The Universal Automobile

Jean-Jacques Chanaron

Although it was during the period between the two world wars that the automobile worked its revolution in North American society and became the symbol of a way of life, it fully conquered "old" Europe only after the Second World War and just now is penetrating the Third World and the communist countries of Europe. The world automobile industry has experienced an unprecedented growth since 1945, trying to satisfy a demand that has grown so wide and so significant that the efforts of governments to channel and control this growth often are overwhelmed by its rapid and uncontrolled advance.

The period 1945–79 represented 35 euphoric years for the industry. World production began its rapid cadence of growth in 1946 (3 million automobiles), passing the figure of 10 million in 1955, 20 million in 1968, and even 30 million in 1972. Adding commercial vehicles to these figures of passenger cars gives these totals: 5 million in 1946, 10 million in 1950, 16 million in 1960, 30 million in 1970, and almost 43 million in 1979. Increasing its output fourteen-fold in thirty-five years, the industry has become one of the major factors in the economic growth of the industrial countries. Its product has served as the symbol of a civilization and of a way of life reserved in large part for the inhabitants of the rich nations, but which is beginning to affect the people of the underdeveloped and communist countries. In 1980 nearly 400 million motor vehicles were on the road all over the world—nearly two-thirds of them in the advanced capitalist countries—compared with 50 million in 1950.

Three periods can be distinguished in the development of automobile production since 1945. The first, ending in the years 1960–61, was characterized by reconstruction and rapid expansion in the five countries where the industry originated and first evolved: the United States, Great Britain, France, the German Federal Republic, and Italy. The second period, 1961–73, was marked by the appearance of automobile manufacturing in new countries, primarily Japan, Spain, Brazil, and some of the communist states. These experienced rates of growth that were spectacular to say the least—more than 20 percent per year in Japan—while a regular but slower growth of automobile production continued in the five traditional manufacturing countries. During the third period, since 1973, the industry has undergone some basic changes.

The Period 1945–1961

The end of the Second World War left the American automobile industry in a situation diametrically opposed to that of Europe. In the United States, the manufacturers had all of their production facilities available. Converted during the war to military needs, they quickly reconverted to produce prewar models to meet the postwar boom in demand. They reached the 1940 output level in 1947. In Europe, on the other hand, the war seriously affected the potential output of the auto industry. Not until 1950 did European auto production regain its prewar level. Delays in rebuilding and re-equipping factories, a shortage of steel, the priority given in reconstruction plans to truck manufacturing, and the general low standard of living that held back demand for cars are the factors that explain the relative slowness of Europe's recovery.

In 1950 the automobile industries in four European countries were of major importance: Britain, where 500,000 passenger cars were produced in 1950; France, 260,000; West Germany, 210,000, and Italy, 100,000. From 1950 on, the industry grew rapidly and regularly in these four countries, though at somewhat different rates. Germany increased its output nine-fold from 1950 to 1961 (spurred by the effects of American aid, the investment effort made by Ford and by GM in its Opel works, and the amazing success of the Volkswagen Beetle) and became the second largest producer in the world after passing the British in 1956. Italian output grew seven-fold, the French quadrupled, and the British tripled. Other European countries, such as the Netherlands and Sweden, also produced their own cars but at a modest level, respectively 13,000 and 150,000 passenger cars in 1961. In Belgium and Spain, plants to assemble foreign cars were established.

Manufacture of commercial vehicles—trucks and buses—was just as dynamic. Ranked according to their rates of growth, the four leading European manufacturing countries end up in the same order. Germany's output rose from 89,000 in 1950 to more than 240,000 in 1961; Italy from 28,600 to 65,700; France from 100,000 to 216,000; and Britain, the second largest producer in the world, from 225,000 to 457,000.

Among the principal characteristics of the European industry during the period 1950–61, is first of all a highly concentrated industry. In Britain, the "big five"—British Motor Corporation, Ford, Standard, Rootes, and Vauxhall—controlled 96 percent of passenger car output in 1960. The four largest French manufacturers—Renault, Citroën, Peugeot, and Simca—accounted for 98 percent. Fiat and Alfa-Romeo turned out more than 85 percent of Italian production, and in Germany four firms—Volkswagen, Opel, Mercedes, and Ford —controlled 87 percent of the total.

More dispersed was the manufacturing of commercial vehicles, though in every country a small number of firms dominated this sector: five in France—Berliet, Citroën, Saviem, Unic, and Simca; two in Italy—Fiat and OM; four in Britain—BMC, Vauxhall, Rootes, and Bedford; and, in Germany—Daimler-Benz, Hanomag, Magirus-Deutz, and MAN. This area of activity became more concentrated as domestic and intra-European competition among producers resulted in many departures, takeovers, and mergers. The consequence gradually reinforced the oligopolistic position of the large manufacturers.

The small-engined passenger cars that appeared in the offerings of English, Italian, and German producers during the 1930s won out in the postwar period, even in France. In ιne late 1940s and the 1950s, new models appeared and the small "people's cars" attained commercial success. They were the spearhead of the expansion strategies and the primary reason for the growth and leadership of some of the major European manufacturers. These included Volkswagen (Beetle), Renault (4CV), Citroën (2 CV), Fiat (500 and 600), and the British Motor Corporation (Mini).

Faced with a market eager to buy, European makers plunged into mass production, in the immediate postwar years feasible only with "economical" cars. This policy, which would permit a true democratization of the automobile, was summed up in a statement made in 1946 by Pierre Lefaucheux, president of Renault: "The idea of the automobile as a luxury product reserved for the wealthy is really outdated and must disappear . . . as far as passenger cars are concerned, our entire effort will be directed . . . toward a car that will be pleasing, of course, but with its low price, its reduced cost of maintenance, and its meagre fuel consumption, will be available to levels of consumers that will grow larger and larger as French purchasing power expands."[89]

The European automobile industry is an export industry. In 1950 Italy exported almost 40 percent of its production, but pressure from the domestic market reduced this proportion to 34 percent in 1960. It found its major markets, in addition to Europe, in Asia and Africa. Britain experienced a spectacular decline in the share of its output exported, from 76 percent in 1950 to 42 percent in 1960. In 1950 the British industry profited from the shortage of dollars elsewhere in the world that hindered American exports, from the need of the automobile industry on the Continent to recover from the ravages of war, and from its key markets in the colonies and Commonwealth.

Various factors help explain the reduction in the share of British production going to exports: the gradual loss of its preferential markets (in 1956 Australia began to limit imports); international competition, especially by manufacturers on the Continent who were now using aggressive sales practices based on more modern products and first-class sales organizations; and a level of domestic demand that exceeded supply.[90] Germany and France expanded their exports significantly during the 1950s: from 30 to 44 percent for Germany, whose exports overtook Britain's in 1956; and from 40 to 46 percent for France. European markets were the principal outlets for these countries, though German manufacturers found noteworthy success on the American market, and the French emphasized colonial markets in North Africa and Black Africa.

The financial structure of European automobile manufacturing featured, on the one hand, powerful nationalized companies—Renault in France, Volkswagen in Germany, as well as Alfa-Romeo in Italy—and, on the other, the part of the industry controlled by the American Big Three. In the British passenger-car market, Ford held on to third place, which it had gained before the war, and its share climbed from 15.4 percent in 1947 to nearly 30 percent in 1961. Vauxhall, a subsidiary of General Motors, and Rootes, controlled by Chrysler, supplied identical and constant shares of British production in this period, about 11 percent each. Therefore, more than half of this country's production of passenger cars in 1961 was made by subsidiaries of the large American manufacturers. The English market for commercial vehicles was likewise dominated by American-owned producers: 43 percent in 1947, and 47 percent in 1961. In the latter year, 31 percent of German passenger cars were made by Opel and

Ford, which produced less than 15 percent of commercial vehicles. Opel, however, gradually dropped from first to third rank in sales revenue. France was different, for the automobile industry remained unbesieged by the Americans. French Ford ended its activities in 1954 and in 1958 sold to Chrysler its 15.2 percent participation in Simca that it had received for its French factory. Chrysler wanted to participate in the European boom. The Italian automobile industry did not appear to interest American capital.

The renaissance of the European manufacturers led to a progressive decline in the American share of world production: from 82 percent in 1950 to 50 percent in 1961. Primarily because of the large size of the cars and of their engines, this country's production more than any other was limited basically to supplying the domestic market. Nevertheless, U. S. cars increased their penetration of foreign markets. In 1960 nearly 7.5 percent of production was exported, as against less than 4.5 percent in 1950. The bulk of these exports went to Canada, Mexico, and South America, but the dynamic European market was unsuitable for the kind of car that American buyers wanted because of Europe's different street and road system, high price of fuel, and lower incomes.

But domestic American demand fluctuated. After the boom engendered by the Second World War's scarcities, which pushed production from 2.1 million vehicles in 1946 to nearly 6.6 million in 1950, the Korean War gradually reduced automobile production to 4.3 million in 1952 because of the use of some facilities for military production as well as price and production control. The end of the war in 1953 terminated these restrictions. This, plus a series of new models, a significant increase in purchasing power, and relaxation of credit restrictions, revived the industry's growth. It reached a new record of 7.9 million passenger cars in 1955, of which nearly 9 percent were exported.

Beginning in 1956 a relative saturation of the American motor vehicle market appeared. Whereas in 1946 vehicles had numbered 200 per 1,000 population, the figure in 1955 was 315 and in 1960 it was 342. Domestic demand was oriented more and more toward replacement, so much so that in 1958 the industry produced only 4.2 million passenger cars. The first effects of the federal government's decision in 1956 to build and finance 90 percent of the cost of the Interstate Highway System, a vast network of about 44,000 miles of expressways, would be felt only after 1960, when some 19,500 miles were in service. The lines of cars offered to the public did not undergo major changes until new models appeared in 1960, in large part because of the European offensive on the American market. These innovations allowed the manufacturers to regain the level of 1950: 6.6 million passenger cars.

The United States was also the largest producer of commercial vehicles, 1.3 million in 1950, or some two-thirds of world output. But, during the following decade, while maintaining world leadership, the United States experienced a relative stagnation in this area. Except for the years 1950–52, when the Korean War boosted production, it remained around 1.1 million per year.

The American industry was highly concentrated. For a long while it had been dominated by the Big Three: General Motors, Ford, and Chrysler. In 1946 there were also six "independents": Crosley, Hudson, Kaiser, Nash, Packard, and Studebaker. Their total share in the market reached 15 percent. The Korean War and the concerted oligopolistic strategy of the Big Three led to the disappearance or regrouping of the independents and the gradual contraction of their importance. By 1956 only two survivors remained: American Motors, the result of the Hudson-Nash merger of 1 May 1954, and Studebaker-Packard, dating from 1 October 1954. Their share of the market reached only 3.6 percent. Kaiser, which had made no profit since 1948, merged in 1953 with Willys-Overland, maker of Jeeps and small trucks that had returned to the passenger-car market in 1952 after a ten-year absence. The major consideration of the two merger partners seemed to be the compensation of the losses of one of them by the profits of the other, for tax purposes. In 1955 Kaiser halted all its production of passenger cars, choosing to devote itself entirely to Jeeps and small commercial vehicles. As in Europe, American production of trucks and buses was more dispersed, though some 70 percent of the market was held by Chevrolet, GMC Truck and Coach Division, Dodge, and Ford. A larger number of firms accounted for the other 30 percent. The most important of these were International Harvester, Kaiser, Mack, and White.

Among the Big Three, GM held absolute leadership; its share of total American automobile production rose from 38 to 47 percent in this period, reaching peaks exceeding 50 percent in 1954 and 1956. Over the same years, Ford's share climbed from 22 to 28.5 percent —and even hit 31 percent in 1954 and 1957. Chrysler held 26 percent in 1946, but steadily declined to 17.6 in 1950, rose to 20.3 in 1953, only to drop to 13 in 1954 and 10.8 percent in 1961. The unhappy fortunes of Chrysler resulted from its policy of less roomy cars and less frequent model changes, which did not pay off, and from a reputation for easygoing quality control.

From 1957 on, the success of the Rambler models of American Motors—the first "compact" cars made in the U.S.—would permit the independents to raise their share of the market to 8 percent in 1961 despite the decline of Studebaker. This improvement was associated with the relative success of imported European cars. The American market for imports remained quite small until 1956—between 0.5 and 1.5 percent of new registrations—but the demand for small models, essentially as second and third cars, allowed foreign machines to gain 3.5 percent of the market in 1957 and more than 10 percent in 1959. The reaction of the American producers came with little delay. The Big Three offered their compacts in 1959, reducing imports to 6.5 percent in 1961 and 4.2 percent in 1962. Volkswagen survived, and imports of other makes began to rise again in a few years.

The marketing policy of the large producers remained rather constant in terms of the numbers of models offered to the public: 243 in 1950 and 244 in 1960. The average duration of each model was three years. Often, however, only the name, body trim, and a few gadgets differentiated two or more models of the same company, and basic mechanical elements, such as the engine, transmission, and chassis, might be retained for twenty or more years.

First in quantity of production, the American automobile industry held first rank in productivity as well. To make a hundred cars in 1950 required ten workers in the United States, compared to twenty-eight in France and thirty in Britain. A decade later, the American figure was eight and the French twelve. The American industry also stood out in the level of its profits. Measuring the ratio of profit after taxes to sales turnover, the average of all companies was about 16 percent over the period 1946–61. Peaks occurred the same years as the highest output, 27.5 percent in 1950, 24 percent in 1955, but under 9 percent in 1958.[91] By comparison, European producers had trouble making more than 5 percent.

American profits stayed at levels very much above the European average because of the absence of real price competition on the American market. It should be noted also that cultural and political factors encourage American companies to arrange to show high profits while the opposite attitudes prevail in Europe. The auto firm that experienced the largest sales turnover, GM, also held the record for profits. They averaged above 20 percent for the period 1946–61, and some especially high peaks occurred: 35 percent in 1950 and 28 percent in 1955, as against 12 percent in 1958. Ford and Chrysler in the same period managed to make an average profit of 12 percent. The independents showed more modest results, comparable to the European figures. American Motors reached a 5-percent average from 1954 to 1961 because of its record performances in 1958 and

1959 (31.6 percent), though it lost money in every other year. Stude-baker incurred heavy deficits from 1954 to 1958, and finally ended auto production in the United States in 1963.

The Period 1961–1973

For three reasons, the year 1961 was a turning point. For the American, French, and British industries, it marked a recession for both passenger cars and industrial vehicles. The year also sounded the end of the quasi-monopoly of production by the countries that traditionally had made most of the automobiles. And, finally, the entry in force of the Treaty of Rome establishing the Common Market in Continental Western Europe brought the end of tariff barriers on automobiles among the member countries.

In the 1961–73 period, the growth of world automobile production accelerated and rose from 14.2 million passenger cars in 1962 to more than 30 million in 1973. Within this growth, a number of developments upset the rules of the game established by the major manufacturers. These included competition and even "invasion" from Japan; the internationalization of markets, including the developing countries and the communist countries; technical innovations that could become competitive, such as rotary engine, electric car, and fuel cell; and the advent of several movements that challenged the dominance of the individual passenger car. To examine world automobile production in this period, it may be best to distinguish three groups of countries: the "old" manufacturers, the new ones, and the communist ones.

The American automobile industry continued to hold first place in the production of passenger cars, a place that it lost to Japan as far as commercial vehicles was concerned. For cars, output achieved new levels: an annual average of 7.5 million in the period 1962–70 and 8.5 million in 1971–73. These averages covered rather large variations: a slump in 1970, when output was 6.6 million, back to the level of 1950 and 1960, and then a record 9.7 million in 1973. As had been true in the years 1946–61, the curve of production fluctuated from 1962 to 1970, but beginning the next year it returned to a regular and accelerated growth. For the entire period 1961–73, the annual rate of growth attained 4.8 percent. Production of commercial vehicles shared in this expansion: 1.9 million units in 1970, as against 1.2 million in 1962. The structure of the automobile industry became even more concentrated around the Big Three. After Studebaker dropped out of the industry, they totaled more than 97.2 percent of production in 1965, and have held this proportion to the present. GM increased its share to between 50 and 55 percent. As for commercial vehicles, the Big Three possessed about 80 percent of the market: GM 37, Ford 33, and Chrysler 10 percent.

Since 1962 the American automobile industry has strengthened its multinational operations through a three-fold policy: (1) the extension and growth of complete production facilities that are relatively independent of the home company, in Canada, Germany, Britain, and Brazil; (2) the establishment of decentralized factories, as illustrated by GM and Ford building factories to make transmissions in France and Ford opening a large assembly plant in Spain; and (3) the acquisition of local manufacturers; for example, Chrysler gradually gained control of Simca in France, of Barreiros in Spain, and a share of Mitsubishi in Japan.

The total number of passenger and commercial vehicles produced under the control of the American Big Three in the world in 1973 reached the astonishing figure of 16.7 million, or nearly 35 percent. This expansion of the international activities of the American firms resulted both from the saturation of the domestic market, which obliged them to find new areas of growth abroad, and from the advantages offered by the host countries, including plentiful and cheap labor along with policies to help and protect the foreign investment that generates jobs. Nevertheless, this foreign expansion did not stop the decline in the role of the American manufacturers in total world production, from more than 85 percent in 1950 to 35 percent in 1973.

The number of models offered to American consumers sharply increased, reaching 370 in 1967. Styling became even more important beginning in 1962, along with a proliferation of options and gadgets. Because the compact cars of 1959 steadily grew larger and more luxurious, they lost a significant place in the market (10 percent of registrations) to foreign cars, primarily from Germany, Japan, and Sweden. The 1960s also saw the success of the pseudo sport cars, best illustrated by the Ford Mustang, which won 11 percent of new U.S. registrations in 1967, and the Chevrolet Camaro.

The most salient characteristic of the 1961–73 period was the emergence of the safety and pollution issues. Pressed by several consumer movements, local governments at first (especially in California) and then the federal finally issued regulations imposing safety and antipollution standards of growing severity. They had to be met by all cars sold on the American market. Despite the vigorous criticism and opposition of the domestic manufacturers, it should be noted that, despite the surface rationales of safety and antipollution, these standards at first appeared as a method of protecting the U.S. market from foreign penetration. The barring of certain kinds of headlights required Volkswagen to remodel the body of the Beetle significantly. In addition, the heavier and larger American cars were more suitable than Japanese and European models for safety improvements by means of strengthening those parts of the structure deemed most important by the authorities and by the manufacturers, and for the addition of catalytic converters.

The Canadian automobile industry, an American preserve, ranked seventh in the world. It produced more than 1.6 million passenger cars in 1973, compared with 330,000 in 1961, a rapid rate of growth averaging more than 13 percent. The American Big Three controlled about 92 percent of Canadian production. A 1964 agreement providing free trade in automobile equipment between the two countries favored the expansion of Canada's automobile industry because its supply of cheaper labor was larger than that of the United States. A substantial share of the output, around 45 percent, went to the American market; the rest was divided, 45 percent to the Canadian domestic market and 10 percent exported primarily to Commonwealth countries such as Australia and South Africa.

The four major European manufacturing countries continued their expansion after 1961 at unequal rates, but, except for Great Britain, always above the United States level. Output in West Germany, third largest producer after the United States and Japan, mounted from 2 million cars in 1962 to more than 4 million in 1973, or a rate of 7 percent annually. France achieved a higher rate of growth, 10.2 percent; passed Britain in 1966; and made 3.3 million vehicles in 1973, compared with 1.3 million in 1962. Just as dynamic was Italian automobile manufacturing. Its average rate of growth of 9.4 percent brought an increase from 878,000 vehicles in 1962 to nearly 2 million in 1973. The British motor industry reflected the country's economy as a whole, experiencing some troubled periods as it gradually expanded. The following figures show its fluctuations: 1.25 million passenger cars in 1962, 1.87 in 1964, 1.55 in 1967, 1.74 in 1971, 1.92 in 1972, and 1.75 in 1973, or an annual average increase of 4.8 percent from 1961 to 1973.

Accompanying this American and West European growth were movements toward decentralization and subcontracting. Even before the First World War, especially in the United States, decentralization of production facilities had begun. It has continued ever since, notably in periods of rapidly expanding output, as in the United States in the 1950s and Western Europe after 1955. The motives for this policy include lower costs of transportation, especially in the United States; finding more or better-qualified labor, especially in Europe; avoidance of overcrowding and the consequent social problems in centers such as Paris, Detroit, Turin, and Moscow; and the lower cost of land and construction in small towns and rural areas.

In consequence, in North America GM operated thirty assembly plants and many factories making components in 1973. In Germany, Volkswagen operated six main plants plus one in West Berlin. Renault in France maintained eleven factories, including three operated jointly with Peugeot, in addition to truck- and parts-making subsidiaries. However, what sometimes appears at first glance to be a policy of factory decentralization in some cases may be the result of a merger of firms located in a number of different places. The British Leyland Corporation illustrates this, for as the end product of a long series of mergers it had more than sixty factories in 1968, and its management was forced to try to reduce the number, not increase it.

Subcontracting, by which an automobile firm buys some of its parts from independent manufacturers, has increased again in Europe since the Second World War. For some firms it reached 15 percent of their purchases and 25 percent of the volume of their sales. The companies employ this technique primarily so they can concentrate their energies on strictly automotive activities.

Three types of subcontracting can be distinguished. The technical type involves parts requiring highly specialized technology and manufacturing skills that the automobile manufacturer purchases so as to save on his own capital investment. This category accounts for some two-thirds of subcontracting purchases. A second type stems from a shortage of capacity. It is used to compensate for a production bottleneck in the operations of a manufacturer. It is temporary and fluctuating. Recently a third type has emerged: obtaining components from factories jointly owned by independent automobile manufacturers. An arrangement in France between Renault and Peugeot in 1966 inaugurated this procedure, and it may become the most important of all. It is used for the production of complex and expensive items such as engines and transmissions. The Peugeot Renault-Volvo factory that builds the same V-6 engine for each of the partners is the most outstanding example so far. Industry observers believe this kind of cooperation will become a leading characteristic of automobile manufacturing. It has also appeared in commercial vehicles, as exemplified by the Franco-Italian Engine Company at Foggia, Italy, which makes diesel engines for Saviem, Fiat, and Alfa-Romeo. By 1980 this plant had reached its capacity of 1,000 engines per day.

In their structures as well as their location policies, the automobile industries in the four major European countries conformed more and more to the American model. For one thing, they became more concentrated. The four largest producers made 94.8 percent of the German output, 89.5 percent of the British, and 99.9 percent of the French and Italian. Such concentration accentuated the worldwide thrust of the industry's production and marketing. The establishment of assembly plants all over the world grew rapidly beginning in 1960, then slowed down after 1968. The number of countries where such factories were located rose from forty-two in 1960 to seventy in 1968 and eighty in 1973. The major manufacturers in the world—American, West European, and Japanese—altogether had more than 500 final assembly lines in operation. They variously assembled completely knocked-down parts, semiknocked-down, those of partial local manufacture, or manufactured under license.

The last is the "modern" and latest type of these installations, especially in communist countries. The European manufacturers in 1970 had 320 of these assembly operations. West Germany had 99 in 39 countries, Italy 39 in 33 countries, France 78 in 41 countries, Britain 89 in 40 countries, and Sweden 15 in 12 countries. The countries were located almost everywhere in the world, including Latin America, Africa, and European states that lacked local producers (Spain, Portugal, and Belgium). In this connection it should be emphasized that Belgium is the world's premier assembler, for it acts as the center of American assembly in Europe with GM and Ford plants in Antwerp (as well as those of Renault and Citroën). Another factor that should also be pointed out is the spectacular progress of Japan, which from seven plants in six countries expanded to sixty in twenty-seven countries.

The European automobile industry is not noted for its high profits. The ratio of profit after taxes to sales turnover is usually under 5 percent, when it is not in deficit, and the period 1961–73 showed a declining rate of return for the manufacturers as a group. An exception was the German firm BMW, but this was unrepresentative because it specialized in luxury cars, usually quite profitable. In the United States, profits were irregular, varying with the level of output, but remained significantly higher than the European averages.

Among the states that have recently joined the restricted world of automobile manufacturing, Japan is remarkable both for the rapidity of its expansion and the total number of vehicles produced. Showing an average annual increase exceeding 26 percent, Japanese output of passenger cars rose from 165,000 in 1960 to nearly 4 1/2 million in 1973. Overtaking Germany in 1971, Japan became the second largest manufacturer in the world. In the first phase of this growth, from

1950 to 1961, Japan followed its prewar path, but at a higher level, building up a supply of commercial vehicles to meet the needs of a rapidly growing economy. Their production rose from 30,800 in 1951 to 553,000 in 1961. It should be pointed out, however, that a large fraction of these were of light and medium-weight. Output of three-wheeled vehicles also resumed earlier trends: 27,500 in 1949, 44,000 in 1951, and 278,000 in 1960. The mass production of passenger cars really began in 1960. Growth came quickly: 700,000 in 1965, 2 million in 1968, and 4 million in 1972. At the same time, commercial-vehicle manufacture continued its advance. When it overtook the United States in this branch in 1967, Japan became the world's largest producer. The 2 1/2 million figure for 1973 represents almost five times the output of 1961.

How can this geometric rate of growth be explained? Several successive events allowed the Japanese automobile industry to forge ahead rapidly. Before the Second World War, it was quite small, except for the manufacture of commercial vehicles. Then the American occupation was a hampering factor until 1949. A very serious deflationary crisis further hindered growth until the Korean War broke out in 1950. That conflict led to American "off-shore" orders, a major stimulus to the recent growth of the Japanese automobile industry. Then, little by little, it installed the production facilities necessary for its rise.

In the first stage, from 1949 to 1955, the industry laid the groundwork by establishing manufacturing standards, importing eqipment, and training a growing number of automobile engineers. From 1956 to 1959, aided by a protectionist policy (100-percent tariff on imported vehicles) that broadened the domestic market, the Japanese industry expanded its capacity for production and assembly. The third period, from 1960 to the present, marks the stage of production on an international scale.

The lowering of tariff barriers beginning in 1960 encouraged manufacturers to expand their output and improve their methods to take advantage of an extraordinary boom in the domestic market, which was encouraged by the improvement and extension of highways. The long period before restrictions on automobile imports were eliminated, finally accomplished in 1971, allowed the Japanese industry to catch up to the levels of productivity of its American and European rivals. It sold its products successfully on international markets by means of very competitive prices—stemming from low labor costs— and new and attractive technologies. The original success in the United States of the Mazda cars, which were powered by Wankel rotary engines, is an interesting example of this approach.

The industry was quite dispersed in structure until 1965. It consisted of eleven firms: Toyota, Nissan, Toyo Kogyo, Mitsubishi, Honda, Fuji, Suzuki, Daihatsu, Isuzu, Hino, and Aichi. Only the last of these restricted production to commercial vehicles. In 1966, however, the industry entered a phase of concentration that allowed the most important companies to achieve a size that would be competitive in the world market. By 1974 only five independent manufacturers had survived: Toyota, Nissan, Toyo Kogyo, Mitsubishi, and Honda, of which the first three controlled 85 percent of the country's output. The Japanese sold an always increasing share of their vehicles on world markets, though not exporting as high a proportion as the West European countries. Although in 1961 less than 5 percent of Japanese output of passenger cars went abroad, in 1965 the figure reached 14 percent; in 1970, 23 percent; and in 1973, 32 percent. For commercial vehicles, the growth of exports was slower, 8 percent in 1961 and 24 percent in 1973, because the domestic market, steadily growing along with the entire Japanese economy, absorbed the bulk of production.

The American and West European markets experienced the major thrust of the invasion of Japanese vehicles, taking respectively 45 percent (U.S. and Canada) and 25 percent of total exports in 1973. The Japanese sold more and more vehicles to Third World countries, and in particular they dominated Asian markets. Consequently, they hold a position of strength on the markets of the future. The domestic Japanese market, on the contrary, remained a monopoly of the country's manufacturers. Imports accounted for 2 percent of new registrations in 1966, 0.8 percent in 1971, and 1.3 percent in 1973. The last figure represented 37,000 passenger cars, of which 21,000 came from West Germany and 12,000 from the United States.

Along with Japan, five other countries developed automobile industries of significance in the 1961–73 period. Two, Sweden and the Netherlands, based theirs on domestic technology; the other three, Australia, Brazil, and Spain, expanded from a base of foreign-owned firms and imported technologies.

In Sweden, passenger-car production rose at an annual rate of 9.6 percent, from 115,000 in 1961 to more than 300,000 in 1973, of which in excess of 64 percent was exported to the United States, Canada, and Europe. Two firms made all of Sweden's cars: Saab, oriented primarily to domestic sales; and Volvo, which enjoyed growing success on sophisticated markets because of its reputation for durability and safety. In the Netherlands, a single domestic firm, DAF, managed to expand by means of a technical innovation, the Variomatic transmission. Nevertheless, the company was ultimately absorbed by Volvo in 1974. DAF, like Volvo, also manufactured trucks.

The Spanish industry grew with exceptional rapidity, from 50,000 passenger cars in 1961 to more than 700,000 in 1973, an annual increase of nearly 25 percent. This was the result of a young industry that was dominated by foreign manufacturers. Seat-Fiat (361,000 in 1973) and Fasa-Renault (173,000 the same year) were by far the largest. Others included Chrysler-España, Citroën-Hispania, British-Leyland-Authi, and Ford. The last of these companies adopted a new international strategy in 1970 that called for Spain to play a major role in its European operations.

Brazilian automobile production rose from 55,000 in 1961 to 729,000 in 1973, or an annual rate of growth surpassing 23 percent. This expansion followed the establishment of production facilities by foreign firms: GM, Ford, and Volkswagen.

As the Brazilian case suggests, the automobile industry was beginning to appear in the Third World. Only three of these countries by the mid-1970s had managed to create a fully domestic industry: Brazil, Argentina (1973 output, 294,000), and India (1973 output, 97,000). A few others required a specific proportion of domestically made components in cars assembled in their territories: Mexico (1973 output, 283,000) and Venezuela (1973 output, 97,000) at 60 percent, Chile 50 percent, Turkey 45 percent, Morocco 35 percent, and Peru 30 percent. Factories in other countries perform assembly only: Bolivia, Columbia, Costa Rica, the Dominican Republic, El Salvador, Ecuador, Guatamala, Paraguay, Trinidad and Tobago, and Uruguay in Latin America; Burma, Ceylon, South Korea, Indonesia, Iran, Cambodia, Malasya, Pakistan, Philippines, Singapore, and Thailand in Asia; Algeria, Egypt, Israel, and Tunisia on the Mediterranean littoral; South Africa, Angola, Cameroon, Ivory Coast, Dahomey, Ethiopia, Ghana, Guinea, Kenya, Madagascar, Mozambique, Nigeria, and Senegal in Black Africa.

In most of these countries, the status of the automobile industry is limited by technical, political, economic, and social factors. Production runs are small because of the large number of producers and the wide diversity in models. It has been argued that the cause of this in Latin America is that many of the large multinational producers wish to be represented in many of the national markets. Their production runs are small, but the high prices they charge provide them with healthy profits.[92] Poor roads and the frequency of defective locally made parts shorten the life of vehicles and increase breakdowns, which are often difficult to repair because of inadequate and poorly organized service facilities as well as a lack of spare parts, except in

Ceylon. High prices, accentuated by special taxes, and lower purchasing power restrict the size of markets in these countries. Rarely do they enjoy an opportunity to reexport. Political and administrative instability is not calculated to encourage the growth of an industry that is very sensitive to economic and financial regulations, which often are incoherent.

In the communist countries, the automobile is, like all other socioeconomic activities, difficult to study because of the lack of quantitative and qualitative information. In the USSR, production of all types of automobiles climbed slowly in comparison with West European and Japanese rates, rising from 363,000 in 1950 to 524,000 in 1960 and reaching 1,142,000 in 1971. Soviet planning long favored the production of commercial vehicles, both trucks and buses, needed for domestic purposes and for export to the important markets in the Comecon (communist Eastern European) countries. These commercial vehicles amounted to 81 percent of the total output in 1950, 72 percent in 1960, and 46 percent in 1971.

Passenger cars indeed rose to a higher proportion, but their output remained modest. In 1969 about 5 Soviet citizens per 1,000 owned a car, compared to 419 Americans, and the bulk of production was devoted to the use of civil servants. Ordinary Russian cars were heavy and sturdy, imitations of American and German models. From 1970 on, as individual purchasing power rose markedly and the demand for cars far exceeded the supply, a large gap appeared between the real price of used cars and the official price. It took a sum equivalent to fifteen years of the average wage in 1969 to buy a two-year-old car, and it required five years' wages to buy a new Volga 2500. Also, delays in delivery of new cars were long, a minimum of two years in 1971.

To meet these problems, Soviet authorities decided to establish the foundations for mass production. To do this, they called upon experienced manufacturers, European ones this time, no longer Americans as before the Second World War. Fiat installed the Togliatti factory on the Volga River, and Renault took part in modernizing the Moskvitch factory in Moscow. The 1971–75 Five Year Plan gave a higher priority to passenger cars. The major manufacturer, Lada, turned out 550,000 in 1973, achieving the rank of ninth in the world as its output rose 64 percent over 1972.

In 1974 four models of passenger cars shared the market: the Zaporojetz (forty horsepower), the Moskvitch (75), and the Volga (100), all completely Soviet designed, and the Jigouli, the Soviet version of the Fiat 124. Output for the year was 1,200,000, of which 650,000 Jigoulis came from the Togliatti factory. Exports to Comecon countries totaled 300,000 and another 300,000 went to government ministries and departments and to taxicab companies. So only half of production reached the public, and 350,000 of these went to the Moscow and Leningrad regions alone. In 1975 production was 1,212,000. Nevertheless, new car prices remained very high.

The expansion of passenger-car production did not stop the Soviet effort with trucks and buses. Renault signed an industrial cooperation contract in 1971, and participated in the construction of a giant truck factory at Kama, for which it supplied a large part of the engineering and equipment, including machine tools and aerial conveyors. The USSR became a major automobile producer, but devoted the bulk of its effort in this period to meet its own domestic demand.

Among the other communist countries, East Germany and Czechoslovakia had significant facilities for making passenger cars and trucks. In Czechoslovakia, two firms, Tatra, which produced luxury models, and Skoda, divided the output of 160,000 cars and 60,000 trucks in 1974. The East Germans built up an automobile industry from what was left after wartime bombing and looting of BMW installations at Zwickau and Eisenach. Hungary chose to concentrate its efforts on trucks and buses, in which it has become the specialist for the Comecon countries. It imports all its passenger cars in the framework of economic cooperation agreements, receiving Polish- and Soviet-built Fiats in return for automotive components and machine tools. The French Renault-Saviem group participated in building a factory at Győr, Hungary, which makes diesel engines on a MAN (West Germany) license. Its capacity is 13,000 annually.

Yugoslavia in 1954, Poland in 1968, and Romania in 1969 called on West European manufacturers to establish plants to manufacture and assemble on license. In Poland, the Fiat Polski factory in Zeran produced more than 100,000 model 125s in 1973. Earlier it had made the Warsawa, on license from the Soviet Pobeda. In Yugoslavia, the Slovenian company Industria Motornih Vozil assembled Renault (2,860 in 1973) and British Leyland cars, Cimos the Citroën 2 CV and Ami 8 (5,700 in 1973) models, and Zastava made Fiats (annual capacity, 60,000). In Romania, the Intreprinderea Autotourisme Potesti assembled 50,300 Dacia 1300 cars (the Renault 12 model) in 1973, and reexported 22,000 to Finland, Greece, Algeria, and Yugoslavia. In return, Renault received transmissions and front ends. In Bulgaria, Moskvitch, Renault, and Fiat cars are assembled. Chart 9–1 shows Fiat's complex relationships with East European and some Third World producers.

The movement of the communist countries into the club of automobile manufacturing countries is taking place by means of close technical cooperation with foreign, basically West European, manufacturers. The latter are thereby increasing the international aspects of their production. In the communist countries, they find markets that are large and stable because they are thoroughly planned and are therefore free from competition. The Western producers are usually repaid in kind, that is, by delivery of assembled cars, parts, components, or by means of reexports.

The Years since 1973

The years since 1973 have been a transition period in the life of the automobile industry, punctuated by two recessions—1973–75 and 1979–81—that are without precedent since the Second World War in their seriousness and length. They were separated by a phase of expansion during which earlier production records were considerably exceeded. Although the two recessions followed the two petroleum "shocks" of 1974 and 1979, they differed in their manifestations and in their consequences.

The first one, extending from the second half of 1973 to mid-1975, affected all the major automobile producing countries, but the new producers were spared (see table 9–1). Negative factors struck one after another. Together, they caused this severe and long-lasting contraction of the automobile market. Of course, a considerable slackening in the demand for passenger cars was to be expected,[93] because of the gradual saturation of markets in highly motorized countries, the weakening of the symbolic value attached to owning a car, and the more rational behavior by car owners as seen in demotorization in highly urbanized areas where competitive transportation became available.

The increase in inflationary pressures all over the world beginning in 1973 caused a shift in the structure of consumer purchases to the detriment of expensive durable goods, especially automobiles. This trend was only aggravated by the unprecedented rise in both car prices and the cost of operating them brought on by the oil crisis and the flare up of raw material prices. Beginning in the second half of 1974, the spread of the recession brought rising unemployment and a slowdown in the growth of nominal wages, whose purchasing power also was squeezed, as were savings, by continued inflation. The uncertainty created by the recession led to a change in family economic behavior in favor of more savings and away from large purchases.

This shift hit automobiles in particular because they are among the

Chart 9-1.
Fiat's Relations with Communist and Underdeveloped Countries, 1970

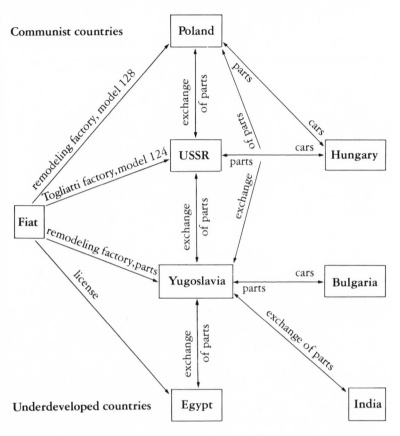

Source: P. Judet, *L'Industrie automobile dans les pays de l'Est* (Grenoble: University of Grenoble II, 1970, I.R.E.P.), p. 8.

most expensive of consumer goods and their replacement, largely a psychological matter, can be delayed more easily than most others. Finally, the wide adoption of speed limits, temporary restrictions on driving, and the higher cost of operating cars (fuel, spare parts, repairs, and insurance) reduced the distance traveled by the average passenger car and consequently increased its longevity. Demand for commercial vehicles acted as might be expected for capital goods of this sort, a decline reflecting the drop in economic activity. The recession in automobiles pulled down related industries also: steel, machinery, chemicals, glass, tires, and other suppliers of equipment.

Table 9-1.
Production during the Recession of 1973–1975, Selected Countries

| | Motor vehicle production (in thousands) | | | Percentage change | |
	1973	1974	1975	1973 to 1974	1973 to 1975
United States	12,674	10,071	8,989	−20.5	−29.1
Japan	7,086	6,553	6,942	−7.5	−2.0
W. Germany	3,948	3,100	3,185	−21.5	−19.3
France	3,218	3,075	2,859	−4.4	−11.2
Britain	2,164	1,937	1,648	−10.5	−23.8
Italy	1,958	1,773	1,459	−9.5	−25.5
Soviet Union	1,600	1,835	1,960	+14.7	+22.5
Spain	822	837	814	+1.9	−1.0
Brazil	729	875	930	+20.0	+27.6

Source: *Argus*, July 1980.

If various countries were affected unequally and at different times by the crisis, it was because their governments reacted differently to the energy problem, to inflation, and economic recession. Actually, the automobile recession was essentially a normal cyclical downswing, characteristic of markets close to saturation. The oil crisis merely accentuated the decline. The year 1975 marked the beginning of widespread and increasing recovery of passenger-car production.

In the next year, truck output also rose, along with the world economy. In 1976 world automotive production regained the record level of 1973, and in 1978 it reached its historic high (42.5 million cars and trucks). This new phase of expansion manifested some characteristics that clearly distinguish it from the pre-1973 period. First, the rate of growth of world production was much less: 2.8 percent per year from 1976 through 1979, as against 6.8 percent from 1960 through 1973. Secondly, although new records were set by the auto industries of the United States (1978), France and Germany (1979), and Japan (1980), their British and Italian competitors continued to decline. In 1977 Italian output of vehicles was at its 1963 level, and in 1979 British production compared with its 1959 figure. Thus, on the world market, the British and Italian companies have been relegated to a secondary position, or even condemned to fall under the control of financially stronger competition.

Among the new producing countries, contrasting developments have occurred, as shown in table 9–2. The Brazilian and Soviet

Table 9-2.
*Annual Average Change in Motor Vehicle Production
in New Producing Countries, 1970s (in percent)*

	1972–75	1975–79
Soviet Union	12.4	2.5
Brazil	15.2	3.6
Spain	5.4	8.4
Argentina	−3.7	1.2

Source: *Argus*, July 1980.

industries have continued their growth, but at sharply lower rates. In the USSR, despite the presence of a potentially large demand, the authorities have chosen to revise their goals downward because of the expense required to expand production capacity and because of the difficulties encountered in organizing the flow of raw materials as well as of parts and accessories.

The slackening of growth in Brazil can be explained by a significant easing of demand caused by the stagnation or even reduction of purchasing power among those social groups likely to enter the auto market. Brazil's economy has been so affected by the energy crisis that the authorities have inaugurated an "Alcohol Plan," which produced some 250,000 alcohol-powered cars in 1980 and expects 400,000 more in 1981. The country is using local technology for this plan, as well as for the production of alcohol from several vegetables, such as sugarcane and manioc. Alcohol fuel in Brazil costs barely half as much as heavily taxed gasoline, so customers are eagerly demanding alcohol cars despite a premium on their price of about 10 percent. A similar plan calls for homegrown palm oil to substitute for diesel fuel.

In Spain, the rising rate of growth from 1976 corresponds to production beginning at Ford-España, which is integrated with Ford operations in the Common Market to produce the Fiesta model. In Argentina, political and social instability explain the fall of production from 1973 (224,000 vehicles) to 1978 (179,000). On the other hand, restoration of order by the military junta lies behind the recovery evidenced in 1979.

During the period 1972–79, some new countries joined the ranks of automobile manufacturers, Mexico and South Korea, and production grew rapidly in the countries of East-Central Europe (table 9–3). In the Third World, conditions changed little from 1973 to 1979.

Table 9-3.
Motor Vehicle Production in New Producing Countries,
1972 and 1979

	1972	1979
Mexico	225,000	444,630
South Korea	18,500	190,000
Poland	156,000	406,000
Yugoslavia	126,000	290,000
East Germany	171,000	220,000
Czechoslovakia	183,000	212,000
Romania	71,000	124,000

Source: *Argus,* July 1980.

Contrary to expectations, the oil-exporting countries—Iran, Iraq, and Algeria, among others—were still not able to establish automobile industries of significant proportions. South Korea, led by a nationalized firm, Hyundai, and helped by technology and know-how from the Japanese Mitsubishi group, and Mexico are the only ones among the developing countries of whom it might be said that their auto industries grew in outstanding fashion. The others remained assemblers only.

When a country's capacity for auto assembly exceeds 50,000 per year, a rather speedy transition can be expected to the stage of manufacturing. In 1980 such a level of output was the case for Portugal and Turkey among European states; Venezuela and Colombia in Latin America; Indonesia, Iran, the Philippines, Taiwan, and Thailand in Asia; and New Zealand in Oceania. These countries, along with India and the Peoples Republic of China, certainly will be major markets of the future, and as such will offer opportunities to establish manufacturing facilities to the multinational companies of the United States, Europe, and Japan, for these firms are anxious to maintain control over most of world auto production and resume their own continued growth and profits. The establishment of political and financial incentives by local governments can lead to an acceleration of such shifts in the location of automobile production.

An interesting occurrence in these years that sprang largely from the sharp boosts in gasoline prices was the widespread interest in diesel-engined passenger cars. Mercedes-Benz had produced almost 2,000 of them in the late 1930s, mostly for taxicab use. This company returned to the field in 1949 and gradually expanded its output. In the mid-1950s Peugeot, the French automaker possessing the most experience with diesel engines, also offered diesel passenger cars. The oil crisis of 1973–74 put the spotlight on these cars because of their 25-percent greater fuel efficiency. Sales of these companies' diesel models soared. Soon other leading producers offered diesel cars: Nissan, Opel, Citroën, Volkswagen, Oldsmobile, Fiat, and Toyota. In 1978 Mercedes-Benz installed a small exhaust-driven turbine to force more air into the cylinders of its diesel cars. This raised their performance to levels equivalent to gasoline models. In 1980 some 4.3 percent of new passenger cars sold in the United States were diesel powered, a proportion that would continue to rise.

Diesel engines had already conquered the heavy-truck market, in Europe by the late 1930s and in the United States during the 1950s. Then this engine began to be used in light trucks too; Europe again led the way because of higher gasoline prices. Daimler-Benz was the most successful of the European heavy diesel manufacturers, and the British Perkins Company made more small diesel engines than anyone else. In the United States, the Cummins firm of Columbus, Indiana, outpaced all the others, even GM, in diesels for heavy trucks.

In the United States, 1979 marked the beginning of a longer and deeper automobile recession than the preceding one, and it had a different character. Added to a normal cyclical drop in demand was a massive movement, caused by the second oil "shock," toward fuel-economic, European-sized cars, hitherto largely absent from the lines offered by the domestic manufacturers. From 1978 to 1979, Chrysler's production dropped by 24 percent, Ford 19 percent, and GM 6.3 percent. From 1979 to 1980, the decline continued, 29 percent for Chrysler, 35 percent for Ford, and 21 percent for GM, while sales of imports, especially from Japan, rose 3 percent. This alarming situation brought Chrysler to the edge of bankruptcy, forced it to appeal to the federal government for financial aid, and required it to sell most of its subsidiaries in Europe, South America, and Australia. Ford and GM announced the most spectacular financial losses in their histories.

The technological and size revolution underway since 1976 by the American giants, aiming toward production of "world cars" and costing an unprecedented amount of new investment, is not over. The first of these "world cars"—that is, those adapted to markets in most regions of the world and assembled from parts supplied by subsid-

iaries all over the globe—the Ford Escort, was launched in the fall of
1980. It joined the Chrysler K cars and in 1981 the new GM J-series
of small cars.

The recession struck the European automotive industries in their
turn in 1980. From 1979 to 1980, French production dropped 6
percent, German 8 percent, British 12 percent, and Italian 20 percent. Even Spain and Brazil were not saved from a recession that
seems likely to continue into 1981 and which, paradoxically, has
allowed Japanese automobile production to continue to advance. In
1980 Japan overtook the United States to become the world's leading
producer of motor vehicles. This spectacular advance was based entirely on exports to industrialized countries. Confronting a stagnant
market at home, the Japanese manufacturers adopted an aggressive
marketing strategy, depending on very competitive prices, springing
in turn from a productivity that surpassed their European and American competition as well as on a chronic undervaluation of the yen. In
1980 Japanese exports of passenger cars rose 35 percent, allowing
the different firms to increase their shares of various markets. In the
European Common Market, their share rose from 7.3 percent in
1979 to 9.6 percent in 1980, despite the maintenance of import
restrictions in Italy, France, and Britain.

In the face of this Japanese tide, European and American governments, anxious over the future of their own auto industries, considered measures to limit Japanese imports by quotas or by agreements with Japan to voluntarily limit exports. These actions seemed
particularly justified because the Japanese market remained virtually
closed to foreign cars. A return to generalized protectionism is not in
sight, at least not in the medium term. Nevertheless, the major
Japanese manufacturers seem to be adopting three new policies: establishing manufacturing operations overseas (Honda and Nissan in
the United States); making coproduction agreements (Honda with
British Leyland, Toyota possibly with Ford in the United States, and
Nissan with Alfa-Romeo in Italy); and buying an interest in a local
company (Toyota with Seat in Spain).

The 1980s will certainly be noted for an accentuation and an
internationalization of competition. The "world cars" of GM, Ford,
and Chrysler are in the first instance the means to reconquer the
North American market, but they are also, looking further ahead,
the beginning of an offensive on a world scale. In 1990 only those
manufacturers having annual capacities of more than 2 million vehicles will survive, along with those specialized in luxury machines,
such as BMW, Mercedes-Benz, and Rolls Royce.

A further move toward international oligopoly in the world automobile industry cannot be avoided. This tendency began after the recession of 1973–75 and has accelerated since 1979 because of the initiative of French and Japanese manufacturers. Renault has taken part control of Mack Trucks, of American Motors (46 percent) and of Volvo (passenger car division); it has raised its shareholding in Diesel Nacional (Mexico), and signed agreements to build factories in Portugal and Colombia. The Peugeot group has begun an arrangement to cooperate with Chrysler on the financial, commercial, and soon the industrial level, after having bought Chrysler's European subsidiaries in 1978 and operated them under the name Talbot. Peugeot has also signed a coproduction agreement with Fiat to make a small engine.

Still, at this point, most knowledgeable observers believe that present trends represent only the first steps of a major reorganization of the industry. As they see it, buyouts, mergers, and coproduction agreements for parts or even entire models will multiply in the next few years, and will eventuate in the continued existence of only a few significant manufacturers on an international scale. The seven names most commonly advanced as the eventual survivors should not be surprising: General Motors, Ford, Toyota, Nissan, Volkswagen, Renault, and Peugeot.

In the history of the world automobile industry, the decades of the 1970s and 1980s will take their place as a phase of fundamental change and upheaval that ended some three decades of euphoric growth. This industry's expansion, until now judged as essential by economists in the developed countries, has been profoundly changed. Prospects for the next decade are hardly optimistic: very slow growth on the European, American, and Japanese markets, and an acceleration, though with a rather small volume, on other markets in conditions of rigorous competition. Although not destined for decline, the world automobile industry is on the brink of a new period of structural and technological change.

The Expansion of Demand

The market for automobiles, like most markets for durable goods, passed through three stages, during which it grew and changed, as the earlier chapters have demonstrated. The United States arrived at the third stage before the outbreak of the Second World War. Europe in turn is about to reach this stage. The communist countries and the Third World are just emerging from the first phase and are about to enter the second, that of rapid growth (see table 9–4).

In the United States, 85 percent of new cars are sold to private persons; the rest to business firms and fleet buyers. These proportions have remained constant over the years 1955–80. Replacement demand forms the bulk of the American market. In 1980 more than 95 percent of the households buying a new car already owned a car, and only 15 percent of them retained it. Eighty percent of the new car buyers sold, traded in, or scrapped an older car when they bought their new one. The same proportions operated for business firms and fleets.

Consequently, the steady growth of total registrations and of the rate of motorization since 1950—one car per 1.9 persons in 1979 against one per 4 in 1950—is attributable for the most part to multi-motorization. About 85 percent of American families owned at least one car in 1980, and more than 45 percent of them owned at least two, an increase from only 15 percent in 1960. The extreme sensitivity of this replacement demand and of multimotorization to such changing economic conditions as variations in purchasing power and credit terms explains the wide variations in annual sales by American manufacturers. They have varied by a ratio of one to two: from sales of 4.1 million cars in 1958 to nearly 9.4 million in 1973. The decision to buy a replacement car or to purchase a second or even a third can be postponed easily from one year to the next.

Actually, as L. J. White has accurately pointed out, "although automobiles may be a necessity in modern American life . . . *new* cars are for the most part in the luxury good category."[94] Except for cases of a "necessity" replacement due to accident or the age of the car, "at any given moment in time, most consumers are able to defer their demand for new cars and get along with their old ones for a while longer."[95] In most American households possessing cars, the average length of car ownership is approximately three and a half years. Scarcely 7 percent of American families purchase a new car every year, 13 percent every two years, and 20 percent every three years, thereby nourishing an active used-car market.

Despite the constant growth in their incomes, the least-well-off social groups find it difficult to become car owners. Those who do succeed usually do so with a used car. Unlike the situation in the household appliance field (television sets, refrigerators, washing machines, etc.), where family ownership may approach 100 percent, it seems impossible that the proportion of families owning cars will rise, for the 15 percent who lack them represent the "unfree" in American society, such as the elderly and the handicapped.

Table 9-4.

Number of Motor Vehicles per 1,000 Population,
Selected Countries, 1950–1979

	1950	1960	1970	1973	1979
United States	260	340	430	475	527
France	40	110	240	265	355
W. Germany	40	90	230	260	357
Britain	50	110	210	240	256
Italy	15	30	190	230	303
Japan	—	5	80	130	185
Spain	—	10	65	100	175
Brazil	—	10	30	50	59
Argentina	5	10	60	75	94
Soviet Union	—	—	10	15	19

Sources: National statistical annuals, *Argus*. Figures have been rounded.

Therefore, the future extension of the American market appears rather limited. During the recession of 1973–75, the registration of new cars dropped more than 26 percent. The annual average increase in total passenger cars from 1960 to 1974 (3.4 percent) will be difficult to reach in the future. Still, yearly demand probably cannot fall below an estimated 5 million automobiles needed for "essential" replacement and to supply the demand from the wealthy.

In Europe, on the contrary, the market has not yet reached the stage where it can be analyzed in terms of "essential" replacements. European markets are much less developed than the American one. The most highly motorized country, Sweden, in 1973 was at the American level of 1956, or one car per 3.1 inhabitants. Also in 1973, West Germany, France, and Switzerland barely reached the American level of 1950, one car per 4 inhabitants. Britain, Italy, and the Low Countries stood at an even lower level, and the less developed countries, Spain, Portugal, and Greece, had yet to pass the level of one car per 5 inhabitants, a figure the United States had reached in 1922.

However, automobile registrations are growing more rapidly in Western European countries than in the United States. On the average, they rose tenfold from 1950 to 1974 in Western Europe and two and one-half times in the United States. Europe's secondary position shows up in figures on family ownership of cars. Although in Sweden some 75 percent of families were motorized in 1979, France, Switzerland, and Italy hardly exceeded 70 percent, West Germany 65 percent, and Britain 55 percent. Only rare European families own two or more cars, about 10 percent on the average in most countries. Because the proportion of families owning cars can still increase and because multimotorization is just beginning, European markets are far from zero growth.

Most studies predicting future European demand rest on the American model. But two significant factors differentiate Europe from the United States. Evident in the major European metropolises is a relative undermotorization, encouraged by the existence of public transit systems and aggravated by a "de-motorization" movement generated and fed by problems of traffic and parking. In Paris, for example, of 100 families that could own cars, taking account of the proportion of people employed and of age and income levels, only 64 actually do.[96] Families that have never owned a car represent three-fifths of the undermotorization, and those who have given up their car are two-fifths, a considerable share. The number that have abandoned the automobile is three times larger than would be expected from normal changes in age and income.

Although the internationalization of European markets resulting from the creation of the European Economic Community (Common Market) and the Free Trade Area did allow a relative homogenization of the style and technology of vehicles, differences remain in the average power of cars. French and Italian models have significantly less power. In France those having engines of less than five fiscal horsepower account for 32 percent of the total, and in Italy nearly 50 percent. Elsewhere in Western Europe, especially in West Germany, the intermediate size (1,000 to 1,750 cc.) is preponderant. Additionally, the average age of French, German, and British cars is relatively higher than elsewhere in Europe. In 1971, about 21 percent of British, 24 percent of French, and 26 percent of West German cars were less than three years old, in contrast to nearly 35 percent in the Low Countries, Switzerland, and Portugal, 31 percent in Italy, and 45 percent in Spain.

The disparities that still exist among the tax systems and technical regulations continue to limit free trade in Western Europe. In that area, taxes weigh most heavily on French cars. The rate of the value-added tax is 33.3 percent of the basic price in France, but only 12 percent in West Germany, 12 or 18 percent according to engine size in Italy, and 23 percent in Britain. Registration taxes are small or nonexistent in most countries except for France—20 francs ($4.50) per fiscal horsepower—and Italy. The annual tax on car ownership is set at the same rate everywhere. In sum, the French automobile owner pays the state 37 percent more than his German neighbor and 16 percent more than the average European.

In both the United States and Europe, the sensitivity of the automobile market to cyclical changes in the ratio of cost of acquisition to income explains the large fluctuations in sales from one year to the next. This sensitivity has led the governments in the major industrial states to pay particular attention to the automobile market in their economic policies. Tax increases, changes in credit arrangements (increases in down payments and reductions in length of loans), and boosts in prices of automobiles and fuels have led to major fluctuations in the demand for cars. These measures usually are associated with antiinflationary policies aimed at holding down consumption by means of temporary regulations, either by raising the price of certain goods or by limiting the increase of purchasing power through wage controls. Although these plans do not affect automobiles alone, they almost always include some specific provisions aimed at automobiles.

The economic slowdown plan in West Germany in 1966, which for the economy as a whole brought a decline of 10 percent in the gross national product in 1967, resulted in a 10-percent drop in new-car registrations. In addition to credit restriction through higher interest rates and larger down payments, the government chose to raise taxes, especially on cars. The Italian and French antiinflation plans of 1963–64 had followed the same policies. The sharp drop in the demand for cars in the 1973–75 period came in part from the various antiinflationary measures decreed by the majority of the West European governments.

In Japan, the real expansion in ownership of passenger cars began only in 1961. Previously, the bulk of motor vehicles comprised trucks and three-wheeled vehicles. For example, in 1955, for 500 inhabitants there were four three-wheelers, two trucks, and only one passenger car. From 1961 to 1973, the number of passenger cars registered increased twenty-two times, an average progression of 27 percent annually, against a 19.5 percent annual growth in commercial vehicles. This boom in domestic demand occurred without interruptions. The rate of increase of new car registrations rose considerably from 1967 but then declined in 1971.

The Japanese market absorbed 500,000 new cars in 1964, 750,000 in 1966, 1,130,000 in 1967, 2,380,000 in 1970, 2,930,000 in 1973 and 3,100,000 in 1979. The level of motorization also rose rapidly, reaching 185 passenger cars per 1,000 inhabitants in 1973, compared with 5 in 1960. The recent date of the automobile revolution in Japan explains the newness of the automobiles in service and the relatively low proportion of families owning cars. In 1973 some 76.4 percent of passenger cars were less than five years old and 46.1 percent less than three years. In 1961 industrial firms, public authorities, and fleets registered 86 percent of new passenger cars; in 1966 the figure was 67 percent. By 1979, however, private families raised their share to 75 percent.

In comparison with the United States and Western Europe, considerably fewer Japanese families own cars: in 1970 only 22 percent of them. But growth has been rapid, for by 1973 the proportion reached almost 36 percent and 50 percent by 1979. Understandably, multimotorization has not yet occurred. The Japanese market, nonetheless, is characterized by some particular physical limits that do not seem to have operated in the United States and Western Europe. Of primary importance, the country has limited space available, further restricted by the extensive mountainous regions that have forced a concentration of activities and population in the coastal regions. A rate of motorization equal to that of Western Europe in 1975 would lead in Japan to a total saturation of its roads, streets, and cities. Unless palliated by a major technical innovation, it would raise the level of pollution and other nuisances to an extent that the public would find unacceptable.

In the communist countries, motorization is at a much lower level: 12 vehicles per 1,000 persons in 1979. Although the level was 19 in the USSR, China brought the average down with 0.8 vehicle per 1,000. The authorities in these countries for many years concerned themselves primarily with fostering the growth of heavy industry. Since 1970, however, they have acted to satisfy an increasing demand for consumer goods, notably passenger cars, by organizing automobile production and an automobile market, both assured of relative stability by the large excess of demand over supply. In this connection, it is interesting to note that the Soviet Union was, along with Brazil, one of the rare major automobile manufacturing countries not hit by the 1973–75 recession. Nevertheless, automobile markets in the communist countries remain rather undeveloped. Access to car ownership is limited both by the level of income, or more exactly by the purchasing power represented by this income, and by the supply of vehicles offered to consumers.

In the Soviet Union, where the annual average wage at present is about $2,667, the purchase of a car requires years of financial sacrifice or the holding of two jobs. In 1974 the small Zaporojetz model (forty horsepower) represented two years' wages, the Moskvitch two and a half years', the Jigouli from three to four years' depending on the model, and the Volga five years' wages. But it is not enough to have saved up the purchase price. The Soviet citizen who wants to buy a car must also be patient. The organization responsible for selling and buying automobiles, Autoexport, in 1974 had only 600,000 vehicles to meet a larger and larger private demand. A prospective buyer needed to sign up on a waiting list in one of the rare state stores specializing in this trade. The delays are long: almost a year in Moscow and three years in Minsk, for example. The full price is paid in cash several days before delivery. Often the final preparation of the car leaves something to be desired. In addition, each auto factory maintains its own priority system, for its management has an annual quota of cars that it delivers to its workers who have signed up on a waiting list.

Used cars are also scarce and expensive. For many years, there was no legal market for them so a black market flourished, but recently the state stepped in. Now, the prospective purchaser of a used car must sign up on a waiting list at one of the few specialized state "Kommission" Stores—there is only one in Moscow—and pay a 7-percent tax on delivery. A sale directly between individuals remains strictly forbidden. All kinds of "arrangements" have grown up to circumvent the official system. For new cars, one method consists in signing up on several waiting lists, and, when the car finally arrives, reselling it immediately at a large profit. On sales between private persons, the seller retains legal ownership, but signs an official document authorizing the buyer to drive his car.

If buying a car is onerous, it is just as difficult to maintain and operate it. Moscow has some 400,000 privately owned cars, but less than 50 repair garages, and the situation in Moscow is better than in any other city. It takes a long time to repair a car: six, seven, or even eight months. Garages also frequently lack spare parts. Such a situation tends to favor black-market repair and do-it-yourself tinkering. Soviet vehicles endure rough treatment, however. Snow and ice make driving dangerous for about five months a year. Accidents tend not to be severe but frequent. The bad state of roads—those having asphalt surfaces remain rare despite a construction program of 15,500 miles per year—and cold weather, which immobilizes cars for many months, results in their rapid deterioration. Vehicle inspection by a special police unit, the GAI, is required annually and further complicates the life of the Soviet motorist. Automobile service stations are infrequent, and, despite the relatively low price of gasoline, it can be difficult and dangerous to undertake long private automobile trips between cities.

Charged for years with being a "symbol of bourgeois property," and then for some time reserved as a means of transportation only for the officials of the Soviet regime, the automobile has become the object of everyone's eager desire. A luxury, it remains a sign of social ascent and even of a kind of social differentiation.

This attitude toward the automobile characterizes not only the communist countries but also the entire Third World. The motor car in the underdeveloped countries fascinates a population whose purchasing power remains quite low. In all the Third World—except for the communist countries of Asia—9 vehicles (5 of them passenger cars) were registered for 1,000 persons in 1968.[97] Little has changed since that date. Population growth has kept pace with the increasing number of vehicles. To understand the true level of motorization in these countries, the fleets of taxicabs, which represent a large share of the passenger cars, should be subtracted. The automobile continues to be a privilege of the well-to-do.

Low average income is not the only hindrance to expanding the demand for vehicles in the Third World. Other factors include the lack of highways in rural areas and their inadequacy in cities, ineffective distribution networks for fuel and repair, and a lack of trained mechanics.

As a generator of employment, as a reputed "leading" industry because it carries on its coattails a group of other activities—steel making, machine tools, and the like—and because its products are necessary for improved transportation, automobile manufacturing appeals to the leaders of the underdeveloped countries as one of the key solutions to their economic problems. As yet, however, the very limited demand in Third World countries usually has not reached a level that would justify the establishment of a local automobile industry. A current estimate suggests that a completely domestic industry is possible in a country where the total annual demand comes close to 200,000 passenger cars and 50,000 commercial vehicles.[98] This would include Argentina and Brazil, which already have reached the levels of motorization very much above the Third World average. These countries are exceptions because for several years they have been in the process of relative industrial takeoff. The large majority of Third World countries remain in a position that justifies only an assembly industry under foreign licenses. Such assembly can be considered where annual demand reaches 10,000 cars and 5,000 trucks.

Nevertheless, the communist countries and the Third World appear to be the major markets of the future. They need trucks to enhance their domestic transportation networks and to overcome the weaknesses of their railway systems, or to avoid extending them.

They need buses to meet the need for public transportation within and among cities. Additionally, the rising incomes of an increasing fraction of their populations ought to advance the market for an expanding number of passenger cars.

Everywhere in the world, except in the communist countries, all the techniques are used to encourage motorization and thereby stimulate the demand for cars. Automobile manufacturers and dealers, banks and other financial institutions, insurance companies, and even governments all find this to be in their interest and earn considerable sums from it. The automobile press attracts readers by using more and more illustrations. Advertising methods are perfected to manipulate consumers. Such methods basically rest on the symbolic values of the automobile and vary according to the social level at which a particular model is aimed. For prestige cars, advertising often focuses, as L. Boltanski points out, "on the principle of contrasting the elegant with the ordinary, such as free space with crowding, elites with the masses. This associates . . . the position of the vehicle in the structure of distribution of goods, and the position of its owners in the structure of classes and in the structure of distribution of the space between classes."[99] Each model receives its own image, a symbolic representation of the social characteristics of those who buy it.

The growth of credit facilities since the Second World War has largely accelerated the spread of private automobiles. Various credit systems—installment loans on the car itself, personal loans, leasing —have brought into the automobile market the less wealthy social groups, who do not hesitate to go into debt to obtain a car even though this may bring privation in other areas, especially their housing. In France, for example, 45 percent of new cars are bought on credit, but this proportion varies according to the size of the car. It reaches 60 percent for small cars of two to four fiscal horsepower rating and only 35 percent for cars at the top of the line. The 1970s have seen the success of leasing, nonexistent earlier, but now accounting for 6-7 percent of new cars in France.

By making automobile insurance obligatory, public authorities have inevitably enhanced the fortunes of insurance companies, who have offered more and more complex and more and more expensive policies.

In the industrialized countries, support for the automobile market has come from the spread of networks of garages and service stations that have become more and more numerous, specialized, and well equipped. Designed to handle the sale and maintenance of complex vehicles for which demand is growing as well as the repair of a ceaselessly increasing number of cars damaged by accidents, the garages have experienced a rapid and steady growth in their business.

Problems have emerged, nevertheless. In this United States, competition among dealers led to more aggressive sales practices. In the mid-1950s a minority of them adopted such amoral sales methods and provided such shabby service that a senatorial committee did not hesitate to speak of "the morality of an oriental bazaar" in reference to their activities.[100] Relations have not always run smoothly between Americn manufacturers and their dealers. In 1953 conflict broke out between them. The dealers complained that manufacturers interfered in the dealers' business, that they cancelled or failed to renew dealers' contracts without justification, that they sold cars in competition with their own dealers, and engaged in other violations of accepted business practice. These strained circumstances led the federal government to intervene in 1956 with the Automobile Dealers' Day in Court Act, which established a higher level of fair dealing and trust in their relations. Primarily, however, it encouraged the manufacturers to take it upon themselves to revise the contracts in a direction more favorable to the dealers.

In Europe, automobile dealers experienced the same difficulties as in the United States. Their professional associations have negotiated directly with the manufacturers about such matters, and, as in the United States, they have worked to obtain favorable legislation. In the 1960s competition among the European producers brought many changes in the signs in front of dealers' showrooms as they jumped from one marque to another following the offers made by the manufacturers. The same struggle in the dealer network goes on in the Third World countries, but it is made more acute by the scarcity of repair facilities.

Another stimulus to the auto market was the spread of new forms of tourism that had originated in the United States. Since the Second World War, camping and the use of trailers made automobiles more attractive as a means of individual transportation. This automobile tourism on weekends and vacations involves nearly half the automobile traffic in Europe today. It is a major factor in the growth of the annual distance traveled per automobile. It can be explained by the extension of express highways and by rising standards of living. In Europe also, the generalization and lengthening of paid vacations have played a part. Automobile tourism has brought new kinds of accommodations and food service: motels and expressway restaurants. It has also made international tourism easier, and for young people who hitchhike made it possible to travel easily and cheaply.

The success of rent-a-car arrangements in the industrial countries since the Second World War has been another spur to demand. Companies specialized in this service, of which Avis, Hertz, and Europcar are the most important, have enjoyed remarkable success and have become powerful multinational operations, aided by the growth of air travel.

Conclusion

The rapid motorization in the industrial countries has led to a considerable democratization of the automobile. This massive spread of cars has worked selectively. In France, for example, studies made by the government statistical office demonstrate that the difference in the amount of motorization between the least motorized groups (farm workers, domestic servants, laborers, and semiskilled workers) and that of the most highly motorized categories (higher executives, professionals, and owners of large businesses) stayed about the same from 1953 to 1969. As L. Boltanski observes, "the spread between the different social classes tends to continue, or, to put it differently, the structure of distribution of automobiles among classes tends to repeat itself" despite some catching up by the middle classes.[101] Multimotorization in France so far affects only the most motorized groups and is just beginning to appear in some others (small businessmen and middle executives). On the other hand, over a quarter of semiskilled workers and laborers are still driving their first car.

Different levels of motorization means that, except for North America, the automobile is not integrated into the banality of daily life—as are refrigerators and washing machines, goods whose usage is customary and arouses no comment. Because large differences remain among different cars as to price, size, performance, and comfort, the spread of the automobile, rapid as it has been, has met social and ideological opposition to the extent that everywhere in the world it has remained a symbol of luxury. It is common for the intellectual sections of the dominant classes to provide the exception that proves the rule. They do this when they try to differentiate themselves from those at the same or higher economic levels, but at a lower cultural level, by buying less prestigious and cheaper cars than their incomes would permit. As to those social categories almost fully supplied with automobiles (where 90 percent own one), these people can always purchase a more luxurious car or a second one.

In the 1970s, the relative difference in the rates of motorization between the underdeveloped and the industrialized nations has persisted. In this regard, Japan figures as in the "middle class." Nonetheless, world demand for cars will continue to grow. It appears likely it will stabilize in the United States, increase slowly in Western Europe, and expand rapidly in the communist nations and the Third World. Because of these prospects, public authorities will have an expanding role. Indeed, it is the governments that will be expected to take the initiative, to an unequal degree except for the United States, where the financial strength of the manufacturers and the principle of government neutrality in the marketplace will hold it back, though the Chrysler case now calls this into question. In the underdeveloped and communist countries, the state handles the creation of an automobile industry. In Western Europe, in addition to Alfa-Romeo three of the four major manufacturers have come under state control or have been nationalized since the war: Volkswagen (1938) and Renault (1944), joined by British Leyland in 1975. Frequently European governments have encouraged mergers among manufacturers. The West European states have acted not only to assure the survival of a national industry by stepping forward to take the place of traditional financial institutions that have admitted their inability to keep it going. They also see in the nationalized companies a special device by which to improve their balance of international payments, to advance economically depressed regions, and to contribute to national economic growth.

Still, since the early 1970s, government interventionist policies have lost some of their effectiveness. Both nationalized and private companies have become multinational in their structures and in their policies. Table 9–5 lists them by size. In their activities abroad, the nationalized firms have gained more autonomy with regard to their own governments. Mergers among manufacturers have become more and more transnational. In sum, it seems doubtful if the European states' control over their automobile industries will remain very effective in the face of this growing internationalization, despite these governments' burgeoning interventions and the results of their actions on the domestic demand for automobiles.

Will the recent and foreseeable expansion in the communist and Third World countries challenge the hegemony of the western manufacturers? It is not impossible. But these latter companies do hold two high trump cards: a mastery of modern technologies, and control of the men who can bring them to fruition.

Table 9-5.
*World's Leading Motor Vehicle Manufacturers, 1979
(including foreign subsidiaries)*

Rank	Company	Nationality	1979 Production
1.	General Motors	United States	8,812,380
2.	Ford	United States	5,501,763
3.	Toyota	Japan	2,996,225
4.	Volkswagen-Audi	W. Germany	2,426,210
5.	Nissan (Datsun)	Japan	2,380,254
6.	Peugeot-Citroën	France	2,283,644
7.	Renault	France	1,867,517
8.	Fiat	Italy	1,432,919
9.	Chrysler	United States	1,231,691
10.	Toyo Kogyo (Mazda)	Japan	971,421
11.	Mitsubishi	Japan	938,517
12.	Honda	Japan	801,869
13.	Lada	Soviet Union	715,000
14.	British Leyland	United Kingdom	628,420
15.	Daimler-Benz	W. Germany	604,859
16.	Isuzu	Japan	424,718
17.	Daihatsu	Japan	366,345
18.	Volvo	Sweden	352,000
19.	Suzuki	Japan	344,845
20.	American Motors	United States	343,194
21.	Fuji (Subaru)	Japan	334,290
22.	BMW	W. Germany	328,281

10. Automobiles and Technical Progress since 1945

Jean-Jacques Chanaron

"Great as have been the engineering advances since 1920, we have today basically the same kind of machine that was created in the first twenty years of the century," wrote Alfred Sloan, former president of General Motors (GM), in 1964.[102] The major advances have not altered the character of the vehicles; they have served primarily to improve the power-to-weight ratio and to extend the durability of cars. True technical innovations have been rare, especially since the Second World War. In passenger cars, only the spread of devices developed earlier, such as automatic transmissions in the United States and front-wheel drive in Europe, has occurred, or the cautious introduction of new materials such as aluminum and plastics or advanced technologies such as electronic components.

Unlike the situation in earlier periods, most technical advances for cars have come from industries outside auto manufacturing, such as steel, petrochemicals, rubber tires, and glass. The few striking innovations by automakers since 1945 have come from Europe and for years were installed only on a few luxury cars: the rotary engine, air suspension, and electronic fuel injection. The use of diesel engines in passenger cars was simply an adaptation of this power plant from light trucks. As for trucks and buses, though they have profited from the considerable improvements in diesel engines and in methods of production and assembly, the industry has not succeeded with the gas turbine, widely viewed in the early 1950s as the technology of the future. Such relative technological stagnation in the industry does not characterize recent years only. It has simply become accentuated after the Second World War, especially in the United States. It affects almost all the auto manufacturers in the West and those in the communist countries as well, so that it appears to be in the very logic and nature of the industry's development.

The Subordination of Innovation

Automobile technology today seems to be the result of a policy clearly subordinating it to considerations of profit and marketing strategy. Widely adopted by the major American manufacturers early in the 1920s, this Sloanist approach flourishes today more than ever. Only at the beginning of the 1960s did most of the European manufacturers adopt it. Earlier, lacking very large markets, they usually had concentrated their production on two models. The leading Japanese automakers followed the Sloan policy, a little later but with less delay than the Europeans. Above a certain level of production, it is a logical response to the requirements of marketing: it aims to provide an outlet for large-scale production and yet adapt the technical characteristics and design of vehicles to a wider variety of useful functions and to a growing segmentation of markets due to differences in purchasers' incomes. Western Europe, however, by its recent success with multifunctional models, has diverged somewhat from the United States and Japan.

Sloanism—the policy of a wide range of models—boils down to multiplying the different combinations of as few as possible standardized parts and covering them with distinct and regularly changing exteriors. This explains the increase in the number of models and variants based on the same mechanical elements, which often remain unchanged for many years. The engine powering the Chevrolets of the 1970s dated from the immediate postwar years, and the one on the recent Citroën CX model is identical to that of the DS of 1954, itself derived directly from that of the 1934 front-wheel-drive model.

The amazing spread of automobiles since 1950 has gradually reduced the symbolic value of car ownership. No longer able to count on the attraction of scarcity alone, manufacturers have come to make the technology of their vehicles reflect social hierarchies and differences. The multiplication of models and versions—"deluxe," "custom deluxe," "sport," etc.—along with "design," "styling," and "gadgetization," exemplify this policy.

While narrowly conceived marketing requirements explain why producers have engaged in as little innovation as possible on their cars, the need to maximize productivity explains why most of their technological effort has aimed at production methods. In this area, they have made important progress, automating a growing number of tasks. Step by step, they have introduced automatic transfer machines to make mechanical parts such as motor blocks and transmissions. Numerically controlled machine tools perform various kinds of metal-cutting jobs, like drilling, boring, punching, and milling. Recently, robot machines have taken over some spot-welding operations. The computerization of many functions—communication among different operations and control of the production of models and options such as color and upholstery according to customer orders—is another outstanding recent innovation in production methods and organization.

The technological policy of almost all manufacturers has become more and more closely tied to the economic and industrial necessities of very large-scale production. This has led to a growing specialization of jobs, even among automobile engineers. Beside research engineers, design engineers try to reach a compromise among the technical, industrial, and sales requirements, and test engineers measure the reliability and safety of the vehicles. Methods engineers translate the plans of the design offices into production operations. The development of this group, some 10 percent of the total engineers, fits exactly into the logic of the contemporary technological strategy of the automobile industry. Production engineers control quality and ensure continuity of manufacture, and customer-relations engineers maintain liaison between the clientele and the factory. Finally, management engineers coordinate all these functions.

A variety of factors all seem to produce technological inertia. The automobile industry's oligopolistic structure limits the circumstances and opportunities for innovation. Twenty huge producers share the world market and compete bitterly, largely over price. But technology often causes higher prices, which cannot be absorbed by a demand especially sensitive to price variations and for which technical factors tend not to determine choices. This is why, at least in part, some significant innovations in recent years have been introduced at the top of the line before appearing on the mass-market cars: the hydropneumatic suspension of Citroën first on the DS and then on the GS, the rotary engine on the RO 80 of NSU and then on the

Japanese Mazda, the variable-assist steering on the Citroën SM and then on the CX, and diesel engines on expensive Mercedes-Benz models.

Hence, supply and demand operate together to leave only a limited opening for the introduction of new technology. This conclusion is confirmed by a number of indications, such as the failure to introduce important devices—antiskid brakes, for example—delays in the adoption of new materials, or the decision of the manufacturers, which seemed natural at the time, to improve the traditional techniques rather than adopting new ones as a way of reducing automobile nuisances such as noise, pollution, and safety hazards.

To explain the industry's technological conservatism, there were powerful factors favoring rigidity, added to the requirements of always more vigorous competition. The automobile industry is, actually, a capital-intensive business, whose investment costs are continually rising. At present, it is estimated that the cost of a complete manufacturing and assembly plant capable of turning out 300,000 vehicles a year would be more than $900 million. Motor car manufacturing also requires much labor. Directly and indirectly, it employs a significant share of the labor force of the countries where it is well established: 4.5 percent in Japan, 5.1 percent in the United States, 7.5 percent in Italy, 9.4 percent in Britain, 9.8 percent in France, and 11.2 percent in Germany. The introduction of major innovations would require expensive alterations in production methods and precedents suggest this probably would bring serious labor difficulties.

The durable nature of automobiles tends to discourage manufacturers from adopting unusual innovations, or even rapid improvements, for the launching of a "revolutionary" model would tend to reduce sharply the value of cars based on older designs. This would be an expensive and socially undesirable cost of technical progress. The favorable aspects of such a new model, a stimulation of demand and a reduction of energy consumption, among others, would not directly offset the negative effects of a collapse of the used-car market, a market whose dynamism has much to do with the health of the new-car business.[103]

Still, the stability of the technical policies of the major manufacturers has been challenged by changes that have occurred in recent years in the economic, social, and political environment of the automobile. One factor, to begin with, is the emergence of a current of thought critical of the classic automobile that may bring public authorities to pressure the manufacturers through rules and prohibitions rather than the usual encouragement. In addition, increases in the price of petroleum fuels may work out to favor alternatives to the internal-combustion engine. Research on entirely new power plants may make them economically feasible at the same time as the seriousness of the problems of urban transportation makes them socially necessary.

So the automobile industry may soon reach a major turning point in its history and insist upon innovation, thereby overturning its rules and traditions so as to ensure its continued existence.[104]

National Divergences

The classic differences between European and American cars were underscored by the situation after 1945. Such differences became more pronounced until the mid-1960s, but then moderated sharply. The application of safety and then antipollution standards, the growing problem of urban automobile congestion, and concern over oil shortages all encouraged American manufacturers to slow down the race for bigger engines, more power, and larger overall dimensions.

The reasons for these transatlantic differences in development seem to spring from geographic and especially socioeconomic factors closely related to differences in the size of the market—both average purchasing power and size of the population—and tax systems. American drivers continue to use their cars more than those elsewhere. In 1978 the average annual mileage per car was about 10,000 in the United States, compared with 8,560 in France, 8,680 in England, and 9,000 in West Germany.

The quality and extent of the American highway network—38,700 miles of interstate expressways in 1978—have helped to orient automobile technology toward cars capable of running for long periods with a minimum of mechanical difficulties, that is, toward large engines with plenty of reserve power. The same is true of West Germany to a lesser degree, but in France the density of the highway network, the winding character of the roads, and the absence of large-capacity highways all work in favor of small cars equipped with reliable brakes, transmissions, and steering mechanisms to meet the heavy demands on them. However, the gap between the average annual mileage of Americans and Europeans has narrowed since the early 1970s.

The differing nature of cities has played an important part also. European cities long antedate automobiles, and so are poorly adapted to them. Growing traffic and parking problems have led European manufacturers to reduce the size of their cars to the minimum compatible with the performance and service their owners expect of them. The younger American cities have been built (and rebuilt) with reference to automobiles. The unprecedented urban and suburban growth of the last two decades has given rise to metropolitan areas dozens of miles across, linked by huge urban expressway systems and broad streets which, among other things, have allowed the widespread use of automatic transmissions.

By encouraging the dispersion of residences to the periphery of cities, by increasing the distances among places of employment, commercial and entertainment centers, and residences, and thereby accentuating the move toward motorization, the automobile has made itself a necessity to the point of creating new problems of noise, air pollution, traffic congestion, waste of energy, and esthetic ugliness. This situation, approaching the threshold of intolerability as in Los Angeles since the 1960s, should by all logic lead manufacturers and buyers to adopt less ponderous cars. It certainly has contributed to weakening the tendencies toward bigger size and horsepower in the United States in the last fifteen years.

Differences in the levels of purchasing power and in the cost of buying and operating cars work in the same direction. In the United States, since the Second World War real prices of automobiles have risen gradually but regularly. Nevertheless, increases in average incomes more than compensated for this trend. Consequently, the replacement demand that provides the bulk of total demand, unlike the situation in Europe, depends on factors other than price: comfort, size, power, and gadgets. European consumers, on the contrary, who enjoy less purchasing power, have reacted much more sensitively to the purchase price of new cars. This accounts for the growth and success of the used-car market there. It acts as a kind of "locomotive" for the new-car market, for four used-car transactions occur for each new car purchased.

The European automobile industry could not take as much advantage as the American from mass production because the individual national markets were much smaller in size and exports among them were sharply limited by tariffs and other restrictions until 1960. Just after the Second World War, Europe experienced a situation where purchasing power was low but the need for cars was high. At the same time, the normal inertia caused by fixed investment was a negligible influence because a large part of the production capacity had been destroyed or completely disorganized.

Consequently, the manufacturers in Germany, Britain, France, and

Italy moved toward producing small, mass-market cars. Gradually, as purchasing power rose and a wider spread of incomes appeared and as the real price of fuel fell and that of cars dropped until 1968, buyers began to move toward more expensive cars offering higher power and better performance. Manufacturers enlarged their lines to include bigger models. An improvement in the ratio of personal income to automobile prices favors an increase in the power and size of cars, but it can also foster the introduction of expensive technical innovations and so encourage progress.

Tax policies concerning the cost of buying and operating cars worked in the same direction as geography, population, and economic factors. In 1946 a gallon of gasoline cost ten times more in terms of purchasing power for a French driver than an American. All over Europe, governments rationed it. These factors could only urge manufacturers to recommence production with "economical" cars. After 1960 the ratio of income to gasoline prices rose noticeably—even more in West Germany than in France or Italy—though it remained far below the American level. In 1972 it stood at four times less in France and Italy than in the United States; that is, speaking very generally, based on twice the average consumption of gasoline, the cost of fuel for the American car was roughly half as much as that of the French or Italian car relative to income levels. In Europe, at least 70 percent of the price of gasoline at the pump comprised taxes, compared with under 40 percent in the United States.

Therefore, in the various countries a direct causal relationship can be found between the price of automobile fuel, including taxes, and the engine size and average annual distance traveled between 1955 and 1962. This relationship was confirmed by two factors: in France, the rather sizable increase in gasoline prices after the closing of the Suez Cenal in 1956 corresponded to a noticeable decrease in average engine size; and the shift to diesel engines by 90 percent of European commercial vehicles and by a large part of the taxicabs clearly stemmed from the impact of gasoline prices on the cost of operation. Taxes levied on the purchase and ownership of cars also play a large role, for in the 1970s they increased the real cost by some 40 percent in France, 30 percent in West Germany, and 15 percent in the United States.

In Japan, the market situation, very similar to that which prevailed in Europe in the 1950s—limited purchasing power, vigorous competition among producers, and cities constructed before the Automobile Revolution—led manufacturers to adopt European styles and technologies. Only at the end of the 1960s did they begin to enlarge their range of models.

As the automobile becomes democratized, it seems to be losing its symbolic value. Functional criteria, the adaptation of vehicles to specific uses in specific conditions, are coming to predominate over those of "prestige." Exemplifying this is the movement toward a convergence in the characteristics of American and European vehicles since the mid-1960s. The structure of the American industry seems to have operated as a unifying and conservative force on automobile technology there, while the still vigorous competition on the European market has left some room for technological rivalry. The still fluid structure of the European industry and the technical dynamism of some manufacturers contrast with the hardened structure of the American industry and its tacit status quo in the technical area. In the Soviet Union, the absence of competition is likewise at the root of a certain technological stagnation, despite some achievements of Soviet engineers, especially with engines.

But the movement toward a world market and the increased competition, dominant characteristics of the 1970s that can be expected to intensify in the next few years, are opposed to divergent technological strategies. These constraints will contribute to speeding convergence in the appearance and character of cars made in various parts of the world, and will ultimately result in a virtual unification of techniques and shapes. The "world cars" already are demonstrating this convergence.

Automobile Research

The automobile industry has not escaped the research and development explosion. Its product is a mechanical device that reached maturity quickly, for it soon approximated its general modern form. Despite intensive and expensive research efforts, it has been difficult if not impossible to produce spectacular technological breakthroughs. On the other hand, the automobile's adaptation to the needs and wishes of the clientele has required a constant effort at improvement in design and comfort, as well as gadgets. Until very recently, and especially in the United States, these minor technical adjustments have absorbed a large, if not the greatest, share of research and development expenditures. In other words, the core of the research effort has been devoted to model changes and has been determined almost exclusively by marketing factors.

The few major exceptions have been rare and have come from the smaller firms. They have not been accepted by the entire industry despite the merits, for example, of Citroën's hydropneumatic suspension, first marketed in 1954 on the DS 19, and the Wankel rotary engine, offered initially in 1962 on an NSU model. Nor did the technical emphasis of these companies bring them much success, for NSU was absorbed by Audi and then fell into the hands of Volkswagen; and Citroën, after a decade of economic and financial problems, was absorbed by Peugeot in 1974. It appears that in a competitive market for a widely consumed product technical innovation will bring profits only if a firm maintains a vigorous marketing effort. Higher production costs result from the need to cover not only the expense of research and development but also the additional cost of the innovation itself and its manufacture in relation to that of the system or part that it replaces. Hence, it becomes essential to increase sales and sometimes to raise prices.

The gradual awakening to the social costs of automobiles and the urgent need to reduce or eliminate such costs have provided new targets for the research and design staffs of the automobile industry. Because almost all the manufacturers have raised their research and development budgets, currently the automobile is the mass-market product that incorporates the highest amount of research input, though it has not yet experienced a very spectacular technological development. And yet the cars of 1980 are safer, quieter, and pollute less than those of 1970; and significant progress has occurred in new power plants.

This research effort is worldwide; both private and public research organizations are at work and receive support from public funds. The traditional manufacturers moved in first, but others have also shown an interest in the evolution of automobile technology. The eventual adaptation to automobiles of technologies foreign to the traditional approach has encouraged those in other industrial areas to devote considerable human and financial resources to the problem.

In consequence, the automobile benefits from the efforts of the electric power and electrical equipment industries in the area of motors and generators. New automobile technology also interests the chemical, petroleum, and aerospace industries; private and public laboratories engaged in fundamental or applied research; the mechanical engineering industry, working on gas turbines and Stirling engines; and the metal refiners, who are particularly interested in the application of aluminum. Automobile research occupies thousands of investigators and technicians all over the world and every year devotes large sums to following numerous lines of approach but no major new technological discovery is clearly apparent. Yet is it not characteristic of research to appear uncertain and chancy?

The research effort in the automobile industry varies from one country to another and from one firm to another according to the resources devoted to it and to the technological options chosen. In the United States, only GM and Ford have established large and significant research programs. The size of GM's earnings permits it to investigate all possibilities. In the world's largest automobile research center, opened in 1956 at Warren, Michigan, GM has since 1970 been engaged in research on various kinds of combustion engines: gas and steam turbines, the Stirling engine (which operates by an exchange of heat between a cold cylinder and a warm one), organic fluid engines, steam engines, the Warren engine (a variant of the classic reciprocating type), the stratified-charge engine, and of course, rotary, diesel, and liquified gas engines.

In collaboration with General Electric, which is working on a fuel cell employing hydrogen and oxygen, GM produced in 1966 two prototype electric vehicles, the electrovan and electrocar. It has also made prototypes of hybrid town cars: gasoline/electric, Stirling/electric, or all-electric. Meanwhile, in cooperation with the National Aeronautics and Space Administration (NASA), the company has continued basic research on batteries made of salts melted at high temperatures. Nevertheless, a major part of the GM research effort has been and remains oriented toward improvement of the traditional vehicle by such means as antipollution catalytic converters and safety devices. GM seems to want to be ready to move in any direction to protect itself against any competitor's innovation and ultimately to "freeze" certain ideas by holding key patents itself.

Although ambitious, the programs at Ford are more modest. Its engineers have worked with steam engines and gas turbines, but priority has been accorded to high-temperature sodium/sulfur batteries and to Stirling engines. In these two promising systems, Ford seems to have a lead over its competitors. In 1976 the company displayed a Torino equipped with the first Stirling engine designed for a standard automobile and claimed it could mass produce these engines by 1985. This experimental engine proved to be outstanding in reducing pollution, noise, and fuel consumption. Laboratory tests indicated a 30-percent improvement in efficiency over a standard V-8 engine of similar size and yet its emissions met the strict California standards. Nevertheless, little has been heard of this effort in recent years.

For a long time, two large firms have dominated research on fuel cells. Allis Chalmers, which specializes in machinery for construction and materials handling, was aided for years by the United States Army. General Electric conducts its research in association with

NASA and GM. Technical difficulties involved in miniaturization and the devising of systems that do not require expensive catalysts brought a slackening of research after 1967. Since 1973, it seems, General Dynamics, Exxon Research, and Union Carbide have resumed investigations in this area.

Japanese automobile manufacturers from the 1960s took an interest in the rotary engine, so much so as to be the first to put it into large-scale production: the Mazda car, made by Toyo Kogyo. The two largest Japanese manufacturers, Nissan and Toyota, have produced operating prototypes of cars employing liquified gas. Public authorities, automobile manufacturers, and battery producers have undertaken major efforts with electric cars. Countless projects and prototypes involve lead batteries. The operation of nearly 300 Daihatsu electric cars of the type at the Osaka World's Fair was the most noteworthy and important result. More basic and more promising research continues on better generators of electricity. Sony is working on air/zinc batteries and Yasa Battery on high temperature sodium/sulfur types.

In Europe, West Germany and France stand out in the number of programs and types of technical systems, as well as the progress made on certain projects despite the relatively small sums devoted to all this work. In Germany, the electric car and the rotary engine have attracted most of the private and public research effort. In addition, MAN is investigating the Stirling engine and the gas turbine. Volkswagen and Klockner-Humboldt-Deutz (KHD) also have sunk substantial sums in gas turbine research. In France, Citroën has always emphasized a "forward looking" engineering policy. Its research on hydraulic suspension and the rotary engine led to practical applications in its cars. At present, it is not only devoting considerable human and material resources to safety, noise, and pollution problems, but it is also trying to develop a power plant using an air/zinc battery featuring a circulating electrolyte. Renault and Peugeot are also endeavoring to reduce the environmental problems created by the automobile. Renault, in collaboration with French Electricity, is studying electric cars powered by lead batteries: small city cars, small delivery trucks, minicars, and buses. Peugeot is preparing prototypes of electric cars using the chasis of sedans and small trucks.

French government authorities have intervened vigorously to ensure that research efforts are coordinated, through the Interministerial Committee on Electric Cars or the Office of Scientific and Technical Research, and to provide financial assistance. They are also supporting research projects in governmental and university laboratories, particularly at the National Center for Scientific Research, the

Transportation Research Institute, and the Research and Testing Office of the army. French automobile research is somewhat ahead of its European and American competitors, an advance emphasizing really new technological systems likely to solve some of the problems of the traditional automobile. Essentially these systems involve fuel cells and air/zinc batteries, which are among the few serious possibilities applicable to electric cars.

In Britain, beyond its research on electric cars, the British Leyland Motor Corporation is continuing work on steam engines and turbines for trucks and buses. Gas turbines for heavy vehicles have also drawn the attention of Fiat in Italy and Volvo in Sweden. The Swedish United Stirling Company and the Dutch firm Philips, holder of the original patents and licenses for the Stirling engine, are trying to develop it. And, finally, in the Soviet Union, several laboratories are dealing with the electric car and turbines for trucks.

The oil "shocks" of the 1970s inaugurated a notable shift in general priorities and in research and development efforts among the leading manufacturers. For the short and medium term, their major aim was to perfect the energy efficiency of traditional internal-combustion engines. As a corollary, the rotary piston engine—except for the Mazda of Toyo Kogyo—would be abandoned, and electric-car projects would be provisionally deferred. General Motors is the only manufacturer that has officially confirmed its decision to market a small electric car by the mid-1980s.

The American producers, spurred by the joint forces of the federal fuel-efficiency requirement of 27.5 miles-per-gallon by 1985 and the major shift in demand toward models similar to those being produced in Europe and Japan, have embarked on research programs of unprecedented expense, without considering for the near future any new lines of technology. Their European and Japanese competitors have already achieved notable progress in energy conservation: the average fuel consumption for 1981 models is about 20 percent below that of 1976. In 1980 six major manufacturers—British Leyland, Fiat, Peugeot/Citroën, Renault, Volkswagen, and Volvo—signed a long-term agreement providing for the systematic exchange of results and the beginning of joint programs for fundamental research on automobiles. The Japanese producers have adopted an identical strategy and have indicated they will continue research on electrical power sources.

So the motives behind research, innovation, and technical improvement have changed their character. The reduction of automobile nuisances, dominant until 1974, is no longer at the top of the agenda, as illustrated by the postponement of the U.S. government's goals for noise and air pollution. Now energy efficiency is the determinant, followed by an increase in the durability of cars, and enhancement of their resistance to collision damage.

For the period since the Second World War, three new lines of automotive technology deserve special attention. The first, although not really new, has been mass produced: the rotary piston engine. The second is just now emerging: automotive electronics. The maturing of the third, which has not been realized for a long time despite expensive research and development programs being carried out in all the industrialized countries, could be the most significant in a new Automobile Revolution.[105]

The Rotary Engine: A Disappointment

In 1588 Agostino Ramelli built an engine powered by a rotary piston for use as a water pump, so the idea is certainly not a new one. During the course of the nineteenth century, experimenters worked sporadically on engines employing reciprocal or rotary pistons energized by steam, gas, or gasoline, but neither system was the obvious one at first. Ultimately, technical problems probably lay behind abandonment of the rotary, but even more persuasive was the rapid success of the reciprocal piston engine after 1860. Nevertheless, occasional research continued and patents were granted for four-cycle rotary gasoline engines to Sansaud de Lavaud in 1938 and Leduc in 1945.

In the early 1950s, Dr. Felix Wankel, director of the Technical Research Institute at Lindau, in West Germany, began working on the problem of gasketing rotary engines. At this point, no automobile firm anywhere in the world seemed to be interested in a rotary engine. Then, a German manufacturer of bicycles and motorcycles hoping to move into motor car production, NSU, showed an interest in a possible market for this innovation. The company quickly hired Wankel and supplied him with researchers and equipment that his university, lacking funds, could not spare him. A Wankel rotary piston engine operated for the first time on 1 February 1957. Not until late 1962 did a car powered by such an engine become operational, and only in September 1963 did production begin on a small batch of NSU Spiders, the first car featuring a single rotary engine offered to the public. Late in 1967, NSU came out with the RO 80, the first birotary car. A major technological event, this vehicle remained for some time the only one of its type available, but at high cost.

The Japanese firm Toyo Kogyo first managed to manufacture rotary cars on a large scale at a cost very close to that of standard models. Its Mazda RX 2 and RX 3 first appeared in January 1968, and by 1973 annual production had reached 300,000. In France, only Citroën became involved, creating with NSU a joint subsidiary, Comotor. Finally, after long and expensive development of the engine and production methods, Citroën unveiled the GS birotary in 1974.

Other manufacturers have thoroughly investigated the rotary engine, and some have built and displayed prototypes. General Motors produced three prototypes on a Corvette chassis, one using four rotors; Ford a prototype birotary Mustang; and Mercedes the C-111 birotary. Others announced the future production of a Wankel-engined car, such as a joint Toyo Kogyo-General Motors 3-litre model, but since 1975 these projects have faded into the background or into oblivion.

In light of the current state of knowledge and of accomplishment, what applications of the Wankel rotary engine can be expected? Very many. The rotary principle can be used both for very small and for very large engines, and the range of power can extend from one or two horsepower to several hundred. The engine can be used on land, sea, and in the air for industrial and automotive purposes. The number of companies that have acquired a Wankel license seems to confirm the unusual potential of this technology. To be sure, not all these licensees are interested in diversifying engine technology and in seizing the opportunities offered by the innovation. However this may be, some twenty-one companies of international scale have purchased licenses to the Wankel and can use this technology. In November 1970 GM did not hesitate to pay $50 million for the license and begin a massive research and development program involving some 500 researchers at its Warren Research Center. Nevertheless, seven years later GM announced a halt to its efforts concerning the Wankel engine.

What are the hopes and what are the limits for using rotary engines in automobiles? The opinions of the experts—engineers, technicians, and managers—are strongly divided, extending from complete rejection to the most passionate infatuation. Although the absence of vibration in the rotary and its logical simplicity (why convert reciprocal motion into rotary motion when one can have rotary motion to begin with?) are universally recognized advantages, many observers see problems in the rotary engine that range from inconvenience to absolute obstacles.

In its present state of development, the thermal efficiency of the Wankel engine is less than that of the traditional type, and no major improvement has occurred since Wankel's first prototype of 1957. To reach a level of output similar to piston engines, two rotors are necessary, with a displacement of at least 1,500 cubic centimeters (92 cubic inches). But this requirement means that the Wankel has to sacrifice its basic advantages, of its technical simplicity and its small number of parts.

In addition, combining several rotors raises complex technical problems. Although the rotary engine causes less pollution than piston engines, it burns the same fuel with tetraethyl lead and requires catalytic converters to remove carbon monoxide and oxides of nitrogen. Moreover, it consumes more fuel. On a standard track, its consumption is 20 percent above a piston engine of similar power and performance. Cooling and lubrication are more difficult, so its reliability and strength are below those of its competitor. Despite these matters, the primary rein on its development is its high cost of production.

The abandonment of this technology, no matter how seductive it is, by all the manufacturers except Toyo Kogyo, even if it cannot be said at this point that it is definitive, does appear to be justified. The chances of Wankel variants, engines designed by Karol, Clarke, and Sarich, are also dim.

Automobiles and Electronics: An Inevitability

During the 1970s, sophisticated electronics entered the automobile industry. This made possible substantial gains in productivity. It has transformed the three major stages in creating an automobile: research and production methods by computer-assisted design; administration and management by computer; and production by industrial robots. Progress has moved rapidly in these areas, and in Japan, which clearly holds the lead over American and European competitors, the first unmanned auto factory has been announced for 1983–85.[106]

Improvement of the energy efficiency of internal-combustion engines is also affected by electronic systems for regulation and control. Most cars are now equipped with an electronic voltage regulator. Microprocessors can optimize the functioning of ignition and carburetion or injection. Since 1975 electronic ignition has been featured in almost all American cars, compared with less than 30 percent in Europe. Electronic injection systems, available since 1970, are still reserved for top-of-the-line models.

But these are separate systems, designed independently of each other. In the future, a small central numerical calculator will integrate all the variables so as to enhance the operation of the entire drive system. Such a computer will make measurements, inspect the mechanism, and transmit information to the driver. Holding back the spread of such integrated systems are economic and technical concerns—that is, the price and reliability of their parts. The major manufacturers of semiconductors and of electrical equipment—Texas Instruments, National Semiconductor, Intermetall, Thomson CSF, Philips, Motorola, Bosch, Ducellier, and others—are making substantial research efforts. By 1990 specialists calculate that electronic devices will account for about 6 percent of the cost of vehicles, about the same as the present cost of electrical equipment. By that date, the first stage in the maturation of electronic systems in motor cars—their close adaptation to the traditional technology of heat engines—may have been completed.

A second stage may be characterized by a movement toward simplification and coherence. The logic of joining electric propulsion with electronic control seems in the very nature of things. Isn't the compatibility of the electric and the electronic almost assured by "nature?"

In a third stage, electronics may bring a radical evolution in the very idea of how cars are used. This would allow a marriage between the qualities inherent in individual transportation—autonomy, availability, and liberty—and the advantages of transportation on fixed routes—performance, regularity, and safety. These would be realized by systems of electronically guided vehicles. The car's computer would handle the tasks hitherto performed by the driver, who would furnish only instructions concerning the destination, route, time of departure and arrival, and speed. He or she would give up the task of driving and retain only control of the decision to travel. In this perspective, a perfect fit would occur between the technology of vehicles and of highways. Individual transportation would become part of an integrated system. A development of this sort obviously would require major changes in the technical design and organization of highways. But it would not necessarily imply the use of some kind of guide-rail arrangement analogous to railways, which would mean giving up the independence of individual transportation.

The Electric Car: Uncertainty

Another major focus of current automobile research, the electric car, is not really a technical innovation. Its early development paralleled that of its continual competitor, the internal-combustion engine. Deficiencies in lead batteries allowed engines burning hydrocarbon fuels to win out. So electric power was restricted to specific and limited uses: in trucks handling industrial materials and making urban deliveries, as well as in various municipal vehicles and in buses.

The technical improvements that the Second World War brought to diesel engines struck a hard blow at electric commercial vehicles. As a result, electric cars almost vanished from the industrial countries, except for Britain. There, a considerable number remained because a regulation forbidding drivers to leave the engine running while their vehicle was stopped allowed electric cars to hold their position among urban delivery vehicles distributing articles such as bread, beverages, and newspapers that required frequent stops. But these were just a small fraction of the total automobiles in Britain.

Although it abandoned the streets to the monopoly of internal-combustion engines, the electric car remained a subject of laboratory research. Investigators continued their efforts on lead batteries and on motors, brakes, and the recovery of energy. Automobile manufacturers, battery producers, electric utilities, and some component makers in the United States, Japan, and Europe built prototype electric cars, most often using standard chassis rather than conceiving an electric car as a unique whole.

Until about 1960, the investigation of more efficient electrochemical power sources than alkaline batteries was almost ignored. As a consequence, one of the major current obstacles to significant progress in this area is a lack of qualified researchers. Only around 1960 did a constellation of circumstances operate to revive interest in the electric car and make it an object of research and development in all the industrialized and motorized countries.

Hopes of rapid development of a practical fuel cell seem to have sparked a revival of interest. Early in the 1960s, the Americans began looking for power generators for space vehicles. The theory of the hydrogen/oxygen fuel cell has been known since 1839. The Englishman Bacon produced one in 1953, and he and his compatriot Forest another in 1959. It seemed to be an especially promising system because in theory it could supply the energy and water needed for manned space flights. The chase was on. In the United States several of the most important companies in the chemical, electrical equipment, and electronic fields, along with many university, military, and private laboratories began research efforts. Some of these were supported by military or space agency grants, but others were conducted on a risk basis so as not to fall behind in a very promising area of technology.

Western Europe could not allow the United States to monopolize a new technology, and quickly plunged into this field, but its objectives were less clear and its financial resources much smaller. This wave of fuel-cell research continued until 1968–69. But, despite several laboratory achievements and the success of spacecraft prototypes where cost considerations were secondary, no fuel cell appeared that was suitable for ordinary private use. The phase of excessive hopes and marvelous budgets was followed by a period of disillusionment crystalizing in a significant reduction of research and a concentration of funds on the most promising systems, especially subsystems such as catalysts, electrodes, and electrolytes. The experts are now saying that only in the decade after 1990 will a fuel cell be evolved that is efficient and cheap enough to compete with hydrocarbon fuels. The best American and French prototypes now show results indicating that in time such competition is possible.

They have not yet succeeded, however, in awakening automotive circles, especially the manufacturers, to the opportunity to prepare for the fuel cell's ultimate arrival by participating in the research effort. Nevertheless, these companies have not completely ignored the progress achieved, for they want to avoid being squeezed out by other industrial sectors currently outside the automotive business, but which, by seizing control of an alternative technology, might gradually take over traditional automotive markets.

Hopes remain bright in scientific and technical circles that eventually an independent source of electrical energy can be delineated. Valuable allies have come from militants in the environmental movement, which emerged at the end of the 1960s. Almost everywhere, public authorities have been forced to invoke regulations requiring the automobile industry to reduce or even end the nuisances associated with its vehicles. As a clean and silent alternative, the electric car quite naturally became one of the solutions favored by the new public attitude.

Research programs on electric cars have been reinforced by the activities of public utilities, which want to maintain their growth by fostering technologies that consume electric power. They have promoted electric kitchen applicances, electric heating, and "all electric" homes so as to expand their sales, and now automobile transportation by electric batteries could become a huge market. The Edison

Electric Institute, the trade association of United States producers and distributors of electric power, since 1964 has supported a significant research effort on air/zinc batteries undertaken by Gulf Electric, which in 1971 tried them on a prototype car. This policy of the institute evidences a psychological shift, which, despite some initial dispersion of effort, led to its founding the Electric Vehicle Council in 1968. The Council was to preside over development and utilization of electric power for all forms of transportation.

In Britain, the Electricity Council of England and Wales decided in 1967 to promote the urban electric vehicle, and prepared several rather theoretical machines. These led to the fruition of one practical type, the Enfield 8000, of which the council ordered 61. In Germany, the Rhine-Westphalian Electric Works and, in Japan, the Tokyo Electric Power Company have vigorously encouraged and coordinated research and have helped finance several prototypes. In France late in 1969, French Electricity decided to enter this field, so as to power its own fleet of vehicles more cheaply, for reasons of prestige, and ultimately to expand its market. These projects, supported by the utility companies, usually aim to speed the promotion of vehicles using aspects of existing technology. Information on the various programs is spread throughout the world by the International Union of Electricity Producers and Distributors.

The urgent need to solve the problem of urban transportation and the consequences of the petroleum crisis of the 1970s are two additional factors spurring research programs in electric vehicles. These machines seem to be the outstanding technological alternative because in the present state of the art their performances limit them to urban usage and because they are quiet, clean, and above all, maneuverable in heavy traffic. Also, electric or diesel-electric vehicles can handle public transportation needs.

The large and rapid rise in petroleum prices should, as long as it remains in effect, powerfully stimulate energy conservation and the investigation of substitute energy sources. The effort of American diplomacy from the beginning of 1975 to set a minimum price for oil so as to encourage research on new forms of energy is an example of this. When compared to the energy available in a primary source, oil, the efficiency of a vehicle in city driving varies by a ratio of 1 to 4 according to the power system used: 7.4 percent efficiency for a four-cycle gasoline engine; 17 percent for a system including a central electric generating system, a lead or air/zinc battery, and an electric motor; and 30 percent for a fuel-cell power source.

The second result of the oil crisis, the awakening of the governments of the industrialized countries to the political consequences of their dependence on imported oil, led them to reconsider their energy policies. Most of them decided to speed up nuclear power development. At the same time, for the last fifteen years, everywhere in the world researchers have pursued the question of using hydrogen as a major energy source. Supplies of it would come either from electrolysis or by splitting water molecules with the surplus heat from nuclear plants. Hydrogen, either burned directly or transformed in the presence of oxygen, may become a basic industrial product. So it is at the center of a variety of converging political and economic forces that may justify a higher level of research effort aiming to produce it in huge quantities cheaply and to manage its transportation and storage. These possibilities for hydrogen favor the chances of the fuel cell and, as a result, those of the electric car.

Active research on such a car is going on in many countries, including mainland China. Knowledgeable observers concede that Japan may hold a lead in this technological race. The Japanese Ministry of Industry and Foreign Trade and the Tokyo Electric Power Company have joined some major automobile firms—Daihatsu, Toyota, Nissan, Toyo Kogyo, and Mitsubishi—and makers of batteries, motors, and control systems to support a large number of projects. All this action springs from the immense pollution and traffic problems in Japan, from the desire of industrial groups to protect themselves from draconian government regulations on conventional cars, and finally from an understanding of the potential advantages of the electric solution.

In the United States, many experiments are under way in addition to the efforts supported by the Electric Vehicle Council. Of the major auto firms, Ford has not progressed beyond the prototype stage, but GM went so far in 1980 as to create a project center to prepare an electric car for large-scale production in 1985–86. GM plans to use a zinc-nickel oxide battery that will provide a range of 100 miles. The Gulf and Western Company in 1980 unveiled a unique zinc-chloride electric power system that promises even better performance, but is far from production for motor cars. By the early 1980s, dozens of American companies were making prototype electric cars, some financed by grants from the Department of Energy. About 2,000 such vehicles operated on streets and roads in 1980.

Across the Atlantic, British Leyland has joined with the Joseph Lucas and Crampton Parkinson groups to develop machines using air/zinc battery systems. Many projects are being carried out in West Germany that link the major truck- and bus-makers with the principal electrical machinery manufacturers.

In France, the major projects concern small vehicles, both for passenger and commercial purposes. French Electricity has allied with Renault to electrify some standard Renault models, and has joined the French General Electric Company and Bertin in making prototypes for city cars, as well as with Sovel to develop a minibus. The French Petroleum Institute and a group comprising Alsthom, Peugeot, and Exxon Research are investigating fuel cells. Both the French General Electric Company and Citroën separately are working on air/zinc batteries using a circulating electrolyte.

In the Soviet Union, several research centers have displayed prototypes since 1970. These include the Central Institute for Automobiles and Automotive Transport of Moscow, the Erivan Polytechnique Institute, the Federal Institute for Electrical Transport of Kaliningrad, and the Kharkov Institute for Highway Traffic. The Soviet interest in electric cars cannot be attributed to pollution problems or to the petroleum crisis, for neither of these have become as pressing there as in the industrialized capitalist countries, but rather as an example of technological competition with the West. Current programs aim to construct city cars providing a range of about fifty miles at normal speeds and usage.

Similar, though modest, research programs on electric vehicles are operating in Italy, Sweden, Switzerland, and Czechoslovakia as part of the vast international effort.

The number and technical variety of power-generating systems being investigated all over the world makes it likely that satisfactory electrical vehicles will appear before long. But that will raise the serious question of a choice of one system for use all over the world, for, unless a single one is chosen, the international system of automotive transport, extending from manufacturer to consumer, will be seriously disorganized. Gasoline is, for the moment, the universal energy source for thermal engines. Electric traction should also be supplied by a single generating system, a choice arrived at either by an international agreement or as the logical result of a compromise between its technical performance and the cost of its manufacture.

The host of research programs currently in operation around the world are not challenging the automobile per se, nor seeking to replace it with some other method of transportation providing all its good qualities and none of its disadvantages. Only the power plant is under attack. Ultimately what system will win out? At the present stage of technology, it is difficult, if not impossible, to judge.

Nevertheless, the various thermal engines can be crossed off the list. The gas (not gasoline) engine only partially solves the pollution problem and hardly improves on noise; it uses hydrocarbons or natural gas and also presents difficulties as to storage and safety. The steam engine as well as the gas or steam turbine, though very clean and relatively quiet, present problems of efficiency, require a heavy and bulky technology, and will take such a long time to develop and money to manufacture that they seem out of the race. The hydrogen engine, which solves the pollution but not the noise problem, has a storage difficulty and is considerably less efficient than electric power. The Stirling engine, quiet, efficient, and emitting little pollution, raises difficult problems of reliability that could make its technical development improbable earlier than that of fuel cells.

Among all the possibilities for thermal engines, manufacturers at present prefer to improve the classic engine by adding pollution controls, silencers, and safety devices. This policy, of course, implies no serious upheaval of their technology. The progress made by two variants of the four-cycle engine, the rotary and stratified-charge engines, tends to strengthen the manufacturers in this policy, for they do not radically challenge traditional production arrangements but do make possible a considerable reduction of pollution and noise.

Among the various electrochemical power systems, it appears that the conventional types, lead and nickel-cadmium batteries, must be eliminated. Nevertheless, they may be developed for test purposes in the expectation of more efficient nonconventional types. The air/zinc system seems to be the most promising.

In the end, the hydrogen fuel cell may well be the most advantageous solution. Its development requires a major effort both concerning the battery itself and on production methods and hydrogen storage.

To try to resolve here such a vast problem, involving politics, economics, ideology, and of course, technology, would be pretentious. The character of automobile technology by the year 2000 will be the product of conflict and ultimately the result of a compromise among the often divergent interests of the various members of a social system in which they are profoundly unequal.

11. Labor and Industrial Relations since 1945

Jean-Pierre Bardou

The automobile industry has experienced an unprecedented growth from the Second World War to the present. From the point of view of labor, this growth has been governed by technical and organizational changes that have affected all the large firms throughout the world. As a result, the global similarity of the manufacturing process appears as the characteristic feature of the automobile industry. In Detroit and Autograd, in Wolfsburg and Liverpool, and in Turin and Billancourt rationalization requires the same manufacturing techniques and the same principles of organization; variation comes only in the degree of administrative centralization or the length of the production process.

Standardization of methods and techniques occurred along with the adoption of long production runs after the Second World War and then from the early 1960s with mass production, which transformed the manufacturing process into a true industrial cycle. The movement from long production runs to mass production brought serious changes in the nature and significance of automobile labor. As the industry necessarily expanded the sectors of the manufacturing process that were not fully mechanized, particularly the assembly lines, it brought together concentrations of labor to a degree unparalleled in history. Then, in the later 1960s a threshold was reached, the new situation suggested new attitudes concerning labor, and new kinds of labor-management conflicts. It also gave an opportunity to apply the principles of job redesign.

The Fabrication Cycle

Two stages comprise the industrial cycle of automobile manufacturing. The first is that of conception in the broad sense of the term; that is, not only the design of the model of the car itself, but also of the technical apparatus and system of organization necessary for its manufacture. The second stage is that of the actual building of the car.

The stage of model design includes three periods, each corresponding to a distinct area of activity. Firstly, the research and design division establishes the technical characteristics of the model, and therefore of each of the assemblies and subassemblies incorporated in it. Included in this phase is the preparation of prototypes. Specialized shops in the factory manufacture the various parts for these prototypes. Although work on some of these parts is handled by ordinary machines, some, especially those involving very precise operations, can be made by numerically controlled machines.

These tools possess the ability to calculate and therefore to determine, after receiving information on the use to which the piece is to be put, not only the optimum technical specifications of the piece (dimensions and tolerances), but even its shape and the type of materials from which it should be made. At present, the large companies have only a few of these machines each, and their use is rather limited in comparison with what can be expected in the future. Still it is true that employment of numerical control could completely change the design stage of production. Now four or five years are required between the original conception and the final production of a new model; using a numerically controlled machine allows a reduction to two years. This occurred at the Citroën company with a recent model. Not only were some parts of the mechanism determined without the traditional calculations by engineers, but even the actual shape of the body was established by the machine without need for drawings and models.

The second period of the design stage is tooling. The specialized services and the tool shops, in close cooperation, design and construct the production machinery needed for the manufacture of the new parts: molds for the foundry, dies for the forges, and punches for the presses. This is small-scale production, determined by the number of machines on which they will be used, and cost problems are significant.

As in the manufacture of prototypes, the fabrication of new machinery brings into use, in addition to universal machine tools, some machines run by computer. In this phase of small-scale production, the computer-controlled machine is useful, obviously for its calculating functions, but especially for its operating ability. By means of its programming, the computer actually directs all the operations of the machine tool, which receives the orders and executes them under its constant control.

It should be noted that until very recently the use of the computer-controlled machine in the automobile industry was limited to the two sectors just mentioned, that is, in making prototypes and in tooling. This is because such machines are profitable compared with traditional machines starting with the first piece when the operation is difficult, and with the second or third piece when the task is moderately difficult.

The third aspect of the design stage is to formulate the general organizational conditions of the fabrication process. First, the methods department calculates production times, which regulate the division of jobs and operations for each point of the process and which define the overall structure. Next, the program office establishes the rate of fabrication (number and type of vehicles per day) and the plan for parts supply. A quarterly or monthly plan is prepared for each factory, and weekly or daily detailed plans for each department or group of shops. The rigorous programming must, in fact, foresee not only the delivery at the right time of approximately 20,000 parts that make up an automobile, but must also arrange for the full employment of the men and the machines.

The second stage of the industrial cycle is the actual fabrication of the vehicles, a process involving two important sequences: first, the manufacture of the mechanical parts (engine and front and rear ends), and then the construction of the frame and body. Once the assembly and the mounting of the mechanical parts and the body are finished, the two sequences converge in the final assembly line. There, the vehicles are equipped with accessories that are usually manufactured elsewhere, such as wheels, tires, radiators, and batteries.

Production of the mechanical parts involves different operations. At the foundry, the molten metal (iron, steel, or aluminum) is poured in molds, which shape the gearbox casings, cylinder heads, pistons, engine blocks, and steering-gear housings. From the forges come crankshafts and connecting rods after hardening by heat treatment. Next comes the machining: engine blocks and the transmissions are machined on transfer machines, which perform all the necessary operations automatically, without human assistance. Lines equipped with specialized machines prepare the other pieces. Small parts—screws, bolts, and nuts—come from specialized machine shops. Then comes assembly. An overhead conveyor helps in the assembly of the engine parts. The completed engine is then tested on a test bench, and finally is mounted on the chassis. Other pieces are added at this stage—front and rear ends, shock absorbers and brakes, steering gear and wheel—so that all the parts of the mechanical system have been assembled.

Body making also occurs in several steps. First, the sheet metal is cut by rows of shearing machines from rolls of flat steel. Next, the panels are formed by enormous machines weighing several dozen tons, arranged in series and equipped with dies that shape the different parts of the body, roof, doors, and fenders. These different panels are assembled in the welding stage by multipoint spot-welding machines. Then the brazing is done manually, with a soldering iron. A conveyor now carries the body to the paint shop, where it undergoes several treatments: degreasing, priming, painting, and drying. The conveyor next brings the body to the upholstery shop, where the interior is installed. The electrical circuits and headlights, grillwork and bumpers, gas tank and windows are added so that the completed body, painted and fully equipped, comes to the final assembly line.

The two principal components of the vehicle, the body on the one hand and the chassis with engine on the other, are then assembled and the last parts are added: wheels and tires, exhaust system and pedals, radiator, and battery. The vehicle next goes to a testing apparatus, is checked for watertightness, and finally is delivered to the marketing department. The time of fabrication averages twelve hours, or seven hours for painting and five for mechanical assembly (excluding time spent on foundry, forge, and press work).

Technical Reorganization

The unprecedented growth in the production of vehicles by large firms throughout the world has become possible through a wide-ranging mechanization in the manufacturing sectors previous to assembly and a tightly integrated production process. The term "technological leap" can legitimately be used to describe a characteristic of the automobile industry following the Second World War as a result of the use of new machines. But, at the same time, the long series of less spectacular innovations, progressively introduced, that led to the technological integration of the whole activity should not be forgotten. By the period of the early 1960s, this integration had generally been achieved. The following years brought no significant technical changes anywhere in the world; a plateau had been reached. After 1965, organizational changes, rising output, and additional final assembly lines enabled the industry throughout the world to reach the stage of mass production.

In the automobile industry, the move from universal machine tools to specialized and semiautomatic machines, which the United States had begun to take even before 1914, was the most salient aspect of technical change in the years between the two world wars.[107] This shift brought with it a sharp transformation of the conditions and nature of automobile labor, mostly in the machine-work sectors, that was characterized by a quickening reduction of skill requirements. The most outstanding technological change after the Second World War, in addition to the general use of specialized or semiautomatic machinery, was the introduction of automatic machines.

The automatic machine represents a precise stage in the evolution of machine tools. The universal machine—lathe, milling machine, boring machine—can accomplish quite different operations according to the speed and position of the tool, for they are usually provided with movable chucks. Therefore, the greater part of the working time of these machines is spent in setting up, for which the operator must first make his calculations. Once the machine is running, the worker directs its operations with intelligence and skill. The universal machine, also called a flexible or polyvalent machine, therefore is most useful in producing single items or a short run of them. These machines are still to be found in toolrooms.

The specialized or semiautomatic machine, on the other hand, does a small number of operations, or even a single one. Calculation and adjustment are reduced to a bare minimum. Once set up and put into operation, the machine runs continuously and gives maximum output. The specialized machines are built for production lines; they are simple and perform a single operation at high speed. Consequently, they must be durable to avoid breakdowns. The widespread use of specialized machines brought with it a new division of labor. The former functions of the skilled workers, capable of making the calculations required to adjust the machine, of changing tools, and of controlling the machine throughout its operations, have been subdivided. Two new categories appeared: the set-up man, whose job is to start the machine's operations and guard against problems, and the semiskilled machine tenders, whose only task is to feed the machine and remove the finished pieces.

In the auto industry outside North America, the use of specialized machines became common after the Second World War. They were introduced especially in forging and shaping and in some other metalworking operations. Highly skilled workers in these sectors gave way to those with less skill, and these in turn to former semiskilled workers promoted to the higher ranks.

Beyond all this, the major technological innovation during the post-1945 years was the automatic machine, corresponding to the third stage in the evolution of the machine tool. It is a combination, or regrouping, of specialized machines. These latter perform simple operations. The automatic machines (large presses for forming sheet metal, forging presses, and systems to machine cylinder blocks) combine formerly separated operations so that a part that in the past had to be produced on three different machines, each of which required an operator, is finished on a single machine run by a semiskilled worker whose only repetitive function has not changed: to feed the machine and remove the finished parts. This has brought a large increase in labor productivity and a comparable rise in output. Although the automatic machine is the major breakthrough of this period, its use did not spread everywhere in the factory. In the production of parts prior to assembly, specialized and automatic machines still coexisted in the 1960–65 period.

How the introduction of automatic machines profoundly transformed the workers' situation, the relations among workers in the shop, and the very meaning of labor is not so obvious if one simply watches the workers at their tasks because the principle of combining several machines into one appears to mean only that fewer workers are employed. But, from the point of view of labor, the new situation created by the complex functioning of the automatic machine is the essential. This complexity derives from the hydraulic, pneumatic, electromagnetic, and electronic systems, without which such a unit would have been impossible. The machine tender could still understand the functioning of the specialized machine doing a simple task, but now the automatic machine is alien to him, and he is not even allowed to understand its operation. The set-up man starts the machine, and in case of malfunctioning the worker is forbidden to touch the controls and must call for special repair services through his supervisor. The automatic machine brutally separates manual and intellectual labor, robs the worker of any remaining trace of shop skill, and cripples his elementary abilities.

Did the general use of the specialized and the introduction of the automatic machine in this period, changing as they did the nature of factory work, succeed in modifying the proportions of workers at various skill levels? One fact strikes all observers of the process: although the change from the universal machine tool to the specialized machine between the world wars furthered the increase of semiskilled workers, the proportions of types of workers in the automobile industry underwent no important changes between 1945 and the early 1960s. An example from the Renault company illustrates this. Semiskilled and unskilled workers accounted for 67.7 percent of factory labor in 1939 and for 67.4 percent in 1964.

The basic reason for this stability is that the elimination of a fraction of the skilled workers through automation was balanced, on the one hand, by a reduction of semiskilled workers because of the use of automatic machines, and also by the elimination of unskilled manual laborers because of the mechanization of materials handling. Things have turned out so that mechanization since 1945 in the preassembly manufacturing sectors (forges, foundries, machine shops, and sheet-metal work) brought no sharp change in the proportions of workers at various skill levels.

An examination of the skilled worker category in more detail reveals that in the preassembly sectors the number of these workers changed slightly over the period 1945–60, despite the spread of mass production and the introduction of automatic machines. The real consequence was a redistribution of skilled work from fabrication to toolmaking and maintenance. In foundries, forges, and sheet-metal shops, the mechanization achieved in Europe between the two world wars tended to replace highly skilled workers by less qualified skilled workers. When automatic machinery was introduced, most of these skilled people were in turn replaced by semiskilled operatives paid at the wages of skilled workers but whose training and knowledge fell considerably below those whom they replaced.

Certain sectors of fabrication, nevertheless, resisted this degrading of skills. In forging, for example, where certain parts are produced from scratch, there remain some old-fashioned professionals who can read blueprints and can make any part asked for. These highly skilled men are aided by semiskilled helpers who have only a minimum of training and by unskilled manual laborers possessing no training. On the other hand, mechanization has encouraged decentralized maintenance and tooling services, where one finds a high proportion of skilled workers along with technical specialists. Using the forges again as an example, highly qualified skilled maintenance and tool men constitute about one-quarter of the total employees in this sector.

Along with the introduction of the automatic machine, the second decisive element in the technical evolution of the automobile industry during this period has been the technical integration of the manufacturing process. The relationships that have been suggested earlier between the changes in the process of fabrication and the stages in the evolution of machine tools clarify certain basic developments in work and among workers in the industry.

This analysis ought to include a study of several innovations that concern not only the machines themselves but also the relationships between the machines and the work stations; that is, the technical organization of the work process. These innovations played a considerable role during these years. They contributed to the almost complete technical integration of fabrication and not just in those sectors prior to assembly. These changes represent the second major advance allowing for mass production.

By technical integration is meant a closer connection not only between the machines but also between work stations, thanks to the mechanization of materials handling: control and feeding of machines, inspection, ejection, handling of parts, and evacuation of scrap. If the impact of the automatic machine occurred mainly prior to assembly, the effect of mechanization of materials handling, constantly growing during this period, was felt everywhere in the fabrication process. Its logic called for a synchronization of all the different stages of the manufacturing process, thereby transforming its structure. This involved a technical evolution at least as meaningful as the introduction of automatic machines. It made possible a centralized control system aiming to speed up the performance of the various production units to a faster rhythm. This allowed a shift from production of large numbers to mass production beginning in the early 1960s.

The first element of this technical integration, its most visible one for it involved changing the appearance of the factory, was the construction of simple systems allowing the transfer of parts from one shop to the next, from one work station to the next. The principles of these systems had been worked out at the Ford Company from 1912 on, but their widespread application came only gradually, and continued to develop after the Second World War. These included conveyors with grasping devices, monorails, traveling cranes, electrically powered block and tackles, conveyor belts, and overhead chains. These different systems formed a web of interconnections among the work stations. They supplied all of them everywhere in the production process, those involving machine work as well as hand work. Other examples include the delivery of small parts where they are needed by containers that drop them into bins, and small trucks that pick up and deliver parts from one station to another.

This movement of parts is closely tied to the growing programming of production. Vehicles of the same model moving on a production line vary according to such factors as style, color, and destination. A system of computer cards and electronic printouts ensures that the parts appropriate for each vehicle arrive automatically in a programmed order at the different work stations. The programming office manages this system. The reorganized factory is not simply a juxtaposition of different shops, assembly lines, and work stations, but rather their technical integration, that is, an interconnected system governed by the programming office that aims at a general synchronization of the fabrication process.

The second element of technological integration is the coordination of machines with each other. Continuous progress has been made in automating the handling of materials at each machine. For example, on transfer machines—automatic machines that move the parts from one post to another between operations—the parts are set in place, locked, and then loosened after completion of the operation, and finally moved automatically to the next machine while the scraps are removed by underground passages. This eliminates almost all handling of parts, and the whole forms a production line checked by an electrical board showing each machine in the unit in order. This allows a surveillance of each machine's action, and eventually provides information for a computer.

The idea of a moving assembly line, first used only for the manual tasks of assembly, began in the interwar period to spread into key manufacturing sectors prior to final assembly and finally permitted synchronized automatic lines. Electronics is the link making possible synchronization between different operations where the times of execution are different. The speed of a continuous operation, such as unrolling sheet steel, can be synchronized with a discontinuous operation such as a punch press. Nonelectronic systems, such as hydraulic or pneumatic controls, are also used.

Installing automatic production lines has occurred more or less rapidly according to the different sectors. At first, workers on the sheet-steel presses fed them manually, positioned the sheet on the die, tripped the press for each operation, unloaded the pieces and trimmings, and finally inspected the quality of the work. The first move toward automation was ejection and removal of the piece automatically while the trimmings were concurrently carried away. An automatic line appeared in two stages. First a worker remained in charge of each press, then one worker controlled the entire line, even if a worker might remain at each machine to oversee its operation.

Production lines that are synchronized and automated gradually have been installed in certain areas of the foundries (remolding), machining (cylinder blocks), large presses, spot-welding, body frames, and painting. Several things should be noted about these lines operating in the processes prior to final assembly. In the first place, automation of an entire sector of production is rarely achieved, for specialized machines still are widely used (screw-cutting lathes and small presses). Still, mechanical conveyors link these machines closely together. Secondly, there never has been an automation "revolution" but rather a continuous progress in technology. Except for electronic systems, techniques have evolved only slightly in their basic principles; they simply have been perfected. Thirdly, and this concerns working conditions, it would be wrong to think that these production lines function very satisfactorily. They employ different control systems, incorporating more and more transistors, but also traditional methods using hydraulic, pneumatic, and mechanical elements.

The junction points of these different systems give rise to frequent breakdowns and to difficulties in repair that often require emergency help from specialists. In addition, the production objectives often interfere with the work of such maintenance services so that the output of these production lines, especially those in machining, can be estimated as seldom above 20 percent of capacity in European car factories, a higher percentage being reached in America and Japan. Contrary to what is usually said of these systems, patching and temporary expedients are commonly used, and the elementary rules of maintenance are frequently neglected in order to hold delays to the minimum and meet production schedules, that is, for the worker to make his pay.

In the early 1960s, technical integration of production seemed to reach its maximum. By breaking the previous autonomy of each sector in the process, flow production also broke up the last of the worker teams, the last vestiges of craft fellowship in the forges for example, and wiped out the last traces of craft work in the fabrication process. The narrowly specialized worker had triumphed. The culmination of these developments in the early 1960s was the disappearance of the work community, whose repercussions would be felt later in the crisis of the existing systems for worker classification. Henceforth, labor would organize itself more around social characteristics: the young, women, immigrants, and those of rural origin. These categories are outside the traditional factory lines of organization, and a second type of reorganization would attempt, in the 1960s, to redefine them.

Organizational Readjustment

From the early 1960s there existed the same phenomenon that previously, between the two world wars, had quickly raised the proportion of semiskilled machine tenders among the labor force in the automobile industry. The industry in Europe entered a new phase in its evolution, moving from production of large numbers to mass production. This did not involve any new type of automation but a massive increase in the output of machines and in labor productivity. It required the large automobile companies to change their organization. The technical integration of production just discussed made possible expanded output per machine in the sectors prior to final assembly, but each such expansion required more final assembly lines, always resistant to further mechanization.

In the period from the 1960s to the present, the goal of reorganization was to establish a compatibility between the increased output of machines and the increasing productivity of narrowly specialized labor. This growth of productivity was made possible by the massive hiring of untrained labor, foreign or "marginal" workers, who were assigned to repetitive tasks. These represented 78 percent of Renault workers by 1970. So, beginning in the early 1960s, the auto industry throughout the world became the focus of an unprecedented concentration of labor. The specific role of the organizational readjustment was to obtain some kind of control over the output of labor force that was quite mobile, whether it was national or foreign.

The first step was geographic decentralization of production units, including the establishment of subsidiaries and further subcontracting. These developments have characterized the large firms, especially in Europe, since the Second World War, and, as shown in chapter 9, have been a key factor in the move to mass production. What has happened has made the auto industry seem to be a hierarchical network of specialized plants, all units in a common manufacturing process.

Next came a rationalizing and centralizing of management. Methods pioneered by Americans in the 1920s have been introduced slowly over the past two decades. These rest on budgetary control over all the units of a factory. Such a unification of accounting methods into a homogeneous system has reduced the administrative and budgetary autonomy of the departments.

At the Renault works in Billancourt, for example, between 1945 and 1949 the department heads managed their affairs autonomously. They maintained their own accounting procedures during a period when cars were ordered three years in advance and when the chief objective was production. In 1950 the creation of a centralized personnel office along with a system of job descriptions took from the departments the flexibility they had enjoyed in allocating bonuses. Between 1950 and 1953, groups of departments were created in the two principal divisions of the works, mechanical and assembly, and production plans were coordinated. The plant was divided into two factories between 1953 and 1959: one for mechanical fabrication, and the other for body making and assembly.

In 1960 these two factories adopted the same managerial system and installed the first central computer, which allowed the central staff to handle in similar fashion for all production units of the works the budget, production, and speed of operations. From 1960 to 1969, general norms were applied to each department and to each shop through local branches of the budget, methods, and personnel systems. The company also added fifteen new computers.

The introduction of rationalized management was paralleled by a centralization of administration that handled for the entire works the different functions formerly treated on the shop level. The central administration henceforth programmed job preparation, the speed of production, and workers' pay. These two aspects of the reorganization, rearranging the production units and central management control, have profoundly affected labor and relationships in the shops. They gradually changed the activities of the skilled workers. The division of labor among these workers could not go any further because the machines they used always left the workers some elements of initiative. So reorganization occurred through a change in preparing, assigning, and inspecting work.

Among skilled people, such as toolmakers, strong tension remained between workers and management. Workers strongly defended their craft autonomy by constantly challenging decisions on standard times, assignment of jobs, work rules, rates of pay, and bonuses. They did not seriously challenge the principle that differences in skill level exist among highly trained workers but only the application of this principle. As the centralized administration took over the foreman's earlier discretionary power of hiring and firing workers, and to a lesser degree his power of adjusting wages, his argument was weak in appealing to workers' "goodwill." He was even less able to impose authoritarian decisions. He had become the weak point in the industrial hierarchy.

The reorganization of labor in these sectors broke the professional autonomy of the skilled workers. Technicians and engineers from the production and methods office took over work preparation and set standard times. This increased the possibility of a further division of operations. The foreman found that he was no longer responsible for preparing the work, which formerly had aroused the permanent hostility of the skilled workers. Production standards became more strict, and rigid time schedules were imposed for complex jobs as well as for simple tasks. To this was added a revision of the system of shop-level supervision: the functions of authority and control were specialized because the machines and tasks could not be. Work assignments were handled by the crew chief, quality control and production delays by the foreman, and the dual tasks of discipline and general management by the shop supervisor.

In this area, then, without a fundamental change in the tasks performed by the skilled workers nor any actual degrading of skill, the new work standards introduced a rigid time schedule, and the new structure of authority and control emptied the system of different skill levels of its traditional content. Payment by results, already begun long before the Second World War, had struck a blow from the outside at the craft system by encouraging competition among workers; reorganization of the job, changing not the task done but the relationship of the worker to his work, attacked the craft system from the inside.

For workers without particular skills, reorganization during this period meant a new system of classification and pay based on job descriptions. This arrangement set the rate of pay for semiskilled workers less by the task they performed, that is, by the quality of their work, than by the post they occupied. The assembly line, like the production line, included a small number of jobs paying a wage significantly higher than the other work posts. In assembly, the most highly paid positions were at the end of the line for inspectors and refinishers. In machine work, whether the output was large or small, the nature of the machine largely determined the pay scale. In sheet metal, the different members of each team working on the large presses were paid according to each one's relation to the machine: as feeder, operator, or remover. In all cases, classification and wage were determined independently of the skills of the individual worker, who could find himself suddenly shifted from one job to another with a consequent drop in pay.

By tying wage, classification, and promotion possibilities to jobs or work posts, this reorganization basically changed the relationship of the worker to his work, defining work as the sum of the conditions that defined him as a member of the organization. In the absence of any possibility of acquiring a personal sense of identification with his work, whether by an anticipated promotion, the hope of increasing pay, or even the simple desire for some stability in his function, absenteeism and turnover in the early 1960s began to climb to considerable proportions everywhere, even in the USSR. This trend revealed the workers' rejection of the new industrial organization, of the industrial firm itself.

With the advent of mass production, the effects of both technical and organizational changes multiplied and augured new attitudes toward work, expressed in unprecedented kinds of labor actions, whose most spectacular demonstrations would be the massive wildcat strikes that began spreading in 1970, especially in Europe.

Technical reorganization, involving automatic machines and the spread of repetitive tasks, has dissolved the relationship between the worker and his job. Work poorly done, slowdowns, and at times even sabotage indicated labor's rejection when it came to repetitive and unwilling labor.

Organizational readjustment, by tying the conditions of employment to the work station, destroyed the workers' loyalty to the company. Absenteeism, turnover, and even indifference to the job indicated labor's rejection when the company proved unable to ensure a minimum of vocational and social integration.

This rejection of the job and of the company actually was only one effect on the semiskilled auto workers of this two-fold movement toward rationalization. The second was the opposite of the first and by definition can not be seen and is not even expressed. This is submission. The unpleasant work and the narrow scope of jobs produced in semiskilled operatives what Daniel Mothé has called the "characteristic damage," by which he suggests "the way everyone remains below his potential, the loss of individuality, the gradual suppression of initiative and responsibility, the premature aging, the acquiescence to routine with a resistance to change even when it is suggested by economic or family difficulties."[108]

The Evolution of Collective Bargaining Systems

One model of the relations between the auto companies in the West and their workers appeared in the United States in 1948. Severely tested by the strike of 1945–46, which lasted 119 days and at the end of which the United Automobile Workers (UAW) numbered one million members, and then by a disturbance in 1947, the GM management proposed a contract to the UAW which incorporated two major innovations that had been under consideration for several years. The first was to move from one year to multi-year contracts, and the second created a pay scale indexed to the cost of living plus an annual improvement factor (originally 2 percent).

Since the inauguration of this contract, there has arisen between the UAW and GM, and generally between the American companies and the unions, a "civilized relationship" whereby the union and management periodically negotiate a renewal of the contract. National strikes have become quite rare. The UAW no longer calls strikes except to force one of the Big Three to concede certain advantages that the other two then accept. These companies have managed to bring what Alfred Sloan has called "relative peace and stability to our labor relations."

At the same time, grievance procedures handled specific complaints. GM dealt with an average of 76,000 of them annually between 1948 and 1962. Sloan said that "some 60 percent of these cases were settled at the first stage . . . by foremen and union committeemen. Another 30 percent . . . at the second stage, in negotiations between the union's shop committee and a management committee . . . Another 10 percent went to the third stage and were settled by a four-man appeal board consisting characteristically of two men from the union's regional office and two representatives of local or divisional management. An average of only 63 cases a year—less than one-tenth of 1 percent of the total—went to the fourth stage for resolution by an impartial umpire."[109]

European automakers waited seven years before achieving an equivalent of this American contractual system. But in 1955, Fiat, Renault, and Peugeot in turn signed wage agreements somewhat similar to this American model, and since that time collective bargaining has tended to spread through the European auto industry. Not all of the companies, however, want to be faced with a strong partner. Certain ones still prefer to keep a company union, or even avoid all unionism within the firm.

In contrast with the American system just after the Second World War where negotiations took place at all levels. ranging from the heads of management and the union down to the individual shop, in Western Europe agreements came only at the highest level. Italy can be taken as an example common to all the countries in that area. An examination of the agreements reached by Italian unions beginning in 1955 reveals the evolution of collective bargaining in these countries, an evolution that was undoubtedly a determining factor in the transformation of industrial relations in the 1960s.[110]

In Italy, for approximately a decade prior to 1954, collective bargaining meant almost exclusively agreements between employer associations and central union confederations. During the period of economic reconstruction and high unemployment, this extreme centralization of negotiations had the effect of raising wages, which the companies would have granted anyway if negotiations by industrial sector or by individual firm had existed. Only from about the years 1958–59 did economic stabilization give rise to some differentiation of increases among industries. While strengthening their membership in various firms, the Italian unions aimed to link decentralization of negotiations with recognition of local unions in specific firms. At the time, workers were represented locally only by works committees, whose negotiating authority was challenged by management and whose role usually was small.

In a period when negotiations turned on the central theme of productivity, the essential concern of management and government at that time, the unions that were fighting for negotiations at the firm level risked playing into the hands of management. In fact, the payments of productivity bonuses became a part of management pressure and an instrument for dividing the unions while at the same time contributing to the general rise of wages. Despite this real risk, the strategy of the unions did bear fruit. Pressure from labor in 1962 gained clauses in the national contract that, by their natures, could be handled better by separate industrial sectors, as well as matters best determined at the firm level. So the unions managed to decentralize collective bargaining and became at the same time exclusive representatives for workers in their own firms. It can be understood why the American system of industrial relations in the auto industry has changed little since the Second World War, for it permitted management to satisfy certain demands at the factory level but avoided any form of union control at this level, and so it preserved the absolute authority of the head of the firm.

The consequences of this decentralization of bargaining to the company level were numerous. Henceforth, union concern over such questions as the size of bonuses, piecework pay, hours of work, job descriptions, and worker classifications meant that the principles of how work was done in the factory would be items for bargaining with management. Another consequence was to bring the company's productivity into negotiations. In the future when management granted demands, they linked them to a union guarantee of labor's cooperation, which meant that the union agreed, if only in a formal way, to ensure worker respect of the company's labor system.

This institutionalization of the union as a guarantor of labor peace as the other side of its involvement with managing the work force, even if it did not recognize it and even if it retained the option of using its power as it chose, placed the union nonetheless in a contradictory situation: between demands from the workers and managing the same workers. This shift in industrial relations when bargaining took place at the company level transferred a fraction of the legitimate authority of management to the union, whether the union recognized it or not. This change also set the stage for the appearance of autonomous forms of labor organization.

When the union imposed company-level negotiations on management, the contractual agreements changed not only in their form but also in their content. In fact, the object of negotiations at the company level was not so much the increase of wages for a certain category of workers but the system by which these wages were calculated. The negotiations that took place at Fiat in the years 1962–63, therefore, concerning payment by results and job descriptions marked a major turning point in industrial relations. By challenging the absolute power of management, these agreements opened a breach through which the workers could demand direct control of the job, no longer on the company level but at the level of the shops and production lines. This came with the movement of the autonomous worker delegates at Fiat in Turin in the course of major strikes during the years 1969–73, a movement that in the beginning took a violently antiunion turn.[111]

In this way, the system of collective bargaining came under fire in the 1960s. At first, the national unions experienced difficulty adapting to the growing multinational character of the auto companies and to the worldwide systematization of their personnel policies. They reacted in two ways. On the one hand, the national unions in the developed countries began to aid unions in the less developed countries. Ford, for instance, in 1968 negotiated its first contract in Peru with a union firmly supported by the UAW.

On the other hand, international organizations of auto workers appeared. Permanent ones were established such as the world councils for the auto industry within the International Confederation of

Free Trade Unions created for Ford, GM, and Chrysler in 1966, for Renault-Peugeot in 1971, and still under development. And there were temporary ones such as the international automobile labor conferences, the first of which met, on a much broader base than the International Confederation just mentioned, in London in December 1974. The major factor changing the situation, however, was the growth, both in numbers and in relative size, of an untrained and youthful labor force, foreign or rural in origin.

The New Automobile Workers

The evolution of collective bargaining in the auto industry during the last three decades is related to the appearance of a new kind of worker consequent to the move from quantity production to mass production. The earlier discussion of the reorganization of the production process in this chapter makes it possible to define the characteristics of this new labor force, that is, in the abstract, as a mass of restless operatives doing narrowly defined tasks. What were these new mass production workers like who crowded into the centers of the auto industry?

As was pointed out earlier, the technical and organizational readjustments in the industry (in the United States from the 1930s onward and in Europe from the end of the war to the 1960s) was paralleled by a profound change in the composition of the labor force, resulting in a massive hiring of rural and immigrant workers, a heterogeneous group without training. These workers lived under tight restraints, first in the work done on the job, where they were allowed little responsibility; and next in their living conditions (social or racial segregation along with a loss of their cultural roots).

This situation exerted considerable impact on the auto industry, for it tended to undermine the system of collective bargaining begun in most industrial countries after the war, but it also challenged the very system of industrial work, for this seemed to be the underlying meaning of a movement such as that of the worker delegates at Fiat.

After the war, an unprecedented flood of workers came to the auto industry, whose rapid expansion caused it to offer relatively higher wages than elsewhere. Everyone knows that Detroit workers, for example, rank among the best paid in the world, and the same holds true, to a lesser degree, for auto workers in Western Europe, Japan, and even in Third World countries. The automobile boom and the broader expansion of industrialism generally in recent decades were associated with agricultural changes that encouraged farm workers to move to vast urban conglomerations.

In Western European countries with neo-liberal economies, the auto industry called upon two sources for labor. The first group consisted of native-born farmers or peasants. The word "native" should be used with care, for even though these farmers do not come from another country, they are not a socially homogeneous group but come from different regions within the frontiers, such as Bretons in France and Calabrians in Italy. Hence they have been called "interior immigrants."

The second type are in fact foreigners: Spanish, Portuguese, Italians, North Africans, Yugoslavs, black Africans, Turks, West Indians, and others. Most of these workers come from the Mediterranean basin as far as the West European auto industry is concerned. The majority of this group found in each country—North Africans in France, West Indians in England, and the like—indicates the relationship between the source of these workers and the former colonial system. Most of these workers of foreign origin come from rural backgrounds even if many lived for a time in cities before leaving their homelands.

This specifically rural origin of the working force moving into the auto industry (never in the past had movements of rural laborers reached such proportions) played an undoubted role in the way labor struggles unfolded, some of which, beginning in the 1960s, echoed the old jacquerie peasant revolts of late medieval Europe. The rural background of the workers collided with the Taylor system of the extreme division of labor. The tasks assigned to semiskilled operatives were far removed from the experience of these former peasants. They had taken part in deciding which crops to plant, which tools to use, and how fast to work. Even when they were not actually masters of their own labor, they often felt themselves to be. But the semiskilled auto worker decides neither how to face his machine nor how to operate it. He uses no particular manual skills nor any "tricks of the trade." He does not use the machine; it uses him. At any moment, he may be replaced by another who will do the work neither better nor worse than he.

The movement to the auto industry induces in this worker, from now on in the majority, two kinds of attitudes and behaviors. In the native-born workers from rural areas, especially in Western Europe, are those who have permanently left their homes and land to come to work in the factories. In addition, now that the factories are moving to the countryside, there exists an extension of the worker-farmers whose agricultural activity is reduced but not ended. Both men and women, after their factory labor, continue to till the land. The former group become city dwellers and appear in the front lines of the labor struggles carried on by the semiskilled workers. This was the case of the Fiat workers from Southern Italy, who lived a strictly segregated social life (lodging, leisure, etc.)[112] in the cities and who played a leading part in the Italian delegate movement. The second group, those who remain on their land, live as farmers and use their factory wages to keep up their homes, buy electrical appliances, and sometimes even to subsidize their farm work. Less directly dependent on their factory work and on the urban surroundings, these people have taken a smaller part in labor action.[113]

In similar fashion, two categories of foreign workers can be distinguished. Arriving in large numbers in the 1960s to fill labor shortages in Western Europe, some—birds of passage—came for several years to make enough money to return to their homes, either to marry, to build a house, or buy a small business and become independent. Others came with their immediate families and, while continuing to send money home each month for other family members, progressively became members of their new communities.

The farmer-workers and the foreign workers who came to build up a stake and return took a different attitude toward labor demands than did the peasants and foreigners who gradually integrated themselves into their communities and factories. The first hesitated in the face of a strike because it threatened their pay. The second group took a leading role in the struggles, especially to improve working conditions. These two opposed attitudes and behaviors of the new workers should be compared with the two kinds of reactions to a production system based on the extreme division of labor: submission or revolt.

It must be noted in passing that these attitudes are quite different from those held by the majority of the native skilled workers, who formed until quite recently the essential core of the production system. Their constant concern has been to negotiate pay and to protect their jobs, which clearly separates them from the extreme attitudes just described. If this difference at present is quite clear and strongly influences labor action and union activity, it seems that in the future the distinctions will gradually fade. The simple tasks of the semiskilled operatives and the complex ones of the skilled are slowly shifting. The skilled workers are moving toward specialized and repetitive tasks under more and more closely timed conditions, even to the point of losing their acquired skills. On the other hand, although most of the work of the semiskilled is repetitive, a number of tasks require a certain apprenticeship, sustained attention, and agility. Consequently, the line between these two kinds of work often is uncertain and will become even more so.

In the United States, the most important source of the labor required by the auto industry (employing directly or indirectly one American out of six) was from rural areas. In distinction to Western Europe, where the new labor came primarily from the national or regional peasantry, in the United States the source was the mass of southern black farm laborers, to which were added certain immigrants of recent arrival. Because class and race coincided more in the auto industry than in other industries, some particularly violent incidents occurred. In the summer of 1967, Detroit experienced the bloodiest American riot in fifty years. This was the "great revolt" of the blacks. One week of rioting left 43 dead, 347 injured, 3,800 arrested, 1,300 dwellings destroyed, and 2,700 stores looted. The majority of the damage was done in the black areas. The estimated property loss was $500 million.[114]

First the Second World War production effort and then the rapid growth of the American auto industry until the recessions of the 1950s brought a large increase of employment, and obliged the companies to call on new sources of labor. One effect of the pause in the growth of the 1950s was to eliminate many of these jobs. The hiring of blacks stopped for several years, and the number of posts available dropped radically, especially at Chrysler. When the industry revived, black workers were again hired in large numbers and were usually assigned to the assembly lines and to the noisiest and most dangerous manufacturing departments where physical labor was most intense. This influx of black labor to Detroit slowed down in the 1960s, but by 1970 the city of Detroit housed 660,000 blacks, 44 percent of its population. Nationally, black workers by 1970 made up 13.5 percent of the labor force in the automobile industry. In Detroit plants, some production and assembly lines had more than 60 percent black workers.[115]

This new labor force also includes other non-European minorities. Black workers in Detroit coexist tensely with mountain people from Tennessee, Kentucky, and West Virginia who are fiercely individualistic and whose working conditions are scarcely better than those of the blacks. In addition, immigration to the Detroit region from Arab countries, until 1966 quite small, grew strongly thereafter. In the Detroit area, the Arab community in 1975, depending on how it is defined, may have numbered between 40,000 and 60,000. Nationally, some 15,000 Arabs were members of the UAW. In 1973 an Arab leader asserted that 2,000 of the 35,000 workers at the Ford

River Rouge plant were Arabs. By one estimate, Chrysler employed some 4,000 Arabs in three of its Detroit-area factories during this period. Perhaps 3,000 Arabs lived in Dearborn in the early 1970s, many of them from Yemen. So the Mediterranean peasantry had come all the way to Detroit.

These changes in the composition of the semiskilled work force created some serious problems because racial issues became intermixed with labor relations. An extreme case was the example of the Dodge Main plant, where in the early 1970s about 90 percent of all foremen were white, 100 percent of the superintendents were white, and 90 percent of the skilled workers and skilled apprentices were white. The majority of the white workers were Polish-Americans. They held the best jobs and controlled the plant's union local. In addition, the factory was located in the town of Hamtramck, an enclave in Detroit peopled by a large number of Polish-Americans. This group dominated the city administration and the police force, which bore the responsibility for keeping the peace in case of riot or strike. Thus, class and race conflict coincided and affected social and labor relations.

The Polish-Americans did not like the working conditions any more than the black and Arab workers, and they too fought for higher wages. Because of their positions of power in the union and the town administration, they also considered the well-being of the company, and therefore their demands differed from those of the blacks and Arabs. The union strategy aimed to defend the interests of the Polish-Americans much more vigorously than those of the blacks and Arabs, chronically unemployed and earning the lowest wages. On this point, the situation of the mass of semiskilled workers in the Western European countries is not fundamentally different.

In the Third World, the educational level of the workers in the auto industry is somewhat higher than that of the general adult population. In India, at Premier Automobile Limited of Bombay, the workers constitute a true "elite" from this point of view. The higher level of education in these countries may be a marked acculturation with western values.[116]

The data available concerning automobile labor in the USSR and Eastern Europe are too fragmentary to allow solid conclusions to be drawn about that area.

Semiskilled Operatives and Unions

From just after the Second World War until the 1960s, unions in the auto industry in Western Europe, Japan, North America, and the Third World constituted a legitimate representation of labor. It can be hypothesized that a serious challenge confronted this system of industrial relations when the companies began to hire massive numbers of rural and foreign workers to fill semiskilled positions. What has become more and more clear, especially in Western Europe, is the lack of agreement between the aspirations of these new workers, thrown in huge quantities into urban and industrial life, and the normal union practices, traditionally defined and organized by native-born, stable, and skilled workers.

The mass of these new, untrained workers, whatever their degree of acceptance at work or of rejection in the urban or national culture, and whatever the degree of their submission or revolt, feel themselves most often outside the world of the union. A certain number of precise reasons explain this phenomenon.

In the first place, the formulation of the semiskilled operatives' demands poses a problem. From the point of view of work done and functions performed, this group is heterogeneous, as revealed for example, by the independent work of warehousemen and parts suppliers, the machine workers paid according to the nature of the machine, or the independent jobs on the lines. This group, moreover, has a high turnover. Restless, but confined to narrowly specialized tasks, these workers have high mobility, which expresses a rejection of work. Because they have collectively lost responsibility for what they do and for their relations with the company, this mass of operatives can find no identity in their occupations nor even less in a social homogeneity. As D. Mothé has said, the semiskilled workers constitute an imaginary category.[117]

In the second place, if stating the demands raises difficulties, the translation of these demands into a progressive and calculated strategy, fitting into traditional union action, is almost impossible. If the essence of the demands of the skilled workers is simply the right to live by their skilled labor, the demands of the semiskilled are, even when expressed in terms of pay, fundamentally the need to be recognized as responsible persons performing useful activities. Hence, they most often place emphasis on working conditions. It can even be asked at this juncture if this is in fact a "demand" in the traditional union sense because such recognition challenges the very principles of the new organization of labor. Another question is whether the job actions of the semiskilled are simply rejection or confrontation, whether they contend against narrowly specialized work or against the company that can no longer assure any vocational or social integration. Yet, by defining these people in purely negative terms, the risk is posed of losing sight of the general and coherent aim that concerns their place in society.

The third reason explaining the recalcitrant attitude of these workers toward the unions is their manner of participation in the actions of organized labor. Rarely are the semiskilled operatives defended by their own kind. First, the skilled men through their seniority and their qualifications monopolize the union leadership so that the semiskilled worker does not even enjoy the opportunity to defend himself. Secondly, when the semiskilled worker does become a union militant, he is no longer a worker without responsibility, whether he puts his work aside for a time or whether his work is only a secondary and uninteresting part of his life in comparison with his union activity. The consequence of this is that the semiskilled worker finds no adequate expression in the union as presently constituted. This explains the appearance of a special mode of worker representation, the delegation, which, emerging only at the time of a job action and usually recognized as temporary, is most often considered as a fighting group rather than a stable negotiating body.

The last reason is that, faced with the apparently diffuse and wide-ranging character of the objectives sought during labor conflicts, no satisfaction can be granted that would guarantee "social peace" in any lasting manner. This has the effect of seriously weakening union power each time that it bases its action on the principle of mutual agreement with management, a principle that was in fact the premise of industrial relations until the 1960s in Western Europe, Japan, and North America.

The complex relationship between the major actions of the semiskilled operatives and the unions during this period becomes more clear if the situation just described is taken into account and summarized. The labor force forms no homogeneous category; the formulation of its problems is in practice almost impossible; the translation of its difficulties into specific demands is most often inadequate; and, finally, a true representation of workers in most cases is not compatible with traditional union practices. For these reasons, management in West European automobile companies sees the struggles of the semiskilled rural and foreign operatives as basically subversive. The various conflicts appear to have a vague and indefinable character, breaking out spontaneously with no regard for deadlines and promises.

It seems more and more clear that if the mass of untrained workers cannot succeed in formulating its demands other than by struggles—daily ones, both individual and collective—this is partly attributable to the lack of adequate structures to represent and act for those workers. The shop delegate movement in Italy, especially at Fiat, therefore, can be seen as a crucial experiment in spite of its decline in recent years. By setting up new structures of this type during the conflicts at Turin from 1968 to 1972, the delegate movement in the Italian auto industry took responsibility for the "indefinable" problems of a labor group that asserted itself as the majority in the production process. The movement was truly innovative in its practice, whether or not it dealt with practical changes in labor relations in the factory or with transportation, housing, and other aspects of life outside the factory.

Although the delegate movement in the period 1968–72 touched all sectors of Italian industry, it reached its apogee in metalworking and its most advanced form in automobiles. It appeared most clearly at Fiat. During the strikes, alongside the union representatives and often in opposition to them, appeared delegates representing "groups of homogeneous and united workers."[118] The term "homogeneous" referred to a group of workers from the same area of production or assembly line, for example, and was meant to be a response to the Taylorist practice of dividing the workers in the same unit so as to arouse competition. The term "united" referred also to the cohesion of the workers, but here not against Taylorist division but against the union rivalries which, in the eyes of the workers, weakened the struggle.

This new structure of representation and worker action, whether it was on the margin of the unions or against them, carried with it a specific demand: insistence on direct worker control of the work process and of decisions on working conditions. Such a demand is nonnegotiable, and therefore the delegate movement was in no way simply a shift of union action from the company level to specific production sections. As it evolved at Fiat, the delegate movement did not seek to create supplementary negotiation at the shop level, but aimed rather at direct worker control over working conditions in all processes, whether this involved such factors as measurements of effective work time or of output, the determination of rest periods or involuntary work stoppages, arranging work stations, or updating work standards.

The movement was strong to the extent that it substituted for negotiations a direct takeover of working conditions and wage determination. This also made it radical to the extent that it took from both management and the unions the right of decision on the nature of the work system. Here also were sources of its weakness and its decline once the open conflicts ended, for at this point the functions of the delegates from the assembly lines changed into special cases of negotiation at the shop level, and in this way integrated themselves quite naturally into the union. These reasons explain the limited character of the delegate movement and an unexpected result: the massive unionization that so far has always followed such an experience.

This situation affected the orientation of the organized labor movement in Western Europe. In Italy, the unions themselves took the initiative (as a kind of response?) of generalizing the institution of worker delegates, as if channeling those labor actions that threatened to escape their control so as to maintain their leadership of the labor movement. In other countries, such as France, the accent put by certain unions on themes such as leveling wages or more generally for worker control brought about a reorientation of their strategies, but not to the point of recognizing autonomous action. Only certain political groups on the extreme Left, outside the factories, fully supported this kind of action and contributed to it.

In the American auto industry, the model of industrial relations established just after the Second World War, which was based on a decentralized system of negotiations, underwent no change in form. Nevertheless, relationships among the different social groups began to shift in the 1960s for reasons analogous to those in Western Europe. A massive hiring of workers new to the industry did indeed occur, though at a less rapid pace than in Europe. Thus, the average age of auto workers remained higher in the United States. But these people worked in more decentralized factories and at higher pay, which may explain the lower frequency of wildcat strikes.

However, the specific trait of this evolution in the American auto industry in which it differs from Western Europe is that the new laborers are almost exclusively non-European in origin. In Detroit, for example, they are composed of southern blacks, and more recently of immigrant Arabs. Consequently, the UAW, in spite of its stated democratic stance, has become somewhat less representative of the workers at the base.[119] By the end of the 1960s, the UAW had lost contact with a good part of these people and especially with the minorities among them. If, at that time, 30 percent of the UAW membership was black, only 2 blacks sat among the 36 members of the executive committee. In 1969 blacks held only 7 of the 100 key posts in the union. Finally, though 14 percent of the UAW were women, the executive committee included only 1.

What was true at the top also held true at the bottom. In the plant locals, those with older European immigrant backgrounds outnumbered young workers of non-European origin, with certain significant exceptions. For example, the local for the GM Technical Center in Detroit representing 4,000 mainly white, well-paid skilled workers, did not hesitate to set up barricades during the 1970 strike at GM and defied some orders isssed by UAW headquarters. It was from this Technical Center also that the first autonomous worker organization hostile to the UAW originated in the 1970s, aiming to take control of the shop. This organization (the United National Caucus) spread to several other companies as a reaction against what it considered too cozy relationships between the UAW leaders and company managements, and as a reaction against the racism at the heart of the union hierarchy, including the plant locals. An example of the UAW understandings with management occurred during the GM strike of 1970. Management granted the UAW a delay in the premium payment for health insurance ($40 million) because of the union's heavy expenditures during the strike. At its conclusion, GM charged the UAW 5 percent interest.

Some autonomous organizations of black workers appeared in 1957. The best known of these was the TULC (Trade Union Leadership Conference), which was started by employees at the Ford River Rouge plant. In 1963 it held a peaceful demonstration march at Detroit in which Martin Luther King led 200,000 persons, the majority black. The lack of results from this kind of peaceful demonstration lay behind the bloody riot of 1967. Even more radical organizations of black workers appeared thereafter, such as the Dodge Revolutionary Union Movement (DRUM), whose actions were not aimed solely at the factory but also at "the most vulnerable point of the American economic system, the assembly line."[120] DRUM was at the origin of the first wildcat strike Dodge had known in many years and which occurred a few months after the black riot of 1967. Later, DRUM gave birth to a movement with a larger audience, the League of Revolutionary Black Workers (LRBW), but the league died away in 1971.

In the United States automobile industry, wildcat strikes were not simply the work of blacks. The case of the famous strike at GM's prestigious plant at Lordstown, Ohio, in January 1972, offered an example. The factory ran the fastest assembly line in the world (104 cars per hour versus 76 at Dodge Main). Production was automated to the maximum and controlled by computers. Engineers organized the work according to the most modern methods. This, however, did not keep 97 percent of the 8,000 workers from spontaneously voting to strike, denouncing the work tempo, discipline, and conditions in general—in this pride of GM—and then go off in the country nearby to play and listen to music. The press spoke of this event as "an industrial Woodstock."[121] Several years later, a careful analysis of this episode by an English investigator sympathetic to labor found its causes not in a changed attitude toward work by a younger generation but in more traditional issues, such as a "speed-up" instituted by a new and authoritarian management team, rivalry among union leaders, and a quarrel over seniority rights.[122]

In many respects, the auto industry of Western Europe and in the United States reflects a common situation and workers movements having similar orientations. Because the difference is only in degree, it can be seen that the conflicts in the United States often represent only a blurred image of what prevails in Western Europe. On the other hand, the particular conditions as well as the particular type of semiskilled labor certainly play a significant role in the form and evolution of the conflicts. Riots in Detroit, the appearance of the Italian delegate movement, and the revolts of Turkish workers in Germany, West Indians in England, and North Africans in France represent many different answers to work situations and types of social existence that are basically similar.

Very little is known in the West about the relations between workers and unions in the auto industries of Eastern Europe, the Soviet Union, and China. Is this because precise information is unavailable or because nothing is happening? One important episode has been described by Adolf Sturmthal. One of the principal centers of the workers' councils movement in Poland that broke out in June 1956 during the strikes at Poznan, and which brought Gomulka to power, was the famous auto factory at Zeran, which employed about 6,000 workers at the time. Long deliberations were held by the Communist party section in the factory, by the factory committee (which was not the union), and in general meetings of workers and salaried employees. These discussions led to proposals that would later be called "worker autonomy."

The secretary of the Zeran factory Communist party cell, who was one of the chief promoters of the workers councils, reported in an October 1957 article in *Nowa Kultura*, "this time we said everything that was on our minds. The meeting was tumultuous. . . . We examined the ways which would permit the working class to have the feeling that it was really administering the enterprise. Many ideas were agreed upon. Many differences appeared. Cautiously we proposed setting up a technical council capable of coordinating our efforts in the economic field. . . . Then we thought that it would not be bad if we had in the plant a workers' council to direct the enterprise, to determine its economic administration and its organization and at the same time to guide it and make recommendations to the directors for execution. We examined this proposal first in the party committee, then in other meetings which in those days occurred frequently. The discussion was often stormy."[123] In fact, the experiment stopped short a few months later. Only when the labor conflicts in Poland broke out in 1980 did an equivalence between unionism and the aspirations of the auto workers reappear.

New Aspects of the Industrial Relations System

The different forms of autonomous workers' organizations—whether they were political movements supporting black workers as in the United States, the emergence of new representation systems as in Italy, or strike committees formed during strikes carried on by immigrant workers in several European countries beginning in the 1960s—all shared a common source: the gap between worker action and union action. The new organizations often expressed themselves in wildcat strikes, movements outside or even against union control.

The union, as an institution, found itself in the midst of the changes in industrial relations in the auto industry that began in the 1960s. The forms of worker autonomy that appeared here and there in the world suggested a new role for the union. As an extreme schematization, everything happened as if the union, in its hand-to-hand combat with management, gradually took over some of the direction of labor that formerly had been monopolized by company officials. This resulted in open conflict within labor and outside traditional channels that revealed a profound crisis in industrial relations.

The following contradiction illustrates this. When wildcat strikes in the auto factories came to play a part in the power struggle in the company, these strikers could not succeed without the organized support of the union any more than the union could take full control of the strikes. Thus, the autonomous action of the semiskilled operatives—peasants, immigrants, women, and blacks—could at the very least result in continued disagreement with the union, if not rejection of it, so long as their fight was aimed primarily against the job while that of the union was aimed against management.

The strikes of these operatives, which spread through the world in 1970–71, often seemed to be revolts characterized by individual and collective actions that again placed the unions in a difficult position, given their own traditions of labor action. The conflicts were, in fact, daily kinds of individual actions, such as the Detroit worker who cracked the skull of his foreman half an hour before the shift change, or the American Ford workers who quit in the middle of the day, leaving the factory and not even coming back to receive their pay. "Quits" were frequent. In 1970 they totaled 25 percent of Ford's workers and 35 percent at Volvo. In the foundry at Fiat, the annual turnover exceeded 100 percent. From 1965 to 1970, some 54,473 workers from southern Italy left Fiat's works in Turin to return home (while 138,000 arrived at Fiat from the same region). Absenteeism reached 25 percent daily at the Fiat factory in Mirafiori and 10 to 15 percent in Detroit. Unorganized and unsystematic groups committed such acts of sabotage as streaking paint and ripping upholstery. This required more inspectors and foremen, and usually brought tighter discipline and antiunion activity. Such kinds of behavior revealed more of social and working conditions than did actual strikes.

When mass production began, in almost all countries strikes occurred. What first catches the attention about these organized collective actions is the apparent diversity of causes, of the motives impelling the leaders, of the objectives advanced, of the character of the struggles as they unfold, and of the reasons for their conclusions. The four following case studies of strikes provide a spectrum of the nature of the conflicts, their progress, and their resolutions:

CASE I. This strike occurred at Ford's Liverpool works in 1973 where the government was trying to freeze wages. Thus, management could not negotiate over wages. The unions asked for pay equivalent to other industries (Ford workers received relatively low pay) and a thirty-five hour week. Management did grant 20 percent of the raise requested. But then immigrant workers—35 percent of the labor force, who came from the West Indies or from Asia and made up a larger proportion of those working on the assembly lines—began a series of job actions against certain speed and output requirements. This caught the union by surprise. It quickly recovered and took leadership of these actions. To guard against work stoppages, management gave special bonuses to key sectors prior to the production and assembly lines, sectors where older workers were employed, whereas the more militant workers came from the presses and final assembly. Management then bypassed the union by sending letters to the workers asking them to pressure the union to sign the agreements. But it seemed that contracts, signed or not, were not the real target for conflicts at the shop level. Work resumed after several weeks of slowdown or stoppage.

CASE II. The second type of conflict appeared at the Volkswagen plant in Hanover in 1969. This factory employed about 10,000 people, including 3,000 women and 5,000 immigrants, comprised of 1,500 Turks, 1,500 Spaniards, 1,200 Greeks, etc. The strike movement originated in the press department, and outbid the union with demands concerning production speed. A pay increase and union-management experiments with reassigning jobs stopped the strike, but worker dissatisfaction found new ways of expression such as absenteeism, which reached a 22-percent daily average; a high rate of turnover; and workers quitting in the middle of the day. When management wanted to fire a large number of immigrant workers, the unions vigorously opposed this. Many of the German workers supported this position, allowing the union to reforge labor unity. Management backed down and allowed the union to set up new working arrangements that were based on homogeneous groups of workers. The workers opposed this change until assured that it would not increase production speeds. Next, they obtained some advantages on skill requirements and a pay hike of 400 marks per month.

CASE III. This occurred at the Renault works in 1973. It concerned job classifications and pay differentials among different posts. Some 400 semiskilled operatives in the press department struck. They were young, and 80 percent of them had immigrated from Algeria, Spain, and Portugal. They wanted promotion to the classification of skilled worker, which would bring a pay increase but especially a minimum-wage guarantee if they were shifted to another job. Achieving the skilled level meant that pay would go to the man, not to machines or work stations. The workers elected their own delegates, who, along with the unions, negotiated with management. The unions decided to support the strike fully, though it caused layoffs in other departments. Management granted some wage increases, but the workers refused to return until their demands on classification were met. The conflict spread, even led to lockouts in some plants, and finally to negotiations. These resulted in the same pay system for all press workers. Since then, wage determination according to work stations has been dropped.

CASE IV. The most unusual conflict took place at the German Ford plant in Cologne in 1973. Turkish operatives began it to protest the firing of 300 of their compatriots who had returned late from vacation. Five hundred workers blocked the lines and set up their own committee, ignoring the union and the factory committee, both dominated by the German majority. The strike committee demanded a rehiring of the fired workers, a slowdown of the work tempo, a raise in wages, and longer vacations. Bitter confrontations occurred between strikers and nonstrikers (mostly Germans) as the latter demanded police protection. Work resumed after a week, and management granted a cost-of-living bonus of 280 marks. But the dismissal of the 300 workers was not rescinded. Important factors in this case were that both union and management accused outside extreme Leftists of intervention, though all the leaders questioned by police did work in the factory; immigrant workers believed that the union paid little attention to their specific problems; antagonisms continued between skilled and semiskilled workers, as well as between Germans and foreigners; and the strike was led by factory delegates, who were members of the union but did not act within the union.

These descriptions of four strikes allow some generalizations to be made about the relations among autonomous work action, union action, and management action. In Cases I and II, the unions took the initiative. Case I is a classic example of "outflanking," where the semiskilled operatives insisted on negotiations—not about wages as the union had done at the factory level, but about working conditions (production speed) at the company level. But unions and workers did join in confronting management. In Case II, the union took the initiative for a strike, this time over working conditions. It obtained satisfaction concerning a series of measures to reorganize jobs about which both workers and management agreed. Summarizing, in both cases the union found it possible to negotiate on the demands.

In Cases III and IV, this did not happen. The movements began outside the unions, and during the strikes autonomous strike committees appeared. In Case III, the strike was led against the union on the principle of wages. The establishment of an autonomous strike committee forced the union to insist that it was the only legitimate bargaining agent with management so as to keep control of the situation. In Case IV, workers outside union control led the movement because they wanted "the moon." In both Cases III and IV, whether the conflict occurred outside the union or against it, the union could not negotiate on the issues.

These results are shown in chart 11–1 in two diagrams, in which W represents workers, U the union, and M the management. The two kinds of relationships are W U and U M. The sign + indicates cooperation; the sign − means opposition.

Chart 11-1.
Four Case Studies of Strikes

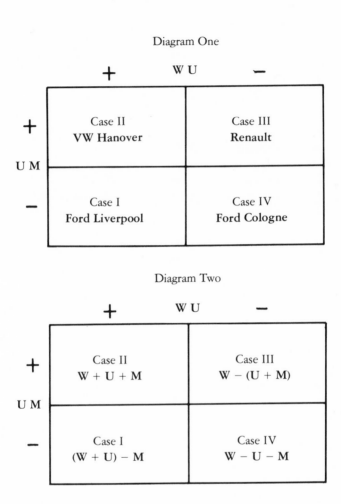

Diagram One

	+	W U	−
+	Case II **VW Hanover**		Case III **Renault**
U M			
−	Case I **Ford Liverpool**		Case IV **Ford Cologne**

Diagram Two

	+	W U	−
+	Case II **W + U + M**		Case III **W − (U + M)**
U M			
−	Case I **(W + U) − M**		Case IV **W − U − M**

In the two diagrams, W represents workers, U the union, and M the management. The two kinds of relationships are W U and U M, with the sign + indicating cooperation, and the sign − indicating opposition.

The first diagram (chart 11–1) shows in Case II that the industrial relations system worked: the union achieved an agreement that satisfied both management and workers. In Case IV, the system broke down, for the union could not serve as mediator. The intermediate cases illustrate situations where alliances are reversed: management isolated in Case I, and the strike committee isolated in Case III.

The second diagram (chart 11–1) shows the relations among these three actors at the end of the strikes, using the same symbols.

Job Redesign

The major labor conflicts that shook the automobile industry in the years before and after 1970 reveal a questioning of the Taylorist organization of labor, which found its most thorough and spectacular expression in this branch of production. This crisis brought a wave of strikes, often wildcat ones, and repressions no less uncontrolled. No one is unaware of private police, company police, and special recruitment activity going on in the large auto firms. Will experiments with job redesign as they have occurred over the past ten years throughout the world operate to change this situation? That is the issue.

The question of how work should be organized is raised everywhere in the modern auto industry—in Western Europe, the United States, Japan, and even in Eastern Europe and the USSR. According to the Labor Institute of Moscow, the most important reason for turnover among workers under thirty in these countries is dissatisfaction with the content of the job. When it is realized that the Soviet Union is the second largest producer of trucks in the world, there is no doubt that this finding applies to the auto industry there. Soviet workers in auto factories—some of which were built by Renault or Fiat—react the same as their comrades in capitalist countries to the assembly line, and the auto plant in Togliattigrad has the longest in the world. Dissatisfaction appears in such forms as slowdowns, absenteeism, and "quits." It seems that Soviet engineers have chosen the same "solutions" as those in capitalist countries: work psychology, economic rewards, studies of pay for work posts, and job classification.

The problem grew particularly acute in the United States. Turnover at Ford approached 25 percent in 1969, and absenteeism in the Big Three auto companies varied between 5.1 percent and 6.8 percent in the early 1970s. Management began to react in this period, and General Motors appears to have accomplished the most. In 1973 the company and the UAW signed an agreement to explore new ways of dealing with the quality of work life (QWL). Irving Bluestone, a UAW vice-president, acted as a prime mover in this and in later developments, making sure that GM's commitment went beyond anodyne verbiage to concrete action.

At the GM assembly plant in Tarrytown, New York, already in 1971 local management had begun to open lines of communication and asked workers for their views on plant reorganization. It accepted many of the hundreds of suggestions received about production methods. Heartened by this success and the parallel decline in labor antagonism toward management, the plant's leadership continued its policy of moving toward the workers and surrendering certain prerogatives that it historically had enjoyed. Despite difficulties springing from frequent changes in production schedules and a massive layoff in 1974, the QWL program continued at Tarrytown and was expanded in 1977. Workers' ideas were incorporated in the changeover to produce the entirely new X car in 1979.

What were the results? Attitudes clearly changed, for the union local reported that by late 1978 absenteeism had dropped from more than 7 percent to 2 1/2 percent, and the number of grievances awaiting decision had fallen from more than 2,000 in 1971 to just 32.[124] The Tarrytown episode, in which emphasis was placed on worker participation in decision making about the working environment, is the best example of GM's QWL movement, but it is far from characteristic of all this corporation's factories. It indicates, however, that a change in labor-management relations is possible, even in this huge enterprise.

Considering the size of the world auto industry, the experiments seeking to respond to problems of labor organization in the early 1970s were for the most part hardly on the same scale as the importance of the conflicts, strikes, and revolts, despite the significant drop in production such belligerence brought. Efforts at reorganization began to spread nevertheless. Examples are Volvo and Saab-Scania in Sweden; Daimler-Benz in Germany; Renault at Le Mans, Choisy-le Roi, and Douai in France; and Fiat at Milan in Italy. At the Swedish Volvo factory in Kalmar, such ventures have been pushed furthest. Perhaps the climate of cooperation peculiar to the Scandinavian countries is a partial explanation. A precise description of the essential traits of these experiments is in order.

Volvo management considers its innovations the most important technological event in the industry since Ford introduced the assembly line. It made the decision to create the Kalmar assembly plant on new principles in 1971. Earlier, in 1966, at the Torslanda factory in suburban Göteborg, came the first attempts at new approaches in labor organization. Thereafter, the company tried several experiments in different plants. First, jobs were rotated so workers might perform different tasks on the same day. Secondly, the content of jobs was expanded, so, for example, a worker might follow an auto body along the line, performing various tasks. Thirdly, decisions were decentralized so a group or team receives a job and distributes tasks among its members.

At Kalmar, all these innovations were combined for the first time, along with an antinoise program and the establishment of many rest areas. To these measures to enlarge the job have been added efforts to enrich jobs by regrouping different kinds of activity, that is, preparation, inspection, retouching, and execution so that the worker acquires some skill in different areas.

The initiative came from management, which created the first study group in 1972, including a project head, production engineers, and architects. A committee comprising representatives of blue- and white-collar unions assisted. These labor representatives sat in on all stages of planning, an example of the climate of cooperation between Scandinavian management and unions. Although nothing was neglected in trying to improve working conditions, the consistent rule was never to make concessions on efficiency or profitability, while also meeting the goal of humanizing work and maintaining productivity. The factory is strikingly modern, far from the traditional sawtooth roof style so frequently seen in industrial suburbs.

The system of job redesign worked out at Kalmar depends entirely on work by teams. Each team, numbering fifteen to twenty workers, exercises full antonomy in performing its tasks and has its own work space and tools. In each of these shops, a particular part of the car is assembled, along with the preassembly of some components. Each member of the team enjoys the opportunity to take a turn at each of the operations assigned to his shop. In this way, the workers quickly can become specialists in a particular area and obtain a general understanding of what they are manufacturing.

Work in teams allows the workers to assume a larger role in technical decisions about their duties. In collaboration with production engineers, assembly workers can suggest and develop the manufacturing system that appears most appropriate to them. They decide how to divide the tasks among themselves and how to rotate them. Within limits, they can change work speeds to suit their own rhythm, independently of activities in adjacent shops. Aided by computers, for the first time the workers are responsible for supplying their shops with parts and also for various quality controls (rigorous at Volvo) and for the maintenance of their machinery. The workers need to detect their own mistakes, and in so doing can increase their ability.

The extreme flexibility of work arrangements is feasible only through extensive use of computers. Four of them coordinate the diverse activities of the factory. This allows a thorough decentralization and a delegation to the workers of technical responsibilities, technical decisions, and technical inspection—functions traditionally handled by foremen. The computers, continuously informed as to the stocks of materials, can transmit instructions on specific assembly jobs to the workers. Because information is handled very rapidly, it is possible to interpolate quality control immediately after assembly. This increases the participation by workers in the manufacturing process by allowing them to inspect their own work (information is transmitted to them by telescreens and teleprinters) as they are doing it and so to continuously improve it. One computer manages production and controls the machines. Another handles quality control. A third relays signals for the screens and printers.

Perhaps the most surprising thing about the Kalmar factory is that it cost only 10 percent more than a conventional factory, for a capacity of 30,000 cars per year. This shows clearly that Kalmar is not just a show window to display the humanist aspirations of management, but is indeed a profitable operation that seems to confront the social problems of labor in the automobile industry. Therefore, it is interesting to find out to what extent it responds to the need to humanize factory work, and to see if it provides, even partially, a worldwide model of the future organization of production in this industry, or in all industry.

At Kalmar, positive results were first obtained in the work environment—quiet shops, elimination of uncomfortable working positions, rest areas, on-the-job safety, and information provided ahead of time. These are important because they can be applied in many factories without breaking the assembly lines and they can reduce physical and mental fatigue.

Volvo next sought answers to the extreme division of labor. By organizing workers around complete jobs, such as assembling the front end, they made operating cycles quite long but involving little repetition, allowing the workers a good amount of autonomy. Frequent rotation of tasks, collectively decided, allows the workers to share the heavy labor. They work at their own rhythm and even modify it in the course of the day, pausing when they desire.

Another key element at the factory, group work, breaks down the isolation of the workers. Their relationship with the product changes markedly when small groups can make complete parts of the auto. Seeing the product helps the worker understand the importance of each movement, for these are seen not in isolation but as part of a concrete result. Significantly, the study group decided that the foreman, as supervisor of technical operations, is no longer necessary; and this function has almost totally disappeared at Kalmar. The foreman now plans and coordinates activities. Hierarchical distinctions have tended to disappear in the production sector, and pay is similar for analogous jobs.

Whatever the extent of modifications at Kalmar, their limits must be recognized and their worldwide application questioned because this is a small factory (600 workers and 30,000 vehicles per year). The first group of limits concerns the conditions at Kalmar before the experiment. Management began it for economic reasons. Turnover at the other Volvo factories had reached 30 percent and the company's biggest problem, absenteeism, measured 20 percent. Reducing absenteeism to 8 percent would cut the unit cost of a car to slightly below the level achieved in a standard factory. (A recent report indicates 15 percent absenteeism at Kalmar, a figure that management blamed on a generous sick-pay policy mandated by the Swedish government.) Fifty percent of the workers quitting the firm's other plants did so because they did not like their jobs. The firm considered carefully before choosing Kalmar, a small town of 53,000 on the Baltic. Unemployment was a problem there before Volvo arrived, and certainly turnover in this quiet provincial town would be less than elsewhere. It is difficult to say which part of the lower turnover would come from enhanced interest in the job and which from the lack of alternative local employment.

It must be noted, on the other hand, that this first factory not using a moving assembly line was built that way, not made over, which allowed free rein to the layout, unhampered by traditional considerations. It is also simply an assembly plant, no fabrication being involved. Heavy and noisy stamping presses are not used at Kalmar, nor is the difficult job of welding body elements performed there.

A second series of limitations results from distrust by labor unions, even though those unions at Kalmar took part in the experiment from the beginning. The unions viewed this type of reorganization with some suspicion and their participation, especially elsewhere in Europe, is far from certain. For example, they fear that such reorganization might eliminate jobs without prior reassignment, and that this sort of thing could also encourage paternalistic labor policies. They fear that management might require an increase in production speed in return for bettering conditions. At the Renault factory in Le Mans, where an experiment of this type was made, management asked for an increase in production. It argued that on the old lines much dead time occurred because tasks did not mesh exactly, and contended that under the new system it should disappear because the workers proceeded without interruption.

A third limitation bears on the education and qualifications of the work force that the new system demands. It is a striking fact that essentially no immigrant workers are employed at the Kalmar factory, though in the other Volvo plants they number 30 percent. It is not by accident, therefore, that the most far-reaching and important experiments in job redesign have taken place in Sweden, where the level of worker education and skill is among the highest in the world.

The Evolution of Techniques and Labor at the Beginning of the 1980s

In the world economic situation of the early 1980s, characterized by persistent difficulties and by an increased movement toward concentration of the automobile industry, manufacturers are beginning to play down the policy of job redesign, which some of them took seriously, and are turning firmly toward a policy of automation.

A review of the period of the late 1960s and the 1970s reveals its real significance. As a result of conflicts with semiskilled workers—in Italy called "the bitter enders"—the labor-intensive automotive industry conducted various experiments to redesign jobs. These experiments brought results that sometimes have been underestimated. In France, for example, at the Renault company, which encountered a decade of labor conflict—1967–77—the policy of redesigning and enlarging jobs, begun early in the 1970s, is continuing in various manufacturing and assembly activities. In 1975, at the factory in Le Mans, certain departments adopted the principle of assembly by groups of eight workers, and in the next year autonomous five-person teams began operating in the manufacturing area. Other experiments by the company currently are under way to enlarge jobs. Similar changes have occurred all over Europe and in the United States. The General Motors Quality of Work Life (QWL) program was discussed earlier in this chapter. It has achieved marked success at GM plants in Tarrytown, Detroit, Bay City, Grand Rapids, and Lordstown. Ford and Chrysler have begun to institute similar programs.

As the 1970s drew to a close, Japanese systems of labor-management relations drew worldwide attention as their cars competed successfully on international markets, both in terms of price and quality. "Can we learn something from the Japanese?" asked more and more industrialists. The answer probably was "yes."

Several rather unique features came to characterize Japanese auto labor in the 1960s and 1970s. Workers were not "marginal" types; rather they were considered among the elite of blue-collar employees. They were envied, not pitied. At the big firms, they enjoyed the probability of permanent employment, and their wages and benefits significantly exceeded those of workers in medium and small enterprises. Pay levels depended partly on seniority, partly on job level. Management took an interest in each worker, not only helping him improve his performance at a particular job, but working with him on a career plan. For this reason, workers responded with unusual loyalty to the firm.

Japanese auto companies accomplished much beginning in the mid-1960s with job redesign. In his brilliant analysis of this movement, Robert E. Cole has shown how Japanese management tried to avoid labor unrest springing from worker alienation by encouraging employee participation in decision making.[125] One method used was the quality-control circle, where a small group of workers, usually led by a foreman or senior worker, studied how to solve a job-related quality problem. Such programs not only improved production methods throughout a company, but they also stimulated teamwork, identified natural leaders, and encouraged the personal status and growth of workers, including the enhancement of leadership abilities, skills, morale, and motivation. By 1978 almost 90,000 quality-control circles had been organized in Japan, involving about ten times this number of workers, along with many other small group activities among industrial workers, such as zero-defect programs and improvement groups. Common to these programs was the principle that they did not immediately reward workers with pay increases, but they did allow them meaningful opportunities to exercise initiative and independent judgment concerning their work.

American labor sociologists currently believe that such opportunities are the major factor in alleviating worker alienation. When the Japanese car industry and its market reach maturity and slow their rate of expansion, it will be possible to ascertain whether the industry can still maintain the policies of permanent employment, rapid promotion, and large-scale worker participation in decisions, and whether these policies will continue to avert bitter confrontations between labor and management.

Unsure of the answer to this question, and seeking even higher productivity, Japanese automakers are playing a leading role in automating production. The priority that has been given to it over job redesign is related to the nature of the labor conflicts that Japanese and other manufacturers saw in the factories of Europe and America. The struggles of the semiskilled workers, which broke out in strikes, have now returned (for how long?) to their earlier form of clandestine, daily, and permanent objection to the job as well as flight from it.

The policy of automation, which is evident from the advanced experiments going on with flexible production or in the introduction of series of robots to handle materials, depends on the use of electronics and computers. It anticipates, by the year 2000 if not before, a shift from the automatic machine tool to the electronic machine tool (usually called "numerically controlled machine tool"). This can be defined as the fourth stage in the evolution of machine tools. Such a shift calls for some comment. In contrast to the classic automatic machine tool, which is set up with mechanized transfer of the work from one machine to the next, and where the action is repetitive and permanently programmed in advance, the electronic machine tool has a calculator and a memory. These give it some autonomy of programming, which allows it, within general guidelines, to arrange its own actions and to inspect its own work.

The experiments and achievements are more or less advanced in various countries. At Renault's factory in Flins, some of the body work is performed by twenty-one robots stationed on the assembly line. Another system performs all body painting automatically. Volvo uses a similar arrangement to assemble motor blocks and GM to install wheels. Chrysler ordered a hundred robots in 1980, and by the end of that year GM employed a total of 425 of them. In Japan, the Nissan plant in Zama employs robots to make from 2,000 to 3,000 welds on various models, or about 96 percent of all welding. Toyota in 1980 ordered 720 robots from a Japanese licensee of an American producer. At the end of 1980, more than 10,000 industrial robots were at work in Japan, two or three times more than in the United States.

The most advanced use of robots requires them to select and distribute parts. The electronic machine tool possessing this ability can handle an almost unlimited number of possibilities and consequently deal with situations that are nearly unpredictable, just as a human operator would. This differentiates it from the classic automatic machine tool, which is programmed only for a small number of operations, well defined in advance. The electronic principle makes it possible to use machines for complex materials handling, not only partially mechanized jobs such as welding and painting, but also operations that heretofore had not been mechanized or automated, that is, assembly. This innovation has historic importance, especially for labor, for ultimately it will transform the final stage of auto manufacturing, assembly operations, where this industry is labor-intensive. According to some estimates, electronic machine tools will lead to the elimination of from 40 to 70 percent of the productive jobs where they are installed.

Flexible production is another major innovation based on the use of electronics. Consisting of a group of machine tools controlled by a computer, this system differs from one comprising a line of machines that are automatically synchronized. The computer determines the movement of parts from one machine to another instead of their following a constant itinerary. Significant gains in productivity are anticipated from this system, but the salient point is that the introduction of electronic machine tools challenges the traditional sequential production process, whether it is a line formed by human operatives or a line formed by a succession of machines. If the assembly line someday disappears, this will not only mark a page turned in the history of the automobile industry, but also in the history of labor.

12.   The Automobile under Fire

Jean-Jacques Chanaron

Until the 1960s, world opinion found the positive consequences of the Automobile Revolution most impressive, that is, the spread of a method of personal transportation allowing an unprecedented freedom and speed of movement. Freedom and speed! Still today this vision prevails in the Third World, and even in the communist countries. It no longer does in the West and in Japan. The extraordinary growth of motorization since 1961 raised to a critical level the social costs and noxious side effects of the automobile. In consequence, movements began almost everywhere, but initially in the United States, to fight against the results of the Automobile Revolution, and even against the automobile myth. As an expert of the Organization for Economic Cooperation and Development (OECD) phrased it, "The automobile is no longer accepted uncritically as an unmitigated blessing."[126]

The Social Costs of the Automobile

From 1960 to 1975, the proportion of the population in the OECD countries (Western and Southern Europe, North America, Japan, Australia, and New Zealand) living in urban areas rose from 58 to 64 percent, most of this growth being concentrated in the larger metropolitan areas. The OECD calculates that at least a quarter of its members' population lived in cities of more than a million inhabitants in 1970. In these cities, the number of vehicles more than doubled over the decade 1960–70. Predictions suggest that this trend will result in sixty cities containing more than a million inhabitants by the year 2000, compared with forty-seven in 1960, and that the number of automobiles will double every two decades. These projections rest on extrapolations from trends prior to the 1973–75 and 1979–81 slumps in the automobile market and are subject to minor changes, especially concerning the trend in the number of cars.

Although the balance of the advantages as against the nuisances of the automobile is shifting toward the latter, most clearly in the older cities of Europe, such is not yet the case in rural areas and small towns, and even in many large cities outside Europe. In these places, the mobility and independence brought by the automobile are still real. The pollution, traffic, noise, and accident problems are not so serious as to be perceived as major disadvantages. At the same time, the low population density of rural and small town areas means that convenient public transportation is not economically feasible, so no alternative transportation to private automobiles is available.

The consequence is a complex political issue. Is the plethora of automobiles a national or a local question? Should regulations designed for overcrowded cities, such as higher taxes on gasoline or emission control, be imposed on rural areas for the sake of uniformity? Does administrative tidiness necessarily bring equity? Once again, the age-old question of the one and the many confronts the societies and their political leaders in the industrially advanced areas. It will be interesting to observe how they try to answer it.

The twin phenomena of growing urbanization and growing motorization accounts for the importance of the negative side effects in the cities and the higher awareness among city dwellers of these problems and their consequences. The noise and air pollution caused by automobiles, the traffic jams and their effect on public-transit systems and on the waste of fuel, many of the accidents, especially those involving bicycles and motorcycles, and, finally, the social nuisances such as the destruction of normal city life and visual ugliness, all these are much more serious problems in the cities. This is why they have a higher priority there.

Most of the disturbing noises in the cities are attributable to automobile traffic. Trucks and buses, motorcycles, sport cars, and standard cars are the noisiest elements, but streetcars and elevated trains should be added. Measurements made in the United States in 1962 established the following results for vehicles equipped with standard mufflers: for a truck traveling at 50 miles per hour, 80–83 decibels A (decibels A—dbA—indicating decibels weighted to the sensitivity of the human ear), for a motorcycle at 65, 81–89 dbA, for a sport car, 65–74 dbA, and for a standard car, 67–71 dbA. Not enough measurements have been made over time to permit historical comparisons. OECD experts have stated that automobile noise in European cities rose 10 decibels from 1954 to 1967. This increase came primarily from the spread of arterial highways carrying rapid and heavy traffic.

Several factors tend to increase or reduce noise levels: climatic conditions, time of day, natural screens such as walls and trees, type of highway pavement, width of streets, character of buildings, design and age of vehicles, nature of the street network, and the type of signals. A vehicle makes noise at neither a constant level nor continuously. It rises with vehicle speed and with acceleration. At a constant speed, it depends on the nature of the pavement. From a fixed reference point, such as a street corner or inside an office or a home, it rises to a peak then recedes as the vehicle moves on. A regular flow of traffic, on the other hand, creates an almost constant background noise, the peaks corresponding to trucks, buses, and motorcycles.

Noise from automobile traffic affects human beings in three ways: their mental states, their physiology, and their activity. The subjective effects, usually described in terms as irritation, annoyance, or disturbance, concern the undesirable effects of automobile noise. Sound level is "a matter of individuals and their sensitivity and is defined more by human values and the environment than by precise physical measurement."[127] The sensitivity to noise and the awareness of its irritation varies among individuals; it is difficult if not impossible to calculate a minimum standard below which the disturbance would not be felt. Still, some correlations have been detected. Sensitivity varies with the energy level of the sound and the frequency of the vibration. It is in the quietest places that sensitivity is the most acute because it is related to variations in sound. This leads to the matter of becoming accustomed to a noisy background. A person's awareness under this circumstance varies with the degree of his activity, whether he is engaged in manual or intellectual activity, whether he is listening to radio or television, or whether he is sleeping.

The numerous studies conducted in France, the United States, the USSR, Sweden, Japan, and elsewhere differ in their results, but it can be concluded that, for a sound level of 40 dbA, the probability of awakening from sleep is around 10 percent, but for a sound level of

70 dbA it reaches 60 percent. The time needed to fall asleep rises with the average sound level—ninety minutes at 50 dbA—and older people are the most affected. The length of the period of deep sleep shortens in relation to the intensity of the sound.

Noise causes psychic reactions that disturb study, or the performance of a task. Because attention is distracted, intellectual effort is affected the most. Two phenomena occur. First, noise arouses strong irritation and a feeling of frustration accompanied by a spectacular drop in efficiency; and, even after the noise stops, the inability to change the situation plays a large part in the level of annoyance. Secondly, the distraction leads to a fall in the intensity of effort and so of the efficiency of the activity.

Noise may have physiological impacts. Although the many studies conducted in all the heavily motorized countries by public, private, and international organizations have not succeeded in proving scientifically that human injuries are sustained from the noise of automobile traffic, medical studies have found irrefutable evidence of sympathicotonic reactions (cardiac accelerations and arterial hypertension), of psychosomatic conditions (pupillary dilatation and insomnia), and of sense changes (lowering of the threshold of hearing perception). The violence of noise, or its unexpected character, induces phenomena of fear and prostration (peristaltic contractions, flow of saliva and gastric juices, and elevation of intercranial pressure); the force of one's involuntary start varies with the degree to which one is accustomed to the background noise. The physiological effects can be cumulative: accelerated weakening of hearing with age (presbyacusia), and qualitative and quantitative disturbance of sleep.

Unfortunately, mechanical and tire noises are difficult to reduce. To achieve more than the 10-percent average reduction of automobile noise gained since 1970 due to long and expensive research, drivers probably will need to accept a considerable increase in the cost of vehicles.

A second major side effect, air pollution, has been produced by urbanization and motorization. Traffic in cities certainly has increased in amount, but it has also spread over more hours of the day, especially since 1960. The quiet periods between the traditional rush hours have shortened because of more serious traffic jams that extend the rush hours and because of the more frequent use of cars for all sorts of trips, such as home to work, home to services, and home to entertainment. In addition, traffic has increased in suburban and outlying areas. Although the intensity of urban traffic has tended to stabilize as saturation has been reached in most of the large cities, its extent over space and time is still growing. Consequently, concentrated pollution and noise levels are felt over wider and wider urban areas, and affect more and more people over longer periods of time.

What exactly are the pollutants generated by motor vehicles and what are their origins and consequences? Despite its high degree of development, the internal-combustion engine emits some gases and particles. In theory, the combustion of light hydrocarbons is inoffensive and nontoxic because it produces only carbon dioxide and water. But the special requirements of driving—flexibility of speed, ease of starting and acceleration, power—cause pollution. All these special attributes required of automobiles are provided by a slight excess of fuel in relation to the theoretical mixture that would produce only water and carbon dioxide.

As a result, exhaust contains the products of incomplete combustion, basically carbon monoxide and unburned or incompletely burned hydrocarbons. To these emissions are added the derivatives of tetraethyl lead, an antiknock substance added to fuel to increase the compression ratio so as to raise performance. High engine temperatures cause the formation of nitrogen oxides (NO and NO_2). From the automobile's exhaust come an estimated 55 percent of the hydrocarbons, and 100 percent of the carbon monoxide, nitrogen oxides, and compounds of lead. Leaks from the crankcase account for 25 percent of the hydrocarbon emissions, and evaporation from the fuel tank and carburetor provide the rest. Other pollutants, also toxic but less well known, are given off by automobile engines. These include phosphates, aldehydes, organic peroxides, ozone, and carcinogenic carbides.

The quantity of pollution depends on the character and design of the cars. A European or Japanese car of the 1972 type emitted annually 770 pounds of carbon monoxide, 88 of nitrogen oxides, 35 of unburned hydrocarbons, and 2 of salts derived from lead and carbon. For an American car, the figures came to 1,650, 494, 88, and 6.6 pounds.[128]

Measurement of the share of atmospheric pollution caused by motor cars depends on a number of variables that make international comparisons risky or even impossible. Still, to illustrate the problem some figures can be offered. For the entire United States in 1977 and as a proportion of all emissions, cars and trucks generated 75 percent of carbon monoxide, 35 percent of hydrocarbons, and 29 percent of nitrogen oxides.[129]

What effect does air pollution have on the health and well-being of human beings? Specialists agree that auto pollution constitutes a growing menace for city people, but they disagree on the gravity of this threat. Its physiological effects are not well understood. Setting minimum standards depends on more knowledge in many scientific areas—such as biology, medicine, chemistry, toxicology, and meteorology—and better techniques of measurement. It also depends on technical innovations capable of reducing or ending unhealthful emissions. Based on what is known at present, then, it remains difficult to calculate the toxicity of various pollutants. It is known that each geographic situation is unique. The real effects of pollution depend on the climate—winds, rains, and temperatures—the layout of the city, the density of traffic, and the several factors that determine the concentration of toxic gases in the air. To all these must be added the subject's length of exposure to determine the risks of the organism changing if not the kind of change.

The many studies carried out in most of the industrialized countries have increased knowledge of the effects of some major types of pollutants. The dangerous effects of high levels of carbon monoxide are well known. A 0.2 percent concentration in the air will kill all organic life in a few minutes. At lower levels, monoxide effects are significant. It reduces the blood's oxygen-carrying capacity, interferes with vision and judgment of time (rate of carboxyhemoglobin), changes psychosomatic performance, and increases cardiovascular difficulties.

Hydrocarbons, the cause of photochemical smogs of the kind first famous over Los Angeles,[130] are directly responsible for eye irritations and significant damage to plant life. The products of the oxidation of hydrocarbons contribute strongly to the formation of aerosols and the consequent reduction of visibility leading to accidents. Ethylene causes lesions on plants and so affects agriculture. Ocular and respiratory difficulties come from these types of pollutants, and some, especially those from diesel engines, may cause lung, throat, and bronchial cancer. Nitrogen oxides are responsible for the photooxidation of hydrocarbons. They also lead to many cases of acute bronchitis among infants and respiratory illnesses among adults. They are associated with lesions on plants and corrosion of parts in electronic equipment.

Photochemical oxidants—ozone and peroxides—have attracted less thorough study and understanding of their effects is more hypothetical than conclusive. Vegetation, human health, animals, and certain materials (rubber, textiles, and dyes) are affected by these substances. Among humans, they cause reduced athletic ability, increased coughing and breathing difficulties, and eye irritation.

Tetraethyl lead and its derivatives clearly are poisonous after prolonged and excessive exposure. They concentrate in the blood and so are transmitted throughout the body. Absorbed primarily through respiration and through the gastrointestinal tract, these pollutants hinder the action of enzymes; disturb metabolism; provoke kidney malfunctions, chronic nephritis, chromosome breaks, anemia, and cancer; and may result in impotence and sterility. Young children, pregnant women, old people, and those whose jobs require lengthy exposure—traffic policemen, auto mechanics, and service station attendants—are the most liable to the harmful effects of lead and its derivatives.

Research is continuing on the other gases and particles emitted by motor vehicles. The surprisingly large variety of toxic emissions and their major consequences for humans, as well as for plants and animals and therefore for the food chain—grass, cow, milk, man, for example—suggests the seriousness of the problem and the urgent need to resolve it.

Emissions can be reduced. Auto manufacturers in 1970 began research in this area under public and governmental pressure. They achieved substantial gains. In Japan, over the decade carbon monoxide levels actually declined, and, in the United States, air pollution did not rise significantly, except for nitrogen oxides. Although newer cars polluted less, more were on the road, and emission control devices tended to lose their effectiveness as the cars aged.

Of the various negative side effects of the automobile revolution, safety is the subject that most rapidly awakened public opinion and led to the establishment of regulations and protective features aimed at reducing the accident risk. As Luc Boltanski has stated it, "the multiplication of automobiles has tended to replace the rarity of vehicles by the rarity of space for them in traffic; this correlates with an increase in the number of traffic accidents."[131] Despite continuing improvement in vehicles and roads, the number of accidents seems to rise, following the increase in cars registered. This is explained by the growth in the "number of new drivers and the increased social heterogeneity of these drivers interacting on the highways."[132]

The number of victims injured or killed in auto accidents alerted the public to the safety issue. In this area, improvements in the safety aspects of automobiles and highways allowed a gradual reduction in the number of victims as compared with the cars in circulation. In the United States, the number of deaths per 100,000 vehicles fell from 134 in 1936 to 71 in 1950, 53 in 1970, and 32 in 1977. In France, 161 deaths occurred per 100,000 vehicles in 1962, 127 in 1970, and 62 in 1979. The Belgian figures show a sharp decline from 175 deaths per 100,000 cars in 1949 to 69 in 1969. Significant differences appear for different countries. Several elements account for this: the recency of mass use of automobiles, the quality of the roads and streets, the types of vehicles commonly used, the nature of driving regulations, and the attitude of drivers toward these rules. Figures from few years back reveal how these factors seem to operate. In 1961 the number of victims killed per 100,000 vehicles reached 266 in Italy, 233 in Germany, 190 in Japan, 165 in France, 71 in England, and 50 in the United States.[133]

Causes of bodily injuries vary. Some stem from the environment of the vehicle: the nature of the road, weather, and light. Others concern the vehicle itself: the active and passive safety features, that is, resistance to shocks, road-holding, brakes, accidental breakage of components, and faulty repair or maintenance. Still others are attributable to the driver: lack of experience, intoxication, poor eyesight, fatigue, poor reflexes, falling asleep, heart attacks, aggressiveness, and failure to respect the rules of the road.

It appears that explanations for accidents that have frequently appeared in recent philosophic, sociological, and psychoanalytic literature and which suggest underlying reasons such as aggressiveness, whether it be sexual or social, may be valid only in a limited number of cases. The large majority of traffic accidents caused by driving error is caused instead by competition among drivers, for, as Boltanski argues, they seek "to maximize their gains in space, equivalent to their profits in time. The intensity of this competition depends on the relationship between the available space and the number of vehicles."[134] The value of time, both objectively and subjectively, varies according to the social position of the drivers and because "they possess a very different amount of mechanical power and aptitude for driving—variables highly correlated with social class—it appears that at least in France the competition to obtain the available road space is largely reducible to a class conflict not perceived as such."[135] Each driver is imbued with an attitude toward automobiles appropriate to his social situation, based on a personal internalized set of driving standards, and therefore has implicit driving habits that sometimes lead him to ignore elementary principles of safety.

The nature of accidents (between vehicles, single vehicle, and vehicle and pedestrian or two-wheeled machine) often determines their seriousness. In Europe, about half of those killed are vehicle drivers or passengers, the other half either pedestrians or cyclists. In the United States, the figures are 70 percent and 30 percent because of the many expressways forbidding access by pedestrians and cyclists. Other factors affect the seriousness of an accident, including the speed of assistance and the location of the collision.

The killed and injured in automobile accidents represent a high cost for society. In order to calculate insurance premiums and also to measure the social costs of highway accidents, many attempts have been made to determine the price of a human life or of a physical handicap, to which should be added damage done to vehicles and to the environment. The issue finally boils down to a political matter, for in all cases the development of an appropriate safety strategy for government requires a quantitative and qualitative judgment of this social cost, a judgment whose determinants can be neither logical nor rational but must be moral and ideological. At the most, the money cost of hospital care and of the retraining and financial aid provided for the permanently injured can be calculated, but this is only the dollar cost. Do health and life really have specific financial values?

The phenomenon of traffic congestion is ordinarily limited to urban and suburban areas, for this problem affects interurban roads only in unusual circumstances, such as vacation periods and holiday weekends. Statistics of automobile registrations in industrial countries show that more than 80 percent are registered in metropolitan areas and consequently are likely to travel and seek parking there. The paralysis of urban centers during rush hours and the slowness of traffic flow on urban expressways can be explained both by the inability of the city to adapt to more and more motorization and by the inability of the manufacturers of the vehicles to adapt their technology and design to the urban street system. Average traffic speed gradually has dropped in Boston, Paris, Rome, London, and Tokyo below that of a horse-drawn bus of the nineteenth century. On some urban expressways, the average speed on weekends falls below that of a cyclist.

The many remedies governments have tried have often aggravated the problem. The multiplication of radial highways and circular links among them, of elevated bypasses, and of ten-lane expressways brings the same result: the more space available on the roads leading in and out of cities, the more cars use them and the more paralyzed is city traffic. However wide and rapid these roads may be, the speed at which cars leave them to reach the central portion of the city can be no greater than the speed with which they spread out in the city street network. The average speed of traffic in the central city therefore determines the rush-hour speed on the expressways feeding into the central city. When the exit ramps are saturated, the slowdown sometimes is transmitted for many miles behind. Traffic speed in the central cities at present is limited by the network of streets, avenues and boulevards, and by the signaling system, which did provide some efficiencies when traffic flowed more rapidly.

Central cities built before the age of the automobile cannot be adapted to its massive and unregulated intrusion. If the car cannot be altered, only one solution remains, eliminate the city, that is, spread it out over dozens or hundreds of miles along monumental expressways. This has happened to some large American conurbations such as Los Angeles. Ivan Illich has described the American situation in these words, "The typical American spends over 1,600 hours a year (or thirty hours a week or four hours a day including Sundays) in his car. This includes the time spent behind the wheel, moving or stopped, the hours of work needed to pay for it and for gasoline, tires, tolls, insurance, fines, and taxes. . . . For this American it takes 1,600 hours to cover a year total of 6,000 miles, four miles per hour. This is just as fast as a pedestrian and slower than a bicycle."[136]

The explosion of the city to suit the automobile multiplied distances, making the automobile indispensable. The home is far distant from the job, services, stores, and schools, which often requires households to own more than one car. Entertainment and friends' homes also are distant, which explains some loss of interest in cultural activities and a growth of individualism and loneliness. The street has lost its social function as a meeting place. To these problems must be added those, also difficult to pin down, concerning the disfiguring of the natural countryside—forests and farmland—and historic sites, and concerning esthetics in general, such as the visual intrusion of modern expressways such as those of Los Angeles or the Left Bank expressway in Paris.

To the traffic problems caused by automobiles can be added those stemming from their competition with city and interurban public transportation, and the more recent and even more pressing issue of wasting energy, where a solution would allow progress on other problems. City buses, imprisoned in the flood of traffic, move only slowly, at speeds below those of the old carriages. Except in the Third World and the communist countries, where absolute necessity makes buses successful, the public has tended to spurn all kinds of bus transportation in large cities. However, when cities provide specific measures to expedite surface transit, including reserved traffic lanes and two-way traffic on one-way streets, usage has revived. Underground transit systems are saturated, and their often unpleasant character has turned some of the public away.

Most cities having streetcar or trolleybus systems abandoned them quickly after 1945 on various pretexts: the danger of mixing these vehicles with automobile traffic and chronic financial deficits, whose cause could only be the automobile itself. Nevertheless, despite its lack of route flexibility, the streetcar offered most of the advantages generally sought for in a public surface transit system: speed, adaptability to changes in the rate of traffic, freedom from traffic jams because of travel on its own right of way, comfort, absence of pollution, and limited noise. Another form of automobile competition was trucks against railways and water transportation.

Most urban and interurban public transit systems encountered difficult financial situations that by 1960 led public authorities to take action such as direct financial aid, encouragement to tighten up management, and pressure to abandon money-losing routes. At the same time, however, they invested public money in huge highway programs. The American interstate highway system is 90 percent financed by the federal government, and everywhere else national budgets support highway construction.

It required the massive increase in oil prices decreed by the Organization of Petroleum Exporting Countries (OPEC) at the end of 1973 to point up the energy-cost aspect of the automobile. But actually it took the second oil "shock" of 1979 to raise the energy issue to the highest priority. At this point, the concerns and self-interests of various socioeconomic groups converged: consumers, whose behavior was now really determined by the cost of operating their cars; governments, concerned to maintain their energy independence and a balance in their international payments; and auto manufacturers, anxious to keep their businesses alive.

In the United States, where every family spends an annual average of $1,500 on gasoline, automobiles use more than half the energy consumed by all forms of transportation and close to 55 percent of the total American consumption of petroleum products.[137] Of this energy, 55 percent is used for urban travel and 30 percent for trips of less than ten miles. The low rate of occupancy of cars and the short trips, combined with traffic congestion, results in a low energy efficiency for cars. In Europe, the energy used by automobiles averages about 20 percent of the total consumption of hydrocarbons, and 40 percent of the energy used in transportation. The differences with the United States figures are explained by the technical design and power of the vehicles, by a lower level of motorization than in the United States, and by a different pattern of use.

In the absence of a vigorous campaign to reduce energy use voluntarily, experts calculate that automobiles will account for 30 percent of all European hydrocarbons used by 1990. In cities, assuming occupancy of only one-quarter of capacity, a car burns eighty grams equivalent of gasoline (geg) per person-kilometer; a motorcycle powered by a 350 cc. engine twenty-five geg; a bus or subway, twenty; a streetcar, sixteen; and a moped with a 50 cc. engine, ten geg. Between the car and public transportation, the ratio is four to one. If the rate of occupancy of public transport rises to one-half, the ratio would be ten to one. For interurban trips, the fuel consumption of a car is thirty geg, compared to nine for a railway train. Only an airplane consumes more than a car, two and one-half times. For freight traffic, estimates are contradictory, some finding that trucks and railways use comparable amounts of energy,[138] and others pointing to the clear (one to two) supremacy of railways.[139] Changes in U.S. energy use for transportation are shown in chart 12–1.

Since 1975 auto manufacturers have made significant progress in fuel consumption without major changes in technology. The European model cars for 1980 consumed about 10 to 15 percent less fuel than those in 1975. In the United States, average fuel consumption for the 1980 models was 27 percent less than those in 1975, but federal law requires a drop of almost as much again by 1985. Nevertheless, if all the automobiles in the world are considered, the results so far are modest because of the many older cars still in service, the larger total number of cars, and the behavior of drivers. When it is realized that, except for the United States, Canada, and Great Britain, all the highly industrialized and heavily motorized states depend for more than 95 percent of their petroleum needs on imports, the extent and seriousness of the energy and the economic problems posed by automobile transportation are clearly apparent.

In this situation, some specialists in the matter of energy conservation have decided to propose a radical, if not a revolutionary, shift in transportation policy for people and for freight. To these specialists, the principle, eminently political, of competition, should be abandoned in favor of the principle, equally political, of complementarity. The supply of public transport should be increased substantially and made more comfortable. A privileged place should be reserved for two-wheeled vehicles—special traffic lanes—and for pedestrians. For some major traffic movements, especially those between home and work, new arrangements should be worked out to raise the average rate of occupancy of private automobiles. The success of such schemes in California offers a good example. Consideration must be given to a limitation on passenger-car use in central cities, a necessary condition for a permanent revival of public transit, two-wheeled vehicles, and pedestrian traffic. These kinds of policies must be followed in future city planning, which must break away from precedents. At all costs, situations must be avoided that render automobiles unusable and thereby compromise the future of the automobile industry.

Finally, worn out and discarded cars present a problem. Until they can be recycled, these cars are assembled in immense graveyards

Chart 12-1.

*Annual Energy Consumption of Different Forms of
Transportation in the United States, 1950–1976*

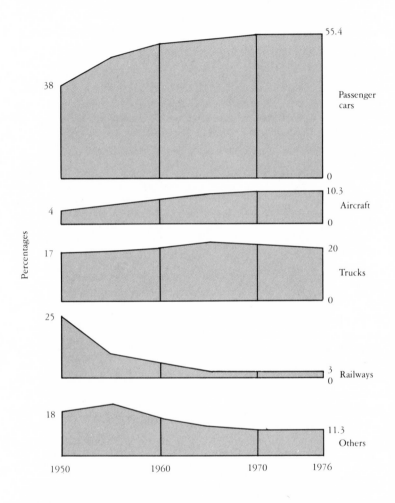

Sources: Pierce, "Fuel Consumption of Automobiles," p. 36; U.S. Department of
Energy, *End Use Energy Consumption Data Base: Transportation Sector*, Tables 1.1A,
1.1B.

outside large cities. Although these have the advantage of keeping the hulks together, they provide an example of a wasteful use of space without even considering their ugliness.

The social costs already enumerated are not the only ones imputable to the automobile. It would be ambitious, and even impossible, to make an exhaustive survey. And factors that bear sociological or ideological significance should also be considered—not the least important among which is the arrival of the automobile at the rank of a myth.

The End of a Myth?

The motor car illustrates the classic example of a luxury product whose spread tends to reduce its attractiveness. The automobile's democratization began with the rise of real income. It speeded up with the relative decline in car prices and the vigorous competition from a well organized used-car market. This democratization accelerated the automobile's ideological devaluation, beginning among those at the top of the social and economic scale. One factor was involved in the case of the automobile that did not affect other consumer durable goods, such as dishwashers or televisions: it takes up so much space. At the very moment when, in the industrialized countries, the least well off socioeconomic groups have managed to obtain automobiles, often at the cost of other aspects of their living standards such as housing, they realize that it is no longer a luxury item and that because of the existing road and street network, when everyone wants to travel at the speed he would like, no one can move. Nowadays, without losing all its prestige, less often is the automobile the focus of obsessions. For many, it has become just another item of personal property, simply a means of transportation.

Other products such as refrigerators, vacuum cleaners, and television sets have spread as widely and rapidly without arousing social or ideological opposition. But the automobile has attracted blame for some of the frustrations and dissatisfactions that have arrived with the consumer society and for which it has become the concrete symbol. More and more rational in their economic choices and concerned about the total costs involved in owning a car, the users-consumers appear willing to change the nature of their "affair" with the motor car and the system of values that its spread has encouraged.

In many countries, but firstly and most vigorously in the wealthy countries, which are also the most motorized and urbanized, the automobile has been challenged as to its usefulness, its necessity, and for some its very existence. Such opposition, even if it is not organized, has become so deep and so well founded that it worries and unsettles those who heretofore have profited so much from automobiles and it provokes them to state their case, to counterattack, or to shift their strategy.

The appearance of criticism targeting especially on the automobile is quite recent. It came first in the United States in the early 1960s; California's first efforts to regulate exhaust emissions date from 1961. It spread then to Japan, particularly affected by the negative side effects of industrialization, and thereafter to all of the industrialized countries. The aim of this opposition campaign has shifted over time. In the 1960s the attack centered on the most obvious side effects: noise, traffic congestion, parking problems, pollution, but especially accidents. The safety matter stirred automobile drivers all over the world the most quickly and strongly, and it also affected cyclists and pedestrians. In the United States arose the consumer movement that had the best organization and strength, the most feared by the industry. From 1965 on its initiatives were frequent and sometimes crowned with success to the point of costing millions of dollars to General Motors (GM) and Ford.

Any discussion of automobile safety must include mention of Ralph Nader, the young lawyer whose activities and name symbolize the awakening of consumers and whose fame spread across the world. His book *Unsafe at Any Speed* appeared in the United States in 1965 and soon in many translations. He assaulted the motor car head-on, and has remained front page news ever since. In the United States, he charged, "In accidents involving all modes of transportation—motor vehicles, trains, ships, and planes—the motor vehicle accounts for over 92 percent of the deaths, and 98 percent of the injuries. This mass trauma represents a breakdown in the relation between the highway transport system and the people who use and control it. From an engineering standpoint, when an accident injury occurs, it is a result of the failure of the technological components of the vehicle and the highway to adapt adequately to the driver's capacities and limitations. This failure is, above all, a challenge to professional engineering, which in its finest work has not hesitated to aim for total safety."[140]

The vigorous campaign Nader waged against the Chevrolet Corvair beginning in 1965—a media enterprise involving print journalism, radio, TV, congressional lobbying, and questions at GM stockholders' meetings—met all kinds of pressure and efforts at intimidation by GM. But the upshot forced GM and in its wake the other American producers to change their cars' designs and begin expensive research programs. It also speeded the establishment of the National Highway Traffic Safety Administration, created in 1966. It has several missions: to inspect new models to see if they conform to current safety requirements, to promote research and encourage manufacturers to continue to improve the safety of their vehicles, and to prepare and issue standards and regulations that become progressively more severe.

Despite all these activities, no fundamental change has occurred in the attitude of manufacturers, governments, or the American public. The manufacturers are content to add some items of passive safety (aimed at protecting occupants in an accident) through reinforcing the structure, and showing the results of their research efforts on experimental safety vehicles without going further than a laboratory prototype utilizing standard components and resembling a monster more than a means of transportation.

Although they have established a complex regulatory structure, the public authorities have continued their concern over the economic interests of the auto industry. This is why the regulations fit in with the existing technical possibilities for passive safety and so can be met at the least cost of adaptation and production. Sensitive to price, auto buyers are not inclined "to pay for safety," but continue to sound drums and trumpets for better protection and security.

Even so, the Chevrolet Corvair controversy in 1965–66, repeated in 1972–73 with the Chevrolet Vega, was a significant step in the debate over automobile safety. The reverberations in the United States and in the rest of the highly motorized countries manifested growing support for the consumer movement and an expansion of its concerns. However, the economic recession into which the industrialized countries fell after October 1973 tended to bring a relative decline in movements of consumers, now more concerned about their jobs and their purchasing power.

Europeans have always been alert to safety matters, but they have not really mobilized or organized around this issue. The auto manufacturers on their own initiative turned their research toward the more difficult and expensive path of active safety (preventing accidents), but this tendency owes as much to tradition as to reflection.

Governmental activity appears to have been more effective on safety in Europe than in the United States. European authorities often conceive their role as expressing the public interest, and impose rules contrary to the interest of the manufacturers, such as speed limits and the regulation and management of traffic. Yet, in

Europe, these kinds of measures often arouse resentment and are characterized as intolerable restrictions on individual freedom, while in the United States they are accepted with less complaint.

Antipollution and antinoise regulations also came in the late 1960s. These issues aroused widespread informal movements, of which certain officials or politicians made themselves the spokesmen in both the United States and Europe. The impact of the provisions of the American Clean Air Act of 1970 was broad. In the United States, automakers counterattacked, claiming they could not meet the standards of a 90-percent reduction in the 1972 average gaseous emissions and that such improvements would bring a substantial increase in the price and operating costs of vehicles. In Japan and Europe, the law at first was considered as a protectionist device because American cars were, for both technical and economic reasons, better adapted to the current methods of pollution control than their foreign rivals.

The intermediate pollution standards set in the United States for the 1975 models required the use of catalytic converters. These devices, which required gasoline without tetraethyl lead, raised the price of cars by $100, but did improve their fuel efficiency. By 1980 the pollution levels set by the Clean Air Act still had not been met completely. American manufacturers have argued that their financial difficulties, which they blame partially on the research and development costs required to reduce pollution as well as the standards of the Energy Act demanding an average consumption level of 27.5 miles-per-gallon by 1985, required a postponement. It is true that, since the emergence of the oil crisis, public opinion has turned away from the matter of automobile nuisances. The psychosociological impact of the spectacular rise of gasoline prices and the very real risk of an interruption of supplies was at the core of a massive shift in demand toward cars of lower price that were more economical of increasingly costly fuel. The research activities of the manufacturers have aimed at the satisfaction of these new requirements. Considerations of air and noise pollution have been somewhat neglected, and the progress achieved so far has been implicitly considered to be sufficient.

In Europe, all the governments tackled the issue and took steps that, without having been decided in common, did follow the same line: reduction of tetraethyl lead in fuel and regulations and standards of an encouraging but not spectacular character. The proposals of the European Economic Community after 1970 tried especially to harmonize standards and deadlines so that the effect would not be too detrimental on the European automobile industry.

Unlike the problems of safety, pollution, and noise, the other negative side effects of automobiles, especially traffic congestion and the waste of energy, have not aroused social protest movements despite the link that can be identified between congestion and noise and pollution. A solution to the first would help the other two.

Traffic problems raise a partial challenge to the existence of the automobile, or at least to some of its implications. But consumers are far from prepared to give up the automobile or even to reduce their use of it and never—or at best only slowly—have accepted restrictive limitations on city traffic. Only indirect action that encourages public transit seems likely to produce some effect. The universal "solution" that finally proved to be a resounding failure was to adapt the city to the automobile by multiplying urban bypasses and expressways and installing devices to manage traffic or to separate various kinds of traffic. A remark the French Minister of Public Works made at the Paris Auto Show in 1973 illustrates in striking fashion the policies of the European, American, and Japanese governments concerning urban auto traffic: "Today we have to learn how to marry the automobile and the city—a city where almost everyone is both driver and pedestrian, resident and traveler, and so has a double reason for wanting this marriage to succeed."[141]

The Mideast Yom Kippur War of 1973 raised the energy problem to a level of urgency. The reactions of automobile owners were to drive less, to buy more small cars and more economical ones, and to reduce or postpone their purchase of new cars. Governments' major concern was their countries' balance of trade and payments, to keep them in equilibrium or reduce the damage caused by higher oil prices. This led the authorities in the rich countries to issue regulations and restrictions on energy use, all the while working out painful revisions in long-term energy development policies. The regulations varied among countries according to the unequal impact of the oil crisis and the different world interests of the various states.

The weight of the economic interests at stake was such that policies devised to respond to the crisis could not be radical, but without radical policies the solutions could only be partial and temporary. The energy crisis could reveal the real problems, which for passenger cars and trucks alike concern transportation policy and not simply the reduction in fuel consumption. But automobile manufacturing and related industries involve at least 7 percent of the gross national product in the major industrial countries, the United States, West Germany, Italy, Britain, France, and Japan. Too rigorous a policy would not find acceptance and would ignite violent social and political conflicts.

It remains true, nevertheless, that the private passenger car, so long considered as a "sacred cow" and as an essential element in economic growth, henceforth raises more questions for society than it solves for the individual. At the moment, it is unthinkable to abandon it because no alternative is available.

General Conclusion

Patrick Fridenson

Among the many industries that in the twentieth century began to manufacture durable consumer goods on a mass basis, has the most important of them—automobile making—seen its best days? The history of its earlier successes and present difficulties leads to this question.

Several promoters of the automobile revolution had seen a glowing future at the very beginning. In 1895 the first automobile magazine in France and in the world, *La Locomotion Automobile*, did not hesitate to contend that "some day the word 'automobilism,' at present a neologism, may well be replaced by the word 'industry.'" That same year, the earliest American automobile magazine, *The Horseless Age*, in its first number predicted, "Those who have taken the pains to search beneath the surface for the great tendencies of the age see what a giant industry is struggling into being there. Everything indicates that the motor vehicle is the next step in the methods of locomotion already established and accepted. The growing needs of our civilization require its arrival, the public believes in it and awaits with the greatest interest its practical application to life on this planet."[142]

Until 1973 the history of the automobile fully justified these early expectations. It became a symbol and motive force for capitalist economic growth—and communist too, in recent years. Like other new consumer products, it went through four successive phases: invention (of an autonomous and marketable means of transportation); product development; rapid expansion of output; and the era of replacement demand. North America started at the same time as Europe, but went through the cycle much faster than its old rival. Advancing at breakneck speed, it reached the final stage in the mid-1920s. Western Europe, much affected by the world wars, has just arrived at this point, and the communist countries of Europe, which are ahead of the Third World, are just reaching the third phase.

In the course of this revolution, the automobile industry has changed more than the car itself. Almost all the technical problems were apparent in the beginning, and subsequently the engineers have dipped into the stock of technical solutions built up before 1914. Basically the improvements worked out after this date that have significantly bettered automobile performance, comfort, and safety, have sprung from minor technical advances rather than from major technological breakthroughs.

The industry has needed to alter its clientele, its labor force, its strategy, and its structure. Starting off by appealing to wealthy urban groups, it then reached the middle classes, and ultimately arrived at the general populace. The industry succeeded in producing enough to bring about this widespread diffusion of cars by combining its growing use of unskilled and semiskilled labor with a small number of highly qualified workers, along with subcontracting for a considerable share of its parts. All this took place in the framework of a complex international division of labor that extended among an always-growing number of countries but that was employed by an always-shrinking number of firms. The progressive decentralization of management structures and the strategy of diversification of output have allowed the companies to succeed.

Because of this industrial evolution, the automobile has gradually changed from the status of a symbolic object to that of a useful product. Yet, if ownership of a motor car has become general and universal, it still remains unequal, depending on income and country. The uniformity of production methods and of type of motive power as well as the structure of the vehicles actually paralleled a differentiation of models. Since the 1930s the Americans have almost monopolized production of large cars because of low gasoline prices and high average incomes, the Europeans and then the Japanese have specialized in small models, and the Third World gives priority to commercial vehicles. Nations, like people, do not make the same social use of cars. It depends on whether they are poor, rich, or somewhere in between.

The automobile made this revolution with its own power. Applicable to other firms and to the entire period is the comment Louis

Renault made in 1920: "If the Renault works were able in such a short time to design and produce all these sorts of products and to supply themselves without the certainty of any outside help, it was solely because of their energy, their will to produce regardless of difficulties, and also because of the boldness and courage with which they confronted all the uncertainties and problems which are the usual result of manufacturing unceasingly new and changing products."[143] The manufacturers came to require, contrary to the early years, a higher and higher amount of fixed capital, but banks played only a minor role in the automobile revolution, as was the case in the iron and steel industry. As for the state, at first it was indifferent to the motor car, then it gave more help to the railways, or even, in the communist countries, for a long time held back the spread of passenger cars. It is only in recent years that governments have granted generous support to the automobile.

It was the automobile industry itself that discovered the organization it needed to adapt itself to fluctuations and changes in demand. General Motors worked this out in the 1920s under the leadership of Alfred Sloan. If the American automobile industry had continued to produce cars that were essentially simple, homely, and cheap—the Model T—the result would have been to stop its own expansion, however desirable this might have been for society.

The effect of Sloanism, however, was to allow one of the major aspects of Fordism to continue. Ultimately, it might well have been possible to automate completely the manufacture of a basic car functionally designed for a mass market, and consequently to free society from the need to furnish workers for the assembly line. But the policy of frequent model changes and diversification of the product line closed out this possibility.[144]

This example suggests that the automobile today is the victim of its own success. In fact, evidence is abundant to support this argument. A means of individual transportation and an encouragement to individualism, the automobile actually fosters an increased intervention by the state to satisfy its needs (such as expressways and fuel supplies), to treat its detrimental side effects, or even to redirect the industry's activities both domestically and abroad. A luxury item at the beginning, it lost that characteristic by its wide diffusion. Along with this diffusion came the effects of congestion, so much so that the criticism that had not been fashionable during the sunny period of scarcity now began to burst forth. Wide usage led to a loss of prestige. But, actually, the automobile is not the true focus of the complaints that are directed toward it; they really aim at certain public policies.

A major center of innovation during La Belle Epoque, before 1914, the automobile has since changed much more slowly because of the complexity of its technology and the cost of the necessary investment in a mature industry. From now on, it will need to appeal for some of its revitalization to those industries that are tending to dethrone it: electronics, aerospace, and nuclear.

The agent of unprecedented progress in the speed and versatility of movement, today the car is held back by its own costs in energy and human lives. A major element in the contemporary accumulation of industrial capital, it now offers a rate of profit in relative decline, especially because of the growing proportion of lower-priced cars and the intensification of competition. The major author of the type of factory organization to which industrial societies owe their prosperity, it now witnesses its own workers challenge this kind of division of labor, especially those on whom its own expansion rests: farmers and immigrants. For many years the liberating answer to social pressure for modern consumer goods—even an automobile trade unionist such as Walter Reuther expressed this view a dozen years ago[145]—it has in recent years heard the thunder of consumer movements in the wealthy countries. Formerly available at prices that in real terms were declining almost continuously because of improving labor productivity, it is now being sold at prices that are rising in real terms just as steadily.

All these challenges and reversals lead to the question: was the crisis of 1973–75 only cyclical or are structural changes on the way? If it is the first, the industry will evolve about the same as before with products somewhat more homogeneous, but will manifest a lower rate of growth in the older industrial countries. Transport by automobile of both people and goods is undoubtedly going to continue to expand in the future, and the least expensive path for the manufacturers is to provide for it with models relatively unchanged from the past.

If the crisis is structural, first of all the car will change. It will become more reliable and durable, quieter and less polluting, but it will be more expensive to buy and operate and eventually it will become heavier and slower.[146] Additionally, a larger proportion of business travel will depend on public transportation (including automobiles), whose comfort, speed, and frequency will improve and which will become more flexible.[147] That is to say, a minor revolution will occur in living styles. Manufacturers will need to prepare to diversify their output, firstly in automobiles other than passenger cars, but also probably beyond automobiles. They will sell fewer simple products and more complex ones, and will export their know-how and their technology. But it is not clear, even in this second scenario, whether the experiments in job redesign popular in Western Europe during the 1970s will spread. They imply substantial investments that will not necessarily enjoy a high priority in the present and near future unless the workers and their unions, as at Fiat since 1971, become leading actors in the policymaking of the companies and force them to advance along this line.

Of these two interpretations, it is not known which is correct, but in any case four things are certain. First, the automobile has a rich future, in itself and through derivatives, even if the industry's growth does slacken. The foreseeable evolution "will certainly reduce the importance of the automobile as a form of consumer investment but it will still remain part of a family's equipment, more frequently rented or obtained second hand."[148] Highways, today built for all types of traffic, will move toward a kind of specialization for different sorts of vehicles, which will permit a reduction of some costs and undesirable side effects. The situation will evolve differently in different countries. Some developed countries possess energy resources that will cover nearly all present and future needs; others, on the contrary, enjoy only slender resources of energy. Some of the Third World countries are thinly populated but have significant energy resources, others are well endowed with both energy and population, and still others lack any source of energy.

Clearly, the outlook for the automobile industry will vary depending on whether permanent confrontation or cooperative agreement exists between the industrial countries and the Third World, and whether the latter countries act independently of each other or create an automobile industry in common in each large geographic region.[149] To other industrial sectors, the automobile industry in many cases will supply the means to optimize their investment capital because of the transfer of its technology. In other words, methods of manufacturing and materials handling devised for mass auto production will be spread to fields further and further removed from their original use through consulting engineering firms that undertake to design and equip factories.

A second tendency will be for even more rigorous competition among motor car makers. It will lead to their focusing on the most profitable activities; to arranging for industrial, financial, and marketing cooperation; and, in the Western countries, to a further increase in the concentration of firms, which will make the automobile industry still more oligopolistic.

In the third place, this competitive struggle will be played out in a larger and larger number of countries. The states of the "golden belt" of the Third World, those that hold the keys to petroleum and/or economic growth and have a minimum of trained labor available and some system of technical education, may establish an automobile industry. At the same time, it is becoming profitable for Western manufacturers to sell in markets beyond the rich countries. The resulting paradox is that the energy and automobile crises may render the automobile even more universal; in short, they may complete the Automobile Revolution.

Finally, the development of the automobile less than ever will be the result of simply the interaction of consumer desires and manufacturers' strategies. The stakes have grown too large. Each citizen's quality of life, and, at another level, the freedom of action of states, depends on it. Whatever the type of society, public authorities will be more and more tempted to step in to further the values and choices of the public, and very probably to move toward control either of the growth of the industry or at least of its structure. The new phase that is opening in the Automobile Revolution, therefore, will be highly political.

Notes

1. Norroy, *André Citroën*, p. 7.
2. Friedmann, *Industrial Society*, p. 395.
3. C. Breer, cited in Burlingame, *Engines of Democracy*, p. 401.
4. The tales that Siegfried Marcus made and then drove a gasoline automobile about the streets of Vienna in the 1860s cannot be credited because of a lack of evidence and consistency. He may have operated a car in Vienna about 1890. See Ickx, *Ainsi naquit*, 2:338–48.
5. This later became the Royal Automobile Club. There were two unsuccessful predecessors, the Self-Propelled Traffic Association of 1895 and H. J. Lawson's Motor Car Club of 1896.
6. The United Motor Cab Company, another large London concern, also was largely French-owned and used French-made cabs.
7. See the discussions in *Automotor Journal* 11 (24 December 1904): 1511–12, and in *La Vie automobile* 5 (1905): 781, 837, 839.
8. Duvignac, *L'Armée motorisée*, p. 179.
9. Ibid., pp. 83–85.
10. Annual reports, P & L archives, Paris.
11. Annual reports, Automobiles Peugeot file, Archives financières, Crédit Lyonnais, Paris.
12. De Dion-Bouton file, Archives financières, Crédit Lyonnais, Paris.
13. Castronovo, *Giovanni Agnelli*, pp. 17–35; *Economist* 67 (22 August 1908): 347–48.
14. Villalon and Laux, "Locomobile," pp. 65–82.
15. National Bureau of Economic Research, *Income in the U.S.*, 1:85.
16. Flink, "Three Stages," pp. 454–57.
17. Montagu and Bird, *Steam Cars*.
18. Chrysler, *Life*, pp. 103–48.
19. Schumann, *Arbeiterschaft in der Automobilindustrie*, p. 34. This study and *Automobile Engineer* (London), 2 (1912): 213–14, provide interesting descriptions of artisanal production. In 1909 Renault, not quite so integrated as Daimler, employed 2,200 persons to make 4,700 cars.

20. Rosenberg, "Technological Change," pp. 414–43.

21. Carden, *Machine-Tool Trade in Germany*, pp. 120, 194–96, 207.

22. Saul, "The American Impact," pp. 23–27.

23. Arnold and Faurote, *Ford Methods*, p. 80.

24. Nevins and Hill, *Ford*, 1:348–51.

25. Kahn would become the premier industrial architect in the United States. Later, his firm would design and build many of the industrial plants in the Soviet Union during the first Five Year Plan.

26. *The Automobile* 18 (19 September 1907): 401.

27. Léon Turcat Papers, in the care of Olivier Turcat, Paris.

28. See Giedion, *Mechanization Takes Command*, pp. 77–96.

29. Arms, "From Disassembly to Assembly," pp. 195–203.

30. *Scientific American* 62 (24 June 1890): 369–70.

31. Arnold and Faurote, *Ford Methods*, pp. 332–50.

32. Ibid., pp. 112–14.

33. Ibid., pp. 103, 142.

34. Calculated from Nevins and Hill, *Ford*, 1:644, 647.

35. For Berliet, Laferrère, *Lyon: ville industrielle*, pp. 375–76, 379; for Sunbeam, *Internal Combustion Engineering* (London), 11 June 1913, pp. 379–80; for Fiat, Castronovo, *Giovanni Agnelli*, pp. 65–67.

36. Carden, *Machine-Tool Trade in Germany*; Watson, *Machines and Men*, pp. 12–13, 90–92.

37. Taylor Papers, Stevens Institute of Technology, Hoboken, N.J.

38. Fréminville to Taylor, 16 January 1914, Taylor Papers.

39. See Friedmann, *Industrial Society*, and Crozier, *The Bureaucratic Phenomenon*.

40. The largest were at the Pope works in Toledo (later the factory of the Willys-Overland Company) during 1906–7.

41. Nevins and Hill, *Ford*, 1:512–67, provides an exhaustive account; the wage increase actually cost $5.8 million in the first year. Critical discussions of Ford include Sward, *The Legend of Henry Ford*, and Russell, "The Coming of the Line," pp. 28–45.

42. Cambon, *Où allons-nous?*, p. 183.

43. Hatry, *Renault: usine de guerre*. For Delage, Petiet, *Organisation rationnelle d'une usine*.

44. French Army Archives, Vincennes, 10 N 73, correspondence with Roussky-Renault, 1917. On Russia generally, see Voronkova, "The Russian Car Makers."

45. Feldman, *Army, Industry, and Labor in Germany*, p. 206; Rist, *Les Finances de l'Allemagne*, pp. 73–75.

46. Chandler, *Strategy and Structure*, pp. 122–24.

47. Meyer, "Adapting the Immigrant."

48. Cuff, *The War Industries Board*, pp. 133–34, 204–19.

49. Motor Vehicle Manufacturers, *Automobiles of America*, p. 65.

50. Marcosson, *The War after the War*, pp. 59, 100; Cote, *L'Automobile après la guerre*, pp. 24–25, 70–71; Cambon, *Où allons-nous?*, pp. 184–85.

51. Chandler, *Strategy and Structure*, pp. 130–61.

52. Sloan, *My Years with General Motors*, p. 64.

53. Reitell, "Machinery and its Effect," pp. 37–43; La Fever, "Workers, Machinery, and Production."

54. *L'Usine* (Paris), 1 July 1920.

55. Ibid., 17 and 24 September 1927; Archives du Tribunal de Commerce de la Seine, "Rapport à messieurs les créanciers de la Société André Citroën," Paris, 1935, pp. 21, 86–87.

56. Boston *Transcript*, 23 April 1923; Detroit *Times*, 15 April 1923.

57. Archives Nationales (Paris), 91 AQ 76, Report of Renault engineers on the German automobile industry, 1927.

58. Sloan, *My Years with General Motors*, p. 325.

59. Hausman, "La Technique automobile."

60. Takagishi, "Japanese Car Industry," p. 537–39.

61. Wik, *Henry Ford and Grass-roots America*, p. 25.

62. Barrett, "Mass Transit and the Automobile in Chicago."

63. Pavie, "Le Code de la route," pp. 346–48.

64. Quoted in Fridenson, *Usines Renault*, p. 248.

65. Rae, *The American Automobile*, p. 48.

66. Ibid.

67. Mathewson, *Restriction of Output*, pp. 34–127.

68. Dubreuil, *Standards*.

69. Barthes, *Mythologies*, p. 169.

70. Flink, *The Car Culture*, pp. 167–81; Thomas, "Pattern of Growth," p. 205; Hickerson, *Ernie Breech*, pp. 64–65.

71. Wiersch, "Die Vorbereitung des Volkswagens."

72. Renault Archives, Pain Papers, agreement with Etablissements Teissier, 18 October 1938.

73. Interview with F. Picard, former president of the Société des Ingénieurs de l'Automobile, October 1974.

74. Centro Storico Fiat, "Fiat 500."

75. Reuther, *The Brothers Reuther*.

76. McGrath, "Chartres in a Chevrolet," pp. 24–28; Bush, *The Streamlined Decade*, pp. 98–128.

77. More information soon will become available in "L'Industrie automobile américaine pendant la dépression," a doctoral thesis in preparation by Gilbert Sugy at the Université de Paris I.

78. Such as spying and informing; see Kraus Papers, box 9, report of F. Corcoran on Flint Chevrolet factory, 1936, in Wayne State University Labor History Archives, Detroit.

79. Friedlander, *The Emergence of a U.A.W. Local*; Keeran, *Communist Party and Unions*; interview with R. Doury, former secretary of Syndicat des métaux de la région parisienne, 16 June 1976.

80. Bernstein, "Automobile Industry and Second World War," pp. 22–33.

81. Interview with M. Fr. Lehideux, former president of the committee, 13 November 1973; Rousso, "Les Comités d'organisation," pp. 133–48, 234–36.

82. Picard, *L'Epopée de Renault*, pp. 134–35.

83. *Ingérences allemandes, Gazogènes*; Borgé and Viasnoff, *Les Vehicules de l'occupation*; interview with M. Tabuteau, of SEV, 11 November 1973.

84. Borgé and Viasnoff, *La Jeep*; von Seherr-Thoss, *Die deutsche Automobilindustrie*, pp. 314, 317.

85. Sloan, *My Years with General Motors*, p. 377.

86. Ibid.

87. National Archives, Washington, D.C., Record Group 243, Renault file; *Ingérences allemandes, Automobile et cycles*, pp. 5–44.

88. Ricci, *Gramsci dans le texte*, pp. 386–87.

89. Press conference of Lefaucheux, 26 September 1946, Archives Renault.

90. Rhys, *Motor Industry*, p. 38.

91. White, *Automobile Industry since 1945*, pp. 153, 251.

92. Jenkins, *Dependent Industrialization in Latin America*, analyzes this.

93. *Industrie et société*, no. 6, 11 February 1975.

94. White, *Automobile Industry since 1945*, p. 93.

95. Ibid., p. 96.

96. Villeneuve, *L'Equipement des ménages en automobiles*, p. 25.

97. Picard, *L'Industrie automobile*, p. 5.

98. Ibid., p. 19.

99. Boltanski, "Usages sociaux," p. 35.

100. A phrase used by Senator Monroney, quoted in Flink, "Three Stages," p. 469.

101. Boltanski, "Usages sociaux," p. 26.

102. Sloan, *My Years with General Motors*, p. 219.

103. Glaude, "La Fin des vieilles voitures."

104. Stoffaes, "L'Industrie automobile."

105. Daniels, "Les Nouvelles techniques."

106. Helidie, "Construction automobile japonaise."

107. Abernathy, *The Productivity Dilemma*, is a basic reference for the United States, and Touraine, *L'Evolution du travail ouvrier*, is essential for France.

108. Mothé, *Les O.S.*, p. 41.

109. Sloan, *My Years with General Motors*, p. 392.

110. Pugno and Garavini, *Gli Anni duri alla Fiat*; Gianotti, *Lotte e organizzazione*.

111. For the Italian delegate movement, see Aglieta, *Révolution dans l'entreprise*.

112. An American comparison can be found in Berger, *Working Class Suburb*.

113. Consult Form, *Blue-Collar Stratification*, especially pp. 75–93.

114. Geschwender, *Class, Race, and Worker Insurgency*, p. 72.

115. Ibid., pp. 44–45. See also Georgakas and Surkin, *Detroit: I Do Mind Dying*, which is sometimes factually inaccurate. Better balanced are Widick, *Detroit: City of Race and Class Violence*, and *Auto Work and Its Discontents*.

116. Form, *Blue-Collar Stratification*, pp. 35–74.

117. See the study by Mothé, *Les O.S.* Mothé is the pseudonym of Jacques Gautrat, who for many years operated a milling machine in Renault's Billancourt works.

118. Aglieta, *Révolution*, p. 109.

119. See Widick, *Labor Today*.

120. Georgakas and Surkin, *Detroit*, p. 24.

121. Rothschild, *Paradise Lost*, p. 102.

122. Ibid., pp. 97–119, presents a shallow account. The definitive study is Child, "The Myth at Lordstown."

123. Sturmthal, *Workers Councils*, pp. 123–24.

124. Guest, "Learning from Tarrytown."

125. Cole, *Work, Mobility, and Participation*, pp. 121–223.

126. Orski, "Impact of the Automobile," p. 31.

127. Wilson, *Noise*, p. 13.

128. Dupas, "Vers l'automobile non polluante," p. 8.

129. *Statistical Abstract*, 1979, p. 212.

130. We now know that the Los Angeles case stems from a unique climatological situation rarely found elsewhere in the world.

131. Boltanski, "Usages sociaux," p. 27.

132. Ibid., p. 41.

133. Rae, *The Road and the Car*, pp. 345–46.

134. Boltanski, "Usages sociaux," p. 29.

135. Ibid.
136. Illich, *Energie et équité*, pp. 26–27.
137. Pierce, "Fuel Consumption," p. 35.
138. Cotta, *Energie et transports*.
139. Pillet, *Les Economies d'énergie*.
140. Nader, *Unsafe at Any Speed*, pp. 170–71.
141. Guichard, "Vivre avec l'automobile," p. 1.
142. *La Locomotion Automobile* 1 (1895): 255; *Horseless Age* 1 (1895): 5.
143. *Bulletin des Usines Renault*, 1 January 1920.
144. "End of the Road," p. 544.
145. Morgan, "Mobility Minus," p. 41.
146. Hupkes, "The Future of the Motorcar," pp. 457–68.
147. Dreyfus, "L'Automobile dans dix ans," pp. 75–76.
148. Ibid., p. 79.
149. Picard, "Prospective de l'automobile," pp. 336–49.

Bibliography

Unpublished Sources

PRIVATE

We have interviewed a number of automobile manufacturers, engineers, workers, and dealers, some of whom are cited in the notes.

We have consulted company and private papers: Ford Motor Company, Dearborn, Michigan; Panhard et Levassor, Paris; Renault, Billancourt, France; various manufacturers trade associations and labor unions; the papers of G. Chereau, Nantes, France; Lucien Loreille, Lyon, France; Gaston Mangeney, Lunéville, France; John Pollitt at the University of London Library; F. W. Taylor at Stevens Institute, Hoboken, N.J.; and Léon Turcat, Paris. We have examined financial records in the Financial Studies section of the Crédit Lyonnais, Paris.

PUBLIC

We have also surveyed the unpublished records of the United States Strategic Bombing Survey at the National Archives, Washington; the records of various French government departments in the Archives Nationales, Paris; and the archives of the League of Nations, the Organization for Economic Cooperation and Development, and the United Nations.

The Press

The contemporary trade and technical press is a crucial source for automobile history. Many references to it may be found in the notes. It has been seconded in recent years by the many publications of the automobile collectors. The Society of Automotive Historians groups several hundred serious workers in this field. Especially helpful from this organization have been Rolland Jerry, W. F. Robinson, Jr., and Michael Sedgwick.

Books and Articles

GENERAL WORKS

Automobile History

Barker, Ronald, and Harding, Anthony. *Automobile Design: Great Designers and Their Work*. Newton Abbot, Eng.: David & Charles, 1970.

Baudry de Saunier, Louis. *Histoire de la locomotion terrestre*. Paris: Editions de l'Illustration, 1936.

Bird, Anthony. *The Motor Car, 1765–1914*. London: Batsford, 1960.

Bloomfield, Gerald. *The World Automotive Industry*. North Pomfret, Vt.: David & Charles, 1978.

Duncan, Herbert O. *The World on Wheels*. Paris: Duncan, 1926.

Ensor, James. *The Motor Industry*, London: Longman, 1971.

Funk, B. "Aspects de la formation des prix sur le marché automobile." *Recherches économiques de Louvain*, September–November 1963.

Georgano, G. N., ed. *The Complete Encyclopedia of Motorcars, 1885–1968*. London: Ebury Press, 1968.

Grégoire, Jean A. *50 ans d'automobile*. Paris: Flammarion, 1974.

Ickx, Jacques. *Ainsi naquit l'automobile*. 2 vols. Lausanne: Edita, 1961. A condensed one-volume edition came from the same publisher in 1971.

International Chamber of Commerce. *A Statistical Survey of World Highway Transport*. Paris, 1931.

Jardin, Antoine, and Fleury, Philippe. *La Révolution de l'autoroute*. Paris: Fayard, 1973.

Mahler, Edouard. *L'Industrie automobile et ses perspectives d'avenir dans le nouvel équilibre européen et mondial*. Lausanne: Ere Nouvelle, 1966.

Montagu of Beaulieu, Edward, and Bird, Anthony. *Steam Cars, 1770–1970*. New York: St. Martin's, 1971.

Nicholson, Timothy R., ed. *The Age of Motoring Adventure, 1897–1939*. London: Cassell, 1972.

Picard, Fernand. *L'Industrie automobile*. New York: United Nations, 1973.

Rhys, D. G. *The Motor Industry: An Economic Survey*. London: Butterworth, 1973.

Seidler, Edouard. *Les Grandes voix de l'automobile*. Paris: l'Equipe, 1970.

Wagner, Jörg. *La Méthode de distribution par concessionnaires et son application dans l'industrie automobile*. Geneva: Georg, 1968.

Automobiles and Technical Progress

Abernathy, William J., and Ginsburg, Douglass H., eds. *Government, Technology, and the Future of the Automobile*. New York: McGraw Hill, 1979.

Chanaron, Jean-Jacques. *L'Innovation dans la construction automobile*. Grenoble: University of Grenoble II, I.R.E.P., 1973.

Christian, Jeffrey M., comp. *World Guide to Battery-Powered Road Transportation*. New York: McGraw Hill, 1980.

Daniels, Jeffrey. "Les Nouvelles techniques de l'automobile." *La Recherche* 11 (September 1980): 938–48.

Dark, Harris E. *Auto Engines of Tomorrow*. Bloomington: Indiana University Press, 1975.

———. *The Wankel Rotary Engine*. Bloomington: Indiana University Press, 1974.

Fridenson, Patrick. "The Coming of the Assembly Line to Europe." In *The Dynamics of Science and Technology*, edited by W. Krohn, E. P. Layton, and P. Weingart, pp. 159–75. Dordrecht: D. Reidel, 1978.

Grosser, Morton. *Diesel: The Man and the Engine*. New York: Atheneum, 1978.

Hillier, Victor A. W., and Pittuck, F. W. *Fundamentals in Vehicle Technology*. London: Hutchinson, 1973.

Jamison, Andrew. *The Steam Powered Automobile*. Bloomington: Indiana University Press, 1970.

Nicolon, Alexandre. *Le Véhicule électrique*. Paris: C.N.R.S., 1977.

Labor

Bezier, P. "L'Industrie mécanique: rétrospective et perspective." *Sciences et Techniques* 20 (15 February 1975): 5–14.

Cole, Robert E. *Work, Mobility, and Participation: A Comparative Study of American and Japanese Industry*. Berkeley: University of California Press, 1979.

Cooper, Cary L., and Mumford, Enid, eds. *The Quality of Working Life in Western and Eastern Europe*. Westport, Conn.: Greenwood Press, 1979.

Crozier, Michel. *The Bureaucratic Phenomenon*. Chicago: University of Chicago Press, 1964.

Dubreuil, Hyacinthe. *Standards*. Paris: Grasset, 1929. Translated as *Robots or Men*. New York: Harper, 1930.

Form, William H. *Blue-collar Stratification: Autoworkers in Four Countries*. Princeton: Princeton University Press, 1976.

Forslin, Jan; Sarapata, Adam; and Whitehill, Arthur M., eds. *Automation and Industrial Workers: A Fifteen Nation Study*. Oxford: Pergamon Press, 1979.

Friedmann, Georges. *Industrial Society*. Glencoe, Ill.: Free Press, 1955.

Kern, Horst, and Schumann, Michael. *Industriearbeit und Arbeiterbewusstsein*. Frankfurt: Europaïsche Verlaganstalt, 1970.

Kujawa, Duane. *International Labor Relations Management in the Automotive Industry: A Comparative Study of Chrysler, Ford, and General Motors*. New York: Praeger, 1971.

Limon, D. "Répercussion du progrès technique sur le niveau de qualification des ouvriers professionnels de l'automobile." *Cahiers d'étude des sociétés industrielles et de l'automation* 7 (1965): 137–82.

Mothé, Daniel. *Le O.S.* Paris: Cerf, 1972.

Sturmthal, Adolf. *Workers Councils*. Cambridge, Mass.: Harvard University Press, 1964.

Automobiles and Society

L'Avenir de l'automobile. Paris: Documentation française, 1976.

Barthes, Roland. *Mythologies*. Paris: Seuil, 1957.

Bhaskar, Krish. *The Future of the World Motor Industry*. London: Kogan Page, 1980.

Boltanski, Luc. "Les Usages sociaux de l'automobile: concurrence pour l'espace et accidents." *Actes de la recherches en sciences sociales* 2 (March 1975): 25–49.

Burlingame, Roger. *Engines of Democracy*. New York: Scribner's, 1940.

Chanaron, Jean-Jacques. *L'Industrie automobile: une industrie motrice?* Grenoble: University of Grenoble II, I.R.E.P., 1980.

Cotta, Alain. *Energie et transports routiers de marchandises*. Paris: Fédération nationale des transports routiers, 1980.

Dreyfus, Pierre. "L'Automobile dans dix ans." *La Nef*, June 1974, pp. 75–76.

Dupas, R. "Vers l'automobile non polluante," *Pétrole Progrès*, no. 88 (summer 1971): 8.

"End of the Road." *London Times Literary Supplement*, 24 May 1974, p. 544.

Glaude, Michel. "La Fin des vieilles voitures." *Economie et statistique*, April 1978, pp. 65–78.

Godart, Albert, ed. *L'Automobile dans la société*. Brussels: Free University of Brussels, Institute of Sociology, 1972.

Grad, Frank P., et al. *The Automobile and the Regulation of Its Impact on the Environment*. Norman: University of Oklahoma Press, 1975.

Grégoire, Jean A. *L'Automobile de la pénurie*. Paris: Flammarion, 1975.

Hublin, R. "La Pollution atmosphérique d'origine automobile." *Analyse et prévision*, April 1971, pp. 421–62.

Hupkes, Geurt. "The Future of the Motor Car: Alternative Scenarios." *Futures* 5 (October 1973): 457–68.

Illich, Ivan. *Energie et équité*. Paris: Seuil, 1975. Translated as *Energy and Equity*. New York: Harper & Row, 1974.

Morgan, John. "Mobility Minus." *London Sunday Times*, 16 June 1974, p. 41.

Nader, Ralph. *Unsafe at Any Speed*. New York: Grossman, 1965.

O.E.C.D. *Le Bruit dû à la circulation urbaine*. Paris, 1971.

———. *The Cost and Effectiveness of Automobile Exhaust Emissions Control Regulations*. Paris, 1978.

———. *Effects of Traffic and Roads on the Environment in Urban Areas*. Paris, 1973.

———. *Evaluation of Traffic Policies for the Improvement of the Urban Environment*. Paris, 1976.

———. *Managing Transport*. Paris, 1979.

———. *The Social Costs of Noise*. Paris, 1976.

———. *The State of the Environment of O.E.C.D. Member Countries*. Paris, 1979.

———. *Techniques d'amélioration des conditions urbains par la limitation de la circulation*. Paris, 1973.

Orski, Kenneth. "The Impact of the Automobile on the Environment." *OECD Observer*, no. 53 (August 1971): 31–35.

Owen, Wilfred. *The Metropolitan Transportation Problem*. Washington: Brookings Institution, 1966.

Picard, Fernand. "Prospective de l'automobile jusqu'à l'an 2000." *Journal de la société de statistique de Paris*, 4th trimestre, 1974, pp. 336–49.

Pierce, John R. "The Fuel Consumption of Automobiles." *Scientific American*, January 1975, pp. 34–44.

Pillet, J. P. *Les Economies d'énergie dans les transports*. Paris: Enertrans, 1980.

Poulain, Hervé. *L'Art et l'automobile*. Zoug: Les Clefs du temps, 1973.

Ricci, François. *Gramsci dans le texte*. Paris: Editions sociales, 1975.

Sauvy, Alfred. *Les Quatre roues de la fortune: essai sur l'automobile*. Paris: Flammarion, 1968.

Townroe, P. M., ed. *Social and Political Consequences of the Motor Car*. Newton Abbot, Eng.: David & Charles, 1974.

Valais, M. "Aspects économiques de l'industrie automobile dans le monde." *Revue de l'Institut française du pétrole* 30 (May–June 1975): 397–444.

Wilson, A. *Noise*. London: H.M. Stationery Office, 1963.

LARGE GEOGRAPHIC REGIONS

Europe

Carden, Godfrey L. *Machine-Tool Trade in Germany, France, Switzerland, Italy and United Kingdom*. Washington: Bureau of Manufacturers, 1909.

Charles, J. "Les Opérations des firmes multinationales automobiles dans les pays socialistes: la voiture particulière." D.E.S. thesis, University of Paris I, 1975.

Hake, Bruno, and Lynch, Philip. *The Market for Automotive Parts in Germany, France, and Italy*. Ann Arbor, Mich.: Institute for International Commerce, 1970.

Hanon, Bernard B. "Impact of Selected Economic Factors on the Automobile Industries of the European Economic Community." Ph.D. dissertation, Columbia University, 1962.

Hu, Y. S. *The Impact of U.S. Investment in Europe: A Case Study of the Automotive and Computer Industries*. New York: Praeger, 1973.

Judet, P. *L'Industrie automobile dans les pays de l'Est*. Grenoble: University of Grenoble II, I.R.E.P., 1970.

Jurgensen, H., and Berg, H. *Konzentration und Wettbewerb im Gemeinsamen Markt: Das Beispeil der Automobilindustrie*. Göttingen: Vandenhoeck und Ruprecht, 1968.

Moneta, Erich H. *Die Europaische Automobilindustrie: Unternehmungen und Produktion*. Baden-Baden: August Lutzeyer, 1963.

Peyrard, Max. "L'Industrie automobile européenne face à la concurrence internationale." *L'Actualité économique* (Montreal), October 1966, pp. 496–627.

Tiraspolsky, A., and Kamenka, I. "Le Développement de la voiture de tourisme en Europe orientale." *Courrier des Pays de l'Est*, January 1976, pp. 42–53.

Tiraspolsky, A. "Camions et autobus en Europe orientale." *Courrier des Pays de l'Est*, April 1977, pp. 19–36.

Vehicle Industry in Europe. Washington: Department of Commerce, Special Consular Report 21, 1900.

Latin America

Behrman, Jack. *The Role of International Companies in Latin American Integration: Autos and Petrochemicals*. Lexington, Mass.: Heath, 1972.

Jenkins, Rhys O. *Dependent Industrialization in Latin America: The Automobile Industry in Argentina, Chile, and Mexico*. New York: Praeger, 1977.

Third World

Baranson, Jack. *Automotive Industries in Developing Countries*. Baltimore: Johns Hopkins University Press, 1969.

————. *International Transfer of Automotive Technology in Developing Countries*. New York: Unitar, 1971.

Establishment and Development of Automobile Industries in Developing Countries. New York: United Nations, 1970.

"Le Marché de l'automobile outre-mer." Special annual issue since 1945 of *Marchés coloniaux*, renamed *Marchés tropicaux*.

WORKS BY COUNTRIES

Algeria

Judet, P. "Le Problème de l'industrie automobile en Algérie." Grenoble: University of Grenbole, I.R.E.P., July 1969 (mimeographed).

Argentina

Automotive Market in Argentina. Washington: Department of Commerce, Trade Promotion Series, no. 84, 1929.

Gale, Richard P. "Industrial Man in Argentina and the United States: A Study of Automobile Workers." Ph.D. dissertation, Michigan State University, 1968.
La Industria automotriz argentina. Buenos Aires: Comisión de Estudios Económicos de la Industrie Automotriz, 1969.

Australia

The Australian Motor Vehicle Industry. Melbourne: Department of Trade, Industries Division, 1959.
Stubbs, Peter. *The Australian Motor Industry: A Study in Protection and Growth.* Melbourne: Cheshire, 1972.

Austria

Seper, Hans. *Damals als die Pferde scheuten: Die Geschichte der Oesterreichischen Kraftfahrt.* Vienna: Oesterreichischen Wirtschaftsverlag, 1968.

Belgium

Ickx, Jacques. "L'Industrie automobile belge. . . ." *Bulletin de la Fédération des industries belges* 25 (1970): 99–118.
Livre d'or de l'automobile et de la motorcyclette. Liège: 1952.

Brazil

Almeida, José. *A Implantação da indústria automobilistica no Brasil.* Rio de Janeiro: Fundação G. Vargas, 1972.
———. "Perspectivas da industria de veiculos no Brasil." *Revista de administrição publica* 8 (January 1974): 297–320.

Canada

Aikman, Cecil H. *The Automobile Industry of Canada.* Toronto: Macmillan, 1926.
Durnford, Hugh, and Baechler, Glenn. *Cars of Canada.* Toronto: McClelland and Stewart, 1973.

China

Automotive Markets in China, British Malaya, and Chosen. Washington: Department of Commerce, Special Agents' Series, no. 221, 1923.
Baranson, Jack. *Automotive Industry–People's Republic of China.* Washington: Rand Corporation, 1973.

Czechoslovakia

Hausman, Jiri. "La Technique automobile au coeur de l'Europe." *Ingénieurs de l'automobile,* October 1972, pp. 559–69.
Jiša, V., and Vanek, A. *Škodowy Žavody (1968–1938).* Prague, 1962.
Štechmiler, R.; Peukert, O.; and Loučkova, D. *Nase Automobily Učera.* Prague, 1957.
Vlasimsky, Jaromir. *75 Years of Czechoslovak Automobile Manufacture, 1897–1972.* Bratislava: 1972.

Denmark

Schmitto, F. *Automobilets Histoire og des Maend.* 2 vols. Copenhagen, 1938.
Thalbitzer, C. *Ford Motor Company: Gennem 25 Aar.* Copenhagen, 1944.

Egypt

"Les Progrès de l'industrie automobile égyptienne." *Marchés tropicaux,* 12 January 1973.

France

Ball, R. V. "The Vocabulary of the Automobile in France, 1860–1914." Ph.D. dissertation, Oxford, 1970.
Bauchet, P. "La Structure d'une branche d'industrie." *Economie appliquée,* April–September 1952, pp. 359–99.
Bird, Anthony. *De Dion-Bouton.* New York: Ballentine Books, 1971.
Borgé, Jacques, and Viasnoff, Nicolas. *Les Véhicules de l'occupation.* Paris: Balland, 1975.
Bertrand, Olivier, and Bonnet, Alain. "L'Evolution des emplois et de la main d'oeuvre dans l'industrie automobile." Paris: La Documentation française, 1978.
Cambon, Victor. *Où allons-nous?* Paris: Payot, 1918.
Castellani, A. "Les Grèves dans l'industrie automobile de la Seine, 1921–1930." Mémoire de maîtrise, University of Paris VII, 1974.
Chanaron, Jean-Jacques, and Nicolon, Alexandre. *Dossier préparatoire à une étude sur la sensibilité de l'industrie automobile française à des changements dans l'usage de la voiture particulière.* Grenoble: University of Grenoble II, I.R.E.P., 1975.
Clarke, Jeffrey J. "Military Technology in Republican France: The Evolution of the French Armored Force, 1917–1940." Ph.D. dissertation, Duke University, 1969.
Cote, Georges. *L'Automobile après la guerre.* Paris: Dunod et Pinat, 1918.
Depretto, J. P. "Les Communistes et les usines Renault de Billancourt (1920–1936)." Mémoire de maîtrise, University of Paris IV, 1974.
Dézert, Bernard. *La Croissance industrielle et urbaine de la Porte d'Alsace.* Paris: S.E.D.E.S., 1970.
Dreyfus, Pierre. *La Liberté de réussir.* Paris: Simoën, 1977.
Dumont, Pierre. *Quai de Javel, quai André-Citroën.* 2 vols. Paris: Editions pratiques automobiles, 1973–78.
Duvignac, Andre. *Histoire de l'armée motorisée.* Paris: Imprimerie nationale, 1947.
Fridenson, Patrick. *Histoire des usines Renault.* Vol. 1. Paris: Seuil, 1972.
————. "Les Premiers ouvriers français de l'automobile (1890–1914)." *Sociologie du travail* 21 (1979): 297–325.
————. "Les Usines Renault de 1898 à nos jours." In *La Terre, l'usine et l'homme au XXᵉ siècle.* Paris: Documentation française, 1974, pp. 30–44.
Garanger, André A. *Petite histoire d'une grande industrie (histoire de l'industrie de la machine-outil en France).* Neuilly: Société d'édition pour la mécanique et la machine-outil, 1960.
Hatry, Gilbert. *Renault: usine de guerre.* Paris: Lafourcade, 1978.
Ingérences allemandes dans l'activité industrielle: Monographie A.I.3, Automobiles et cycles; Monographie A.I.8. Gazogènes. Paris: Imprimerie nationale, 1948.
Krutky, Judy B. "The Impact of International Influences on the Domestic Distribution of Power: The Situation in the French Automobile Industry." Ph.D. dissertation, Columbia University, 1977.

Labourdette, J. H. *Un Siècle de carosserie française.* Lausanne: Edita, 1972.

Laferrère, Michel. *Lyon: ville industrielle.* Paris: Presses universitaires de France, 1960.

Laux, James M. "Les Capitaux étrangers et l'industrie automobile." In *La Position internationale de la France,* edited by Maurice Lévy-Leboyer, pp. 371–76. Paris: Editions de l'Ecole des Hautes Etudes en Sciences Sociales, 1977.

———. *In First Gear: The French Automobile Industry to 1914.* Montreal: McGill-Queen's University Press, 1976.

———. "Rochet-Schneider and the French Motor Industry to 1914." *Business History* 8 (July 1966): 77–85.

Loubet, Jean Louis. "La Société André Citroën (1924–1968)." Thesis, University of Paris-Nanterre, 1979.

Naville, Pierre; Bardou, Jean-Pierre; et al. *L'Etat entrepreueur: le cas de la Régie Renault.* Paris: Anthropos, 1971.

Norroy, Maurice. *André Citroën, le précurseur.* Paris: Librairie Desforges, 1973.

Nuu, Thi Nguyen. *Le Part automobile des ménages.* Paris: INSEE, 1978.

Nwafor, James C. *L'Evolution de l'industrie automobile en France: Une étude de géographie industrielle et d'aménagement du territoire.* Thesis, University of Paris I, 1974.

———. "La Structure et l'évolution spatial de l'industrie française d'équipement automobile." *Annales de géographie* 83 (1974): 190–202.

Pavie, André. "Le Code de la route—voitures, bêtes et gens." *L'Illustration,* 6 October 1923, pp. 346–48.

Pelle, Pierre. "L'Industrie automobile française et l'Empire colonial durant la crise des années trente." Mémoire de maîtrise, University of Paris-Vincennes, 1978.

Pérot, Benoit. *Panhard, la doyenne d'avant garde.* Paris: Editions practiques automobiles, 1979.

Petiet, Aimé. *Organisation rationnelle d'une usine travaillant. . . .* Paris, 1920.

Picard, Fernand. *L'Epopée de Renault.* Paris: Albin Michel, 1976.

———. "Les Gadzarts dans l'industrie automobile." In *Ecole nationale supérieure d'arts et métiers,* pp. 143–52. Paris: I.P.F., 1969.

Rousso, H. "Les Comités d'organisation, aspects structurels et économiques: 1940–1944." Mémoire de maîtrise, University of Paris I, 1976.

Schweitzer, S. "Partis et syndicats aux usines Renault de 1936 à 1939." Mémoire de maîtrise, University of Paris VIII, 1975.

Schweitzer, Victor. *Die Französische Automobilindustrie.* Langenthal-Zurich, 1952.

Seidler, Edouard. *The Romance of Renault.* Newfoundland, N.J.: Haessner, 1977.

———. *Le Sport et la presse.* Paris: A. Colin, 1964.

Serre, Michel, *La Demand d'automobiles.* Paris: INSEE, 1971.

Soares-Ferreira, Silverio. *Le Commerce éxterieur et la production française des vehicules utilitaires.* Paris: Prospective et amenagement, 1975.

Spinga, Nicolas. "L'Introduction de l'automobile dans la société française entre 1900 et 1914: étude de presse." Mémoire de maîtrise, University of Paris-Nanterre, 1973.

Stoffaes, C. "L'Industrie automobile." *Annales des mines,* December 1979, pp. 21–33.

Touraine, Alain. *L'Evolution du travail ouvrier aux usines Renault.* Paris: 1955.

Vallin, Jacques, and Chesnais, J. C. "Les Accidents de la route en France." *Population,* May–June 1975, pp. 443–70.

Vennin, Bruno. "Pratique et signification de la sous-traitance dans l'industrie automobile en France." *Revue économique,* March 1975, pp. 280–306.

Villeneuve, A. *L'Equipement des ménages en automobiles.* Paris: INSEE, 1972.

Wasservogel, François. *L'Auto immobile.* Paris: Denoël, 1977.

Yvelin, Paul. *Delage: Levallois-Courbevoie, notes et souvenirs.* Viroflay: P. Yvelin, 1972.

Germany

Baürle, Peter. *Die Entwicklung der Automobilindustrie in der B.R.D.* Stuttgart, 1966.

Busch, Klaus. *Strukturwandlungen der westdeutschen Automobilindustrie.* Berlin: Duncker und Humblot, 1966.

The Economist Intelligence Unit, "Notes on the East German Motor Industry." *Motor Business*, September 1966.

Feldman, Gerald. *Army, Industry, and Labor in Germany, 1914–1918.* Princeton: Princeton University Press, 1966.

Heuss, Theodor. *Robert Bosch: Leben und Leisting.* Tübingen: Wunderlich, 1946.

Horch, August. *Ich baute Autos: von Schmeidelehrling zum Autoindustriellen.* Berlin: Schutzen, 1937.

Ludvigsen, Karl. *Opel: Wheels to the World.* Princeton, N.J.: Automobile Quarterly, 1966.

Müller, Peter. *Ferdinand Porsche: ein Genie unserer Zeit.* Stuttgart: Leopold Stocker, 1965.

Olley, Maurice. *The Motor Industry in Germany during the period 1939–1945.* London: British Intelligence Objectives Sub-committee Overall Report, no. 21, 1949.

Overy, R. J. "Cars, Roads, and Economic Recovery in Germany, 1932–8." *Economic History Review* 28 (1975): 466–83.

——. "Transportation and Rearmament in the 3rd Reich." *Historical Journal* 16 (1973): 389–409.

Rist, Charles. *Les Finances de guerre de l'Allemagne.* Paris: Payot, 1921.

Schildberger, Frederick. *75 Jahre Nutzfahrzeug-Entwicklung.* Stuttgart: Daimler-Benz, 1971.

Schumann, Fritz. *Auslese und Anpassung der Arbeiterschaft in der Automobilindustrie.* Leipzig: Duncker & Humblot, 1911.

Siebertz, Paul. *Gottlieb Daimler.* Munich: Lehmans Verlag, 1940.

——. *Karl Benz.* Stuttgart: Reclam Verlag, 1950.

Uhland, R. "Die Fabrik der Daimler Motoren Gesellschaft in Stuttgart-Untertürkheim." *Zeitschrift des Vereines Deutscher Ingenieure* 56 (1912): 981–85.

United States Strategic Bombing Survey. *German Motor Vehicle Industry.* Washington, 1945. There are also separate reports on individual cases, including Auto-Union, Bussing, Nag, and Henschel und Sohn.

von Brunn, Johann H. *Ein Mann macht Auto-Geschichte: der Lebensweg des Robert Allmers.* Stuttgart: Motorbuchverlag, 1972.

von Fersen, Hans H. *Autos in Deutschland, 1885–1920.* Stuttgart: Motorbuchverlag, 1965.

——. *Autos in Deutschland, 1920–1939.* Stuttgart: Motorbuchverlag, 1963.

von Seherr-Thoss, Hans C. *Die deutsche Automobilindustrie.* Stuttgart: Deutsche Verlaganstalt, 1974.

Wachtel, Joachim, comp. *Facsimile Querschnitt durch frühe Automobilzeitschriften.* Munich: Scherz, 1970.

Werner, Oswald. *Autos in Deutschland, 1945–1966, eine Typengeschichte.* Stuttgart: Motorbuchverlag, 1966.

Wessels, Karl Dieter. *Die Struktur und Wettbewerbssituation des Kraftfahrzeuger-satzteils.* Osnabrück: University of Fribourg, 1967.

Wiersch, Bernd. "Die Vorbereitung des Volkswagens." Dissertation, Hannover Technische Universität, 1974.

Great Britain

Andrews, Philip, and Brunner, Elizabeth. *The Life of Lord Nuffield*. Oxford: Blackwell, 1955.

Bhaskar, Krish. *The Future of the UK Motor Industry*. London: Kogan Page, 1979.

Church, Roy A. *Herbert Austin: The British Motor Car Industry to 1941*. London: Europa, 1979.

———. "Innovation, Monopoly, and the Supply of Vehicle Components in Britain, 1880–1930: The Growth of Joseph Lucas, Ltd." *Business History Review* 52 (1978): 226–49.

Church, Roy A., and Miller, Michael. "The Big Three: Competition, Management, and Marketing in the British Motor Industry, 1922–1939." In *Essays in British Business History*, edited by Barry Supple, pp. 163–86. Oxford: Clarendon Press, 1977.

Clack, Garfield. *Industrial Relations in a British Car Factory*. London: Cambridge University Press, 1967.

Clegg, Hugh; Fox, A.; and Thompson, A. *History of British Trade Unions, 1889–1910*. Oxford: Clarendon Press, 1964.

Culshaw, David J., and Horrobin, Peter. *The Complete Catalog of British Cars*. London: Macmillan, 1974.

Dunnett, Peter. *The Decline of the British Motor Industry*. London: Croom Helm, 1980.

Friedman, Andrew. *Industry and Labour*. London: Macmillan, 1978.

Goldthorp, John H., et al. *The Affluent Worker*. 3 vols. London: Cambridge University Press, 1968–69.

Jefferys, James B. *The Story of the Engineers, 1800–1945*. London: Lawrence & Wishart, 1946.

Lloyd, Ian. *Rolls Royce*. 3 vols. London: Macmillan, 1978.

Matthews, John. *Ford Strike: The Workers' Story*. London: Panther, 1972.

Maxcy, George, and Silberston, Aubrey. *The Motor Industry*. London: Allen & Unwin, 1959.

Nixon, St. John C. *The Story of the Society of Motor Manufacturers and Traders, 1902–1952*. London: The Society, 1952.

Plowden, William. *The Motor Car and Politics, 1896–1970*. London: Bodley Head, 1971.

Rhys, D. G. "Concentration in the Inter-war Motor Industry." *Journal of Transport History* 3 (1976): 241–64.

Richardson, Kenneth. *The British Motor Industry, 1896–1939*. London: Macmillan, 1976.

Saul, S. B. "The American Impact on British Industry, 1895–1914." *Business History* 3 (1960): 19–38.

———. "The Motor Industry in Britain to 1914." *Business History* 5 (1962): 22–44.

Turner, Graham. *The Leyland Papers*. London: Eyre and Spottiswoode, 1971.

Turner, Herbert; Clack, Garfield; and Roberts, Geoffrey. *Labour Relations in the Motor Industry*. London: Allen & Unwin, 1967.

Ware, Michael E. *The Making of the Motor Car, 1895–1930*. Buxton: Moorland, 1976.

Watson, William F. *Machines and Men: Memories of an Itinerant Mechanic*. London: Allen & Unwin, 1935.

Young, Stephen. *Chrysler U.K.: A Corporation in Transition*. New York: Praeger, 1977.

India

American Automotive Products in India. Washington: Department of Commerce, Special Agents Series, no. 223, 1923.
Les Industries de construction de véhicules routiers. New Delhi: French Embassy, 1975.

Italy

Aglieta, Roberto, et al. *Révolution dans l'entreprise: le mouvement des délégués ouvriers en Italie*. Paris: Economie et humanisme, 1972.
Barbiroli, Giorgio. "Dinamica della produzione e del mercato della automobile." *Rassegni economici*, November 1971, pp. 1281–1409.
Bigazzi, Duccio. "Gli Operai della catena di montaggio: la Fiat (1922–1943)." *Annali dell Instituto G. Feltrinelli*, 1979.
Burnier, Michel. *Fiat: conseils ouvriers et syndicats*. Paris: Editions ouvrières, 1980.
Castronovo, Valerio. *Giovanni Agnelli*. Turin: U.T.E.T., 1971.
Centro Storico Fiat. "Breve storia del modello Fiat 500." Typewritten memorandum. Turin, 1975.
Gabert, Pierre. *Turin: ville industrielle*. Paris: P.U.F., 1964.
Gianotti, Renzo. *Lotte e organizzazione di classe alla Fiat (1948–1970)*. Bari: De Donato, 1970.
Lanzardo, Lilana. *Classa operaia e partito communista alla Fiat: la strategia della collaborazione, 1945–1949*. Turin: Einaudi, 1971.
La Valle, Davide. *Le Origini della classe operaia alla Fiat*. Rome: Coines, 1976.
Luppi, Laura, and Reyneri, Emilio. *Lotte operaia e sindicato in Italia (1968–1972)*. Bologna: Il Mulino, 1974.
Musso, St. "L'Operaio dell' auto a Torino," *Classe*, October 1977, pp. 87–143.
Pugno, Emilio, and Garavini, Renzo. *Gli Anni duri alla Fiat*. Turin: Einaudi, 1974.
Sedgwick, Michael. *Fiat*. New York: Arco, 1974.
Wherry, Joseph H. *The Alfa Romeo Story*. Philadelphia: Chilton, 1967.

Japan

Allinson, Gary D. *Japanese Urbanism: Industry and Politics in Kariya, 1872–1972*. Berkeley: University of California Press, 1975.
Cole, Robert E. *Japanese Blue Collar*. Berkeley: University of California Press, 1971.
De Vos, George. "Achievement Orientation, Social Self-Identity, and Japanese Economic Growth." In *Modern Japan*, edited by Irwin Scheiner, pp. 151–64. New York: Macmillan, 1974.
Helidie, Jean Yves. "Construction automobile japonaise." *Bulletin Sedeis*, 6 June 1980, pp. 331–42.
Japan as an Automotive Market. Washington: Department of Commerce, Special Agents Series, no. 217, 1922.
Japan Automotive Industrial Association. *Motor Vehicle Statistics of Japan, 1961, 1974*. Tokyo: 1962, 1975.
Japan: Its Motor Industry and Market. London: H.M. Stationery Office, 1971.
Japanese Bank for Industrial Development. "History and Speciat Characteristics of the Japanese Automobile Industry." *Industrial and Financial Bulletin*. Tokyo, 1950. (In Japanese)
Kamiya, Shotaro. *My Life with Toyota*. N.p.: Toyota Motor Sales Co., Ltd., 1976.

Motor Vehicles in Japan, China, and Hawaii. Washington: Department of Commerce, Special Agents Series, no. 170, 1918.

Nakamura, Seiji. *The Automobile Industry*. Tokyo, 1957. (In Japanese)

Osako, Masako. "Auto Assembly Technology and Social Integration in a Japanese Factory." Ph.D. dissertation, Northwestern University, 1973.

Sanders, Sol. *Honda: The Man and his Machines*. Boston: Little Brown, 1975.

Satoshi, Kato. *Toyota, l'usine du désespoir*. Paris: Editions ouvrières, 1976.

Shimokawa, Koichi. "Sales Marketing and Financing in the Automobile Industry: U.S. and Japan." In *Marketing and Finance in the Course of Industrialization*, edited by Keiichiro Nakagawa, pp. 121–42. Tokyo: University of Tokyo Press, 1978.

Takagishi, Keiichiro. "Development of the Japanese Car Industry." *Ingénieurs de l'automobile*, October 1972, pp. 537–39.

Takezawa, Shin'ichi. "The Quality of Working Life: Trends in Japan." *Labour and Society* 1 (1976): 29–48.

Ueno, Hiroya, and Muto, Hiromidu. "The Automobile Industry of Japan." *Japanese Economic Studies* 3 (1974): 3–90.

Mexico

Fleming, Al. "Mexico's Auto Industry." *Ward's Auto World*, September 1980, pp. 48–54.

Netherlands

Asten, H. A. M. van. "De Spyker van de Weg Gereden." *Economisch- en Sociaal-Historisch Jaarboek* 33 (1970): 67–118.

Nederlandse Vereniging de Rijwiel. *En Automobiel Industrie Jaaverslag*. The Hague, 1974.

Poland

"The Establishment of the Modern Automobile Industry in Poland." *Geography* 63 (1978): 362–63.

Piatkowski, D. "Les Perspectives de l'industrie automobile." *Perspectives polonaises* 14 (June 1971): 19–25.

South Africa

Griffiths, Ian C. "The South African Motor Industry." *Standard Bank Review*, June 1968.

Rosenthal, E. *The Story of Holmes Motor Company*. Capetown, 1957.

Spain.

Castro Vicente, M. de. *Historia del automóvil*. Barcelona: C.E.A.C., 1967.

Ciuro, J. *Historia del automóvil en España*. Barcelona: C.E.A.C., 1970.

Sweden

Chatterton, Mark. *Saab: The Innovator*. North Pomfret, Vt.: David & Charles, 1980.

Gyllenhammar, Pehr. *People at Work*. Reading, Mass.: Addison-Wesley, 1977.

Nicol, Gladys. *Volvo*. New York: St. Martin's, 1976.

Switzerland

Schmid, Ernest. *Automobiles suisses des origines à nos jours*. Grandson: Editions du Château de Grandson, 1967.

Waldis, Anton. "Les Débuts de l'industrie automobile en Suisse." *L'Anthologie automobile*, July-August 1969, pp. 17–21, and September-October 1969, pp. 11–16.

Wallach, Francis. *Die Bedeutung des Personenautomobils für die schweizerische Wirtschaft*. Winterthur: P. G. Keller, 1960.

Wittmann, W., and Bülte, U. *Les Coûts sociaux de l'automobile en Suisse*. Zuirch: Institut Gottlieb Duttweiler, 1973.

United States

Abernathy, William J. *The Productivity Dilemma*. Baltimore: Johns Hopkins University Press, 1978.

Abernathy, William J., and Wayne, K. "Limits of the Learning Curve." *Harvard Business Review*, September–October 1974, pp. 109–19.

Arms, Richard G. "From Disassembly to Assembly." *Bulletin of the Historical and Philosophical Society of Ohio* 17 (1959): 195–203.

"The Automobile, Its Province and Its Problems." *Annals of the American Academy of Political and Social Science*, November 1924, pp. 1–292.

Arnold, Horace, and Faurote, Fay. *Ford Methods and the Ford Shops*. New York: Engineering Magazine, 1915; reprint, New York: Arno, 1973.

Barrett, Paul. "Public Policy and Private Choice: Mass Transit and the Automobile in Chicago between the Wars." *Business History Review* 49 (1975): 473–97.

Belasco, Warren James. *Americans on the Road: From Autocamp to Motel, 1910–1945*. Cambridge, Mass.: MIT Press, 1979.

Berger, Bennett M. *Working Class Suburb: A Study of Auto Workers in Suburbia*. Berkeley: University of California Press, 1960.

Berger, Michael L. *The Devil Wagon in God's Country: The Automobile and Social Change in Rural America, 1893–1929*. Hamden, Conn.: Archon, 1979.

Bernstein, Barton J. "The Automobile Industry and the Coming of the Second World War." *Southwestern Social Science Quarterly* 47 (1966): 22–33.

Borgé, Jacques, and Viasnoff, Nicolas. *La Jeep*. Paris: Bolland, 1974.

Boyd, Thomas. *Professional Amateur: The Biography of Charles Franklin Kettering*. New York: Dutton, 1957.

Bryan, E. James. "Work Improvement and Job Enrichment: The Case of Cummins Engine Company." In *The Quality of Working Life*, edited by Louis Davis and A. B. Cherns, vol. 2, pp. 315–29. New York: Free Press, 1975.

Bush, Donald J. *The Streamlined Decade*. New York: Braziller, 1975 .

Chandler, Alfred D., Jr. *Giant Enterprise: Ford, General Motors, and the Automobile Industry*. New York: Harcourt, Brace and World, 1964.

———. *Strategy and Structure*. Cambridge, Mass.: MIT Press, 1962.

Child, John. "The Myth at Lordstown." *Management Today*, October 1978, pp. 80–83, 177, 183.

Chinoy, Eli. *Automobile Workers and the American Dream*. Garden City, N.Y.: Doubleday, 1955.

Chrysler, Walter. *Life of an American Workman*. Philadelphia: Curtiss Pub., 1938.

Cormier, Frank, and Eaton, William J. *Reuther*. Englewood Cliffs, N.J.: Prentice Hall, 1970.

Crandall, Robert. "Vertical Integration and the Market for Repair Parts in the U.S.

Automobile Industry." *Journal of Industrial Economics* 16 (1968): 212–34.

Cuff, Robert D. *The War Industries Board*. Baltimore: Johns Hopkins University Press, 1973.

Davis, Louis. "Job Design: Overview and Future Direction." *Journal of Contemporary Business*, spring 1977, pp. 85–102.

Dettelbach, Cynthia G. *In the Driver's Seat: The Automobile in American Literature and Popular Culture*. Westport, Conn.: Greenwood Press, 1976.

Editors of Automobile Quarterly. *The American Car since 1775*. New York: Dutton, 1971.

Edwards, Charles E. *Dynamics of the United States Automobile Industry*. Columbia: University of South Carolina Press, 1965.

Erskine, Albert. *History of the Studebaker Corporation*. South Bend, Ind.: Studebaker Corporation, 1924.

Fine, Sidney. *The Automobile under the Blue Eagle*. Ann Arbor: University of Michigan Press, 1963.

————. *Sit Down: The General Motors Strike of 1936–1937*. Ann Arbor: University of Michigan Press, 1969.

Flink, James J. *America Adopts the Automobile, 1895–1910*. Cambridge, Mass.: MIT Press, 1970.

————. *The Car Culture*. Cambridge, Mass.: MIT Press, 1975.

————. "Three Stages of American Automobile Consciousness." *American Quarterly* 24 (1972): 451–73.

Foner, Philip. *History of the Labor Movement in the United States*. 4 vols. New York: International Publishers, 1947–65.

Ford, Henry, and Crowther, S. *My Life and Work*. Garden City, N.Y.: Doubleday, 1922; reprint, New York: Arno, 1973.

Friedlander, Peter. *The Emergence of a U.A.W. Local, 1936–1939*. Pittsburgh: University of Pittsburgh Press, 1975.

Georgakas, Dan, and Surkin, Marvin. *Detroit: I Do Mind Dying*. New York: St. Martin's, 1975.

Geschwender, James A. *Class, Race, and Worker Insurgency*. Cambridge, Mass.: Harvard University Press, 1978.

Giedion, Siegfried. *Mechanization Takes Command*. New York: Oxford University Press, 1948; reprint, New York: Norton, 1966.

Guest, Robert H. "Quality of Work Life; Learning from Tarrytown." *Harvard Business Review* 57 (July 1979): 76–87.

Hickerson, J. Mel. *Ernie Breech*. New York: Meredith, 1968.

Jardim, Anne. *The First Henry Ford: A Study in Personality and Business Leadership*. Cambridge, Mass.: MIT Press, 1971.

Keeran, Roger. *The Communist Party and the Auto Workers Union*. Bloomington: Indiana University Press, 1980.

La Fever, Mortimer W. "Workers, Machinery, and Production in the Automobile Industry." *Monthly Labor Review* 19 (1924): 735–60.

Langworth, Richard. *Kaiser-Frazer: The Last Onslaught on Detroit*. Kutztown, Pa.: *Automobile Quarterly*, 1975.

Leland, Mrs. Wilfred C., and Millbrook, M. D. *Master of Precision: Henry M. Leland*. Detroit: Wayne State University Press, 1966.

Lewis, David. *The Public Image of Henry Ford*. Detroit: Wayne State University Press, 1976.

MacDonald, Robert. *Collective Bargaining in the Automobile Industry*. New Haven: Yale University Press, 1963.

Marcosson, Isaac. *The War After the War*. New York: John Lane, 1917.

Mathewson, Stanley. *Restriction of Output among Unorganized Workers*. New York: Viking, 1931.

Maxim, Hiram P. *Horseless Carriage Days*. New York: Harper, 1937.

May, George S. *A Most Unique Machine*. Grand Rapids, Mich.: Eerdmans, 1975.

———. *R. E. Olds*. Grand Rapids, Mich.: Eerdmans, 1977.

McGrath, R. L. "Chartres in a Chevrolet." *Dartmouth Alumni Magazine*, December 1974, pp. 24–28.

Mercer, Lloyd J., and Morgan, W. Douglas. "Alternative Interpretations of Market Saturation: Evaluation for the Automobile Market in the Late Twenties." *Explorations in Economic History* 9 (1972): 269–90.

Meyer, Stephen. "Adapting the Immigrant to the Line: Americanization in the Ford Factory, 1914–21." *Journal of Social History* 14 (1980): 67–80.

Motor Vehicle Manufacturers Association of the United States. *Automobiles of America*. Detroit: Wayne State University Press, 1974.

National Bureau of Economic Research. *Income in the United States: Its Amount and Distribution, 1909–1919*. 2 vols. New York: The Bureau, 1921–22.

Nevins, Allan, and Hill, Frank E. *Ford*. 3 vols. New York: Scribner's, 1954–63.

Ozanne, Robert. *A Century of Labor-Management Relations at McCormick and International Harvester*. Madison: University of Wisconsin Press, 1967.

———. *Wages in Practice and Theory: McCormick and International Harvester, 1860–1960*. Madison: University of Wisconsin Press, 1968.

Phelps, Dudley M. *Effect of the Foreign Market on the Growth and Stability of the American Automobile Industry*. Ann Arbor: University of Michigan, School of Business Administration, 1931.

Pound, Arthur. *The Turning Wheel: The Story of General Motors through Twenty-Five Years, 1908–1933*. Garden City, N.Y.: Doubleday, 1934.

Rae, John B. *The American Automobile*. Chicago: University of Chicago Press, 1965.

———. *American Automobile Manufacturers: The First Forty Years*. Philadelphia: Chilton, 1959.

———. *The Road and the Car in American Life*. Cambridge, Mass.: MIT Press, 1971.

Reitell, Charles. "Machinery and its Effect upon the Workers in the Automobile Industry." *Annals of the American Academy of Political and Social Science*, November 1924, pp. 37–43.

Reuther, Victor G. *The Brothers Reuther and the Story of the U.A.W.* Boston: Houghton Mifflin, 1976.

Rose, Mark H. *Interstate: Express Highway Politics*. Lawrence: Regents Press of Kansas, 1979.

Rosenberg, Nathan. "Technological Change in the Machine Tool Industry, 1840–1910." *Journal of Economic History* 23 (1963): 414–43.

———. *Technology and American Growth*. New York: Harper and Row, 1972.

Rothschild, Emma. *Paradise Lost: The Decline of the Auto-Industrial Age*. New York: Random House, 1973.

Russell, Jack. "The Coming of the Line: The Ford Highland Park Plant, 1910–1914." *Radical America* 12 (May 1978): 28–45.

Seidler, Edouard. *Let's Call It Fiesta*. Newfoundland, N.J.: Haessner, 1976.

Seltzer, Lawrence H. *A Financial History of the American Automobile Industry*. Boston: Houghton Mifflin, 1928; reprint, Clifton, N.J.: Kelley, 1973.

Serrin, William. *The Company and the Union: The "Civilized Relationship" of the General Motors Corporation and the United Auto Workers*. New York: Knopf, 1973.

Sloan, Alfred P., Jr. *My Years with General Motors*. Garden City, N.Y.: Doubleday, 1964.

Snyder, Carl D. *White Collar Workers and the U.A.W.* Urbana: University of Illinois Press, 1973.

Swados, Harvey. *On the Line*. Boston: Little, Brown, 1957.

Sward, Keith. *The Legend of Henry Ford*. New York: Rinehart, 1948; reprint, New York: Russell and Russell, 1968.

Thomas, Robert P. "An Analysis of the Pattern of Growth of the Automobile Industry: 1895–1929." Ph.D. dissertation, Northwestern University, 1965.

Thompson, George V. "Intercompany Technical Standardization in the Early American Automobile Industry." *Journal of Economic History* 14 (1954): 1–20.

U.S. Bureau of Labor Statistics. *Wages and Hours of Labor in the Motor Vehicle Industry: 1928*. Bulletin 502. Washington, 1930.

U.S. Department of Commerce. *Statistical Abstract of the United States, 1979*. Washington, 1979.

U.S. Department of Labor. *Industry Wage Survey: Motor Vehicles and Parts*. Washington, 1971.

U.S. Senate. Committee on the Judiciary. *Automotive Repair Industry. Hearings before a Subcommittee on Antitrust and Monopoly*, 90th Cong., 2d session, 1969.

U.S. Senate. Committee on Small Business. *Planning, Regulation, and Competition: Automobile Industry. Hearings before Subcommittees on Small Business*, 90th Cong., 2d session, 1968.

U.S. Senate. Committee on Small Business. *Role of Giant Corporations. Hearings before a Subcommittee of the Committee on Small Business*. 4 vols. 91st Cong., 1st session and later, 1969–75.

Villalon, L. J. Andrew, and Laux, James M. "Steaming through New England with Locomobile." *Journal of Transport History* 5 (September 1979): 65–82.

Walker, Charles R., and Guest, Robert H. *The Man on the Assembly Line*. Cambridge, Mass.: Harvard University Press, 1958.

Weisberger, Bernard. *The Dream Maker: William C. Durant, Founder of General Motors*. Boston: Little, Brown, 1979.

White, Lawrence J. *The Automobile Industry since 1945*. Cambridge, Mass.: Harvard University Press, 1971.

Widick, B. J., ed. *Auto Work and its Discontents*. Baltimore: Johns Hopkins University Press, 1976.

———. *Detroit: City of Race and Class Violence*. Chicago: Quadrangle, 1972.

———. *Labor Today*. Boston: Houghton Mifflin, 1964.

Wik, Reynold M. *Henry Ford and Grass-roots America*. Ann Arbor: University of Michigan Press, 1972.

Wilkins, Mira, and Hill, Frank E. *American Business Abroad: Ford on Six Continents*. Detroit: Wayne State University Press, 1964.

Wright, J. Patrick. *On a Clear Day You Can See General Motors*. Chicago: Wright Enterprises, 1979.

USSR

Greyfie de Bellecombe, Laurence. *Les Conventions collectives de travail en Union soviétique*. Paris: Mouton, 1958.

Holliday, George D. *Technology Transfer in the U.S.S.R., 1928–1937 and 1966–1975: The Role of Western Technology in Soviet Economic Development*. Boulder, Colo.: Westview Press, 1979.

"L'Industrie automobile en U.R.S.S." *Courrier des pays de l'Est*, January 1976 and March 1977.

Kramer, John M. "Soviet Policy toward the Automobile." *Survey* 22 (1976): 16–35.

Parker, W. H. "The Soviet Motor Industry." *Soviet Studies* 32 (1980): 515–41.

Sutton, Antony C. *Western Technology and Soviet Economic Development, 1917 to 1965.* 3 vols. Stanford: Stanford University Press/Hoover Institution, 1968–73.

Voronkova, S. V. "The Russian Car Makers 1914–1917." *Istoriceski Zapioki* 75 (1965): 147–69 (in Russian).

Yugoslavia

Biro Proizwodaca Motornih Vozila. *Motorna industrija Jugoslaviji/The Yugoslav Motor Industry.* Belgrade, 1974.

Index

Absenteeism: in U.S., 263–64
Accidents, road, 116, 278–80, 286
Adler Company, 145; begins auto making, 35; during First World War, 83
Advertising for autos, 117–18
AEC Company, 144
AEG Company, begins auto making, 35; makes NAG cars, 35
Agnelli, Giovanni, 147, 164; and Fiat, 36–38, 108; visits U.S., 37, 73; indicted for fraud,38; cleared of fraud, 73; during First World War, 82; and mass market car, 108; death, 167
Aichi Company, 184
Aircraft manufacture by auto firms: in First World War, 80–83; in Second World War, 162
Airflow design: by Chrysler, 151
Air pollution by autos, 275–78, 286, 288
Air/zinc batteries, 218, 219
Albion Company, 33, 144
Alcohol Plan: in Brazil, 191
Alfa Romeo Company, 147, 173, 174, 181, 194, 206; nationalized, 141
Allis Chalmers Company: and fuel cells, 217
Alsthom Company, 228
Amalgamated Society of Engineers, 64
American Automobile Association: founding of, 19
American Locomotive Company: buys license from Berliet, 28
American Motors Company, 176; Rambler model, 176–77; profits, 177–78; and Renault, 195; production in 1979, 207
AMO Company, 148; begins in Moscow, 82 Annual model change: in U.S. in 1920s, 94–95
Anonymity: and autos, 119
Aquila Company, 36
Arbenz Company, 87
Argyll Company, 33
Arrol-Johnston Company, 33
Artisanal production of autos, 56–57, 63
Assembly line production, 238; by meat packers, 60; introduced at Ford, 60–61; in France, 81, 103; in U.S., 85
Associated Equipment Company (AEC), 81
Association of Licensed Automobile Manufacturers: and Selden case, 43–44
Aster Company: supplies engines to Renault, 28
Atkinson Company, 144
Auburn Company, 118
Audi Company, 144, 216
Austin, Sir Herbert: enters auto busi-

ness, 31; in 1920s, 105–6; death, 167
Austin Company, 71, 102, 143–44; in
   First World War, 82; in 1920s, 104–6;
   Seven model, 105, 146; and U.S.S.R.,
   148; and labor, 155
Australian auto industry: in Second
   World War, 161
Austro-Daimler Company, 38; in First
   World War, 83
Austro-Tatra Company, 148
L'Auto (newspaper), and De Dion, 27
Autobahnen, 145. *See also* Expressways
Auto bodies: specialist builders of, 56
Auto Club de France, 17; founding of,
   16, 27
Auto industry, world: and Second
   World War, 159–69; growth after
   1945, 171–72; development during
   1961–73, 178–88; decentralization,
   180–81; subcontracting, 181; de-
   velopment since 1973, 188–95
Automatic transmission of GM, 151
Automation. *See* Robots
Automobile Club of America (New
   York City), 18
Automobile Club of Great Britain and
   Ireland, 17
Automobile Manufacturers Association
   (France), 80
Automobile Organization Committee
   (France), 160, 166
Automobile press: in France, 15
Automobiles de Place, 21
Automotive Council for War Produc-
   tion, 160
Auto parts making: France, 29; U.S., 40,
   42; Detroit, 46
Auto shows: in France, 16–17; in
   Frankfurt, 17
Auto-Union Company, 144–45
Avis Company, 205
AVO Company, 148
Avro Company, 166

Bacon, 224
Banks: and auto industry to 1914, 75
Bantam Company: and Austin Seven,
   150
Barreiros Company: and Chrysler
   Company, 179
Barth: and scientific management, 67

Barthes, Roland, 120
Bedaux system of industrial pay, 142
Bedford, 144, 173
Belgium, auto industry in, 30, 109;
   center of foreign assembly plants, 182
Benz, Karl, 34, 35; early experiments, 5
Benz Company, 17, 25, 30, 33–35, 73;
   engines made by P & L, 7; early cars,
   8–11; cars in U.S., 13; expansion,
   1909–14, 71–72; production 1913,
   74; during First World War, 83; air-
   craft engines, 83; merges with
   Daimler, 107; and diesel engines, 107
Benz Sohne, C., 34
Berliet, Marius: founds auto company,
   28
Berliet, 70, 173; new methods of pre-
   1914 production, 62; 1913 production, 74; trucks during First World
   War, 81; assembly line, 81; in 1920s,
   103; trucks, 123; diesel trucks, 145
Berna Company, 87
Bertin Company, 228
Bezier, Pierre, 166
Bianchi Company, 36
Bicycles: safety, 6; prepare a market for
   autos, 6–7, 15; 1894 show in Paris,
   11; industry in France, 25–26;
   influence on French automakers, 26;
   industry in Britain, 33
Biscaretti di Ruffia, Carlo: and Fiat, 36
Bluestone, Irving, 264
BMW, 182, 187, 194; and aircraft en-
   gine production in Second World
   War, 164; 1979 production, 207
Board of Trade (U.K.), 166
Bollée, Amédée, 3; steam omnibus, 12
Bollée Company: and Morris, 105
Boltanski, Luc, 203, 205
Bosch Company, 223
Boulanger, Pierre: and Citroën, 146
Bouton, Georges: designs high-speed
   gasoline engine, 10, 26
Brandt Company: and U.S.S.R., 148
Brasier, Henri: and Mors Company, 25
Brasier Company, 26
Brayton, George: gas engine, 4
Brazil, auto industry: during 1961–73,
   185; since 1973, 190–91
Brennabor Company, 72
Bricherasio, Emanuele: and Fiat, 36

Briscoe, Benjamin, 37; founds Maxwell-Briscoe, 46; founds U.S. Motors, 53

Briscoe Brothers, 40, 57

Britain, auto industry: early interest in cars, 12–13; delay in production, 30–31; location, 33; 1909–14 development, 71; Ford in England, 71; small cars, 71; during First World War, 81–82; in 1920s, 104–6; concentration, 105; in 1930s, 142–44; during Second World War, 162; during 1945–61, 172–75; decline, 190

British Leyland, 187, 227; decentralization, 181; and Honda, 194; and 1979 production, 207; and research since 1945, 219

British-Leyland-Authi, 185

British Motor Company, 173; Mini model, 173

British Motor Syndicate, 30–31

Brown, Donaldson: and GM, 97

Brown and Sharpe Company: and Henry Leland, 45

Budd Company, 99; and Morris, 105

Buick, David D., 45

Buick Company, 45, 51–52, 54; model 10, 45, 46, 53, 54; controlled by GM, 46; in Canada, 48; and assembly line, 69, 85; 1913 production, 74; and Liberty engine, 88; in 1920s, 96

Buses: and De Dion-Bouton, 27

Bussing Company: during First World War, 83

Cadillac Company, 67; and Selden case, 43; origin, 45–46; controlled by GM, 46, 52; and self-starter, 49–50; and electric ignition, 49; 1913 production, 74; and Liberty engine, 88

Canada, auto industry: to 1914, 48; during First World War, 87; in 1920s, 100–101; in 1930s, 154–55; during Second World War, 161; during 1961–73, 180

Capital requirements in early auto industry: before 1914, 75

Capitalism: and 1920s auto industry, 120

Catalytic converters, 217

Caterpillar Tractor Company, 149

Ceirano, Giovanni and Matteo: and Fiat, 36

Central Engineering Institute, Paris, 7, 27

Central Institute for Automobiles and Automotive Transport, Moscow, 228

Chalmers Company, 67; 1913 production, 74; and installment loans, 84; during First World War, 88

Chapin, Roy: and Olds, 18; president of Hudson, 89

Chenard et Walcker Company, 26

Chevrolet Company: enters industry, 84–85; 1913 production, 74; and GM, 85, 93; in 1920s, 96, 98; in 1930s, 151; trucks, 176; Camaro model, 179; models since 1945, 209; Corvair model, 286–87; Vega model, 287

Chrysler, Walter: and GM, 52; and American Locomotive, 52; and Maxwell, 93–94; and Chrysler, 98; retires, 151

Chrysler Company, 95, 174–77, 206; and Maxwell, 53, 98; founding, 93–94; buys Dodge, 98; product policy, 98; foreign assembly plants, 100; and Canadian branch, 101, 154; in England, 104; and German plant, 106; and Swiss plant, 148; in 1930s, 151; and Simca, Barreiros, and Mitsubishi, 179; Chrysler-España, 185; and recession of 1979, 193; and K cars, 194; and Peugeot, 195; 1979 production, 207; and labor, 246–47; and job redesign, 269; and robots, 270

Cimos Company, 187

Citroën, André, 103–4; as head of Mors, 25; in First World War, 81; foreign assembly plants, 104

Citroën Company, 102, 105, 106, 108, 146, 164, 173, 182, 187, 210–11, 231; in Russia, 82; during 1920s, 103; and Italy, 108; in Belgium, 109; and Renault, 141; 2CV model, 173; Citroën-Hispania, 185; and diesel cars, 193; recent models, 209–11; research in 1970s, 218; rotary engine, 221; research on electric car, 228

Clarke, 222

Clean Air Act of 1970, U.S., 288

Clément, Adolphe, 25–26, 30

Clément-Bayard Company, 70

Clément Company: Italian branch, 36

Clerk, Dugald, 5; and Selden case, 44

Closed bodies: in U.S. in 1920s, 94–95

Clyno Company, 105

Coffin, Howard, 87

Cole, Robert E., 269

Cole Company: and annual model change, 94

"Columbia" bicycles: of Pope, 38

"Columbia" electric cars: of Pope, 38

Common Market, 178; and Ford, 191. *See also* European Economic Community

Communist countries: and auto industries, 186–88, 189

Comotor Company, 221

Computer-aided design, 231

Consumption society: and autos, 117

Cord, E. L.: and Auburn Company, 118

Coudert, Frederic: and Selden case, 44

Couzens, James: and Ford Company, 42, 54

Coventry: center of British motor industry, 31

Crampton Parkinson Company, 227

Crane Company: and conveyors, 61

Criticism of autos: pre-1914, 22–23; post-1945, 285–89

Crosley Company (U.S.), 176

Crossley Company (U.K.): cars in Russia, 82

Cross-licensing agreement, U.S., 44

Crozier, Michel, 68

Cultural effect of autos: in 1920s, 117–120

Cummins Company: and diesel truck engines, 193

Czechoslovakian auto industry: in 1920s, 108–9; in 1930s, 147–48

DAF Company, 184–85

Daihatsu Company, 227; 1979 production, 207; and electric cars, 218

Daimler, Gottlieb, 33, 44; invented gasoline engine, 5; first car, 6; sells license to P & L, 7; shows car in Paris, 8; license to Simms, 12; license to Steinway, 13

Daimler, Paul, son of Gottlieb, 34

Daimler-Benz Company, 131, 145, 173, 194; aircraft engines in Second World War, 164; diesel cars, 193, 211; 1979 production, 207; rotary engine, 221; job redesign, 264

Daimler Company (England), 31, 33

Daimler Company (Germany), 8–9, 17, 18, 25, 30–31, 71–72, 75; during 1895–1907, 34–35; Mercedes model, 34; pre-1914 output and employment, 57; during First World War, 83; aircraft engines, 83; merges with Benz, 1926, 107

Darracq, Alexandre: early work in cars, 25–26

Darracq Company, 27, 33, 60, 70; 1913 production, 74

Dealers, relations with U.S. manufacturers: in 1920s, 99–100; in 1930s, 141; post-1945, 204; Automobile Dealers Day in Court Act, 204

De Dion-Bouton Company, 26, 29, 33, 35, 36, 60, 70; early autos, 26–28; tricycle, 26–27; special steels, 27; small cars, 27

Delage, Louis, 29, 104

Delage Company: shell making during First World War, 81; during 1920s, 104

Delahaye Company, 70

Delaunay-Belleville Company, 25, 75

Denmark: end of auto making, 109

Department of Energy, U.S., 227

Depression of 1929: auto industry as a cause, 120–21; effect on auto industry, 139–42; and concentration, 141; and government policies, 141–42

Design of autos: national divergencies, 212–15; in manufacturing process, 231–32

De Soto: and Chrysler, 150

Detroit: as center of U.S. auto industry, 46

Detroit Automobile Company: and Henry Ford, 42

Deutz Gas Motor Factory: founded, 5

Diesel engines, 142, 144–45, 211, 217; in Britain, 144; in Germany, 144–45

Diesel Nacional: and Renault, 195

Diesel passenger cars, 192–93

Diesel trucks, 193

Dion, Count (later Marquis) Albert de, 26–28, 30; steam cars, 8, 10, 11; early gasoline engine, 10; and Auto Club de France, 16

Discarded autos: problem of, 283, 285

DKW Company, 144–45

Dodge Brothers Company, 40, 93–95, 104; supplies Ford, 42; makes car, 84–85; in First World War, 88; and Henry Ford, 92; in 1920s, 96; division of Chrysler, 150; trucks, 176

Dodge Revolutionary Union Movement, 256

Downsizing American cars: in 1970s, 137

Dubreuil, Hyacinthe, 119

Ducellier Company, 223

Du Cros, Harvey: and Dunlop, 12, 25–26

Dunlop, John Boyd: and pneumatic tire, 12

Dunlop Tire Company, 12, 25

Du Pont, Pierre: and GM, 93, 96

Du Pont de Nemours Company: and GM during 1915–16, 85; and GM during 1918–23, 89–90, 92–93, 96

Durant, William C., 37, 103; buys out Buick, 45; and GM, 51–52, 89, 92–93, 96–97; and Chevrolet, 84–85; and Mathis, 150

Durant Company: foreign assembly plants in 1920s, 100

Dürkopp Company: begins auto making, 35

Duryea, Charles and Frank: early cars, 13

Earl, Harley: GM styling director, 99, 153

Economic benefits: and costs of autos in 1920s, 113–14

Edge, Selwyn F.: and Napier, 31–32

Edison Electric Institute, 225–26

Electric cars: in U.S. before 1914, 13, 21, 38–40, 48–50, 224; De Dion-Bouton, 27; post-1945, 217, 218, 220, 224–29; research, 227–28

Electricity Council of England and Wales, 226

Electric Vehicle Company, 39; and Selden patent, 43

Electric Vehicle Council, 226, 227

Electronic machine tool. *See* Robots

Electronics: and autos, 220, 222–23

EMF Company: bought by Studebaker, 53

Employers Association of Detroit, 19, 68

Employers' Federation of Engineering Associations (U.K.): and strike of 1897–98, 68

Energy cost of automobiles, 282–83, 284, 289

Energy crises of 1970s, xv, 191, 193, 282–83, 289, 295–96

ERF Company, 144

Erivian Polytechnique Institute, 228

Esso Company, 164

Ethyl gasoline, 99

Europcar Company, 205

European auto industry: during 1908–14, 70–75; begins to adopt U.S. methods, 101–2; small cars in 1920s, 102; in 1930s, 139–49; during 1945–61, 172–75; during 1961–73, 180–82; in 1960s and 1970s, 240–43; and recession of 1980, 194–95

European Automotive Committee, 160

European Economic Community, 288

Evans, Oliver: and conveyors, 60

Everitt, Byron, 40

Expressways, xiv, 142, 145–46, 212, 280, 281, 289, 293; in Italy, 114, 147; *Autobahnen*, 145; Queen Elizabeth Way in Canada, 155

Exxon Research: and fuel cells, 218, 228

Faccioli: at Fiat, 36

Fasa-Renault Company, 185

FBW Company, 87

Fedden, Sir Roy, 160

Federal Institute for Electrical Transport, Kaliningrad, 228

Fessia, Antonio: at Fiat, 147

Fiat Company, 75, 181, 187, 263; during 1899–1907, 36–38; moves toward flow assembly, 63; during 1908–14, 73; taxi-cab, 73; U.S. branch, 73; 1913 production, 74; during First World War, 80, 82; plant in France, 103; in 1920s, 107–8; in Spain, 109; "Topolino," 132, 147; in 1930s, 147; during Second World War, 164; 500 model, 173; 600 model, 173; in U.S.S.R., 186; diesel cars, 193; and Peugeot, 195; 1979 production, 207; research in 1970s, 219; labor, 244, 246, 254–55, 295; and worker-delegates, 246; job redesign, 264

Fiat Polski Company, 187

Fisher Body Company: bought by GM, 92

Five-dollar wage. *See* Ford, labor policy, five-dollar wage

Five Year Plans (U.S.S.R.), 148

Flanders, Walter: and Maxwell, 53

Flexible production, 270, 271

Flink, James J., 121

Floating engine: of Chrysler, 151

Flow production: pre-1914, 59

FN Company. *See* National Armament Company

Foden Company, 144

Ford, Edsel, 95, 115

Ford, Henry, 13, 101, 104, 115, 117, 152; career to 1908, 41–45; Selden case, 44; refuses to sell to GM, 52; and five-dollar wage, 69; tractors, 89; policies in 1920s, 92–96; and Model T, 104; death, 167

Ford Company, 46, 51, 52, 53, 54, 58, 62, 75, 81, 102, 176, 177, 179, 182, 195, 227, 237, 259, 263, 264; marketing, 19–20; beginning, 42; Model N, 43, 44, 45; and Selden case, 43–44; Model T, 45, 46, 71, 79, 84, 90, 91–96, 102, 108, 111, 293; pre-1914 Ford of Canada, 48, 56; branch assembly, 54, 55; single model policy, 54–56; price policy, 54–55; share of U.S. market, 55; pre-1914 Ford of England, 56; moving assembly line, 56; development of mass production, 59–62; Highland Park factory in 1910, 60–61; profits during 1911–16, 61; production and employment during 1913–15, 62, 74; pre-1915 labor policy, 65, 66; five-dollar wage, 69; during First World War, 80, 81, 84–85, 87, 88; Rouge

plant, 85, 92, 98; tractors, 89; in 1920s, 91–100; Model A, 98; black workers, 100; exports, 100; overseas plants, 100; Ford of Canada in 1920s, 101; and Australia, 101, 111; other foreign operations, 101; in France in 1920s, 103; Ford of England in 1920s, 104–05; in Germany, 106; in Italy in 1920s, 107; overseas operations in 1920s, 109–12; in Latin America, 110–11; in Japan, 111–12; Fordson tractor, 117; immigrant workers, 122; assembly lines in 1914, 125; foundry in 1914, 126; semiautomatic machine tool in 1914, 127; Ford of England in 1930s, 143–44; Ford of Germany in 1930s, 145, 146; in U.S.S.R. in 1930s, 148–49; operations in 1930s, 151, 152; adopts annual model change, 152; V-8 engine, 152; transfer machine, 152; overseas operations in 1930s, 154; Ford of Canada in 1930s, 154, 155; labor in 1930s, 156; Jeep, 161; aviation manufacture, 162; Ford of Germany during Second World War, 163–64; during Second World War, 165; Ford of England during Second World War, 165; Ford of Canada during Second World War, 165; post-1945 Ford of England, 173, 174; post-1945 Ford of Germany, 173, 174–75; post-1945 Ford of France, 175; Mustang model, 179; Ford-España, 185; Fiesta model, 191; recession of 1979, 193; Escort model, 194; 1979 production, 207; research since 1945, 217; rotary engine, 221; labor since 1945, 246, 247; job redesign, 269; safety movement, 286

Fordism, 120, 157, 167, 293

Foreign assembly plants, 182

Forges de Douai (Arbel), 57

Fornaca, Guido, 108

Four-stroke gasoline engine: invented by Otto and Daimler, 5

France, auto industry: dominance to 1908, 14–15, 24; exports to 1914, 20–21, 70; location, 29–30; entrepreneurship, 30; 1908–14 production, 70–71; small cars, 70–71; during First World War, 80–81; in 1920s,103–4; in 1930s,145–46; during occupation, 164; during 1945–61, 172–75; research since 1945, 218–19

Franco-Italian Engine Company, 181

Franklin Company: and scientific management, 67

Fréminville, Charles de: and scientific management, 67

French Electricity Company, 226, 228; and electric car, 218

French Petroleum Institute, 228

Friedmann, Georges, 68; quoted, xiii–xiv

Front-wheel drive, 145, 146

Fuel cells, 217–19, 224–27, 229

Fuji Company: 1979 production, 207

Future of auto industry, 295–96

Gasogene, 161

Gasoline engine: invented by Otto and Daimler, 5

Gas turbine engine, 218, 219

Gautier, 4

General Dynamics Company: and fuel cells, 218

General Electric Company (U.S.): fuel cell research, 217–18

General Electric Company (France), 228

General Motor Cab Company, 21

General Motors, 102, 176, 177, 179, 182, 195, 208; founded, 46; and Kettering, 50; during 1908–15, 51–53; Durant resumes control, 85; acquires McLaughlin, 87; in First World War, 88; refrigerators, 89, 152; reorganization in First World War, 89–90; in 1920s, 91–100; policies in 1920s, 96–99; product policy, 97; annual model change, 97; closed body, 97; decentralization with central staff, 97; technical innovations, 99; 1920s foreign assembly plants, 100; Canadian branch, 101; McKinnon, 101; in Britain in 1920s, 104; buys Vauxhall, 104; and Germany in 1920s, 106–7; and Italy in 1920s, 107; overseas operations in 1920s, 109–12; in Latin America, 110–11; in Japan, 112; GM Technical Center (Warren, Michigan) in 1975, 136; in Britain in 1930s, 143; in Switzerland, 148; withstands Great Depression, 151; diesel-electric locomotives, 152; aviation, 152; in Canada in 1930s, 155; labor, 156; and Second World War, 160–63; 1941–45 profits, 165; planning for post-Second World War, 166; and Australian subsidiary, 166; post-1945 decentralization, 181; recession of 1979, 193; J cars, 194; 1979 production, 207; Warren Research Center, 217; research since 1945, 217–19; rotary engine, 221; research on electric car, 227; labor since 1945, 244, 246–47; and Quality of Work Life, 264, 268–69; robots, 270; safety movement, 286; management innovations, 293

General Motors Acceptance Corporation: established, 92

Germain Company, 30

Germany, auto industry: early disinterest in cars, 8–9, 18; to 1907, 33–35; during 1908–14, 71–72; during First World War, 83; in 1920s, 106–7; motorcycles, 107; in 1930s, 144–45; during Second World War, 163–64; during 1945–61, 172–75

Giffard, Pierre, race promoter, 10–11

GMC trucks, 176

Gomulka, W., 257

Gothic cathedrals: autos as, 120

Government policy toward autos: pre-1914, 22–23; in 1920s, 119; in 1930s, 141–42; during Second World War, 160; since 1945, 199, 206, 293, 295–96

Gräf und Stift Company: in First World War, 83

Graham Paige Company: foreign plants, 100

Gramsci, Antonio, 167

Grégoire, J. A., 166

Guardian Frigerator Company, 89

Guillet, Léon: and research laboratory, 27; and scientific management in France, 67

Gulf and Western Company: electric car, 227

Gulf Electric Company, 226
Guy Company, 144

Hampton, Ellis, 110
Hanomag Company, 173
Haynes, Elwood: early cars, 13
Henry Ford Company, 42; germ of
    Cadillac, 45
Hennessy, Patrick, 160
Hercules Motor Company: and
    U.S.S.R., 148
Herrington, Colonel: and Jeep, 161
Hertz Company, 205
Highways. *See* Expressways; Roads
Hillman Company, 143
Hino Company, 184
Hispano-Suiza Company, 38, 81; and
    aircraft engines, 80
Hitler, Adolf, 164
Honda Company, 184; factory in U.S.,
    194; and British Leyland, 194; 1979
    production, 207
Horch, August: begins making cars, 35
Horch Company, 144
Horseless Age, 291
Hotchkiss Company, 25
Howie, Captain: and Jeep, 161
Hudson Company, 88, 89, 93, 94, 150,
    176; production in 1913, 74; Essex
    model, 95, 96; foreign assembly
    plants, 100; merger with Nash in
    1954, 176
Humber Company, 31, 33, 71
Hungary: auto industry, 109
Hupmobile Company: 1913 produc-
    tion, 74
Hydropneumatic suspension, 210, 216
Hyundai Company, 192

Ignition: electric, 4; incandescent tube,
    5
Illich, Ivan: quoted, 281
Imbert Company: and gasogenes, 161
Imperia Company, 148
Imperial Preference, 143
Independent front-wheel suspension:
    and GM, 151
Industria Motornih Vozil Company, 187
Innovation, technical: dearth since
    1920, 208, 211–12; advances since
    1945, 208–9, 210, 216

Installment selling of cars, 20, 94, 118,
    203
Intermetall Company, 223
Interministerial Committee on Electric
    Cars (France), 218
International Confederation of Free
    Trade Unions, 246–47
International Harvester Company, 149,
    176
International Union of Electricity Pro-
    ducers and Distributors, 226
Interstate Highway System (U.S.), 175
Intreprinderea Autotourisme Potesti,
    187
Invention of gasoline auto, 4–6
Ishikawa Company, 87
Isotta-Fraschini Company, 29, 36,
    72–73
Isuzu Company, 184; 1979 production,
    207
Itala, 36, 73; in First World War, 82
Italy, auto industry: during 1895–1907,
    35–38; location, 36; during 1907–14,
    72–73; during First World War, 82; in
    1920s, 107–8; in 1930s, 146–47;
    during Second World War, 164; dur-
    ing 1945–61, 172–75; decline, 190

Japan, auto industry: beginning, 87; in
    1930s, 149–50; during Second World
    War, 165; since 1945, 182–84; during
    1979–80, 194; becomes leading pro-
    ducer, 194
Japanese Ministry of Industry and
    Foreign Trade, 227
Jeep military vehicle, 161, 176
Jeffery: and Selden case, 43; bought by
    Nash, 89
Jellinek, Emil: and Daimler Company,
    34; and Mercedes model, 34
Jigouli car. *See* Lada Company
Job redesign: in 1970s, 263–68
Johnson, Claude, 17
Jordan, Edward: and Playboy car, 118
Joy, Henry B.: and Packard Company,
    46
Junior Company, 36

Kahn, Albert: industrial architect,
    59–60
Kahn, Albert Company: and U.S.S.R.,

149

Kaiser Company, 176

Kama (U.S.S.R.): truck factory, 187

Karol, 222

Keim, J. R., Company, 57

Kettering, Charles F.: early career, 49–50; self-starter, 49; and GM in 1920s, 99

Kharkov Institute for Highway Traffic, 228

King, Charles B.: makes first car in Detroit, 41–42

King, Martin Luther, Jr., 256

Klockner-Humboldt-Deutz Company: and research, 218

Knight, Charles Y.: and rotary valves, 50

Knight, J. H., 12

Knudsen, William, 152, 160

Korean War: and auto business, 175, 176; and Japanese auto industry, 183

Krupp Company, 57; during First World War, 83

Kubelwagen: in Second World War, 161

Labor in auto industry: pre-1914, 64–69; women during First World War, 80; in U.S. in 1920s, 100; blacks, 100; during 1920s, 119; mass unionization, 155–57; in U.S. during Second World War, women and blacks, 160, 163; forced labor and prisoners in Germany during Second World War, 160; in Europe since 1945, 240–45; collective bargaining since 1945, 244–47; new workers in Europe, 247–50; new workers in U.S., 250–51; black workers in U.S., 250–51, 255; unions and new workers, 252–57, 258–63; Lordstown strike, 256–57; Labor Institute of Moscow, 263; in Japan in 1960s and 1970s, 269–71; changes in organization, 292. *See also* Strikes, in auto industry

Lacquer paint, 99

Lada Company, 186, 200; 1979 production, 207

Lanchester, Frederick, 32

Lanchester Company, 32

Lancia Company, 36, 73, 108, 147; during First World War, 82; plant in

France, 103

Langen, Eugene: and Deutz Company, 5

Lanza, Michele, 36

Latin American auto industry: during Second World War, 161

Laurin-Klement Company, 83, 108

Lawson, Harry J.: financial promoter, 30–31

League of Revolutionary Black Workers, 256

Le Chatelier, Henry: and scientific management in France, 67

Leduc, 220

Ledwinka, Hans, 109

Lefaucheux, Pierre: quoted, 173

Lehideux, François, 160, 166

Leland, Henry M.: and origin of Cadillac, 45–46; and self-starter, 49; founds Lincoln, 88

Leland and Faulconer Company, 40

Lend-Lease: U.S. to U.S.S.R., 163

Lenin, V. I., 117

Lenoir, Etienne: and gas engine, 4–5

Levassor, Emile, 30; and early cars, 7, 8, 9–12; wins 1895 race, 12

Leyland Company, 81, 144

Liberty aircraft engines, 88

Lincoln Company, 88, 93

Liquified gas engine, 217, 218

Locomobile Company, 60; steam cars, 39–40; in First World War, 87

La Locomotion Automobile, 11, 291

Loewy, Raymond, 153

Lorraine-Dietrich, 27, 70; begins auto making, 28–29; expands, 29; new methods, 62; and Isotta-Fraschini, 72–73

Loughead (Lockheed): and brakes, 88

Lucas, Joseph: electrical parts, 105, 227

Lutzmann, 17

Lyon: as a center of French auto industry, 28

McGregor, Gordon: and Ford of Canada, 48

Machine tool industry, 57–58

Machine tools: in French auto industry, 27; changes after 1945, 234–36; effects on labor, 235–36

McKenna Duties, 80

McKinnon Company: and GM, 101

Mack Truck Company, 176, 195
McLaughlin Company: acquired by GM, 87
Magirus-Deutz Company, 173
Malcomson, Alexander: and Ford, 42
MAN Company, 173, 187, 218
Management: of auto firms (U.S.), xiv; rationalizing and centralizing in 1960s and 1970s, 240–42. *See also* Sloan, Alfred P., Jr.
Market: for autos since 1945, 195–205
Marketing: pre-1914, 15–21, 22
Marmon Company, 88
Martini Company, 109, 148
Mass consumption society: role of Ford and mass production, 69
Mass market cars: pre-1914, 22; in 1930s, xiv, 142–48; post-1945, 173, 213–14
Mass production of autos, xiii–xiv; in U.S., 50, 51; work of Ford, 59–62; in Europe, 62–63, 79, 173–74; in Japan, 182–84; and labor, 230; becomes world-wide, 234. *See also* Assembly line production
Matford (Ford subsidiary in France), 146
Mathis Company, 146
Maudslay Company, 33
Maxim, Hiram P., 13, 38
Maxwell, Jonathan, 46, 53
Maxwell-Briscoe Company: founded, 46; and U.S. Motors, 53
Maxwell Company: 1913 production, 74; installment sales, 84; in receivership, 93; and Walter Chrysler, 93; renamed Chrysler, 94
Maybach, Wilhelm, 5, 34
Mazda cars, 183, 211; and rotary engine, 218. *See also* Toyo Kogyo Company
Mercedes model. *See* Daimler Company (Germany)
Mercedes-Benz. *See* Daimler-Benz Company
Merrick: and scientific management, 67
Metal Federation of General Confederation of Labor (France), 156
Mexico: auto industry, 191–92
Michelin, Edouard and André, 12
Michelin Company, 12, 16, 139

Middle West: as center of U.S. auto production, 40–41
Mid-European Automobile Club, 17
Military orders: for auto industry in 1930s, 157–58
Military use of automobiles, 23
Minerva Company, 30, 148
Mirabaud (bank), 21
Mitsubishi Company, 87, 184, 192, 227; and Chrysler, 179; 1979 production, 207
Mobile Company: steam cars, 46
Morris Company, 71, 75; Cowley model, 79, 105; during First World War, 81; plant in France, 103; in 1920s, 105–6; Minor model, 143; moving assembly, 143–44; labor, 155
Mors Company, 25, 29, 81
Moskvitch Company, 186, 187, 200
Mothé, Daniel, 243, 252
Motorization, world, 20, 47, 72; in 1927, 112; during 1950–79, 197; in 1970s, 205
Motorola, 223
Multimotorization, 116, 196, 198, 200
Mussolini, Benito, 107
My Life and Work (Ford), 117
Mythologies (Barthes), 120

NAG cars. *See* AEG Company
Napier, 22, 31–32, 75
Nader, Ralph, 286–87
Nash, Charles, 52, 89
Nash Company, 93, 150; merges with Hudson in 1954, 176
National Aeronautics and Space Administration, 217
National Armament Company (FN) (Belgium), 30, 79
National Association of Automobile Manufacturers (U.S.), 19
National Cash Register Company, 49
National Center for Scientific Research (France), 218
National Highway Traffic Safety Administration, 287
Nationalized auto manufacturers, 206
National Metal Trades Association (U.S.), 19, 68
National Semiconductor Company, 223
Nesseldorf Company, 83

Netherlands: auto making ceases in, 109
Neubauer Company, 43
New England: as early leader of U.S. auto manufacturing, 38–40
New York Motor Cab Company, 21
NIRA legislation: in U.S., 141–42
Nissan Company, 149–50, 184, 195, 227; Datsun cars, 149; diesel cars, 193; factory in U.S., 194; and Alfa-Romeo, 194; 1979 production, 207 1970s research, 218; robots, 270
Noise pollution, 273–75, 286, 288
Norroy, Maurice: quoted, xiii
Norway: auto industry, 109
*Nowa Kultura,*257
NSU Company, 72, 210, 216; and rotary engine, 220–21
Nuisances, 116, 273, 282
Numerically controlled machine tools. *See* Robots

Oakland Company: and GM, 52; 1913 production, 74
Office of Scientific and Technical Research (France), 218
Olds, Ransom E.: steam car, 13; early career in auto industry, 40–42
Olds Company, 46, 54, 60; Oldsmobile cars, 18; marketing, 19; electric cars, 40; as assembly operation, 42; influence on Ford, 42; Selden case, 43; supplied by Leland, 45; controlled by GM, 46, 52; division of GM, 150; diesel cars, 193
OM Company, 173
Opel Company, 72, 145, 173–75; begins auto making, 35; 1913 production, 74; during First World War, 83; in 1920s, 106–7; GM buys control, 107; during Second World War, 163–64; diesel cars, 193
Organization for Economic Cooperation and Development, 272–73, 274
Organization of Petroleum Exporting Countries (OPEC), 282
Osaka World's Fair: electric cars at, 218
Otto, Nicholas: invents gas engine, 5
Overdrive: of Chrysler, 151

Packard Company, 44, 150; moves to Detroit, 46; factory reorganization

during 1912–13, 67; in First World War, 87; Liberty engine, 88; merges with Studebaker in 1954, 176
Paige Company: 1913 production, 74; and installment sales, 84
Panhard et Levassor Company (P & L), 18, 24, 25, 26, 29, 30, 33, 70, 156, 166; early work in autos, 7–12; marketing, 19, 20; special steels, 27; Selden case, 43–44; in First World War, 79; 1922 advertising, 128
Paris: as center of French auto industry, 14–15, 29–30
Paris Exposition of 1889, 8
Peerless Company, 87
People's cars. *See* Mass market cars
Perkins Company: diesel engines, 144, 193
Peugeot, Armand: begins auto making, 7–12
Peugeot Company, 18, 24, 73, 146, 164, 166, 173, 181, 195, 216, 228; early work in autos, 7–12; marketing, 19; during 1896–1905, 24–25; Italian branch, 36; small cars, 70; 1913 production, 74; during First World War, 79, 80–81; in 1920s, 103; foreign assembly, 104; diesel cars, 193; and Fiat, 195; and Chrysler, 195; 1979 production, 207; research, 218, 219; labor, 244, 247
Philips Company, 219, 223
Picard, François, 166
Pic-Pic Company, 87
Plymouth models of Chrysler Company, 151
Poland: auto industry, 109
Pollution issue, 179
Pomey, Jacques: as engineer at Renault, 146
Pons Plan (France), 167
Pontiac division of GM, 150
Pope Company, 75; bicycle and auto making, 38–39; sells Toledo plant to Willys, 53; special steels, 58
Porsche, Ferdinand: and Daimler, 107; and VW, 145
Porsche Company, 161
Praga Company, 83, 109
Premier Automobile Ltd., 251
Production methods: new by 1914,

57–62, 74–76; fabrication cycle in 1970s, 231–33; technical integration in 1970s, 237–40. *See also* Assembly line production

Production of autos: during 1895–1907, 15; leading firms in 1913, 74; leading firms in 1979, 207

Prosperity, 139

Protos Company: bought by Siemens-Schuckert, 35

Quality-control circle (Japan), 269

Quantity production in U.S.: pre-Ford, 40

Races: Paris-Bordeaux in 1895, 11–12; Chicago in 1895, 13; Gordon Bennett, 16, 18; in U.S., 18

Ram, Georges de: and scientific management, 67

Rambler-Jeffery Company: 1913 production, 74

Ramelli, Agostino, 220

Rapid Company, 36

Raskob, John J.: and GM, 92

Recession: of 1920–21, 93; of 1973–75, 188–90, 200; of 1979, 193–94

Red Flag Law, 13, 17, 30

Reliability trials: Paris-Rouen in 1894, 10–11; British 1,000-mile in 1900, 17, 33; Herkomer, 18; Glidden, 18

Renault, Louis, 29, 30, 117, 145–47, 292–93; early work in autos, 27–28; in First World War, 80; in 1920s, 103, 104; death, 167

Renault Company, 35, 54, 60, 70, 73, 75, 105, 108, 166, 174, 182, 187, 195, 206, 240, 241, 263; marketing, 19; taxicabs, 22, 28, 124; founding, 27–28; becomes largest in France, 28; as assembly operation, 42; compared with Ford, 43; new production methods before 1914, 62; strike of 1913, 69; 1913 production, 74; during First World War, 80–81, 82–83; in 1920s, 103; foreign assembly plants, 104, 109; transmission assembly in 1938, 130; and Citroën, 141; in 1930s, 145–46; 4 CV model, 173; decentralization, 181; in U.S.S.R.,

186–87; and Mack Truck, 195; and American Motors, 195; and Volvo, 195; and Diesel Nacional, 195; 1979 production, 207; research, 218, 219; and electric car, 228; labor, 244, 247; job redesign, 264, 268; robots, 270

Renault-Saviem Company, 187

Rent-a-car arrangements, 205

Reo Company, 150; and R. E. Olds, 41, 42, 43; 1913 production, 74

Research and Testing Office (French Army), 219

Research efforts in auto industry: in 1970s and 1980s, 216–29

Research laboratories, 27

Reuther, Walter, 294

Reuther brothers, 149, 156

Rhine-Westphalian Electric Works, 226

Richard, Georges: founds and leaves Georges Richard, 26; founds Unic, 26

Richard, Georges, Company: changes name to Brasier, 26

Rigoulot: and Peugeot, 9

Riot: Detroit in 1967, 250, 257

Roads: construction in 1920s, xiv, 114; before 1914, 9, 18, 23; French, 9; U.S., 9, 18, 89; German, 9; improvements before 1914, 23; during First World War, 89; need for improvement, 90. *See also* Expressways

Robots: industrial, 222; in auto manufacture, 268, 270–71

Rochet-Schneider Company, 28, 70

Roger, Emile: as agent for Benz cars, 7–8

Rolls, Charles S.: installment sales, 20; career and death, 32–33

Rolls Royce Company, 25, 194; beginning, 32; aircraft engines, 32, 81–82

Romeo, Nicola: and Italian Darracq, 82

Roosevelt, Franklin D., 141–42, 159

Rootes Company, 143–44, 173, 174

Roper, Sylvester, 13

Rosengart Company, 146

Rotary engine, 183, 210, 216, 217, 218, 220–22, 229. *See also* Wankel, Felix

Rothschild, Henri de: and Unic, 26

Rover Company, 31, 33, 71

Royce, Henry, 32; compared with Henry Ford, 41

Rubery Owen Company, 57

Russell Company, 48, 87
Russia: auto industry during First World War, 82–83
Russo-Baltic Company, 82

Saab Company, 184
Saab-Scania Company: and job redesign, 264
Safety issue, 179–80, 287
Sankey Company, 57
Sansaud de Lavaud, 220
Sarich, 222
Saurer Company, 87
Saviem Company, 173, 181
Scania-Vabis Company, 86
Scat Company, 36
Schrodter, 9
Scientific management (Taylorism), 67–68, 120, 167, 248, 254, 263; in Europe during First World War, 80
Seat-Fiat Company, 185
Second World War: and the auto industry, 159–69
Seddon Company, 144
Selden, George B.: patent of, 4, 13, 19, 39; legal case, 43–44
Self-starter: invention of, 49–50
Serpollet, Léon, 7, 48
Sertilanges, Father: and scientific management, 67
Service station: U.S. in 1920, 129
SEV Company: and gasogenes, 161
"Shadow" factories: in Britain, 160
Shopping centers: in 1920s, 115
Siemens-Schukert Company, 35
Simca Company, 156, 173; and Fiat, 146; and Topolino, 146; and Chrysler, 179
Simms, Frederick R., 12, 17
Singer Company, 31, 71, 105
Sit-down strikes, 155–56
Size of cars: divergence between U.S. and Europe, 102–3
Skoda Company, 108–9, 148, 187
Sloan, Alfred P., Jr., 107, 151–52, 162–63, 208, 293; and United Motors, 85; and GM policies, 92, 96–98; and labor, 244
Sloanism, 121, 157, 167, 209–10
Smith, Adam, 60
Smith, A. O., Company, 57, 100

Social changes, wrought by autos: in 1920s, xiv–xv, 113–120; in rural areas, 114–15; tourism by auto, 115; cars and cities, 115; loosening of social ties, 116–17
Social costs of autos: in 1960s and 1970s, 272–85
Society of Automotive Engineers, 88; standardization of parts, 44
Sony Company, 218
South Korean: auto industry, 191–92
Sovel Company, 228
Spa Company, 36
Spain, auto industry: decline in 1920s, 109; rise in 1960s and 1970s, 185, 191
Special steels, 145; early use in France, 27; general adoption, 58
Spyker Company, 38
Stalin, Joseph, 117
La Stampa, 108
Stamping of auto parts, 57
Standard Company, 33, 105, 143–44, 173; labor, 155
Standardization of parts: in U.S., 44
Stanley, Francis and Freelan: steam cars, 39
Stanley Company, 39; steam cars, 49–50
Star Company, 31
Steam cars: early experiments, 3–4; Peugeot-Serpollet, 7, 8; defeat in 1894, 11; De Dion-Bouton, 27; Stanleys, 39; to 1914, 48–49
Steinway, William: and Daimler engines, 13
Stirling engine, 217–19, 229
Stoewer Company, 35
Storrow, James: and GM, 52–53
Stratified charge engine, 217, 229
Strike of metal workers: British engineering during 1897–98, 31
Strikes, in auto industry: pre-1914, in Britain, 68, in U.S., 68, in France, 68–69; at Ford Liverpool in 1973, 259–63; at VW Hanover in 1969, 260–63; at Renault in 1973, 260–63; at Ford Cologne in 1973, 260–63
Studebaker Company, 75, 93, 150; in Canada, 48; enters auto business, 53, 54; 1913 production, 74; installment sales, 84; foreign assembly plants,

100; merges with Packard in 1954, 176; leaves auto industry, 178–79

Studebaker-Packard Company, 176, 177, 178

Sturmthal, Adolf, 257

Styling: GM Art and Color section, 99; of autos, 118

Subcontracting: since Second World War, 181

Sunbeam Company, 31, 71; approaches moving assembly in 1913, 62–63

Sun Yat-sen: and Ford, 110

Suzuki Company, 184; 1979 production, 207

Sweden, auto industry: in 1920s, 109; during 1961–73, 184

Swift Company, 31

Switzerland: decline of auto industry, 109

Synchromesh transmission of GM, 99

Talbot Company: and Clément cars, 26, 33; and Peugeot, 195

Tanks: made by auto firms in First World War, 80

Tariffs on cars: to 1914, 21, 47; protective, 102

Tarrytown, N.Y.: GM assembly plant and QWL, 264

Tatra Company, 109, 147–48, 187

Taxation: of motor vehicles, 23, 198

Taxicabs, 21–22; Unic, 26; at Battle of Marne, 90

Taximeter, 21

Taylor, Frederick W.: high-speed tools, 58; scientific management, 67–68

Taylorism. *See* Scientific management

Texas Instruments Company, 223

Third World auto industries, 185–86, 189, 191–92

Thomson-CSF Company, 223

Tires: low pressure balloon, 99

Togliatti factory (U.S.S.R.), 186

Tokyo Electric Power Company, 226, 227

Touring Club de France, 16

Tourism: after Second World War, 204

Toyo Kogyo Company, 184, 227; 1979 production, 207; Mazda car, 218, 221; rotary engine, 221–22

Toyota Company, 184, 194, 195, 227; in

Second World War, 165; diesel cars, 193; and Seat, 194; 1979 production, 207; research, 218; robots, 270

Tractors: by Ford, 89

Trade Union Leadership Conference, 256

Traffic problems: in U.S. after 1914, 86; general, 280–81, 286

Transfer machines, 238; at A. O. Smith Company, 100; Morris, 106; Ford, 152

Transportation Research Institute (France), 219

Treaty of Rome (Common Market), 178

Truck purchases: by U.S. farmers, 115; at Verdun in 1916, 90

Tudhope Company, 48

Turcat, Léon: designs Lorraine-Dietrich factory, 48

Unic Company, 22, 26, 70, 173

Union Carbide Company: and fuel cells, 218

U.S.S.R. auto industry: in 1920s, 109–10; in 1930s, 148–49; during Second World War, 163; from 1961 to 1974, 186–87; trucks, 187; since 1973, 190–91; market, 200–203; research, 219

United Automobile Workers (U.S.), 156, 163, 244, 246, 255–56

United Motors Company: and GM, 85

United National Caucus, 256

United States: early interest in cars, 13; 1895–1907 production, 38–47; pre-1914 demand, 47; pre-1914 production, 47; growth of production during 1905–14, 51; low-priced cars before 1914, 74; auto industry during First World War, 84–90; 1919–23 production, 91; market changes in 1920s, 94–95; all-steel bodies, 99; exports in 1920s, 102; dominance of world industry in 1920s, 120–21; 1930s, 150–54; Second World War, 162–63; during 1945–61, 175–78; during 1961–73, 178–80

U.S. federal aid: and road construction, 86

United States Motors Company, 53

United Stirling Company, 219

Unsafe at Any Speed, 286
Used cars, 94, 116, 141, 201

Valletta, Vittorio, 108
Variable-assist steering, 211
Vauxhall Company, 33, 143–44, 173, 174
Vickers Company: buys Wolseley, 31
Vivinus, Alexis, 30
Voisin, Gabriel, 104
Volga car, 186, 200
Volkswagen Company, 141, 148, 173, 174, 177, 195, 206, 216; Beetle model, 133, 173, 180; origin of, 145; in Second World War, 161; decentralization, 181, diesel cars, 193; 1979 production, 207; research, 218, 219
Volvo Company, 148, 184–85, 259; beginning, 109; cars assembled on carriers, 134; assembly accommodated to workers, 135; joint factory, 181; and Renault, 195; 1979 production, 207; research, 219; job redesign at Kalmar plant, 264–68; robots, 270

WAF Company: in First World War, 83
Wanderer Company, 72, 144
Wankel, Felix, 216, 220
Wankel engine. *See* Rotary engine
War Industries Board (U.S.), 90
Warren engine (GM), 217
Warren Research Center (GM), 221
Westinghouse Air Brake Company, 60–61
White, L. J., 196

White Company: and steam cars, 49; in First World War, 87; trucks, 176
Wills, C. H., 42
Willys, John N., 53
Willys-Overland Company, 93, 176; in Canada, 48; founded, 53, 54; moving assembly, 69; 1913 production, 74; during First World War, 84–85; installment sales, 84; acquires Russell, 87; in 1920s, 96; foreign assembly plants, 100; Jeep, 161
Winton, Alexander, 18; early gasoline cars, 40; Selden case, 43
Wolseley Company, 31, 33, 71, 105
Wolseley Sheep Shearing Machine Company, 31
Women auto workers: in First World War, 80, 89; in Second World War, 160
Worker delegate movement: in Italy, 254–55, 257
Workers Councils movement: in Poland, 257–58
"World cars," 193–94
World market. *See* Market
World War, effect on European auto industry in First, 79–83
Wright aircraft: Rolls crashes, 33

Yasa Battery Company, 218
Yom Kippur War of 1973, 289

Zaporojetz car, 186, 200
Zastava Company, 187